# A History of English Language Teaching

## A. P. R. Howatt

Oxford University Press

Oxford University Press
Walton Street, Oxford OX2 6DP

Oxford New York Toronto
Delhi Bombay Calcutta Madras Karachi
Petaling Jaya Singapore Hong Kong Tokyo
Nairobi Dar es Salaam Cape Town
Melbourne Auckland

and associated companies in
Berlin Ibadan

OXFORD and OXFORD ENGLISH are trademarks of
Oxford University Press

ISBN 0 19 437075 5
© A. P. R. Howatt 1984

First published 1984
Second impression 1985 (with corrections)
Fourth impression 1991

Set in 10½/12 Linotron Sabon by Promenade Graphics
Limited
Printed in Hong Kong

To the memory of my father

# Contents

# Illustrations

# Acknowledgements

First of all, I should like to acknowledge a deep sense of gratitude to Ronald Mackin, my teacher at the School of Applied Linguistics at the University of Edinburgh twenty years ago. In the autumn of 1962 he delivered a series of lectures on the history of language teaching with a grace, wit, and seriousness that left an indelible memory. To a young teacher of English as a foreign language, for whom the attraction of the job lay in its rootlessness, he showed that there were roots, in a tradition that was sufficiently weighty with achievement to command allegiance and sufficiently unpredictable to retain affection. I should also like to thank my present colleagues and past students in the Department of Linguistics and the Institute for Applied Language Studies for their patience in tolerating sabbatical terms and other disappearing acts. I am grateful in particular to Professor David Abercrombie for agreeing to work with me on the translation of the Viëtor pamphlet included in this book and for other comments and observations that have indirectly moulded certain views expressed in the book. I am also greatly indebted to Alan Kemp (Edinburgh is dauntingly proficient in this field) for his many instances of help and advice, and to Professors Pit Corder and Jim Hurford for their enthusiasm and encouragement.

I should like to express my particular gratitude to the Main Library of Edinburgh University, not only to the present staff for their quiet efficiency in many practical instances associated with the preparation of this book, but also to the many librarians in the past who have seen to it that Edinburgh possesses an amazingly rich collection. The day that it fails to be exciting to handle a sixteenth-century copy of Holyband, a copy of Comenius published in his lifetime or the folio edition of Johnson must surely be the day to give it all up.

Finally, I should like to thank Oxford University Press for asking me to do something I have long wanted to do, and for their support and patience.

Aside from the many valuable references which have been acknowledged in the normal manner in the text, there are four sources to which I am particularly indebted and which played an essential role in the preparation of this book. The first is the bibliography prepared in 1888 by W. H. Widgery for his pamphlet *The Teaching of Languages in Schools* and, more recently, the comprehensive bibliography by L. G. Kelly in his *25 Centuries of Language Teaching* (1969), sources which started many other searches. Third is Kathleen Lambley's *Teaching and Cultivation of the French Language in England in Tudor and Stuart Times* (1920), and, finally, and most important of all, the *Bibliography of the English Language from the Invention of Printing to the Year 1800*, edited by R. C. Alston and published in Yorkshire between 1965 and 1974. The associated series of 365 facsimile editions (*English Linguistics 1500–1800*, published by the Scolar Press, Menston, Yorkshire, 1967–72) allowed me to maintain a strict principle of commenting only on works studied at first hand. This series, also edited by Alston, and the *Bibliography* itself made this present work possible, and, without them, it would have been quixotic to have attempted it at all.

Stern's *Fundamental Concepts of Language Teaching* (1983) appeared too late to act as a major source, but it has been very helpful with some late details. Its general historical perspective is of great interest, and its coverage of North American events is particularly useful.

I should also like to express my thanks to the French Embassy and the Ministry of Foreign Affairs in Paris for their detailed assistance on the career of the unjustly neglected Claude Marcel, to the Berlitz Organization in New York for supplying a photograph of their founder, to Mrs Elizabeth Uldall for permission to use the picture of Harold Palmer taken at the 1935 Congress of Phonetic Sciences, and to the Department of Linguistics at Edinburgh for lending the photograph of Henry Sweet from their splendid collection of pictures of noted phoneticians made by David Abercrombie.

The publishers would like to thank the following for their permission to reproduce the following material.

Almqvist and Wiksell for the extracts from *John Hart's Works on English Orthography and Pronunciation*, Part 1 by Bror Danielsson, Stockholm: 1955, pp. 239, 241 (Figs 15 and 16).

Berlitz Organization for the photograph of Maximilian Berlitz (Fig. 24).

Cambridge University Press for the extract from *The French Littleton, with an Introduction by M. St. Clare Byrne*, Cambridge: 1953 (Fig. 3).

Professor J. Hurford of the Department of Linguistics, The University of Edinburgh for the photograph of Henry Sweet (Fig. 23).

Johnson House for the section of the page from the Johnson Dictionary with the 'oats' definition (Fig. 18).

The Main Library (Special Collections Department), Edinburgh University Library for Klinghardt's transcriptions and Sweet's Broad Romic, Lesson 50 of Ollendorff's German Course for English speakers (Fig. 21), 'The Labyrinth' from Thomas Prendergast's *Mastery of Languages* (1864) (Fig. 22), and the title-page of Wilhelm Viëtor's *Der Sprachunterricht muss umkehren!* (Fig. 28).

The Scolar Press for facsimiles EL 51 (Fig. 1), EL 141 (Fig. 2), EL 74 (Fig. 4), EL 222 (Figs 5–7), EL 152 (Fig. 8), EL 216 (Fig. 9), EL 276 (Figs 12, 13, 14) EL 119 (Fig. 17) and EL 18 (Figs 19, 20) from their facsimile editions in the series *English Linguistics 1500–1800* (EL) edited by R. C. Alston.

Mrs Elizabeth Uldall for the photograph of Harold E. Palmer (Fig. 25).

# Note on Spelling

The basic principle in the main text of the book has been to use modern spelling and punctuation conventions. The following points should, however, be noted:

1 Where English and foreign language texts are presented together, for example in the dialogues of Caxton, Bellot, etc., the original spelling has been preserved in both languages.
2 Some well-known titles such as Ascham's *Scholemaster*, for example, have become so well-known in their original spelling that modernizing seems unnecessary. However, for the sake of consistency, and somewhat reluctantly, they have been modified. The one exception is Mulcaster's *Elementarie* in which he used his own system and to change it would be like modifying the Initial Teaching Alphabet or some similar self-contained system.
3 Original spellings have been preserved in the bibliography, a compromise that permits their appearance at least once in the book.

# Preface

The history of English teaching is a vast subject, and this is a relatively short book which of necessity has had to adopt a specific and therefore limited perspective. The spread of English round the world in the wake of trade, empire-building, migration, and settlement has ensured the teaching of the language a role, sometimes central, sometimes peripheral, in the educational history of virtually every country on earth. The European focus of this book is, therefore, only a small part of the history of the subject, hence the indefinite article in the title. From time to time, the narrative touches on events and their consequences outside its immediate concern, but it can do so only briefly, since they reflect cultural and educational patterns that require to be explored in their own time and context.

The reader will also notice that, in the earlier sections of the book in particular, some of the familiar dividing lines between modern specialisms have been deliberately blurred. The teaching of languages other than English, for example, has been treated in some detail. The bilingual, or in some cases multilingual, format of language teaching manuals was a standard procedure for a long time and it was also common for such books to 'work both ways', teaching French to English speakers, for instance, and vice versa. More generally, however, it would be wrong in principle, I believe, to divorce English language teaching from its broader educational and intellectual context.

Another contemporary distinction that cannot be projected back into the past too uncritically is the separation of English 'as a mother tongue' from English 'as a foreign language', and the present book places considerable emphasis on the relationship between the teaching of English, whether to native or non-native audiences, and the need to develop linguistic descriptions which reflect the generally agreed norms of the standard language. The phoneticians and spelling reformers of the late sixteenth century, for example, addressed their proposals as much to the foreign learner as to the native, and many of the early grammars, such as Wallis's *Grammatica*, which eventually became major sources for the influential eighteenth-century mother-tongue grammars, were originally intended for non-native students of the language.

It is really only in the present century that we can begin to discern a separate identity for English as a foreign language which derives in part from the 'applied linguistic' principles of the late nineteenth-century

Reform Movement, and in part also from its relative freedom from restrictions imposed by the demands of secondary school curricula and examination systems.

It is not part of the purpose of this book to explore any specific theme of historical development. It will serve, I hope, as a source book as much as anything else. Nevertheless, if there is a latent point of view beneath the surface, it is a belief that progress in the teaching of languages, as in many practical arts, is neither a function solely of the application of theoretical principle, however persuasive, nor of an unthinking reaction to the demands of the immediate market, but of the alchemy which, whether by accident or by design, unites them to a common purpose.

# PART ONE

# Practical language teaching to 1800

# 1 The early years

The teaching of modern vernacular languages began in England towards the end of the Middle Ages when French died out as the second language of the kingdom and gradually surrendered to English. The processes of linguistic change in England from a bilingual feudal community ruled by the Anglo-French Plantagenet dynasty to a largely monolingual nation under the Tudors were slow but irreversible. In 1385 John of Trevisa complained that English children knew no more French than 'their left heel' and it was necessary for them to construe their Latin lessons in English. He blamed the Black Death of 1356 for this dislocation of traditional linguistic patterns, but saw certain advantages in the change: 'they learneth their grammar in less time than children were i-woned (*used*) to do'. However, there were also disadvantages in this new linguistic independence when Englishmen 'shall pass the sea and travel in strange lands and in many other places'.[1] From now on French was a foreign language and would have to be learnt. So, *mutatis mutandis*, was English.

Trevisa was writing in the reign of Richard II and was a contemporary of Chaucer who traditionally represents the waxing mood of English self-confidence at the end of the fourteenth century. Before the end of Richard's reign the earliest extant manual for the teaching of French in England had been written by an unknown East Anglian author in Bury St. Edmunds on Whitsun Eve, May 29th 1396.[2] It is a collection of useful everyday dialogues for travellers to France and was the first of a number of similar manuals, or *manières de langage* as they are usually called, which appeared during the fifteenth and early sixteenth centuries, and were the forerunners of the situational language teaching textbooks of the Tudor period which we shall discuss later.

The break with the past, represented by the usurpation of the throne from Richard II by the House of Lancaster in 1399, expressed itself in overt linguistic terms. The order deposing Richard was read in English and Henry IV himself elected to use English both in claiming the crown and later in his acceptance speech.[3] The tradition was carried on by his son Henry V who adopted English as the language of royal correspondence in place of French. If there is a fulcrum in the swing away from French and Latin as the normal means of written communication towards their replacement by English, it is probably the reign of

Henry V which witnessed a rising consciousness of nationhood engendered by Henry's legendary victory at Agincourt in 1415. Although Shakespeare's portrait of Henry is obviously an Elizabethan glamorization of 'the star of England', the touches of linguistic self-consciousness that he gives his hero in his dealings with his French bride ('Fie upon my false French! By mine honour, in true English, I love thee, Kate')[4] are not without some historical reality. The first extant council record written in English dates from his reign (1417),[5] and his decision to follow his father's example and publish his will in English also made a public impact.[6] The London brewers, for instance, adopted Henry's attitude as a precedent in making their decision to record their proceedings in English in 1422:

> Whereas our mother tongue, to wit the English tongue, has in modern days begun to be honourably enlarged and adorned, because our most excellent lord, King Henry V, has in his letters missive and divers affairs touching his own person, more willingly chosen to declare the secrets of his will, and for the better understanding of his people, has with a diligent mind procured the common idiom (setting aside others) to be commended by the exercise of writing: and there are many of our craft of Brewers who have the knowledge of writing and reading in the said English idiom, but in others, to wit, the Latin and French, used before these times, they do not in any wise understand.[7]

By the end of the fifteenth century even the statutes of the realm were written in English, and the affairs of state handled through the royal secretariat were conducted in the vernacular. During the same period the dialect of the East-Central Midlands established itself as the prestige variety of English pronunciation used among the nobility and others associated with the power that gathered round the new Tudor dynasty.[8] Orthographical standardization was also well advanced in so far as it was subject to the scribal disciplines of the royal chancery, but suffered a setback after the introduction of printing (1476) which, in the early years of the trade, had no tradition of uniformity in craft training or practices. To the Tudors, English was the language of the nation, spoken by all from the King himself downwards. French was seen as a prestigious accomplishment necessary for anyone with ambition towards culture or advancement in high places, and Latin remained secure as the mark of a properly educated man or woman. Going to school meant learning Latin grammar and, in a sense, Latin was the only language that had a grammar. French was about to acquire one in John Palsgrave's monumental *Lesclaircissement de la langue francoyse* published in 1530. English, on the other hand, had to wait until the beginning of the next century before any serious attempt was made to produce a scholarly description of the language, though William

Bullokar's *Pamphlet for Grammar*, a brief sketch for a longer work, had appeared a little earlier in 1586.[9]

In the absence of grammatical and other descriptions of vernacular languages, it is not surprising to find that early language teaching materials relied mainly on texts, and the dialogue form as a 'slice of linguistic life', was the obvious type to choose. There were, however, other reasons. In the first place, the use of dialogues was a long-established tradition in the teaching of spoken Latin in the Middle Ages. The best-known example of a Latin-teaching dialogue, or colloquy, as they were usually called, is one by Aelfric, Abbot of Eynsham, written in the eleventh century, before the Norman Conquest.[10] The Latin text, which is accompanied by an interlinear translation in Anglo-Saxon, consists of a series of questions and answers relating to topics and activities of everyday rural life, farming, hunting, trading, and so on. These were familiar to the youngsters who were being trained in elementary Latin before moving on to higher studies in grammar and rhetoric. The question-and-answer format itself derives from an even more basic teaching technique common in orate communities where verbatim learning of written texts is required in the education of the young to preserve essential texts from the linguistic variation which otherwise accompanies oral traditions of learning. This is the catechistic technique whereby questions are used as prompts to the memory and serve to break the text into digestible chunks which can be learnt by heart. It was a common procedure in textbooks throughout the whole period to 1800, and sometimes later as well. Joseph Priestley's *Rudiments of English Grammar* written in the late eighteenth century (1761) is a typical example:

Q What is Grammar?
A Grammar is the art of using words properly.
Q Of how many parts doth Grammar consist?
A Of four: Orthography, Etymology, Syntax, and Prosody.
Q What is Orthography?
A Orthography is the art of combining letters into syllables, and syllables into words.[11]

Modern language teaching dialogues did not of course adopt all the features of the catechistic method, but they grew out of the same procedural tradition and shared some of its advantages for the teacher. The learners had to do all the work of memorization and the teacher merely had to prompt them with questions in order to 'hear' the lesson. The following extract shows traces of a catechistic origin. It comes from a *manière de langage* written in the same year as Agincourt (1415). The battle is actually mentioned in an earlier section of the text, underlining the interest of these manuals in contemporary life and events. In this section, it is quite clear who the manual was written for: merchants in the all-important wool trade as well as other traders in agricultural products. I have included the rather lengthy list of things for sale in order to emphasize the importance of commerce in the early stages of modern language teaching. It is likely that the book was written by William of Kingsmill, a noted teacher of French in fifteenth-century Oxford.[12]

> Lady, where is your master?
> By God, sir, he has gone to the fair at Woodstock, which is ten miles from here.
> Lady, what goods does he wish to buy or sell there?
> Sir, he has to sell there, bulls, cows, oxen, calves, bullocks, old and young pigs, boars, sows, horses, mares, foals, sheep, rams, and ewes, tups, lambs, kids, she-kids, asses, mules, and other beasts. He also has to sell there 20 sacks, 3 tods, 4 stones, and 5 cloves of wool, 200 woolfells, 14 long cloths and 10 dozen Oxford mixtures, 20 Abingdon kerseys, 10 Witney blankets, 6 Castlecombe reds, 4 Colchester russets, scarlets, celestial blues or perses, sanguine and violet plunkets in ray grain, Salisbury motleys, and other various colours of several kinds of cloth to be delivered as well to lords, abbots, and priors, as to other folk of the countryside.'

The first textbooks designed solely to teach English as a foreign language do not appear until the late sixteenth century after the arrival of large numbers of French Huguenot refugees in the 1570s and 1580s, but there are signs of an interest in learning the language among members of the mercantile community on the other side of the Channel, particularly in Flanders, well before this. Double-manuals in the *manière* tradition aiming to teach English to French-speakers as well as the other way round, started to appear at the end of the fifteenth century, though it is unlikely that the market for English was particularly extensive. The customers for these manuals may have included merchants using French as a *lingua franca* as well as native French speakers. Perhaps they found the French of their English counterparts difficult to understand at times and so decided to learn English themselves. More likely, however, they recognized the old truth that even a smattering of your client's mother tongue works wonders in business. It also helps to safeguard against sharp practice.

The first of these double-manuals was a short book of dialogues and other texts prepared by William Caxton and printed on his newly-established printing press in Westminster in 1483 or thereabouts. The title-page of the book has been lost but it is known by its sub-heading as *Tres bonne doctrine pour aprendre briefment fransoys et engloys* or *Right good lernyng for to lerne shortly frenssh and englyssh*. According to Henry Bradley, who prepared an edition of the work for the Early

English Text Society in 1900, it was almost certainly a reworking by Caxton of a much older Flemish-French manual written in Bruges in the fourteenth century. Caxton had been a leading member of the English merchant community in Bruges for much of his life and had presumably brought the manual back to England with him. Perhaps his experience in the textile trade in Flanders convinced him that there was a market for English, and he may have wanted to do his former associates a good turn by promoting their language. There is no doubt, however, that he had the commercial needs of his learners in mind: 'Who this booke shall wylle lerne may well enterprise or take on honde marchandises fro one land to anothir'.[13]

The Caxton manual follows the traditions of the older *manières* except that, unlike them, it is bilingual. It is severely practical in its aims and contains no linguistic information about either French or English. It opens with a set of customary greetings: 'Syre, god you kepe! . . . I haue not seen you in longe tyme . . . Syre, gramercy of your courtoys (*courteous*) wordes and of your good wyll',[14] and so on. It then moves on to very simple texts which are designed to introduce useful vocabulary for household equipment ('ketellis, pannes, basyns')[15], servants, family relationships, etc. A shopping dialogue follows with lists of words for meat, birds, fish, fruit, herbs, etc. and a very detailed dialogue on the buying and selling of textiles of various kinds, mainly wool but also hides, skins, and other materials.

The second half of the book is more interesting and original. It contains an alphabetically arranged series of vignette portraits, mainly of trades-people, such as 'Agnes our maid', 'Colard the goldsmyth', 'David the bridelmaker', 'George the booke sellar' and the following extract concerning 'Martin the grocer':

| | |
|---|---|
| Martin le especier | Martin the grocer |
| Vent pluiseurs especes | Selleth many spyces |
| De toutes manieres de pouldre | Of all maners of poudre |
| Pour faire les brouets, | For to make browettys, (*broths*) |
| Et a moult de boistes pointes | And hath many boxes paynted |
| Plaines de confections, | Full of confections, |
| Et moult de cannes | And many pottes |
| Plaines de beuurages. | Full of drynkes.[16] |

After a dialogue about finding and paying for lodgings, the book ends with a short prayer that it will enlighten the hearts of its readers.[17]

Caxton's assistant in his printing shop, Wynken de Worde, produced another double-manual about fifteen years later along similar lines called *A Lytell treatyse for to lerne Englisshe and Frensshe* (c.1498). The text is laid out in alternating lines of English and French rather than in columns. The opening is interesting because of the reference to the use of French as a commercial *lingua franca* in the last three lines of the extract: 'so that I may do my merchandise in France, and elsewhere in other lands, there as the folk speak French':

> Here is a good boke to lerne to speke Frenshe
> Vecy ung bon livre apprendre parler françoys
> In the name of the fader and the sone
> En nom du pere et du filz
> And of the holy goost, I wyll begynne
> Et du saint esperit, je vueil commencer
> To lerne to speke Frensshe,
> A apprendre a parler françoys,
> Soo that I maye doo my marchandise
> Affin que je puisse faire ma marchandise
> In Fraunce & elles where in other londes,
> En France et ailieurs en aultre pays,
> There as the folk speke Frensshe.
> La ou les gens parlent françoys.[18]

There were other signs of a growing interest in learning English in the early sixteenth century. The polyglot dictionaries and phrasebooks, which were a popular device for acquiring a 'survival knowledge' of foreign languages in Renaissance times, began to include English alongside the more widely-known languages like French, Italian, and Latin. The earliest listed in the Alston *Bibliography* is a seven-language dictionary of 1540[19] (Latin, French, Dutch, Italian, Spanish, and High-Dutch[20] as well as English) published, as one might expect, in Antwerp, the busy multilingual meeting-place of north European cloth merchants in the sixteenth century. It was followed by many others.

Double-manuals originating on the continent are perhaps a rather better guide to the demand for English as a foreign language than those produced in England itself. An early example is by a Frenchman called Gabriel Meurier who made his living as a language teacher in Antwerp in the mid-sixteenth century. Meurier can claim to be the first teacher of English as a foreign language we know by name since the other books we have been discussing were written anonymously, though it is unlikely that he had as many customers for English as for French. Meurier's double-manual was called *A Treatise for to Learn to Speak French and English* and was orginally published in Antwerp in 1553. The last known copy unfortunately perished in the bombing of Nuremberg during the last war, but a later edition, published in Rouen in 1641, survives and the title-page includes the further information that the book contains: 'a form for making letters, indentures and obligations, quittances, letters of exchange, very necessary for all Merchants that do occupy trade of merchandise'. The commercial interests of Meurier's students are very clear from this list of extras that the book promises.

The final example of early handbooks for the teaching of English to foreigners before the more serious work with the Huguenot refugees began was a manual discovered by Alston in his bibliographical research called *A Very Profitable Book to Learn the Manner of Reading, Writing and Speaking English and Spanish* (1554). It is reproduced in the Scolar series along with a vocabulary found bound with it. The background to the *Very Profitable Book* is rather curious. It is, as the title indicates, a double-manual, but both the languages have been translated from different earlier editions, the Spanish from Flemish and the English probably from Latin. It is a version of a famous sixteenth-century manual known as 'the Vocabulary of Barlement' which appeared in various guises at different times. According to Alston, the original of this version was probably a Flemish-Latin edition of 1551. It was clearly a rush job brought out to catch the market in 1554, when large numbers of Spaniards were expected in London to attend the wedding of Philip II of Spain and Mary I, a kind of Tudor Royal Wedding souvenir. The signs of haste are evident enough. The vocabulary list at the end of the book claims to be 'set in order of the Alphabet a.b.c.d.' It was in alphabetical order in the original Flemish but in translation the order disappeared and nobody bothered to rearrange it. More importantly, the situational background to the dialogues and commercial texts was reproduced unaltered, with the bizarre result that students are asked to arrange the sale of houses in Antwerp to landlords posing as Flemish entrepreneurs:

> I John of Barlement witness that I have let out to Peter Marschalco my house at Antwerp in the market, being at the sign of the Hare, with the ground and well, for six years.[21]

The 'John of Barlement' mentioned in the text is, presumably, an indirect reference to the author of the original *Vocabulaire* on which the manual was based, Noël de Barlement. He was another Antwerp language teacher working in the city a little before Meurier. Once the Spanish learners got used to addressing Tom of Wapping, for example, rather than some Low-Dutch property agent, they would find much of practical value in the book. It is fairly short and most of the first part is taken up with a conversation over dinner which gives all the useful phrases of everyday communication. The second half is almost entirely concerned with commercial affairs including buying and selling, ways of 'calling upon your debtors' and 'writing epistles', etc. It concludes with the vocabulary list already mentioned, and the standard church texts including, diplomatically enough, the Ave Maria.

Compared to some of the later manuals the dialogues are rather primitive, but serviceable. The following is part of the dining scene (the Spanish text is printed in a parallel column as usual):

**Hermes**   John, I pray God send ye a good day.
**John**       And I, Hermes, wish unto you a prosperous day.
**Hermes**   How do you?
**John**       Ask you how I do? I fare well, thanks be to God, and will be glad to do you pleasure. I say, Hermes, how go your matters forward?
**Hermes**   Verily I fare well.[22]

By the end of the century, teaching-dialogues were to become very much livelier and more entertaining than the efforts of John and Hermes.

The next stage in the development of English language teaching after these humble beginnings on the Antwerp quaysides was determined by major events in the mainstream of late sixteenth-century religious politics.

## Notes

1  *Polychronicon* quoted in Trevelyan (1956:234).
2  Myers (ed. 1969: 1212), Doc. 714. The title of the manual is *La manière de language qui t'enseignera bien à droit parler et escrire doulz françois*. A considerable number of manuscript copies have survived, indicating the popularity of the book (see Lambley (1920: 35–8)).
3  Baugh and Cable (1978: 148).
4  *Henry V*, Act V, scene ii.
5  Myers (ed. 1969: 1084), Doc. 634, footnote.
6  Baugh and Cable (1978: 153).
7  Myers (ed. 1969: 1084), Doc. 634.
8  Baugh and Cable (1978: 191–6). The East Midlands district was a large area taking in most of eastern England between the Thames and the Humber. Of particular importance for the development of Standard English was the dialect spoken in and around London.
9  The *Pamphlet for Grammar* is sometimes referred to, inappropriately, as the *Bref Grammar*, a sub-title taken from the running page-heading. See Turner (ed. 1980).
10  Garmonsway (ed. 1947).
11  Priestley (1761: 1).
12  Unlike the later manuals, the original has no English gloss. The translation comes from A. R. Myers (ed. 1969: 1195), Doc. 701. See also Lambley (1920: 39–40). The text includes some unfamiliar terms, mainly connected with the wool trade: *tups* (rams), *tods* and *cloves* (units of measurement of weight), *kerseys* (lengths of coarse narrow cloth), *perses* (dark purple cloth), *plunkets* (blankets), and *ray* (striped) *grain* (scarlet).

13 The exact date of the Caxton manual is unknown. Bradley (ed. 1900: 3–4) and Lambley (1920: 42–6) give 1483 as the probable date. Others have placed it slightly earlier, around 1480. There is also an argument that Caxton may have printed a translation written by another (unknown) Bruges merchant rather than his own, (see Blake (1965)).

14 Bradley (ed. 1900: 4–5).

15 Ibid.: 7.

16 Ibid.: 41.

17 Ibid.: 51–2.

18 Quoted in Lambley (1920: 48–9).

19 The dictionary was called *Septem Linguarum*.

20 (Low) Dutch = modern Dutch or Flemish; High Dutch = modern German.

21 Anon., *A Very Profitable Book* (1554: Dv verso).

22 Ibid.: Aii verso – Aiii recto.

# 2 'Refugiate in a strange country': the refugee language teachers in Elizabethan London

From about 1560 onwards, as Catholic reaction to the Reformation gathered momentum under the leadership of Philip II of Spain, the Low Countries, and particularly Flanders, were singled out for an exemplary show of Counter-Reformation power. The Duke of Alva bludgeoned the Flemings into choosing between submission and flight, and the younger and more enterprising among them elected exile. They arrived in large numbers in friendly neighbouring countries including England and were later joined by increasing numbers of their French co-religionists. Queen Elizabeth made them welcome for the skills and conscientious attitudes they brought with them to England, though many of her subjects were less enthusiastic about the threat these zealous foreigners brought to their own livelihoods. There were complaints and protests from guilds and apprentices, but Elizabeth and her ministers had little time for chauvinistic grumbles and restrictive practices. Besides, she had support from the more educated, and less threatened, sections of society who had sympathy for those who had 'suffered for religion', and welcomed them into their homes and communities. Serious unrest was inhibited to some extent by the impact of the St. Bartholomew Massacre in Paris in 1572 which provoked a mass exodus of Protestants from France to safety in the countries of the reformed church. St. Bartholomew was one of those events that crystalize complex historical processes and movements into a single indelible image, like Passchendaele, Auschwitz, or Stalingrad in our own century. The details of the massacre need not detain us here but the impact on life in England in the last quarter of the sixteenth century was considerable.

The French Huguenot and other Protestant refugees from Flanders, Italy, and even Spain itself, were for the most part skilled craftsmen and artisans, dyers, weavers, smiths, lacemakers, diamond-cutters, and so on, though some had a more intellectual 'middle class' background, among them of course the teachers. The numbers who came across in the 1570s and 1580s were formidable. It has been estimated that aliens registered in England (not all refugees, of course) rose from 300,000 to 360,000 between 1570 and Armada year (1588) to bring the total close to 10 per cent of the population, assuming the latter to be something of the order of three-and-a-half million.[1] This would be equivalent in modern terms to a foreign population of five-and-a-half million. After the Edict of Nantes in 1598 which, for a time at least, settled the religious question in France, many Huguenots returned, including almost all of those who had made a living and a reputation for themselves by teaching languages in London and other major English cities during the previous three decades.

We shall look in detail at the work of three of the refugee teachers who represent a cross-section of the language teaching community of the time. The first, *Jacques Bellot*, was the most significant in the present context since he devoted himself more seriously than the other two to the teaching of English to the immigrant French community in London, though, like the others, he also taught his mother tongue to the native population. The second is *Claudius Holyband*, the leading professional language teacher of his day and therefore the man whose work and teaching methods we know most about. Although he claimed to be 'a professor of the English tongue', his principal work was teaching French to young children at a succession of schools he founded in and near London. Holyband's career gives us a clear picture of the high level of pedagogical expertise that the immigrant group at its best brought to their language teaching activities. The third teacher, *John Florio*, is complementary to Bellot and Holyband in the sense that he represents the private tutors of languages who were adopted into large households by the gentry and aristocracy. Florio was, however, much more than a language teacher and textbook writer. His interests and talents took him into virtually every aspect of linguistic and literary studies in the 'Golden Age' of the English Renaissance in the decades on either side of the Union of the Kingdoms. Like the other two, Florio was a Protestant but he was a second-generation immigrant and the only one to remain in England until his death.

One interesting feature of the refugee teachers, which is of relevance to our own time, is that, leaving aside Bellot's English-teaching activities, they were native speakers of the languages they taught. Unlike their twentieth-century counterparts, however, they did not adopt a monolingual approach, but continued the traditional bilingual method of the earlier manuals. The ability to look at one's own language through the eyes of someone attempting to learn it requires what might be called a 'reflexive imagination', and the skill and knowledge to put its insights into practice. This in turn implies a need for reliable linguistic descriptions from which models, examples, and explanations can be drawn to clarify the teacher's native intuitions. In the sixteenth century there were substantial descriptions of French, including Palsgrave's magnificent *Lesclaircissement de la langue francoyse* (1530) mentioned earlier, but there was no comparable study of English. This helps to explain why the linguistic information in the manuals of Bellot and Florio is so scanty, and also, perhaps, accounts for the absence of native-speaking teachers of English.

As we have seen, most of the refugees were craftsmen and, provided they could find employment or the resources to set up on their own, would survive and even prosper without a detailed knowledge of spoken English. Most of them would pick the language up informally through their contacts in the local community. They would not, however, be able to pick up literacy skills in the same way and, although the demands made on them would have been slight compared to their counter-parts at the present time, it would have been difficult to maintain the status of a skilled craftsman without some ability to handle the written language.

For the wives and other members of the family, however, with little opportunity for full-time work, the situation would have been more distressing. Literacy skills would not have had much importance, but the ability to speak English would have been even more essential for them than for the men. Not only were there all the obvious situations such as shopping and getting about the city, but there were social needs as well. Local grassroots hostility to foreigners could break out at any time. With both the most powerful nations of Europe, France and Spain, ranged against them, the English were suspicious and 'jumpy'. Rumours of foreign spies, Catholic agents, and conspiracies of every kind were flying about and small incidents frequently flared into ugly scenes in the overcrowded streets. The women and the elderly in particular would have been exposed to insults, if not outright physical danger, and a knowledge of everyday English was some protection against mindless scare-mongering.

The two small English manuals that *Jacques Bellot* wrote for the French-speaking refugees in the 1580s reflect these priorities of basic literacy and everyday conversation quite closely. Unlike the books for teaching French, they contain very little about commercial transactions or other aspects of business life. They are much nearer home and concentrate on the needs that have just been described. The first book that Bellot published after his arrival in England (some time in the late 1570s) was *The English Schoolmaster* (1580), obviously echoing the title of Roger Ascham's famous educational treatise of 1570. *The Schoolmaster* was dedicated, rather unexpectedly, to the brother of the King of France, Duke Alençon, presumably because he was a well-known suitor for Elizabeth's hand, though she was far from enamoured of her 'little Frog' as she called him. It shows that Jacques Bellot, the self-styled 'Gentleman of Caen', who had arrived without a penny some years before, was aiming high. His second book, *Familiar Dialogues* (1586) is, as the title suggests, a collection of everyday dialogues and conversations.

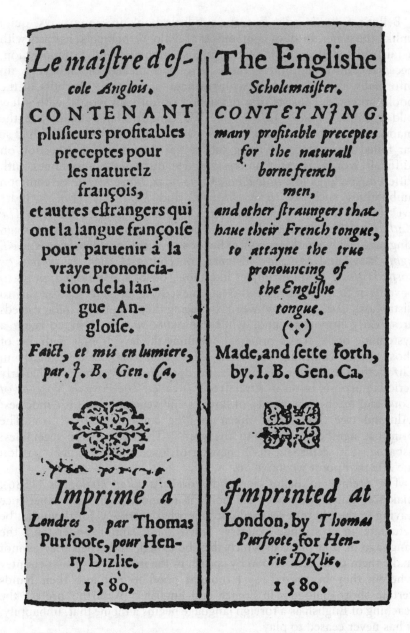

*Le maiſtre d'eſ-* | The Englishe

cole Anglois. | Scholemaiſter.

CONTENANT | CONTEYNING.

pluſieurs profitables | *many profitable preceptes*

preceptes pour | *for the naturall*

les naturelz | *borne french*

françois, | *men,*

et autres eſtrangers qui | *and other ſtraungers that*

ont la langue françoiſe | *haue their French tongue,*

pour paruenir à la | *to attayne the true*

vraye prononcia- | *pronouncing of*

tion de la lan- | *the Engliſhe*

gue An- | *tongue.*

gloiſe. | (∵)

*Faiɫt, et mis en lumiere,* | Made, and ſette forth,

*par. J. B. Gen. Ca.* | by. I. B. Gen. Ca.

Imprimé à | *Jmprinted at*

*Londres* , *par* Thomas | London, by *Thomas*

Purfoote, *pour* Hen- | *Purfoote,* for Hen-

ry Dizlie. | rie *Dizlie.*

1580, | 1580.

Figure 1 *Title-page of the earliest extant manual specifically designed for the teaching of English as a foreign language, Jacques Bellot's* English Schoolmaster *published in 1580. The letters I.B. are the author's initials (J and I were interchangeable), and Gen. Ca. stands for Gentilhomme Cadomois, or Gentleman of Caen, the town in Normandy where Bellot came from. The book was written to help Huguenot exiles in England who had arrived in great numbers during the previous decade.*

Bellot's *Schoolmaster* is a curious little book in many ways, quite unlike the general run of contemporary dialogue manuals. It starts with a fairly detailed account of the English alphabet and pronunciation, necessary information for those who had picked the language up informally and needed help with reading and writing. The bulk of the book, however, consists of a discussion of 'difficult words' with a few odd grammar points thrown in. We cannot blame Bellot for the inadequacy of these grammar notes, considering that the English had so far failed to produce anything substantial themselves. The section on 'difficult words' is more interesting. He discusses homophones with different spellings like *hole/whole*, *bore/boar*, *horse/hoarse* or common ambiguities such as *right*, *straight*, and *hold*. He even includes everybody's favourite minimal pair: *David was a keeper of sheep / The Katharine of England is a fair ship*. Every teacher of English as a foreign language today would recognize Bellot's choice of problem-words: *well*, *light*, *stay*, and *fast*, for instance, or contrasts such as *fill/feel* or *cost/coast/cast*. With examples like these, Bellot's main aim appears to have been to help learners who had picked the language up 'by ear' to distinguish easily confused words by seeing them in print. Literacy needs are clearly important and, while the *Schoolmaster* is in no sense a systematic book, it is a practical one none the less. It ends with one of those rather charming collections of sayings that occur regularly in Elizabethan language textbooks. It does not have any particularly serious purpose, but it is attractive. It is called *The Posy or Nosegay of Love* and teaches the names of flowers and vegetables in little mottoes: 'Almond tree flowers are taken for "be content in love" ' or 'The primrose signifieth "I begin to love you" '. Then he turns to vegetables: asparagus, it seems, means 'renewing of love' and the radish 'pardon me'. At that point we move on.

The preface to Bellot's second work, *Familiar Dialogues* (1586), makes it quite clear who the book is intended for: 'The experience having in the old time learned unto me what sorrow is for them that be refugiate in a strange country, when they cannot understand the language of that place in which they be exiled, and when they cannot make them to be understood by speech to the inhabiters of that country wherein they be retired . . . I thought good to put into their hands certain short dialogues in French and English.'[2] With this preface the teaching of English as a foreign language begins a theme that, unhappily, it has never ceased to play.

Bellot's dialogues have a domestic setting with a strong emphasis on shopping. His characters visit the poulterer, the costermonger, the draper, the fishmonger, and the butcher in a lengthy sequence of shop scenes in the middle of the book, which follows more or less the sequence of a single day. It begins with getting up in the morning and seeing the children off to school. Then comes the shopping and, in the evening, friends call in for dinner, and the conversation gets round to their present depressing predicament:

| The master | What news? |
| The neighbour | There is no other news but of the sickness and the dearth, which be nowadays almost throughout all France . . . |
| The master | Is the number of them great, that are come over into this country? |
| The neighbour | Very great, and there be many of them which do live very hard, so great is their poverty.[3] |

Later their spirits revive and they play dice and cards. The book ends with some useful travel phrases.

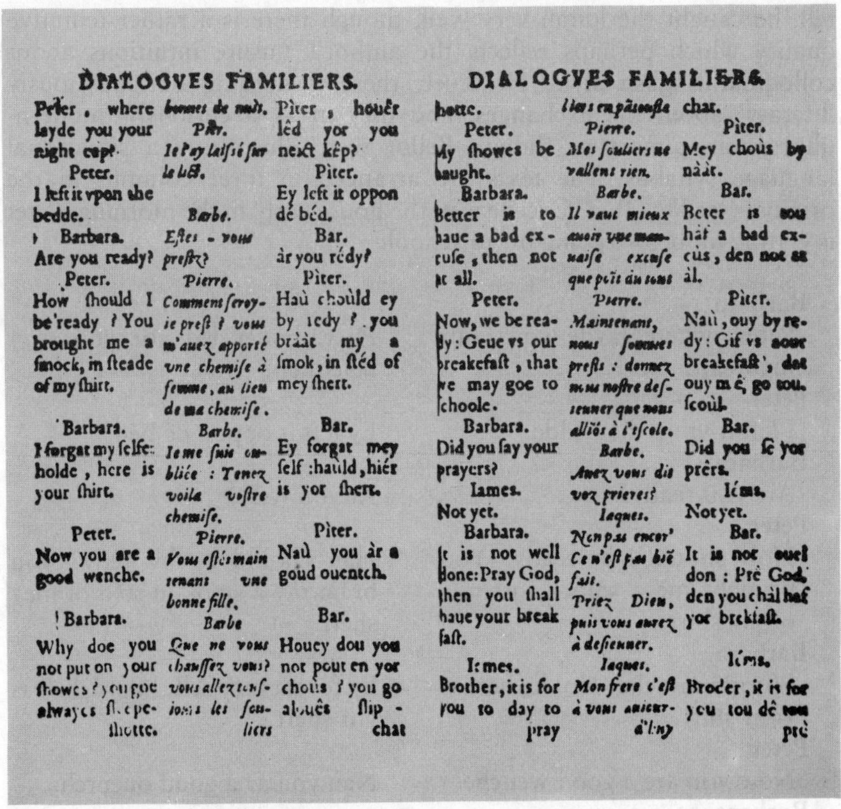

Figure 2   Extract from Jacques Bellot's Familiar Dialogues, written in 1586 to help the Huguenot refugees with everyday spoken English. It depicts one of the standard situations in dialogue manuals of this kind, Getting up in the Morning. The 'semi-phonetic' pronunciation in the third column is of special interest.

It is quite likely, though we cannot be sure, that Bellot assumed his dialogues would be used mainly for self-instruction at home. At all events, he included a 'semi-phonetic' transcription of the English texts which would obviously be useful for such purposes and it was not a standard procedure. The transcription has been studied by experts (Bjurman 1977) and I shall not comment on it in detail here. To a non-specialist ear the transcribed phrases seem to have a French 'flavour' to them, especially expressions like *oppon de bed*, or *you go alouês slip-chat* (French *ch* = English *sh*), but it does not appear to be entirely consistent. *Breakfast*, for instance, is transcribed in two different ways. Perhaps this was a printer's error, although the printer in question, Vautrollier, also a Huguenot refugee, had a high reputation. He was Holyband's printer, at least for some of his publications. The following extract gives some idea of the transcription and how it worked. It also shows the kind of language Bellot considered representative of ordinary conversation in everyday situations. So far as one can tell, he caught the idiom very well, though there is a rather tentative quality which perhaps reflects the author's unsure intuitions about colloquial English style. However, there is nothing self-consciously 'literary' about the exchanges, and they make a curiously 'modern' impression, almost as though Bellot were illustrating a situational language syllabus. The texts are arranged in three columns in the original (see Fig. 2). The scene is in the house early in the morning. Peter is getting up before going off to school:

**Barbara**
  Peter, where layde you your nightcap?

  Pìter, houêr lêd yor you (*sic*) neict kêp?

**Peter**
  I left it vpon the bedde.

  Ey left it oppon dé béd.

**Barbara**
  Are you ready?

  Àr you rédy?

**Peter**
  How should I be ready? You brought me a smock insteade of my shirt.

  Haù choùld ey by redy? you brààt my a smok in stéd of mey shert.

**Barbara**
  I forgat myselfe: Holde, here is your shirt.

  Ey forgat mey self: haùld, hiér is yor shert.

**Peter**
  Now you are a good wenche.

  Naù you àr a goud ouentch.

**Barbara**
  Why doe you not put on your showes? You go always slepe-shotte.

  Houey dou you not pout on yor choùs? You go alouês slip-chat.

**Peter**

| | |
|---|---|
| My showes be naught. | Mey choùs by nàat. |

**Barbara**

| | |
|---|---|
| Better is to haue a bad excuse then not at all. | Beter is tou hàf a bad excùs den not at àl. |

**Peter**

| | |
|---|---|
| Now, we be ready: Geue vs our breakefast that we may goe to schoole. | Naù, ouy by redy. Gif vs aour breakefast, dat ouy mê go tou scoùl. |

**Barbara**

| | |
|---|---|
| Did you say your prayers? | Did you sè yor prêrs? |

**James**

| | |
|---|---|
| Not yet. | Not yet. |

**Barbara**

| | |
|---|---|
| It is not well done: Pray God, then you shall haue your breakfast. | It is not ouel don: Prê God, den you chàl haf yor brekfast.[4] |

Bellot's English manuals are not as thorough or as ambitious pedagogically as many of the contemporary French textbooks. On the other hand, they take their task seriously and were no doubt of practical benefit to their customers. In addition, they are of considerable interest historically as the earliest extant textbooks intended solely for the teaching of English as a foreign language.

The second of our group of language teachers working in London during the last quarter of the sixteenth century is *Claudius Holyband*, in many ways the most successful and certainly the most professional of them all. Our knowledge of Holyband before and after his London work is scanty. We do not know when he was born, or when and where he died. It is not even clear exactly when he arrived in England. All we know is that he came from the town of Moulins in Central France and that he was already a teacher when he fled with his family to escape the rising religious tensions. His home town was a centre of Huguenot activity and was 'visited' by the King and his mother Catharine de Medici in 1565. In the view of M. St. Clare Byrne (1953) it is more than likely that the royal interest in the town prompted Holyband's departure around Christmas 1565.[5]

Holyband was granted letters of denization (citizenship rights) in January 1566 under the name of 'A Sancto Vinculo, Claud.'. And he appeared in the Register of Aliens for the City of Westminster in 1568 under the name of 'Claudius Hollybrande, scholemaster, denizen'. This is an anglicization of his original name Claude de Sainliens (sometimes spelt as one word Desainliens) which is usually preferred by historians of linguistics. We shall, however, stick to the name he chose to adopt in his new country, Claudius Holyband. These details are of more than academic interest since they show that Holyband, alone among the refugee teachers, went so far in assimilating to his new country as to take a new name. Of course, he might also have thought it good for business, given the undercurrents of hostility that the increasingly large numbers of immigrants tended to generate. Holyband was a relatively early arrival and perhaps he wanted to distance himself somewhat from the influx after St. Bartholomew.

Secondly, Holyband's date of arrival in England is important since it relates to the order in which he wrote his major textbooks, *The French Schoolmaster* and *The French Littleton*. The date on the title-page of the latter is given as 1566, which would make it the first. However, if he only arrived in the country in that year, and the book clearly shows evidence of considerable experience of teaching French in England, it lends weight to other arguments which we need not go into, that 1566 is in actual fact a misprint for 1576, making *The French Littleton* the second work. It makes much more pedagogical sense.[6]

During his time in London, Holyband opened three schools at different times in which he taught French to young children as well as offering the standard Latin curriculum which parents would want and expect. The first was at Lewisham, at that time a small village to the south of the city, in the late 1560s, and the other two were in St. Paul's Churchyard, the precinct round the Cathedral which still exists under that name, in the early to mid-1570s. The Churchyard in Elizabethan times was the centre of the book trade and full of printers, stationers, and booksellers all identified with signs, a device that only survives today with pubs. Holyband's first school at St. Paul's was at the Sign of Lucrece and the second at the Sign of the Golden Ball. We do not know why he moved, but he may have needed larger premises since his school seems to have done very good business in spite of the high fees. He charged fifty shillings a year, a large sum if you consider that a headmaster might expect to earn around twenty pounds a year. Holyband's critics had a point when they accused him, and other refugee teachers, of making exorbitant charges. Nevertheless, he found customers, mainly among the wealthy mercantile classes – the aristocracy did not send their children to school – who were evidently anxious that their sons should be able to speak French. These commercial interests were prominent in Holyband's teaching materials, as we shall see.

Between giving up the Lewisham school and opening the new one at St. Paul's, Holyband spent some time in the household of Lord Buckhurst, a member of the influential Sackville family and a relative by marriage of the Queen. Elizabeth herself visited Lewisham school at one point, and Holyband later dedicated one of his books to her. She also accepted the dedication of a French manual by Bellot. Incidents of this kind, though small, lend weight to the view that the Queen took a close and sympathetic interest in the activities of the immigrant community in

London and helped, indirectly anyway, to counteract the grumbling of the populace. Holyband's time with the Sackvilles meant that he had experience of both kinds of contemporary language teaching, as a schoolmaster teaching classes of youngsters and as a private tutor to a noble family. The two textbooks we have already mentioned clearly reflect this breadth of experience. The earlier of the two, *The French Schoolmaster*, appeared in 1573 at more or less the time he entered the Sackville household, and the second, *The French Littleton*, was produced as the new textbook for his school in St. Paul's which he opened in 1576.

The *Schoolmaster* and the *Littleton* have much in common. They are both teaching manuals not linguistic studies, and they both make great use of dialogue work. The *Schoolmaster* (another conscious echo of Ascham) is organized rather differently from the *Littleton*, however, because it was intended as much for self-instruction as for class use. This reflects its origins during Holyband's service with the Sackville family. It was 'set forth for the furtherance of all those which do study privately in their own study or house'. The principal difference between the two books is that the linguistic information on pronunciation and grammar comes at the beginning of the *Schoolmaster* whereas in the *Littleton* it is put in an appendix at the back of the book. In most other respects the books are very similar, though the *Schoolmaster* has perhaps more of a social slant whereas the *Littleton* concentrates on commercial French. Both books contain lengthy vocabulary lists arranged in topic areas (Holyband later collected these lists together and expanded them into his *Dictionary French and English* (1593)) as well as proverbs and sayings.

Holyband's dialogues are well-known to social historians of the period for the minutiae of everyday life they portray. They are not like dialogues in modern courses but much longer sequences of scenes and events that follow one another in quick succession. 'Picture after picture is flashed upon the mind in vivid, breathless sequences as the talk shifts momently from group to group', as St. Clare Byrne puts it.[7] One is also reminded of Shakespeare's hectic battle scenes: part of the field, the King's camp, another part of the field, etc. Held together in a broad thematic context such as 'School', these short, self-contained episodes not only have an artistic impact, they also serve a more prosaic pedagogical purpose which helps to clarify Holyband's classroom methods. Each episode contains enough material for one lesson – he worked very thoroughly and slowly – while the context keeps a situational thread running through from one lesson to the next. This technique has certain advantages not available to modern authors who use either very short dialogues illustrating a new language point or longer, more discursive 'playlets' which can sometimes be difficult to break down into sections for classroom use.

We shall look at an extract from one of the *Littleton* dialogues shortly, but first a word or two about the book itself and its audience. The rather unusual title is taken from a famous basic law textbook of the time by Sir Thomas Littleton called *Tenures*, and, like its namesake, it is very small. It was designed to fit neatly into a satchel along with the quills, penknives, ink-horns, conkers, and everything else that the 'whining schoolboy' might carry about with him. Not that there is much evidence in Holyband's school of any unwillingness to attend, and if the children arrived 'creeping like snails', the most likely explanation is they were half-asleep. School started at seven in the morning and finished at five in the afternoon with an hour off for lunch. In the winter it was dark at both ends of the school day, and Holyband closes his school dialogue with a late departure: 'Blow out the candle for the tallow stinketh; snuff the other . . . go to supper without playing the fools by the streets. Light your lanterns'.[8] One can almost see him bustling the children out of the door with all these reminders and afterthoughts following them down the draughty alleyways of St. Paul's Churchyard.

The children in Holyband's school were worked hard. They not only had their French lessons but also followed a regular Latin course which, it seems, Holyband left mostly to his assistant, or usher. They were very young, about eight or nine years old, and the atmosphere of the school that comes across in the dialogue is youthful, exuberant, and high-spirited. There is a lot of dire talk about thrashings and the like, but they rarely happen; it is all in the bantering tradition of 'right, you scruffy urchin'.

The extract from the school dialogue ('Of Scholars and School') (Fig. 3) comes about halfway through the text. In earlier episodes, a new boy arrives with his father and there is a discussion about fees, the equipment the boy needs, and so on. Then there is the first of a series of interruptions from Master John Nothingworth, the school ruffian, who, it is alleged, 'hath sworn by God, lied twice, played by the way',[9] and committed sundry other misdemeanours. In the extract, he breaks another rule by speaking English, which implies strongly that Holyband used French as a medium of instruction in the class. Suddenly, the scene switches to another boy, Peter, who oversleeps. The extract begins as he is leaving home already very late.

After the parting scene at Peter's house, in which Holyband uses the substitution table to introduce personal pronouns *lui, elle*, etc., there is a 'filmic' switch to the late arrival at school. In the short 'bribery' episode of the ring, the substitution table has a second function, namely to show that there is not always a one-to-one correspondence between words in French (*anneau, bague, cachet, signet*) and English (*ring*). Next come the excuses for being late, which are also presented in a tabular form, this time for the more traditional purpose of vocabulary teaching. There are two further examples on pp. 22–3, the second describing more

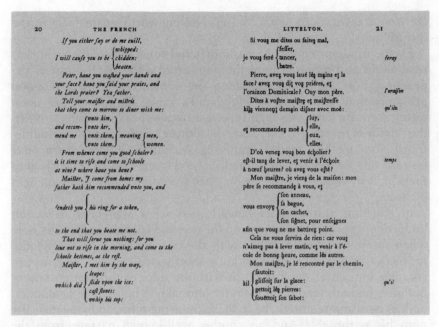

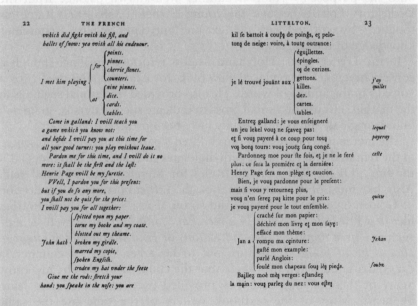

Figure 3  Extract from the dialogue 'Of Scholars and School' in Claudius
Holyband's French Littleton, though it was not included in the first edition of 1576.
Most of the text deals with the late arrival of Peter, one of the boys, and his excuses.
At the bottom of p. 22, there is one of the periodic incidents involving John
Nothingworth, the class ruffian. It is interesting to see that speaking English in class
was discouraged.

classroom disruptions with Master Nothingworth again leading the disturbances.

Each episode provided the basic material for a lesson. The text was read aloud and repeated until the pupils had a thorough grasp of the pronunciation and could produce the sentences fluently. A good pronunciation was one of Holyband's chief aims and his main justification for charging high fees as a native-speaking teacher. Next, the children practised the text in writing, following the 'double-translation' method made famous by Ascham: 'Children, turn your lessons out of French into English, and then out of English into French'.[10] By the end of the lesson, they would probably know the text by heart.

In teaching grammar, Holyband used what was later called an 'inductive' approach, starting from the text and consulting the rules only when the pupils were familiar with the new material. 'If the Reader meaneth to learn our tongue within a short space,' he said 'he must not entangle himself at the first brunt with the rules of the pronunciation; but after he hath read them over, let him take in hand these Dialogues; and, as occasion requireth, he shall examine the rules, applying their use unto his purpose'.[11] And, in another well-known passage from the Dedicatory Epistle, he says 'the young learner . . . shall first frame his tongue'[12] by working with the text and only later acquire a conscious knowledge of the language.

In the French texts, Holyband used a reformed spelling, though a conservative one. He replaced a qu by k, for example, and used z for a voiced s in the middle of words. He also provided traditional spellings in the margin. His use of a small cross to indicate silent letters is, so far as I know, original, and could usefully have been preserved.

The mercantile interests of the children's parents are well-represented in the remainder of the book with dialogues such as 'For Travellers', 'Of the Inn', 'Of the Weight', and 'Rules for Merchants to Buy and Sell'. Also, like most of its contemporaries, the Littleton contains a collection of Golden Sayings, Bon Mots, and so on. These include short mottoes like In a Prince loyalty and In a merchant faith-keeping as well as 'sets' such as Three things odious and tedious or Four things which ought to always be at home (these turn out to be a hen roost, a chimney, a cat, and a good wife). It is likely that the children would already know many of these sayings and they provided excellent material to learn by heart. Most of the textbook writers of the time use the same examples and Florio collected hundreds of them for use in his Italian courses.

After the sayings come the vocabulary lists and a lengthy reading text on dancing (not such an odd subject in Elizabethan times as it might be today) and, finally, the grammar and pronunciation rules. The former are very detailed, but the syntax is sketchy since Holyband considered that grammar really belonged in a more advanced course than the *Littleton*.

By the time he left England in the late 1590s Holyband had completed most of his textbook scheme which, besides the two elementary courses we have discussed, included a study of French phonology called *De Pronuntiatione Linguae Gallicae* (1580), a grammatical work called *A Treatise for Declining of Verbs* (1580), and a dictionary which started out as *A Treasury of the French Tongue* and was later enlarged into *A Dictionary French and English* (1593). This work later formed the (unacknowledged) nucleus of Randle Cotgrave's famous English-French dictionary of 1611.

Holyband had spent thirty years of his life in England when he returned to France, as we assume he did, after the Edict of Nantes in 1598. He had changed his name to suit his adopted country and he had married an English woman, his second wife Anne Smith. He, and his many fellow refugee teachers working in St. Paul's Churchyard and elsewhere in London and other English towns, had established high standards for the teaching of languages in England and their published work survived for many years into the next century.

The work of *John Florio* (*c.*1553–1625), the last of our trio of sixteenth-century language teachers, shows language teaching in a rather different light. Unlike Bellot and Holyband, Florio cannot really be called a refugee. His father, Michaelangelo Florio, had come to England during the Protestant regime of Edward VI to be pastor of the Italian Church in London. He was also Italian tutor to the unfortunate Lady Jane Grey and therefore under suspicion after the accession of Mary I to the throne in 1553. After the failure of the Wyatt rebellion against Mary in the following year, the Florio family fled abroad to join one of the exiled English Protestant communities in Strasbourg. They later moved on to Switzerland. John Florio was a baby when the family left England and an adult of about twenty or so when he returned in the early 1570s. There is some evidence that he attended Tübingen University for a time but his movements during the period of exile are unclear. Having had an English mother he was a bilingual speaker of English and Italian but, though it is unlikely that he ever went to Italy, he is said to have preferred Italian. Like Joseph Conrad he was a writer whose expert but unusual control of the English language allowed him to develop a prose style that eventually enriched the literature of his second language.

Florio, like his father, moved in circles close to power and therefore danger. Immediately on his return he entered Magdalen College, Oxford, and made a living tutoring in Italian, a very popular language among the cultured aristocracy of the time. It had all the right associations of Machiavellian politics and Renaissance art, and Florio made the most of them. He was brought to London to work in the

French Embassy, a post he held in spite of a change of ambassador after the Mary Stuart affair, and later we find him employed as tutor in the household of the Earl of Southampton, the probable addressee of Shakespeare's sonnets and the rather worrying ward of Sir William Cecil, Elizabeth's chief minister. Frances A. Yates, in her excellent biography *John Florio, the Life of an Italian in Shakespeare's England* (1934) suggests that Florio had connections in high places in Elizabeth's administration, including Sir Francis Walsingham, whose intelligence network may have included Florio while he was nominally a secretary at the French Embassy, and even Cecil himself. Cecil needed ears and eyes (particularly around Southampton) and if Florio was a Cecilian 'mole' he was a good choice: a loyal Englishman who could if necessary be branded as a foreigner, a superb practical linguist, a tutor who could mix with the family and still keep in touch 'downstairs', and a squirrel of a man with a passion for collecting things: words, proverbs, sayings, mottoes—and gossip.

Florio survived the Essex rebellion and went on to become Italian tutor to the Royal Family itself in the next reign. He also acted as personal secretary to the Queen, Anne of Denmark, whose name he used in the title of the revised version of his great Italian–English dictionary *Queen Anna's New World of Words* which came out in 1611. When the Queen died in 1619, Florio lost his job and spent the last years of his life in poverty with fees due to him from King James unpaid. He died of the plague in 1625 at the age of 72.

All Florio's work as a language teacher was as a private tutor to high-ranking aristocratic patrons, and the textbooks he wrote for them suited their interests and tastes. Even the titles of his two principal double-manuals, *First Fruits* and *Second Fruits*, have a sense of style not found in the ordinary *Schoolmasters* and *Treatises*. Written in 1578 and 1591 respectively, they consist of Italian and English dialogues, some of them quite long and discursive, dealing with the topics of artistic and intellectual interest. There are no commercial texts, though he does find room for everyday phrases and the practical language of the 'Grand Tour': finding the way, arranging accommodation, dealing with landlords, etc. He also includes some interesting dialogues that explore different modes of address: how to talk to a gentleman, a lady, a servant, a merchant, and so on. The later dialogues are written in an elaborate, almost euphuistic, style that would have appealed to the young noblemen who employed him.

Florio was certainly a serious student of language as his collections of proverbs and his lexicographical work proves, but his vocation as a language teacher is more doubtful. His textbooks were mostly a means of survival in the years after his return from Europe. Essentially he was an intellectual with literary talents of the highest order and his genius did not find its full expression until he embarked on his famous translation of Montaigne's *Essays* (published in 1603) in which he produced one of the masterpieces of English prose. He made close friends with Ben Jonson, and Yates points to some interesting evidence linking him to Jonson's *Volpone*.[13] The absurd English milord and his lady who find themselves trapped in Mosca's schemes may well have been based on some of Florio's sillier pupils.

Although he is best known as a teacher of Italian, Florio also claimed to be a teacher of English as a foreign language. Presumably his students were drawn from the small but not insignificant group of Italian refugees resident in London. Both his *Fruits* were advertised as double-manuals, and in the *First* he took his English-teaching role seriously enough to include an Italian-language summary of linguistic points, mainly concerned with English spelling and pronunciation. In the *Second Fruits*, 'to be gathered of twelve trees of divers but delightsome tastes to the tongues of Italians and Englishmen',[14] he is less convincing. There are no linguistic notes and he attaches a list of six thousand proverbs in Italian without any attempt at an English gloss, which he called rather fancifully *Il Giardino di Ricreatione* (*Garden of Recreation*).

In the *First Fruits* Florio starts out with some practical dialogues giving examples of 'familiar speech' which are followed by a series of less successful conversations into which he weaves as many proverbs, golden sayings, mottoes, and the like as he can. In the latter half of the book he adopts a more serious tone and the discussions range over such matters as peace and war, fortune, beauty, virtue, and so on. One of the less expected strands in Florio's work is his dislike of England. How serious he was in his criticisms is difficult to tell, but he seems to have felt a sense of grievance at the hostility shown to him and other foreigners by the local population. These attacks were resented and he paid dearly for them in an incident which we shall come to shortly.

*Second Fruits* is more calculated to appeal to his new aristocratic patrons, the Earl of Southampton and his friends. The puritanical streak of the earlier book is missing and there are many scenes depicting riding, tennis, card games, fencing, and so on. It is full of gossip and rhyming couplets extolling the joys of love and the beauty of women. Although there are some useful dialogues providing the language needed for a tour of Italy, much of the material feeds the author's insatiable appetite for proverbs as this very short extract from Dialogue 9 shows:

What is become of your neighbour? . . .
As old as you see him. He hath of late wedded a young wench of
  fifteen years old.
Then he and she will make up the whole Bible together, I mean the
  new and old testament.
To an old cat, a young mouse.
Old flesh makes good broth.[15]

In the early 1590s the publishing activities of the refugee teachers reached their climax, and the simmering resentment of the native-born teachers finally boiled over in the publication of an extraordinary 'spoof' manual called the *Ortho-epia Gallica* by John Eliot in 1593.[16] It is easy to understand the strength of local feeling at what was becoming a foreign monopoly in the language teaching business. Holyband's *French Schoolmaster* was in constant demand, so much so that it attracted a special tax in 1600 'for the benefit of the poor'. Florio's *Second Fruits* appeared in 1591, the same year as a new edition of the *Littleton*. In 1592 a new refugee author called de la Mothe came on the scene, and the only work by an Englishman was William Stepney's *Spanish Schoolmaster* in 1591. The time had come for a counter-attack by the aggrieved locals.

John Eliot's mock French manual, the device chosen for his 'revenger's comedy' at the expense of the immigrant authors, is an amazing publication, made more deadly because it is a textbook that can be taken seriously as a teaching instrument. Eliot was a man of considerable literary talents in the style of Rabelais, a writer he did much to popularize in England, and he knew exactly what he was doing. It is quite clear from the title-page onwards who his chief target was. The Latinate over-title *Ortho-epia Gallica* is immediately revealed as a decoy and the real title is printed in capital letters underneath: *ELIOT'S FRUITS*. Eliot continues: 'Interlaced with a double new Invention. Pend for the practice, pleasure and profit of all English Gentlemen, who will endeavour by their own pain, study and diligence to attain the natural Accent, the true Pronunciation, the swift and glib Grace of this noble, famous and courtly Language'. He then throws out a direct challenge to the 'teachers and professors of noble languages, who are very busy daily in devising and setting forth new books and instructing our English gentlemen in this honourable city of London'.[17] If they attack him in return, it will be because he is an Englishman:

> I pray you be ready quickly to cavil at my book, I beseech you heartily calumniate my doings with speed, I request you humbly control my method as soon as you may, I earnestly entreat you hiss at mine inventions, I desire you to peruse my periodical punctuations, find fault with my pricks, nicks and tricks, prove them not worth a pin, not a point, not a pish: argue me a fond, foolish, frivolous and fantastical author, and persuade everyone that you meet, that my book is a false, feigned, slight, confused, absurd, barbarous, lame, unperfect, single, uncertain, childish piece of work, and not able to teach, and why so? Forsooth because it is not your own, but an Englishman's doing.[18]

Warming to his subject, he pitches into the teachers themselves, reviling them as 'beasts and serpents' who have poisoned England with the works of Machiavelli and other devilish writers. They should be banished from the kingdom like any other plague. Eliot knew how to keep up the vituperation for pages at a time and the book is a tour-de-force of insult.

If Eliot's attack was effective, it also seems to have been destructive. Florio himself, the prime target, never wrote another language manual, though he may have been preparing a Third Fruits when he died in 1625. Textbooks by other refugee teachers also dried up, but many of them were beginning to drift back home from the mid-1590s onwards as the religious situation in France improved. Significantly, however, Eliot's assumption that native textbook writers were being discriminated against proved groundless and no English-born author came forward to fill the place of the maligned foreigners.

After the departure of the refugees, foreign language teaching seems to have gone into a decline in the early seventeenth century, though well-established works like Holyband's *Schoolmaster* continued to be reprinted. Perhaps part of the explanation lies in the fact that England by and large stood aside from close involvement in European affairs. The debilitating violence of the Thirty Years' War, which broke out in 1618, made little practical impact on everyday life in the United Kingdom, though both England and Scotland provided a source of mercenary soldiers who sought fame and fortune in the armies of both sides. One such was a Scotsman called John Wodroephe who managed to exploit the side-effects of his war experience in the Netherlands by publishing a double-manual called *The Marrow of the French Tongue*[19] in Dort in 1623. It was republished two years later in London and dedicated to the new King Charles I, but, if Wodroephe hoped that Charles' marriage to Henrietta Maria would increase the demand for French in England, he must have been disappointed. The Queen succeeded in making herself and her language very unpopular in a series of studied insults. She refused to learn English herself and, to make matters worse, insisted on employing troupes of French actors who bored the court to tears with lengthy and unintelligible performances of French dramas.

The royal French connection did nothing for the teaching of English as a foreign language, either. There was, however, one new author, a French merchant called George Mason who produced a small manual called *Grammaire Angloise* in 1622. It is a disappointing work that adds little to the achievements of the previous century, being both pedagogically thin and linguistically unreliable. It contains comments on a rather oddly chosen selection of pronunciation problems followed by a lengthy set of grammatical paradigms and a small collection of dialogues at the end. The topics covered in these dialogues do not reflect Mason's interest in commerce and seem to be aimed specifically at a female readership, including one dialogue 'For Women', and others on 'The Kitchen' and 'At the Shambles'. The book has some interest for students of early seventeenth-century English pronunciation since, like Bellot, Mason uses a system of imitated pronunciation in some of the dialogue texts. But there is one particular linguistic point that makes his grammar of interest to teachers of English as a foreign language. This is the prominence he gives to the verb form which today would be called the progressive or continuous aspect: *I am going, I was writing*, etc. This is not a form that occurs in Latin and hence does not fit easily into a Latin-based description of English. It is noteworthy that writers of pedagogical grammars who were either foreigners themselves like Mason and later Miège, or who had a professional interest in teaching English to foreigners like Christopher Cooper (1685), should consistently have given this feature of English more emphasis than native-speaking writers who tended to treat the *-ing* form as a present participle separate from the verb *to be*. While Mason and the others failed to give *be + -ing* a special label, they clearly recognized it as a distinct verbal unit peculiar to the structure of English.

Apart from Mason there was very little activity in the teaching of English to foreigners until a new generation of teachers and writers emerged from about the middle of the century onwards. Some, like Ben Jonson and John Wallis, were interested in writing scholarly grammars for private study while others, particularly after the arrival of another wave of refugees in the 1680s, picked up and developed the traditions of Bellot and Holyband in teaching a practical command of the spoken language.

## Notes

1  King (1971: 259).
2  Bellot (1586: A2 verso).
3/4  Ibid.: no page references.
5  St. Clare Byrne (1953: viii–ix).
6  Ibid.: 213.
7  Ibid.: xxvi.
8  Holyband (1609 edition: 28).
9  Ibid.: 16.
10  Ibid.: 26.
11  Ibid.: 7.
12  Ibid.: 2.
13  Yates (1934: 277–83).
14  *Second Fruits*, title-page.
15  Ibid.: 141.
16  Eliot (1593: title-page).
17  Ibid.: 'Epistle to the French Teachers', A3 verso.
18  Ibid.: A3 recto.

19  Wodroephe claimed on the title-page that his work could be used to teach English as a foreign language as well as French: 'the meanest capacity either French or Englishman, that can but read, may in a short time by his own industry without the help of any Teacher attain to the perfection of both Languages'. And later, 'Ce livre est aussi utile pour le François d'apprendre l'Anglois, que pour l'Anglois d'apprendre le François'.

# 3 Towards 'The great and common world'

Apart from brave attempts by men like Holyband and his fellow-refugees to run schools in which classical and vernacular languages were taught side-by-side, the teaching of modern languages remained a small-scale enterprise, usually with a private tutor but occasionally in small classes, throughout the seventeenth century. The main concern of the schools was the teaching of Latin and to some extent Greek, and until the private schools and academies put down strong roots in the early eighteenth century, the classical curriculum was dominant and unchallenged. Young children arrived at the grammar school at about the age of eight having, in theory at least, acquired basic literacy skills in the mother tongue, and were immediately force-fed with a diet of unrelenting Latin grammar rules and definitions. Their grammar book was for the most part in Latin and there was no alternative but to rote-learn the text, dimly understood if at all, or risk a beating. Schoolroom violence is a constant theme throughout the literature of reform right up to the present century, and it was clearly very prevalent in the sixteenth and seventeenth centuries.

The source of these infamous rules was what must be the best-selling language teaching textbook ever written, *A Short Introduction of Grammar*, generally credited to William Lily (1468–1522), the first headmaster of St. Paul's School which was refounded by John Colet in 1509. Colet also made a contribution to the *Short Introduction* but he was usually omitted in the popular name for the book, 'Lily's Grammar'. It was also known as the 'Royal Grammar' since it originated in a committee set up by Henry VIII in the late 1530s to establish a uniform method of grammar teaching in schools. It appeared in 1540 with the royal injunction that it was 'to be used in the Kynges Maiesties dominions', an injunction repeated by Edward VI in 1547 and Elizabeth in 1559. With that kind of support it is not surprising to find it selling around 10,000 copies a year at a time when the size of any 'edition' of a book was limited to 1,250 copies only.[1] It continued without a serious rival until the middle of the eighteenth century and was still in occasional use in the nineteenth. It also prompted many other publications, introductions, simplifications, teaching manuals, and so on. But for over 250 years 'Lily' and 'language teaching' were virtually synonymous, at least in the minds of generations of little boys.

The book is in two parts, one much longer than the other. It begins with a 'Short Introduction to the Parts of Speech', written in English, followed by the 'Brevissima Institutio', which is a description of Latin syntax written entirely in Latin and, in defiance of its title, extremely long. It was here that all the 'Concords' and the other dreaded rules were to be found.

It is against this background of mindless rote-learning and the custom of writing sample sentences, or 'Latins' as they were known, that the reform movements in sixteenth and seventeenth-century language teaching have to be seen. The various reforming groups adopted different philosophies and theories of education at different times, but a common concern for text rather than precept or rule was evident among them all.

There were, broadly speaking, two schools of thought on the role and function of language studies in late sixteenth and early seventeenth-century education. The first represented the humanist tradition established earlier in the century by Erasmus and Vives and reiterated in Roger Ascham's influential book *The Schoolmaster* (1570). The other was a more puritanical philosophy set out at some length in Francis Bacon's *Advancement of Learning* (1605) which reached its most elaborate expression in the work of Jan Amos Comenius.

Like John Locke's famous essay on education a century or more later, Ascham's *Schoolmaster*, published posthumously in 1570, was inspired by the need to advise on the education of a specific child, in Ascham's case the young Richard Sackville, grandson of Lord Buckhurst, with whom Holyband lodged in the early 1570s. *The Schoolmaster* is in two parts of almost equal length, the first entitled 'The Bringing Up of Children' which discusses the general aims and purposes of an education for the offspring of a noble family attending on the Elizabethan Court. Culture and sensibility, derived from close familiarity with the great literature of the ancient world, receive considerable attention, and also what he calls 'eloquence', which implies a more subtle and complex control of the use of language than mere 'public speaking' in the modern sense. Practical accomplishments also feature in Ascham's programme for the child, but the central role is played by language and the nurture of an elegant and flexible style for courtly use. Quintilian's 'good man skilled in speaking' (*vir bonus dicendi peritus*) was the ideal to aim at, and the study of classical texts, Latin first and Ascham's beloved Greek authors later, was the way it would be properly attained.

Part Two of *The Schoolmaster* ('The Ready Way to the Latin Tongue') is the pedagogical plan for achieving the educational intentions of Part One. In it Ascham sets out six teaching procedures which should start as soon as the child has mastered the basic parts of speech, presumably the 'Short Introduction' in the English-language section of

Lily. The best-known of these procedures, and the technique which is always associated with him though in fact he did not invent it, is the device of 'double-translation' which we have already noted in connection with Holyband. The particular advantage of 'double-translation', in the hands of a skilful teacher, is that it gives equal status to both the foreign language text and the equivalent text in the mother tongue. It will not do to produce a hurried and half-hearted gloss if the ultimate aim is to recreate the original Latin text accurately. The method is intended to make the learner equally conscious of the structure and resources of his own language. Content is held constant while the resources of both languages are manipulated to express, as far as possible, a common array of meanings.

Once the child had acquired a basic knowledge of Latin grammar and usage inductively through the study of simple but authentic texts (mainly by Cicero in Ascham's programme), he should be ready to move on to the heart of the method which was called *Imitatio*. The learner had to create Latin and Greek texts of his own on the model of the great authors, a demanding task but one which concentrated his attention very closely on the stylistic and rhetorical devices used by the model writers in order to achieve 'a faculty to express lively and perfectly that example which ye go about to follow'.[2] In addition to *Translatio* and *Imitatio*, Ascham recommended four further procedures designed to exercise stylistic flexibility even more rigorously. These were *Paraphrasis* (reformulation), *Epitome* (summarizing), *Metaphrasis* (transforming a text from poetry to prose and vice versa) and, at an advanced stage, *Declamatio*, or public eloquence. All these techniques are clearly intended to develop and refine a sensitivity to stylistic and textual variation which, as we have said already, applied as much to English as to Latin and Greek. In expert hands, they add up to a sophisticated approach well-suited to the needs and aspirations of the aristocracy for whom Ascham was writing. However, there are also certain dangers, in particular an overly fussy concern for style at the expense of content. 'Delicate learning', as Bacon called it in his critical review of contemporary education in the first part of *The Advancement of Learning*, consisted merely of 'vain affectations' and, he concluded, 'Substance of matter is better than beauty of words'.[3]

It is important to follow the 'anti-grammar' strand of language teaching methodology to its conclusion in the work of an extraordinary writer called Joseph Webbe who designed a language textbook format of great originality and applied it in a series of publications in the late 1620s. While Ascham had made the learning of grammar subservient to the study of original texts, Webbe dispensed with grammar altogether: 'no man can run speedily to the mark of language that is shackled and ingiv'd with grammar precepts',[4] he stated uncompromisingly in his treatise on method called *An Appeal to Truth* which appeared in 1622.

It is very interesting to observe how this contrast between Ascham (inductive grammar) and Webbe (no grammar) repeated itself in virtually the same form in the late nineteenth century with Henry Sweet playing, as it were, the role of Ascham and the Direct Method teachers that of Webbe.

Not a great deal is known about the life of Joseph Webbe (*c.* 1560–1633) before the publication of *An Appeal to Truth* though it has been thoroughly researched by Vivian Salmon in an interesting article about him called 'Joseph Webbe – some seventeenth-century views on language-teaching and the nature of meaning'.[5] However, we know from the *Appeal* and other works that he was heavily influenced by Georgius Haloinus Cominius (i.e. from the town of Comines in Belgium, not to be confused with Comenius), who was writing about a hundred years earlier, and by his German contemporary Wolfgang Ratke (Ratich). Cominius had argued that grammars were either long and tedious or short and confusing, and useless either way. In addition, they were by definition imperfect since language was in a state of constant flux and change, from one regional dialect to another, and from one year to another over the course of time. This concern for dialectal variation over both space and time strikes a very modern note, and Webbe's use of the term 'habit' in the subtitle to his textbook of Latin dialogues *Pueriles Confabulatiunculae* (*Children's Talk*) (1627) carries rather similar connotations. The work, he says, is 'claused and drawn into lessons, for such as desire to breed an habit in themselves (either by their own industry, or by the help of Masters) of that kind of dialogical or common-speaking Latin'.[6] What Webbe meant by 'claused and drawn into lessons' we shall come to in a moment. First, however, we should outline the rationale for his method and his belief that languages should never be taught by learning grammar rules but 'by use and custom'. 'Custom', he said, 'is the best approved school-mistress for languages'.[7]

Webbe began from the views on grammar expressed by Cominius which have already been noted above. Grammars were bound to be inadequate as descriptions, and their study merely 'shackled' the learner's progress. The proper starting-point for language learning in his view was the exercise of communication skills which would ('whether we will or no') lead to a knowledge of the grammar through use. This is such a modern notion, or so we like to think, that it is worth quoting Webbe's point in full:

> By exercise of reading, writing, and speaking after ancient Custom, we shall conceive three things which are of greatest moment in any languages: first, the true and certain declining and conjugating of words, and all things belonging to Grammar, will without labour, and whether we will or no, thrust themselves upon us.[8]

| 62 | | |
|---|---|---|
| when he dare tell such [lyes?] | q. 15. | quum hic talia andeas prædicare? | |
| Why should I not dare | q. 16. | Quidni andeam | R. |
| when it is true? | q. 17. | cùm sit verum? | |
| O false speaker! | q. 18. | O falsidice! | S. |
| But — — — — — — — when heardest thou me speak English? | q. 19. | — — — Quando — — vērò audiuisti me — — loquentem An- glicè? | |
| Wilt thou know? | q. 20. | Vis scire? | R. |
| Yea verily — — — — — —I desire (it.) | q. 21. | — — — — volo — — enimverò. | S. |
| Some where — — — — — — —of late. | q. 22. | Nuper — — — — alicubi. | R. |
| Heare. | q. 23. | Audio. | S. |
| Of all good fel- lowship tell [me,] | q. 24. | I n hm, | |
| what day? | q. 25. | quo die? | |
| or | q. 26. | aut | |
| in what place? | q. 27. | vbi gent um? | |
| I haue forgot the day, | q. 28. | Dies excidit mihi, | R. |
| I doe not remem- ber the place. | q. 29. | locum non comme- mini. | |
| Tell [me] | q. 30. | Dic | S. |
| | | who | |

Figure 4   *Extract from Joseph Webbe's* Pueriles Confabulatiunculae (Children's Talk) (1627), *a book of dialogues for the teaching of Latin in schools. It is part of a dialogue in which one of the children (S) has been accused (by R) of speaking English in school, which was not allowed. Webbe's ideas on textbook design are unique in language teaching history, and were patented for thirty-one years by Parliament in 1623.*

Once the grammar has been unconsciously assimilated ('thrust upon us', 'without labour'), it is time to investigate variations of style:

> Secondly, we shall taste of the manner of speaking used by the ancients, together with the elegancy, grace, pleasure, and delightfulness of the Latin.[9]

Finally, he makes a point about auditory memory (retaining 'the judgement of the ear') which was not to emerge again until the revival of interest in the spoken language in the nineteenth century:

> Thirdly, we shall get the judgement of the ear, and retain the same for ever: which Grammar cannot help us to; in that it is imperfect and beguileth us.[10]

While one must be wary of reading more into the statements of writers of a previous age and cultural context than their words will actually sustain, there is, I believe, every reason to suppose that Webbe was proposing a form of 'direct method'[11] of language teaching, without the use of reference grammars, which would depend heavily on spoken interaction ('dialogical and common-speaking Latin') and aim to develop an internalized knowledge of the language through the exercise of communicative activities ('reading, writing, and speaking after ancient Custom') conducted in the foreign language.

In order to put his ideas into practice, Webbe devised a completely original layout for his textbooks which he patented after submitting a *Petition to the High Court of Parliament* in 1623. In this he outlined his views and asked for his method to be protected in law. Taken aback by the unusualness of the request, Parliament gave him his patent, which was to run for thirty-one years, and Webbe set about producing his textbook series. He published four in all, including *Children's Talk*, which has already been mentioned. They are adaptions of classical texts, by Cicero and others, each of which is 'claused and drawn into lessons' according to his patented system, which is outlined below.

The similarity between Webbe's methods and certain features of contemporary methodology stops short at the use of translation to teach the meaning of the new language. He retained a bilingual, comparative approach, but he interpreted it in a radically different way from most of his contemporaries, a reinterpretation which underpinned his novel ideas in textbook design. Webbe rejected the common notion that foreign language texts should be translated word-by-word in order to emphasize the importance of accuracy and the 'correct choice of words'. 'Construing word-for-word', he said in his *Petition* to Parliament, 'is impossible in any language', giving as an example 'the barbarous English of the Frenchman, *I you pray, sir* for *je vous prie, monsieur*'.[12] Translation equivalence, he believed, existed at the level of the clause, not the level of the word, and he based his method on this insight. Take, for example, the following sentence, which comes from *Children's Talk*:

> Unless some body raised me, I should not wake, I believe, before noon, I sleep so sweetly.[13]

Webbe analysed the sentence into five clauses (though we might want to quibble over the precise definition of 'clause') and set them out on the page with their Latin equivalents in a parallel column:

| Unless some body raised me, | c.22 | Nisi quispiam suscitet me, |
|---|---|---|
| I should not wake, | c.23 | non evigilem, |
| I believe, | c.24 | credo, |
| before noon, | c.25 | ante meridiem, |
| I sleep so sweetly. | c.26 | ita suaviter dormio. |

The middle column indicates that it is Dialogue C and each clause is given a number, here clauses 22–26. Drawing 'boxes' round the clauses was entirely original and has some of the connotations of early 'programmed learning' techniques of the 1960s. A further refinement of the system is exemplified in the illustration (Fig. 4), also from *Children's Talk*. In order to draw the learner's attention to the differences between Latin and English word order, Webbe divided his more complex 'boxes' into columns and rows. The translation equivalents are always in the corresponding columns, but the order in which they are translated is indicated by the rows, starting from the top and working downwards. For example, in Clause q.19 on p. 62, (Fig. 4), the connective *but* comes at the beginning of the English clause whereas the Latin equivalent *verò* comes second, after *quando* (*when*).

Webbe opened a school in London at the Old Bailey, at that time still an ordinary street, but he left no successors and his ideas died with him. In many ways he is close to the individualistic nineteenth-century reformers. One thinks of Prendergast and his 'mastery sentences', for example, or Gouin and his 'series'. In the end, their insights into language learning were ill-served by the ingenious materials they devised in order to realize them. Originality became a trap that imprisoned their ideas in techniques which acted as a substitute for a richer understanding of underlying principles.

Webbe's achievement was considerable but it was also sterile, isolated from the context of educational thought and philosophy that surrounded it. He took one strand of contemporary thought, language use as opposed to linguistic rule, further than any other teacher of his time, but he lost sight of the fabric as a whole. Meanwhile, the Baconian tradition moved past him and found its fullest expression in the work of Comenius.

As we have seen, Bacon and the Puritan movement disapproved of the 'delicate' literary interests of humanists like Ascham with their stress on rhetoric, style, and eloquence. 'Words', in Bacon's view, were 'but the images of matter; and except they have a life of reason and invention, to fall in love with them is all one as to fall in love with a picture'.[14] The real world of things and events was the proper object of study and investigation, not its insubstantial reflection in language. Language was merely the means whereby we come to a knowledge and understanding of the world through reason. It was an instrument for action, not an object of contemplation.

Bacon admitted, however, that the humanist tradition was an improvement on the despised Schoolmen with their 'vermiculate' (tortuous) argumentation and their fondness for abstraction, who 'bring forth indeed cobwebs of learning, admirable for the fineness of thread and work but of no substance or profit'.[15] 'Substance' and its investigation were his chief concerns, not 'the monstrous altercations and barking questions of the Schoolmen in the universities'. Learning should be directed outwards towards the perceptible world of the senses and experience, not inwards towards words and their logical or stylistic properties. The error of both humanists and Schoolmen, as Bacon saw it, quoting from the Greek philosopher Heraclitus whom he much admired, was that 'Men sought truth in their own little world, and not in the great and common world'.[16]

It was towards this 'great and common world' that Comenius, following Bacon, wanted to lead his pupils in their exploration of nature through the senses. Language, or 'the right naming of Things', was the means whereby these perceptions would be transformed into knowledge and an understanding of the unity of God and nature in universal love and wisdom. He expressed this philosophy very simply in the opening statements of his first schoolbook, the *Janua Linguarum*:

1  God save you, friendly Reader.
2  If you demand, what it is to be a good Scholar? I answer, to know the differences of things, and to be able to mark out each thing by its own proper term.
3  Is there nothing else? Nothing sure: he hath laid the ground of all scholarship, who hath thoroughly learnt the right-naming of things.
4  For words are the notes (marks) of things: words being (then) understood aright, things are understood: and both are better learnt together, than asunder.[17]

We shall return to the *Janua* later, but Comenius is such a central and complex figure in the history of language teaching that it is important to set his work in the context of his unquiet life.

Jan Amos Comenius (1592–1670) was a genius, possibly the only one that the history of language teaching can claim, and like many geniuses, his practical achievements fell a long way short of his aspirations. He produced two major works of lasting educational significance in his late thirties, the *Janua Linguarum Reserata*, an intermediate-level textbook for the teaching of Latin, which was completed in 1631, and the Czech version of his *Great Didactic*, though the latter was not published in its final Latin form until 1657. Thereafter, he wrote nothing of importance for the classroom for over twenty years when suddenly, or so it seemed, he devised one of the most imaginative language teaching textbooks of this, or any other century, the *Orbis Sensualium Pictus* published in Nuremberg in 1658.

To many of his contemporaries, however, Comenius would have appeared in quite a different light. To them he was a reformer searching for a new pattern of faith and a new framework of practical ethics in the political and philosophical confusion that followed the breakdown of traditional Christendom. They would have regarded his religious writings and his new philosophy of pansophy, or universal wisdom, as the most serious contribution he could make to the welfare of the reformed church in Europe.

The two sides of Comenius's genius, the teacher and the philosopher, never really came together. Many of his educational plans were too ambitious and unrealistic to survive the pressures of everyday reality and they were never put to a real test. They were the dreams of an exile preparing the perfect scheme for the day of return when it finally dawned. It never did, and the only opportunity that came his way to put his ideas into practice was short-lived. The pansophical philosophy that aroused so much interest in his time died with him and it is doubtful whether his methodological ideas exerted much influence until they were re-discovered in the nineteenth century. The *Janua* and *Orbis Pictus* did survive, however, and were widely used. Through them some of the educational and pedagogical innovations which he had sought to bring about filtered through into the schools.

The first twenty-eight years of Comenius's life were spent in his homeland of Moravia, apart from a brief period of study in Germany. He was born in a small village called Nivnice in the north of the country near the border with Poland. After he lost his parents at the age of twelve his guardians neglected him, sending him to the local school where the educational standards were appallingly low and life was brutal. He was sixteen when the church to which he was to give so much of his life, the Unity of Brethren, rescued him and sent him to the town of Přerov to study at the grammar school.

Later, after further study in Heidelberg and Herborn, he returned home and was ordained into the Brethren. He took up his pastoral and teaching duties in Fulnek, not far from Přerov, and it seemed that the rest of his life would be spent in the calm backwaters of northern Moravia. This prospect was shattered by the outbreak of hostilities in Prague in 1618 which were to usher in thirty years of war in central Europe. In 1620 events reached a crisis with the defeat of the Protestant forces at the Battle of the White Mountain, and he was forced to flee with his wife and young family. For the next seven years he was a refugee on the run in the mountains along the border with Poland. In 1628 Comenius himself finally managed to escape to join the Brethren in the Polish town of Leszno, about halfway between Wroclaw and Poznan. He was alone – neither his wife nor his children had survived the ordeal.

The war was to drag on in a desultory series of outrages, sackings, plunder, murder, and burnings for another twenty years. But in 1628 the outlook for the Protestant cause looked bright. It was led by the charismatic King of Sweden, Gustavus Adolphus, the only leader who succeeded in maintaining any degree of discipline over his troops and who refused to sanction indiscriminate violence and looting. For the next four years Gustavus dominated events and looked set to bring them to some kind of resolution. Then, in 1632, the Catholic forces regrouped under Wallenstein and fought back at the Battle of Lützen, losing the battle but killing the King, and the war continued. These four years, from 1628 to 1632, must have been years of optimism for the Brethren in exile. At all events, they were certainly the most creative in Comenius's life. He completed the *Great Didactic* (in Czech) and wrote the first two textbooks in the series that was planned to accompany it: the *Janua Linguarum* and the more elementary *Vestibulum*. He also produced a large number of religious and philosophical writings.

*The Great Didactic* was an ambitious study that attempted to outline a complete curriculum for a reformed educational system to be implemented in the free Moravia that would arise from the war. His aim was nothing less than a universal system of education through which we may 'seek and find a method of instruction by which teachers may teach less, but learners may learn more; by which schools may be the scene of less noise, aversion and useless labour, but more of leisure, enjoyment and solid progress; and through which the Christian community may have less darkness, perplexity and dissension, but on the other hand, more light, orderliness, peace and rest'.[18] It offers a philosophy of Christian education in the framework of a curriculum 'that the entire youth of both sexes, none being excepted, shall quickly, pleasantly and thoroughly become learned in the Sciences, pure in Morals, trained to Piety and in this manner instructed in all things necessary for the present and for the future life'.[19]

The Comenian curriculum is founded on the concept of natural order as the true reflection of divine order, a seventeenth-century concept which finds an echo in all contemporary science from Kepler to Newton.

Its appeal in our own time lies in the parallels that can be drawn between Comenius's notion of growth and modern concepts of maturational development, but we have to be wary of such parallels. The Comenian child grows towards wisdom and a knowledge of God in nature through a gradual 'unfolding of the objective world to the senses'. Comenius expressed the journey towards wisdom in terms of a metaphor of the Temple: the young child approaches the porch (*Vestibulum*) and, with proper preparation, is permitted to enter the gates (*Januae*). On the inside he finds himself in the great court (*Palatium*) and ultimately progresses to the wisdom of the inner sanctum or treasure house (*Thesaurus*). This four-stage progress towards knowledge was to be the framework for all learning, including the learning of languages.

Comenius envisaged two textbooks for each of the four stages of the journey through the Temple, a basic manual and a reference guide. In his language teaching scheme the *Vestibulum* should contain a few hundred words, sufficient for simple conversation on everyday things with an accompanying word list. The *Janua* was to be the basic school textbook and should aim at teaching about 8,000 words in a series of graded texts of intrinsic interest and educational value. There should also be a small dictionary. The *Palatium* was to concentrate on style and the proper use of language while the advanced *Thesaurus* stage would be principally concerned with translation and the comparison of languages. Comenius never got very far with this scheme. During the early years at Lezno, he wrote the *Vestibulum* and the *Janua* which was published in Leipzig in 1633 (though an earlier version had appeared in London as early as 1631 under the title of *Porta Linguarum* edited by John Anchoran): it quickly became one of the most widely used textbooks in European schools. The English translator of Comenius, Charles Hoole, put it on the syllabus at his school in London as suitable for third-form pupils, i.e. aged ten or eleven.

The *Vestibulum*, or to give it its full title *Januae Linguarum Reseratae Aureae Vestibulum*, is about forty pages in length and arranged in parallel columns giving the Latin teaching text alongside the various vernacular equivalents (all Comenius's textbooks regularly appeared in polyglot editions). Comenius's philosophy of the supremacy of 'things' over 'words' is evident from the titles of the seven chapters which make up the work. It starts with a section on 'The Accidents of Things' and teaches the names of colours, tastes, smells, and other qualities of objects through short sentences like *The grass is green, The chimney is full of smoke, The mountains are high* and so on. Since he also includes comparatives, he effectively covers the grammar of simple sentences with the pattern *be + adjective*. In the second chapter he moves on to 'Things Concerning Actions and Passions' which concentrates on the simple present tense of verbs: *The stars shine, The farmer ploughs, In spring he sows*, etc. 'Circumstantial Things' related to time and place follow, which provides an opportunity to introduce adverbs and prepositional phrases in short dialogues: '*Where have you been?*' '*Where are you returning from? – From the town*'. The last four chapters are concerned with the vocabulary of the school, the home, the city, and moral virtues. All the words introduced in the texts are collected together in an 'Index Verborum' at the end and there is an appendix of grammar notes.

In many ways the *Vestibulum* is a kind of 'first draft' for the much more ambitious *Orbis Pictus*. There are, however, no connected texts, which are such an important feature of the later book, and no pictures. The carefully organized and graded introduction to the structural features of simple Latin sentences is a notable and original aspect of the *Vestibulum* and one that obviously caught the attention of teachers in the twentieth century. But the grammatical grading is never permitted to obscure the wider educational principles behind the book, in particular the value of language in promoting exploration of the outside world.

It is rather ironical that Comenius should be remembered for writing Latin textbooks when what he really wanted was a system of education in which the mother tongue would play the central role and foreign languages would be learnt as and when they were needed for practical purposes. He believed that foreign vernacular languages should be taught as a means of communication with the people of neighbouring countries, and that the classical languages, which were still required for certain academic and professional purposes, should not claim more than their fair share of curriculum time. In the introduction to the *Janua Linguarum*, he says explicitly that Latin studies should be completed in a year-and-a-half 'at the farthest', and there was no need for excessive zeal and thoroughness: 'the complete and detailed knowledge of a language, no matter which it be, is quite unnecessary and it is absurd and useless on the part of anyone to try and attain it'.[20] He was particularly angry with teachers who tried to 'improve' the *Janua* by stuffing it with 'uncommon words and with matter quite unsuited to a boy's comprehension'.[21] To Comenius, content and not form was of overriding importance. In this he agreed with Milton who said in his essay *Of Education* in 1644: 'though a Linguist should pride himself to have all the Tongues that Babel cleft the world into, yet, if he have not studied the solid things in them as well as the Words and Lexicons, he were nothing so much to be esteem'd a learned man, as any Yeoman or Tradesman competently wise in his Mother Dialect only'.[22]

'Solid things' are at the heart of the *Janua*. It consists of one hundred texts arranged in topic-groups. The first group deals with the natural world – the elements, the earth, trees, animals, and so on leading up to man. Then there is a set of ten texts on parts of the body, the senses, etc. before the longest topic-group in the book consisting of thirty texts which discuss everyday work and activities such as baking, tilling, hunting, trade, navigation, building, and so on, finishing at Text 60 with the church. The next group deals with social organization (the law, good government, etc.) and the book concludes with discussions on moral issues like wisdom, prudence, friendship, and fortitude. Finally, there is a coda of texts on death, God, and the angels. Comenius's famous 'principle of gradation' is very evident from the outline of the *Janua*: he starts from the creation and ends with salvation, taking in every aspect of human life on the way.

The *Janua* texts are arranged like verses in the Bible, short sections which allowed the teacher to handle the ideas step-by-step in class. As a classroom teacher Comenius was revolutionary. He rejected the traditional role of the teacher as a supervisor who handed out self-study tasks that could be tested ('heard') later on. Comenius believed in class teaching with the children grouped round him. The starting-point of the lesson was the topic itself and what it meant. Only when he was satisfied that the children really understood what it was about did he move on to learning the new language of the texts. To some modern teachers, Comenius's approach may seem 'teacher-centred'. In fact he would almost certainly have approved of teachers who remained at the centre of things. In his eyes they had great responsibilities as the source of light and knowledge. He was as much a pastor as a pedagogue.

In 1641 Comenius left Leszno and travelled to England at the invitation of Samuel Hartlib, a German merchant from Elbing on the Baltic coast of what is now Poland. Hartlib was converted to Baconianism while an undergraduate at Cambridge and, finding himself barred from returning to his home town, settled in London. He busied himself acting as a kind of entrepreneur for the reformed faith, raising funds for refugee relief work, disseminating ideas, and generally promoting the cause. His network of connections among the puritan élite included such leading Parliamentarians as John Pym and intellectuals like Milton whose *Essay*, quoted earlier, was addressed to Hartlib. In an interesting article on Comenius, Hartlib, and his associate John Drury, the son of a Scots minister, Hugh Trevor-Roper (1967) goes as far as to say that 'the intellectual world which surrounded Cromwell was very largely the world of these three men'.[23]

The principal reason for Comenius's visit was to explore the possibility of setting up a pansophical school in England where he could put his ideas in the *Great Didactic* into practice. Things went well to begin with, and he was encouraged by his welcome. Soon, however, the political climate deteriorated and England began to move towards civil war. He was approached by the Swedish government with the offer of a post to write textbooks and, in spite of feelers from Cardinal Richelieu in France and from America, he accepted the job and left to start work in, curiously enough, Hartlib's home town of Elbing, now in Swedish hands. It was a disastrous decision and an example of self-deception by both parties. The Swedes, a major European power at this time, wanted to employ the most famous and best textbook writer in Europe for their schools. They knew of Comenius's philosophical interests but persuaded themselves that these could be put on one side for a time. Comenius, for his part, was equally unrealistic. His ulterior motive in accepting the Swedish job was to bring what political influence he could to bear on Sweden to help the Bohemian cause in the negotiations leading to the end of the war. This was likely to come soon as Europe declined into an exhausted stalemate. However, neither the Swedes nor Comenius were really playing fair, and the results were dismal. There were no new textbooks, apart from some ideas for a revised *Janua* and a few bits and pieces. There was, however, a new theoretical study called the *Linguarum Methodus Novissima* (Newest Method of Languages) of which Chapter 10 has become famous as the *Analytical Didactic*.[24] But this was not what the Swedes had in mind after six years' work. Comenius for his part was equally disappointed. In the peace talks in Westphalia which finally brought the war to a close the Swedes, who were leading for the Protestant cause, failed to secure a free Bohemia–Moravia. 'They have sacrificed us at the treaties of Osnabrück',[25] Comenius wrote, bitterly angry.

This must have been the lowest point in Comenius's life. He was now 56 years old. For twenty-seven of those years he had been either an exile or on the run. He had wasted the last six years working on a fruitless project for a government which had now betrayed him. His second wife had died on the journey back from Elbing to Leszno. All the work he had done to prepare for his return had been in vain. His exile was permanent. In circumstances of despair as deep as this, what Comenius did next was astounding.

He accepted a commission to found a pansophical school in a small rural town in north-east Hungary called Saros Patak. One reason for his acceptance was his admiration for the Prince of Transylvania, Sigismund Rakoczi, who had invited him. Rakoczi was a kind of surrogate Gustavus Adolphus for the Protestant cause and Comenius wanted to do him a good turn. However, it was a long way from Leszno to Saros Patak across hostile territory (the fact that the war was over did not mean that the fighting had stopped), and leaving Leszno meant abandoning his newly-married third wife as well as the Brethren. Nevertheless, he set off on this rather quixotic trip, crossed the Carpathian mountains and arrived in Saros Patak. He felt encouraged at first. The buildings were adequate and more extensive than he had expected, the rector of the school was affable, and Comenius sat down to prepare for the new term. When the pupils arrived, however, he was shocked at their backwardness and general unpreparedness for school. He had taken their knowledge of basic literacy for granted, and now realized he had made a mistake. The teachers were unhelpful, bored with their work and filling in between jobs, and the rector's attitude began to cool. To cap it all, Rakoczi died and Comenius was on his own.

Faced by a situation that seldom faces venerated elderly European intellectuals, Comenius did what few if any of them would have done. He started to teach the children. If the Swedish government had had the same insight into Comenius as Rakoczi, they would have given him a school instead of asking him to write textbooks. The practical problems forced Comenius to rethink the structure of the elementary curriculum in the light of his pansophical principles, and the result was the *Orbis Sensualium Pictus* (literally, The World of the Senses in Pictures), a work of great pedagogical strength founded on intellectual rigour and deeply considered philosophical and spiritual values.

The starting point of each *Orbis* lesson is a picture with numbered objects which refer to words in the accompanying text. The purpose of the picture is not to 'illustrate' the meanings of the words but to represent the real world, the world of the senses from which, in Comenius's philosophy, all knowledge originates. The teacher should begin by talking about the picture, and, if possible, bringing the real objects into the classroom. The children should talk about their ideas and feelings, and think deeply about the objects in the picture before moving on to the text. Comenius suggested they should try and draw the objects for themselves, or at least colour in the picture in the book. Only when the experience was thoroughly absorbed should it be associated with the language.

The opening sections of the book provide an introductory course in what today would be called 'phonics' (see Fig. 6). Comenius associated the sounds of the letters with the noises made by animals. Ducks, for instance, 'say' *kha-kha*, which helps to introduce the letter K. Unfortunately for Charles Hoole, who prepared his translation in 1659, English ducks do not speak German, so the sounds do not fit the animals very well. Hoole was unable to afford new woodcuts, so had little choice but to leave the teacher to make the best of it. Similar problems arose with some of the pictures in the main body of the work which depicted objects or events that were unusual or even unknown in England. Also, the English text did not match the Latin in the parallel column as exactly as the German, so the layout was not as helpful as it might have been. Hoole apologized for all these things in his Introduction,[26] but they are minor blemishes.

The main body of the *Orbis* texts follows the *Janua* pattern, starting with the Creation and moving through human life to heavenly wisdom. There are, however, more topics (150 in all) and they are, of course, described more simply. It is important not to think of the book as a kind of 'picture dictionary'; the texts are all coherent passages in Latin. Figure 7 is an early one about domestic animals:

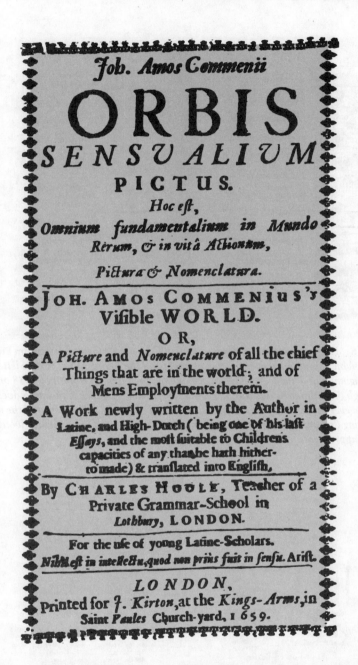

*Figure 5   Title-page of Charles Hoole's translation of Comenius's* Orbis Sensualium Pictus, *published in London only one year after its appearance in Nuremberg. Hoole was one of the best-known schoolmasters of his day and an ardent Comenian. The following year, he published his famous book on school teaching,* A New Discovery of the Old Art of Teaching School *(1660). Notice Comenius's emphasis on Things in his subtitle.*

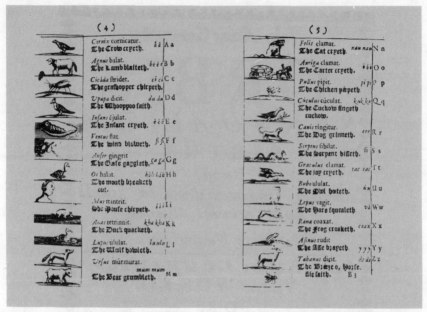

Figure 6　Extract from the opening section of Comenius's Orbis Sensualium Pictus (1659) which is intended to teach the alphabet and the sound-values for the letters. The original woodcuts were made to accompany the German edition of 1658 and, although the 'animal noises' suit the Latin text, Hoole's English translation does not work in every case. Cats, for example, do not 'say' nau-nau in English, and the use of a snarling ('grinning') dog to illustrate the r-sound suggests a velar r which would not be appropriate for English.

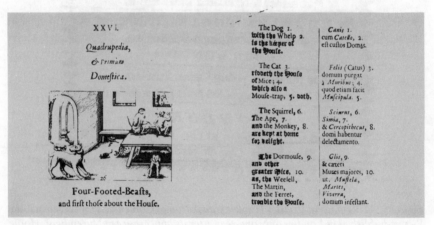

Figure 7　Lesson 26 from Orbis Sensualium Pictus, dealing with pets (rather a wider range than would be common today), and vermin. Comenius encouraged teachers to discuss the content of the texts (including, if possible, bringing the animals into the classroom) before studying the language.

The Dog (1) with the Whelp (2) is the keeper of the House. The Cat (3) riddeth the House of Mice (4); which also a Mousetrap (5) doth. The Squirrel (6), the Ape (7) and the Monkey (8) are kept at home for delight. The Dormouse (9) and other greater Mice (10) as the Weasel, the Martin and the Ferret trouble the House.[27]

There is plenty to talk about and some, if not all, the animals could be brought into the classroom.

Comenius left Saros Patak in 1653 before the *Orbis* was finished and returned to Leszno, but the political hopes that brought him back were, as usual, dashed and a few years later in 1656 the town was razed in a Catholic assault and many of his papers were burnt. Shattered, exhausted and gravely ill, he left central Europe for the last time and travelled via Hamburg to Amsterdam. In the following year, 1657, his collected educational works, *Opera Didactica Omnia*, were published including, for the first time, the Latin version of the *Great Didactic* originally written nearly thirty years before. Comenius continued his philosophical work until he died, still in Amsterdam, in 1670 at the age of 78. He entrusted his last works to his son, but they were lost until the 1930s when they turned up in Halle in Germany. It was only in 1966 that they finally came to Prague itself. True to the Comenian destiny this was only two years before the events of 1968. No doubt they will survive.

It is difficult to assess the contribution Comenius made to the general development of educational thought or to the more particular concerns of language teaching. His own inconsistencies, and the discrepancies between his almost limitless ambitions and his relatively modest practical achievements, stand in the way of a precise assessment of his historical significance. His contemporary influence was powerful but at the same time diffuse and unfocused. His failure to found a school, either in the literal or in the more extended sense, meant that for most practical purposes his work died with him. There is no evidence, for example, that John Locke, who might have been expected to find at least some of his ideas congenial, was familiar with Comenius, other than as the author of the *Janua Linguarum*. Against that, however, one has to recognize the importance of Comenius in moulding the aims and priorities of the nonconformist educational tradition which eventually came to play a central role in the development of the eighteenth-century academy.[28] His re-discovery in the latter half of the nineteenth century coincided with the need of 'modern' methods for the ballast of historical authority, and he became something of a cult figure.

Put rather crudely, people tend to mine Comenius for what they can get out of him, and his technique of listing principles and precepts lends itself easily to selective quotation. Adherents of a rationalist approach to language teaching, for example, like to adopt his emphasis on gradation, moving step-by-step from the known to the unknown, and his concern for an ordered, hierarchically-organized curriculum. Those, on the other hand, who believe in a natural approach can also discover much to sustain their case in his belief in the primacy of nature and experience, and his stress on the relationship of the curriculum to the inner development of the individual child. Both would be right, yet both would also undervalue the coherence of Comenius's philosophy in the context of the intellectual and theological preoccupations of his own time. Systems of universal wisdom derived from interpretations of man's relationship to God and nature are not easily assimilable to the secular traditions of the twentieth century.

From the more practical point of view, there is no doubting the success of his two major textbooks, the *Janua* and the *Orbis Pictus*. Both books continued to be reprinted for a century or more after his death. Yet, strangely enough, neither of them stimulated other writers to emulate his techniques and methods. It is particularly disappointing that his pioneering work in using pictures failed to attract the interest it deserved. Part of the explanation may lie in the cost of producing illustrations. On its own, this is not a particularly convincing argument, considering the large number of artists and craftsmen employed in illustrating chapbooks and other types of popular reading material in the eighteenth century. Much of it was hack-work, it is true, but it proves that the resources existed. What was lacking was the will to use them: pictures were not considered 'serious', and while they might be used with infants or to amuse the semi-literate working classes, they were not appropriate in the schoolroom. It is only in the past twenty years or so that this prejudice has been dented with the arrival of audio-visual methods in the teaching of languages and many other subjects, but it would still be rather naïve to claim that it has been completely overcome.

Pictures, as images of concrete experience, lay at the heart of Comenius's philosophy of learning, though even they were second best to the 'real thing'. It is here that the abiding challenge of Comenius lies for the teacher of languages: how can the teacher come to terms with the fact that language is not the object of learning but the outcome, the product of interplay between the learner and 'the great and common world'?

## Notes

1 Charlton (1965: 108). See also Watson (1908: 243–75).
2 Ascham (1570: 45).
3 Kitchin (ed. 1973: 23–5).
4 Webbe (1622: 9).
5 Salmon (1961/79).

6  Webbe (1627), title-page.

7  Webbe (1622: 26).

8–10  Ibid.: 38.

11  'Direct method': Webbe emphasized the use of spoken Latin in class and avoided grammatical explanations. He stressed the use of language rather than linguistic form. He did not, however, share the modern 'direct method' rejection of translation.

12  Quoted in Lambley (1920: 31), footnote.

13  Webbe (1627: 6).

14  Kitchin (ed. 1973: 25).

15  Ibid.: 26.

16  Ibid.: 33.

17  *Janua Linguarum* (1662 edition:1).

18  Keatinge (1910: 4).

19  Keatinge (1910), *The Great Didactic*, title-page.

20/21  Keatinge (1910: 204).

22  Patrides (ed. 1974: 183). Milton himself wrote a short Latin grammar in English called *Accedence commenc't Grammar* published in 1669.

23  Trevor-Roper (1967: 281).

24  See Jelinek (1953).

25  Wedgwood (1957: 460).

26  Hoole (1659: iii) 'The Translator, to all judicious and industrious School-Masters'.

27  *Orbis Sensualium Pictus* (Hoole's translation, 1659: 55).

28  Comenius was also influential in 'advanced' educational thinking in eighteenth-century Germany, notably in the work of Basedow (see Biographical notes).

# 4   Guy Miège and the second Huguenot exile

The second half of the seventeenth century was a richly productive period in the history of theoretical and practical linguistics in England, but, paradoxically, it was also, after the Restoration of 1660, a fiercely reactionary period so far as education was concerned. Innovatory ideas that had emerged during the Cromwellian revolution, under the influence of thinkers like Comenius and others in the Hartlib circle, were frustrated by the reassertion of the traditional grammar school and university system controlled through the established Anglican church. Radical plans to set up a string of new universities, for example, in cities like London, York, Norwich, and Manchester were shelved for the next two or three centuries, and the power of Oxford and Cambridge was deliberately diluted by the incorporation of the Royal Society in 1662 as an alternative forum of intellectual activity under the direct royal patronage of Charles II. The Society succeeded in attracting ambitious intellectuals such as John Wallis, Professor of Geometry at Oxford and author of the *Grammatica Linguae Anglicanae* (1653), Bishop John Wilkins, whose work on the development of a universal language in his *Essay* of 1668 was one of the Society's early achievements, and many others. It is ironic, however, that the Society should have been interested in promoting a universal alternative language to Latin at exactly the same time as the old-fashioned, Latin-based classical curriculum was being given a new lease of life in the grammar schools. Besides, the realistic alternative to Latin as an international *lingua franca* was not an artificial language, however well-made, but French, the language of the leading cultural and political power in Europe. Needless to say, French was not taught in the grammar schools.

The absence of French from the public school curriculum (though it was marginally more successful in the private sector) is all the more remarkable considering the prestige which the language enjoyed after the Restoration both as a social accomplishment and, more seriously, as an essential element in the training of court officials, diplomats, and the like. The case for French was supported by Lord Clarendon, the Lord Chancellor, who maintained that it was 'too late sullenly to affect an ignorance'[1] of the language, partly because the French themselves had no intention of learning English, and partly because 'it would be a great

Dishonour to the Court if, when Ambassadors come hither from Neighbour Princes, nobody were able to treat with them . . . in no other language but English, of which not one of them understand one word'.[2] Since, in Clarendon's view, 'Latin hath ceased to be a language, if ever it was any', and 'French is almost naturalized through Europe',[3] the inclusion of French in the education of the future leadership of the country was essential, but it was not a task for the grammar schools. What Clarendon had in mind was private education through the employment of tutors living with the family, the kind of arrangement discussed by John Locke in *Some Thoughts Concerning Education* (see Chapter 14).

The result was a healthy demand for native-speaking teachers of French, some of whom also turned their attention to the teaching of English as a foreign language to speakers of French, particularly as the number of religious refugees rose steadily during the 1670s and 1680s. After Louis XIV revoked the Edict of Nantes in 1685, which had protected the Huguenots since 1598, the stream of exiles expanded to a flood even greater than had been experienced a hundred years earlier. Among the French teachers who contributed most to helping the new refugees with learning English were Paul Festeau, a native of Blois on the River Loire, not far from Holyband's home town of Moulins, and a Swiss from Lausanne called Guy Miège whose *Nouvelle Méthode pour apprendre l'Anglois* (New Method of Learning English) (1685) raised the teaching of English as a foreign language to a standard of expertise and professionalism it had not enjoyed before.

Festeau was the first of the two men to make a mark in the field. He was a member of a circle of French teachers in London called 'Little Blois', the undisputed leader of which, Claude Mauger, was another exile from the same city. In 1667 Festeau had written a French textbook called *A New and Easy French Grammar* in direct competition with Mauger's best-selling *True Advancement of the French Tongue*, which had appeared for the first time back in 1653. In 1672 he adapted the *Grammar* to the teaching of English, using the same dialogues and vocabulary lists, and published it under the title of *Nouvelle Grammaire Angloise*. He later joined forces with Mauger and together they published a double-grammar, *Nouvelle Double-Grammaire Françoise-Angloise et Angloise-Françoise* (1693). This was one of the principal sources of English for French speakers in the early eighteenth century, though it was later overtaken by a similar enterprise, using exactly the same title, by Miège and his French co-author, Abel Boyer.

The Francomania of fashionable society in post-Restoration London with its French chefs, dressmakers, wig-makers, dancing-masters, and the like provided a very different atmosphere for learning the language from the serious-minded mercantilism of Tudor England, and this is reflected in both the style of the teaching dialogues and the sort of topics they deal with. Most of the students were, of course, adults rather than the youngsters who had attended Holyband's schools in St. Paul's Churchyard, and a great many of them were ladies intent on keeping up with everything *chic* and *à la mode*.

Since frivolous salon chit-chat had provided the starting-point for Festeau's original French course, its adaptation to teach English to newly-arrived immigrants was not entirely satisfactory. The dialogues tend to be long set-piece 'playlets' rather than scenes of everyday life, and the language they contain is not very practical for the newcomer. One of them, for example, chronicles the activities of a group of 'Gentlemen that go to be merry abroad' (i.e. tavern-crawling in Greenwich) and while this may be entertaining enough it would not be immediately helpful to the beginner in the language. Another represents a 'Dialogue between two Gentlewomen: whether it is necessary for Women to be learned'. This is exactly what the Restoration ladies wanted from their French lessons, witty conversations on such diverting topics as in this instance, the battle of the sexes:

> They say that man was created first, and that the woman was made of one of his ribs, as it is true.
>
> It doth not follow for all that, that they have got more wit than we: for beasts that have got none were created before man. God created the noblest last of all.
>
> . . .
>
> But St. Paul will not have women speak in the Church. It is a sign that he doth not hold them so capable as men.
>
> No, it is not that. The thing only is, that he doth not hold it so convenient that women be mix't with men in a Church counsel. For he foresaw that this might cause some disorder by reason of the small account that men make of women's judgement and wit.[4]

Amusing enough, but as material for learning the language of a newly adopted country, unnecessarily complicated and over-elaborate. By comparison, Guy Miège's *Nouvelle Méthode*, published about twelve years later in 1685, is written in a much more appropriate manner and is a landmark in the development of English language teaching.

Miège came to England shortly after the Restoration in 1661. He was a talented practical linguist with a gift for international diplomacy in the true Swiss tradition. He would no doubt have felt at home today working for the United Nations or some similar body. He spent two years (1663–65) travelling to Sweden, Denmark, and Russia as under-secretary to the Earl of Carlisle, the English ambassador, and another three in France preparing a report of his diplomatic experiences. He returned to England in 1669 and made a living teaching geography, French and, later, English as a foreign language to the immigrant community.

His writing career started in lexicography and he published three dictionaries of French and English between 1677 and 1684, completing the task with his *Great French Dictionary* of 1688. He also wrote textbooks of French along much the same lines as Mauger and Festeau, though he was never a member of the 'Little Blois' circle. With the arrival of large numbers of refugees after 1685, which coincided with the publication of the *Nouvelle Méthode*, he became more closely associated with the teaching of English. He was also courageous enough, as a non-native speaker, to bring out an adapted translation of the *Nouvelle Méthode* which he called *The English Grammar* (1688), which did not have the success it deserved. Although Miège normally merits a brief mention in histories of the development of English grammar, his work tends to be overshadowed by that of his more academic contemporaries like John Wallis and Christopher Cooper. For pedagogical purposes, however, what he wrote is more accessible to learners and much better presented. The latter point was an important one to Miège. As he says in the Preface to his French grammar, he would rather use ten pages than five if this meant giving room for 'all those advantages of Braces and Columns, which make the Matter both pleasant to the eye, and obvious to the understanding'.[5] Miège's lack of commercial success with the *English Grammar* may have had something to do with his being a foreigner, but perhaps the venture was a little ahead of its time. The demand for 'middle-brow' grammars did not emerge in any strength until the expansion of English-based alternatives to the classical school curriculum in the eighteenth century.

The original *Nouvelle Méthode* itself is a substantial work, over 270 pages long, and brings together a grammar, a compact dictionary (derived from his earlier lexicographical research), and a dialogue manual. Either alone or in tandem with Boyer's French course, it went through around thirty editions between its appearance in 1685 and the end of the following century.

Miège was able to benefit from the considerable advances made in the understanding of English grammar and pronunciation since the sixteenth century, some of which are discussed in a later section of this book. His own grammar section (119 pages) consists of a description of English orthography and pronunciation as well as a detailed study of the basic paradigms and word forms in the language. Like most of his contemporaries, he considered English an easy language to learn once the student had mastered the complexities of the sound and spelling systems. In his view there were three main difficulties, which he lists at the beginning of the book. The first was a small set of troublesome 'letters' as he called them (he meant consonant sounds):[6] *th* as in *think*, *ch* as in *church* and the 'soft' *g* in words like *ginger*, *jest*, and *judge*. The second was the vowel and diphthong system, and the third the difficulty of knowing where to place the stress in individual words.

His emphasis on spelling led him to include a series of interesting lists which give a valuable picture of the 'state of play' in late seventeenth-century orthography. For example, the following list (taken from his *English Grammar* of 1688) shows that some of the 'modern' spellings of his time have reverted back to earlier forms. Most, however, have remained:

| Instead of | | now we write | |
|---|---|---|---|
| chaunce | fourty | chance | forty |
| summe | * choose | sum | chuse |
| * money | moove | mony | move |
| murther | peece | murder | piece |
| * fathom | * flood | fadom | floud |
| * loath | | loth | |

(*Forms which returned as standard spellings)

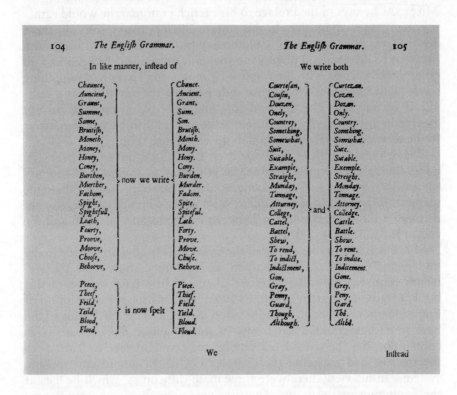

*Figure 8   Two pages from* The English Grammar *by Guy Miège, published in 1688, which was an adapted translation of his* Nouvelle Méthode *of 1685 (see Fig. 9). It is interesting to note that some of Miège's 'modern' spellings failed to become standard (e.g. mony, chuse, and bloud). Most of his variants (p. 105) have stabilized, though* tunnage/tonnage *and* grey/gray *still exist.*

Miège also has a list of spellings which admitted more than one form, such as *cousin* and *couzen*, *onely* and *only*, *something* and *somthing*, *gon* and *gone*, etc. In addition, some words are 'indifferently' spelt with *y* or *i*, (e.g. *ayd/aid* and *boyl/boil*), with *u* or *w* (*persuade/perswade*), *s* or *z* (*to prise/to prize*), and *em* or *im* as (*employment/imployment*).[7]

The second half of the *Nouvelle Méthode* consists of a long vocabulary list, more of a short dictionary than a traditional word list in fact, organized in topic areas, which is followed by a collection of everyday dialogues ('Dialogues Familiers') on situations like shopping, coping with landlords, and the like. While they are very ordinary compared with Festeau's dramatizations, they suit the needs of their audience rather better. The book closes with a set of 'Dialogues Choisis' which are more original. They depict scenes of English life loosely connected by a narrative thread describing a journey from the south coast and a trip round London. The coffee-house conversation (see Fig. 9) is fairly typical. It is not as imaginative as some of the Holyband dialogues of London life, but it gives a useful picture of an everyday activity which would have been unfamiliar to a French immigrant at the time.

Miège's teaching methods are evident from the layout of his book. He believed in a thorough grounding in the basics of pronunciation, spelling, and grammar followed by practice and language study using the dialogues and phrases. He disapproved of learning a language without grammar rules, referring to it as 'properly building in the Air. For whatever progress one makes that Way, unless he sticks constantly to it, the Language steals away from him; and, like a Building without a Foundation, it falls insensibly'.[8] However, he took a tolerant view of the argument and allowed that if the learner were 'so very averse from Grammar-Rules as to look upon them as so many Bug-bears', he could begin by learning texts by heart and come to the rules later, by which time they will appear 'very plain, easy, and delectable'.[9]

The teaching of English as a foreign language came of age with Miège's *Méthode*. Earlier books had been short and their linguistic information was incomplete. By drawing on the work of the native phoneticians and grammarians, Miège was able to provide a substantial manual for a more discerning and sophisticated public than had existed during the earlier exile of Holyband and Bellot. He also incorporated original work of his own, and his insights in some instances complement those of the native grammarians. As we have already noted in discussing the grammar of George Mason earlier in the century, non-native writers were sensitive to aspects of English such as the 'progressive aspect' which the natives tended to overlook. Miège's account of the 'past continuous' is acute: 'when we speak of a Thing that was a doing, but interrupted upon some Incident, then we properly use the Verb *I was* with a Participle of the Present Tense. As, *I was speaking of you when*

## CHOISIS.                                    109

V. L'un vaut l'autre.

V. *They are both alike for that.*

M. Et, si vous alliez decrier l'Ail en Guienne & en Gascogne, pensez vous que l'on ne vous traitât pas de ridicule?

M. *But, if you went about to cry down Garlick in Guienne and Gascongne, don't you think you would be ridiculed for your pains?*

V. J'avouë que la Bienseance des Choses ne depend pas tant de leur Nature, que de leur Etablissement dans le Monde.

V. *I confess, that the Decorum of Things do's not so much ly in their Nature, as in the Acceptance they find in the World.*

---

### DIALOGUE.

### A DIALOGUE.

Des Cabarets à Caphé, & des Usages qu'un Etranger en peut faire.

*Of Coffee-houses, and of the Uses a Stranger may make of them.*

M. VOulez vous savoir, nôtre Ami, ce qui m'a beaucoup servi à apprendre l'Anglois.
Ce sont les Cabarets à Caphé.

M. WILL ye know, our Friend, what has been no small help to me to learn the English by?
*The Coffee-houses.*

V. Comment cela?
M. C'est que dans ces Cabarets les Compagnies se mêlent, de sorte que chacun a la Liberté de parler & d'ecouter.

V. *How so?*
M. *Because in those Houses the Companies do intermix together, so that every one has the Liberty both to speak, and to hear what others say.*

V. Et que fait on dans ces Cabarets?
M. En y beuvant une Tasse ou deux de Caphé, ou de Thé, on y apprend ce qu'il y a de Nouvelles, soit veritables ou fausses.
On y trouve la Gazette à lire tous les Jours qu'elle se publie, qui sont le Lundi & le Jeudi.

V. *But what is it that Men do in those Houses?*
M. *Whilst a Man drinks a Dish or two of Coffee or Tee, there he learns what News there is, either true or false.*

*There one may read the Gazet every Day it comes out, viz. on Munday and Thursday.*

Si

IIo    *DIALOGUES*

Si l'on veut fumer du Tabac, on y trouve non feulement les Pipes & la Bougie, mais auffi en quêques Endroits le Tabac même, gratis. Le Caphé & le Thé payent pour tout.

*If you will take Tobacco, you find not only Pipes and Candle, but in fome places the Tobacco, gratis. So that the Coffee, or the Tee, pays for all.*

*V.* Combien fe vend donc la Taffe de Caphé, ou de Thé?

*V. How much then do they fell a Difh of Coffee, or Tee?*

*M.* Un Soû.

*M. A Peny a Difh.*

*V.* En verité, cela eft commode.

*V. Truly, 'tis mighty convenient.*

Pour un Soû ou deux, on fe met à couvert, on boit, on fume, fi l'on veut, & on a l'avantage d'apprendre ce qui fe paffe dans le Monde.

*For a Peny or Two-pence, one gets a fhelter, drinks and fmokes at will, and has the benefit befides of learning how the World go's.*

Ne vend on pas auffi du Chocolate dans ces Cabarets?

*Don't they fell Chocolate alfo in thofe Coffee-houfes?*

*M.* On en fait pour ceux qui en veulent.

*M. Thofe that want it may have it quickly made.*

Et ceux qui ne fe foucient pas de ces Sortes de Breuvage, y peuvent avoir du Cidre, de l'Hydromel, du Mum de Brunfwick, de l' Ale, & en Eté du petit Lait.

*But, if you are not for thofe Sorts of Liquour, you may be fupplied with Cider, Mead, Brunfwick Mum, Ale, and Whay in Summer-time.*

*V.* Voila bien de la Varieté.

*V. That's Variety enough.*

*M.* En fin ce font des Endroits fort commodes pour fe rencontrer.

*M. In fhort, thofe Coffee-houfes are mighty convenient Places to meet in.*

Ils font plus honnêtes que les Cabarets à Biere, & l'on peut mêmes s'en tirer à meilleur marché.

*They are much genteeler than Ale-houfes, and yet one may come off cheaper.*

*Figure 9    The coffee-house dialogue from Guy Miège's* Nouvelle Méthode pour apprendre l'Anglois *(1685). Like the Tudor manuals (cf. Fig. 2), the materials were intended for Huguenot refugees, but they are more sophisticated. The small cultural details of coffee-house life, free newspapers, and tobacco, for example, would have been important for his students newly arrived from France. In this respect, Miège's work is much more practical than the rather 'showy' language teaching manuals of some of his contemporaries.*

*you came in; I was writing a Letter when you knock't at the door*'.[10]
These examples, taken from the *English Grammar*, could almost have
been lifted straight out of a modern structure drill.

After Miège, there were few textbooks for English as a foreign
language written and published in England. The initiative passed
abroad. It is one of the curious features of the subject that native-
speaking authors of coursebooks for English as a foreign language were
virtually unknown before the late nineteenth century and the work of
Henry Sweet, whereas today native speakers tend to dominate the
market. There were, of course, many examples of native grammarians
like Wallis whose books had foreign learners in mind, but no authors of
manuals like the *Nouvelle Méthode* for beginners in the language, in
spite of the fact that dialogues, which are an important feature of such
books, would have greatly benefited from a native-speaking author.

## Notes

1–3  Quoted in Lambley (1920: 393).
4  Festeau (1667: 244–5).
5  Miège (1688: Preface, A2 verso).
6  See Abercrombie (1949c) 'What is a 'letter'?' for further discussion
   on this point.
7  Miège (1688: 104–7).
8  Miège (1685: Preface, A3 recto).
9  Ibid.: A3 verso.
10  Miège (1688: 70).

# 5 The spread of English language teaching in Europe

The teaching of English as a foreign language was a rather less common activity in Britain during the eighteenth century than it had been in the seventeenth. The religious and political upheavals which had brought large numbers of foreigners to Britain during the two periods of Huguenot exile did not occur again until the arrival of the emigrés in the aftermath of the French Revolution in the 1790s. The interest abroad in English philosophy and literature that had prompted the grammars of writers like John Wallis continued to grow, but the textbooks needed to teach the language were no longer written by native speakers. Wallis and his contemporaries had written in Latin and its decline as a scholastic *lingua franca* left their successors without a generally recognized means of communication with foreign readers. There was, however, a shift of interest among grammarians themselves and a growing demand for mother tongue grammars to meet the needs of the new English Schools which were expanding in competition with the traditional Latin Schools (see Chapter 10).

None of this meant a slackening of interest in learning English abroad, however. It grew, slowly at first and rather more quickly after the middle of the century, spreading out from Britain in a kind of 'ripple effect'. First there were the countries immediately bordering the Channel: France, the Netherlands, Denmark, and Germany, all of which had examples of locally-produced English grammars before 1700. Then came the 'outer circle' of the Mediterranean and Baltic countries, finishing in the late eighteenth century with Russia, and in 1797 the first non-European textbook for teaching English appeared in Serampore in Bengal. The map (Fig. 10) illustrates this pattern clearly, though the fact that it is based on publications (derived from the Alston *Bibliography*) may well mask earlier local activity.

As we have already seen, the teaching of English outside Britain had begun in the Netherlands and the tradition had continued strongly throughout the seventeenth century reflecting the closeness, if not always the amity, between the two nations. Alston mentions, for instance, the Elizabethan-sounding *English Schoolmaster* published anonymously in Amsterdam in 1646, a manual by François Hillenius called *Den Engelschen ende Ne'erduitschen Onderrichte ... The*

*English and Low-Dutch Instructor* (Rotterdam 1646, and reissued five times before 1686), J. G. van Heldoran's *Een nieuwe en gemakkelijke Engelsche Spraakkonst . . . A new and easy English Grammar* (Amsterdam 1675) and, in the eighteenth century, a very popular book reissued many times called *Korte Wegwyzer der Engelsche Taale . . . A Compendious Guide to the English Language* by William Sewel published in Amsterdam in 1705.

France was the only other European country besides the Netherlands with a history of English language teaching before 1600. The seventeenth-century textbooks such as Festeau's *Nouvelle Grammaire Angloise* of 1672 and Miège's *Nouvelle Méthode* of 1685 were both reissued in the form of double-grammars, Festeau with Mauger in 1693 and Miège with Boyer in 1718. Both were successful, particularly the latter which came out for the first time in the Netherlands, an important printing centre, and was republished in Parish in 1745.

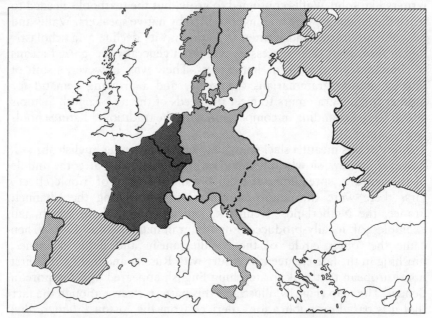

*Figure 10    The Spread of English as a Foreign Language in Europe to 1800 (Political frontiers c.1750)*

English as a foreign language, for speakers of:

1. Before 1600    French, Low-Dutch, Flemish
2. 1600–1700    German, Danish, Norwegian
3. 1700–1750    Italian, Swedish Portuguese
4. 1750–1800    Spanish, Russian

Dates based on earliest locally produced textbooks mentioned in R. C. Alston (ed.) *Bibliography*, Vol. II, (1967).

Figure 11  Selected late-seventeenth and eighteenth century works for the teaching of English as a foreign language, to speakers of [1]:

| | French | German | Dutch | Italian | Spanish/Portuguese | Danish/Swedish | Russian |
|---|---|---|---|---|---|---|---|
| To 1700 | FESTEAU (1672) MIÈGE (1685) MAUGER-FESTEAU (1693) | OFFELEN (1687) | 'Schoolmaster' (1646) HILL-ENIUS (1664) Van HELDOR-AN (1675) | | HOWELL (1662) | BOLLING (1678) (Dan.) | |
| 1700–1725 | BOYER-MIÈGE (1718) (11*) | KÖNIG (1706) (18*) ARNOLD (1718) (10*) | SEWEL (1705) | | | | |
| 1725–1750 | | | | ALTIERI (1728) (7*) | de CASTRO (1731) (Port.) (7*) | KULLIN (1744) (Sw.) KRAAK (1748) (Sw.) BERTRAM (1749) (Dan.) | |
| 1750–1775 | PEYTON (1761) (10*) SIRET (1773) (18*) | | SMITH (1752) | BARKER (1766) (10*) | | | PERMSKII (1766) ZHDANOV (1772) |
| 1775–1800 | | SAMMER (1783) MORITZ (1784) CANZLER (1787) EBERS (1792) FICK (1793) KÖHLER (1799) | | | CONNELLY (1784) (Sp.) | | KRYAZHEV (1791/95) |

* = no. of editions to 1800.

In the second half of the century the two most successful courses were V. J. Peyton's *Elements of the English Language, explained in a new, easy, and concise manner, by way of dialogue* (1761, and sixteen editions before the end of the century including one in Philadelphia in 1792), and Siret's *Élémens de la Langue Angloise, ou méthode pratique pour apprendre facilement cette langue* (originally published in Paris in 1773). Siret's course appeared in eighteen editions before 1800 and the last edition mentioned in Alston was as late as 1877. Like Peyton, Siret was also published in Philadelphia in 1792.

Many learners of English acquired the language through the medium of French. It was the language of the Enlightenment, spoken by the largest and most powerful nation on the continent. Most important works originally written in English found their way into a French translation and thus gained a wider audience. However, for some people, this was an inadequate and unsatisfactory way of studying English philosophy and literature and they attempted to learn the language so that they could read it at first-hand. Also, as we have already seen in discussing the work of Comenius and Wallis, England was regarded among 'progressive' theological and intellectual circles as a country of more than usual interest from which challenging new ideas in divinity and philosophy could be expected. After the Restoration and the failure of the Puritan experiment, this interest may have waned a little, but the development of the Baconian tradition of pragmatic philosophy in the work of John Locke and, later, David Hume, continued to attract the interest of foreigners. Britain was in some respects a political maverick, even vaguely 'subversive' in a century of hierarchies and absolute monarchs. After a 'glorious' revolution that resolved itself in the creation of a constitutional curiosity, the joint-monarchy of William and Mary, and a dynastic switch that had passed off with scarcely a murmur of dissent, Britain was the object of some envy among those frustrated by the claims of continental absolutism. King George I's benign lack of both charisma and English proved positively beneficial and new forms of state power and patronage began to emerge round the ministers of the Crown, providing the romantic House of Stuart with very little hope of success outside the Catholic-Celtic fringe. Green (1964) describes this fascination with things English among members of the French intelligentsia as 'Anglo-mania' and it prompted a healthy trade in French translations of English books printed in the Netherlands and smuggled over the border into France.

The real breakthrough for the English language came towards the end of the century in Germany where an interest, almost an obsession, grew up round the dramatic works of English literature, and particularly Shakespeare. As the map shows, there was a regular pattern of interest in English among Germans throughout the century and then a sudden explosion of publications in the last twenty years. Among the earlier works was Henry Offelen's *Double-Grammar for Germans to Learn English and for Englishmen to Learn the German Tongue* (1687), a book discussed in a bicentenary article by Viëtor in *Englische Studien* in 1887.[2] Johann König's *Volkommener Englischer Wegweiser für Hoch-Teutsche* (1706) is of some interest since it was later translated into Danish and also Swedish, and therefore counts as one of the earliest English courses in use in Scandinavia. König (who liked to anglicize his name to John King) was a teacher of German in London and the *Wegweiser*, as the name suggests, is a practical guide to the language including everyday dialogues and model letters. It also provides a City Guide to London for travellers and visitors. Theodor Arnold's *Grammatica Anglicana Concentrata, oder Kurz-gefasste englische Grammatica* (Summary of English Grammar) (1718) is another course that achieved a considerable number of new editions during the century. When the Germans turned from the formal classicism of French drama and its measured Alexandrines to the free-wheeling lyricism and passionate romanticism of Shakespeare and other English dramatists, interest in learning the language quickened and it even began to earn a place for itself in the schools towards the end of the century. There was a strong interest among German textbook writers in English phonology and prosody which reflected these concerns, for example Ebers' *Englische Sprachlehre für die Deutschen* (1792) has the subtitle 'following Sheridan's and Walker's basic rules', and Alston lists a large number of smaller works devoted to stress and rhythm in English. As well as new editions of older works by men like König and Arnold, grammars appeared in large numbers from about 1780 onwards, by Sammer (1783), Moritz (1784), Canzler (1787), Ebers (1792), Köhler (1799) and Fick (1793), who wrote the first of the new grammar-translation method courses which we shall look at in more detail later.

Denmark completed the 'inner circle' of neighbouring countries with a grammar by Frideric Bolling in 1678. Moving to the 'outer circle', interest is evident first in Italy with a grammar called *Gramatica Inglese per gl'Italiani* by Ferdinando Altieri, published in Livorno in 1728. Altieri was a teacher of Italian in London, his principal customers being young noblemen about to set out on the Grand Tour. Another Italian teacher was one Evangelista Palermo who wrote a particularly entertaining textbook called *The Amusing Practice of the Italian Language* (1779). The first part consists of 'a choice Collection of humorous Stories, Bon-Mots, smart Repartees, etc.' in which 'are inserted some well-digested Grammatical Notes'. In the second part there are Italian stories to translate into English and in the third part 'some very pretty Novels' to translate into Italian. In addition, there are thirty-six 'familiar Dialogues', mainly to do with travelling and ensuring social success during the trip to Italy. It is nice to see the Florionian touch is still alive: 'Two Gentlemen admire the Beauty of a Lady' is one dialogue; others include 'Two Gentlemen in a Coffee House' and 'Between an Italian Master and a Young Lady his Scholar'. Ironically, many of Palermo's pupils will have been well-bred young girls who would never have gone off on Italian adventures like the heroes in the dialogues. The travelling sounds pretty tough going sometimes, what with lazy postilions and bumpy roads. The most successful English course in eighteenth-century Italy was a dialogue textbook called *Nuova e Facile Grammatica della Lingua Inglese* (New and Easy English Course) (1766) by a Carmelite priest called Eduardo Barker.

Still on the 'outer circle', Portugal showed an interest in English earlier than Spain, possibly because of its status as 'our oldest ally', with Jacob de Castro's *Grammatica Lusitano-Anglica*, a double-grammar published in London in 1731. The earliest grammar for Spanish speakers mentioned by Alston was written by an expatriate native speaker called Thomas Connelly and appeared in Madrid in 1784. There had, however, been a much earlier publication in both Portuguese and Spanish brought out in 1662 by James Howell to coincide with the marriage of Charles II to Catherine of Braganza called *A New English Grammar, prescribing as certain Rules as the language will bear, for Foreigners to learn English*. It contains practical dialogue material, including 'a perambulation of Spain and Portugal, which may serve for a direction how to travel through both countries'.

Apart from the early grammar by Bolling (1678) already mentioned, there appear to have been few, if any, original English textbooks in Scandinavia until the 1740s (though a translation of König's course had appeared in Stockholm around 1730). *Et Kort och Tydeliget Begrep af en Engelsk Grammatica* (A Short and Clear Outline of an English Grammar) by Lorents Jul. Kullin was published in Stockholm in 1744, followed four years later by Ifvar Kraak's *Essay on a Methodical English Grammar for the Swedes* (Gothenburg, 1748). In Denmark Carl Bertram produced *Rudimenta Grammaticae Anglicanae* (1749) followed by a reader in 1751 and the *Royal English-Danish Grammar* in 1753. Textbooks continued to appear during the rest of the century, but they were mainly small-scale studies and practice manuals of specific features of English rather than major courses and grammars.

Finally, there was Russia, which was in some respects a special case. The country veered between a determined self-sufficiency in which foreigners were unwelcome, and 'openings to the West', when they were invited in large numbers. French was, of course, the principal foreign language and approached the status of a second language among the aristocracy and nobility, a tradition of Francophilia that lasted for a long time. It is interesting to read, in Sweet for instance, that the Russians had the reputation of being particularly 'good at languages', rather as the Scandinavians and Dutch do today. However, as Sweet said

*Sweet on Russians:*

'the Russians were obliged to be good linguists, partly because their retarded civilization obliged them to be imitative and adaptive with regard to the older civilizations of Western Europe, partly because the newness and inaccessibility of their own language prevented foreigners from acquiring it', and he concluded, 'we may safely prophesy that as the national life of the Russians develops, they will become worse and worse linguists'.[3]

The principal role of English was in naval affairs and the earliest books for teaching the language were written for the cadets at the Naval Academy for Young Noblemen in St. Petersburg. The first course mentioned by Alston is a translation from an unknown English original made by Mikhail Permskii in 1766 called *Prakticheskaya Angliskaya Grammatika* (Practical English Grammar) followed by Prokhov Ivanovich Zhdanov's *Angliska Grammatika* (1772), both authors being members of staff of the Academy. Zhdanov was obviously a leading author since he produced a second course four years later, also a translation, this time from an original by Thomas Dilworth called *New Guide to the English Tongue* (1751). Intended for young learners, it contains a number of everyday phrases and dialogues as well as more descriptive material. Finally, there was a rather more academic approach by Vasilii Stepanovich Kryazhev in two grammars, *Rukovodstvo k aglinskomu yazyku* (Handbook of English Grammar) (1791) and *Aglinskaya Grammatika* (English Grammar) (1795). These textbooks were written for 'pupils of noble birth at the pension of the Imperial University of Moscow' and used a catechistic technique of question-and-answer:

Teacher   When is *g* pronounced soft?
Pupil     *G* is pronounced soft when it precedes *e*, *i*, and *y*, for example, *gender, ginger, gipsy* . . . .
Teacher   Are there exceptions?
Pupil     The letter *g* is pronounced hard before *e* and *i* in the following words: *gelderland, gibbons, gibson, gilman, huggins, seager*.[4]

Presumably the slightly curious list of exceptions includes the names of foreign teachers at the university.

I should like to close this survey of the spread of English language teaching in the eighteenth century on a completely different note with a book that was not produced in Europe at all but in India. Published in Serampore in 1797 and printed by the author John Miller himself, *The Tutor* is possibly the earliest example of a book written to teach English in what would today be called the Third World. It is one of Alston's most fascinating discoveries, the only known copy being in the library of Calcutta University.

*The Tutor, or a New English and Bengalee Work, well adapted to*

*teach the natives English*, to give Miller's book its full title, begins, as
one would expect, with the English alphabet, but also includes features
that only a printer's professional eye would notice, namely the special
digraphs used for *fi, fl*, and so on. Next it moves on to the teaching of
pronunciation and uses a technique which is unusual for the time, a kind
of phonic practice which Miller may possibly have experienced as a
child learning to read at home. He provides extensive lists of
phonetically contrastive sets, for example, *lip, nip, pip, rip, sip*, and so
on, and includes 'nonsense syllables' for further practice. The following
list is particularly interesting. It shows quite clearly that Miller was
working phonetically, and not orthographically, as most of his more
academically educated contemporaries would have done:

*chur, scur, spur, ker, fir, stir, bur, cur, hur, pur, blur, flur, spur.*[5]

Miller's vocabulary list, which follows next, is also remarkable for the
period in that it avoids all the 'worthy' and 'over-literate' words which
other authors of the time would almost certainly have included as
evidence of their own erudition and to 'improve' the natives. Miller's
word-list is amazingly modern and practical as a result. It is arranged in
alphabetical order with Bengali translation equivalents. Here is part of
the list for the letter *T: tin, trip, them, then, try, thy, that, thus, tar, trap*,
and *thin*.[6] The inclusion of *thy* betrays the only area of language
teaching where Miller's self-confidence and commonsense deserts him,
the grammar. Presumably he was trying to recall what he had been
taught at school and he provides some rather curious paradigms and
lists. For example, he has a list of 'Verbs Neuter' which includes *to me*,
*to you, to him, to us, to her*, and *to it*, which is an oddly-named set, and
also omits *to them*. Under 'Active Verbs' he gives the past tense of *be* but
not the present. His paradigm for *to speak* seems to be traditional
enough, but includes the arcane *he speaketh*, as well as *thou speakest*.
The inclusion of *thou* is understandable since it provided a parallel form
for the Bengali, but *speaketh* had been dropped from even the most
old-fashioned English grammars by the end of the eighteenth century.

The grammar, however, is incidental to the main content of the book
which is a set of practical dialogues relating to river-boat trading (see
Fig.13).

At the end of the book there is some handwriting practice based on a
rather nostalgic set of sampler sentences that Miller must have recalled
from early childhood *Delight and some care, will make us write fair;
Good manners in a lad, will make his parents glad; Fraud in childhood,
will become knavery in manhood* and so on (see Fig.14). After the
straightforward practicality of the vocabulary lists and the dialogues,
these copperplate mottoes seem strangely inappropriate, but perhaps
they served their purpose well enough.

The appearance of Miller's *Tutor* is an appropriate place at which to

THE

*TUTOR,*

OR A

*New English & Bengalee Work,*

WELL ADAPTED TO TEACH

THE NATIVES ENGLISH.

IN THREE PARTS.

শিক্ষা গুরু

কিম্বা এক নুতন ইংরাজি আর বাঙ্গলাবহি

ভালো উপহুক্ত আছে বাঙ্গালি দিগেরকে ইংব৷

শিক্ষাকরাইতে তিনখণ্ডে

COMPILED, TRANSLATED, AND PRINTED,

*By* JOHN MILLER.

1797.

Figure 12   *Title-page from John Miller's* The Tutor, *printed by the author in Serampore in Bengal in 1797. It is possibly the earliest textbook for the teaching of English in what today would be called the Third World.*

( 113 )

ক্রিয়রচা ন্যাগে হি
সও মোন ভণ্ডুল চালা
নক্করিতে

S. Sir, the expences
are great; the boat hire,
the mangees and dandees'
wages, ghaut duties, &c.
from Bakurgunge amount
to about four annas, and
the expences from Patna
come to a little more or
lefs than fix annas per
rupee.

মহাঁশয থরচ বিস্তর
লৌকাভাড়া ওঁ মাঝির
ও ঁ ডারির মাহিনা ঘা
ঢের হাশিল ওগযরহো
বাথরঙ্গ হইতে দাড়া
য চারিআনা আর পাঊনা
ইতে থরচ হয কমবে
সজযআনা ছিতঙ্কে

M. How does the rice
of Burdwan and Raur
come to Calcutta?

কেমন ক্রুযা বঙ্মান
আরবাডেরতণ্ডু লক্লি
ক্লাতায অইসে

S. In the rainy feafon
they bring it in boat loads,
and in dry weather on
bullocks.

বরসাক্কালে তাহারা
লৌকায আর ঘযন্
সময বলদেক্রযা আন

M. What differ-nce
is there in the expence of
bullocks and that of
boats?

থরচেরকিত্তভাঊ হয
লৌকায আরবলদে

S. Conveying rice on
bullocks is attended with
double the expence of
boats.

বলদে ভণ্ডুল পান্া
নো নৌকাহইতেদ্বিগুন
থরচ হয

M. Where does the
greateft quantity of rice
grow?

কোন্ম্ানে ভণ্ডুল বি
স্তুরহয

S. In Bengal, towards
Moorfhedabad, Poornea,

*Figure 13　An extract from one of the dialogues from Miller's* The Tutor, *depicting the work of river traders in the Ganges delta. Presumably, these commercial activities were important in the lives of his students.*

bring this part of the story to a close. From this point on, the history of English language teaching forks into two streams which, for over a century, have little if anything to do with each other. One follows the path of imperial expansion and traces the role that English was destined to play in the development of education in the Empire. This is a vast subject that requires a separate series of studies in its own right. The other, to which we shall return in Part Three, is more limited in scope and is primarily concerned with the response of language teaching methodology to educational and social change in nineteenth-century Europe.

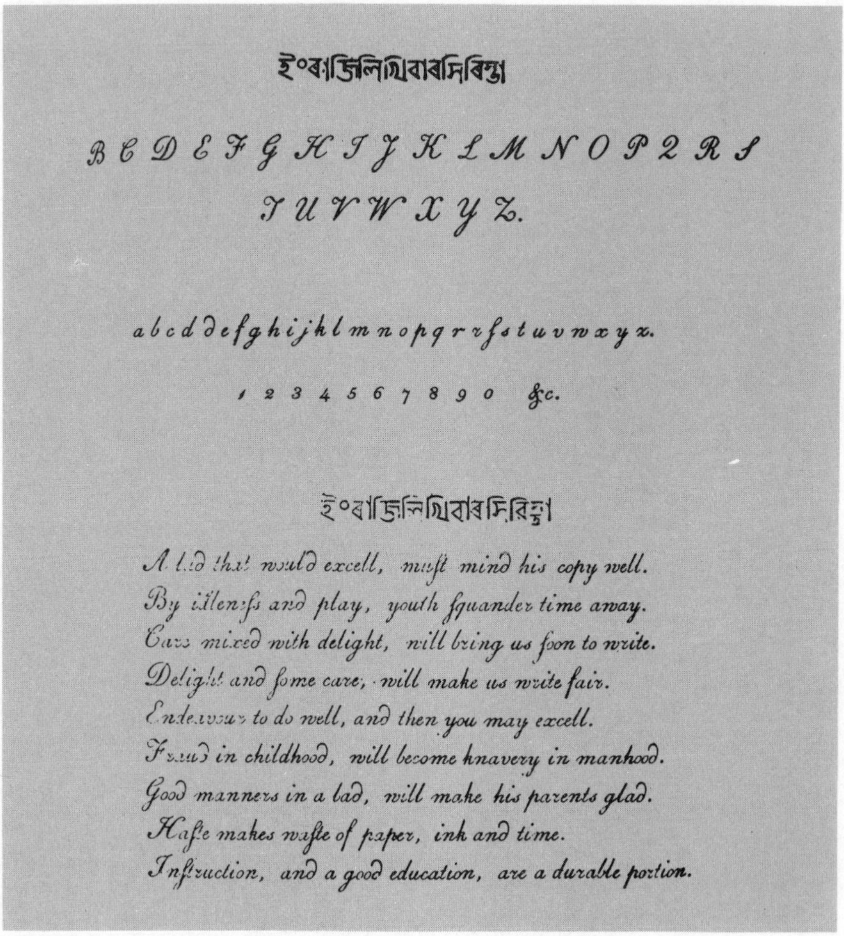

*Figure 14   A set of sentences for handwriting practice from Miller's* The Tutor. *Uncharacteristically, Miller did not attempt to adjust the content of the sentences to local interests and conditions.*

## Notes

1  Source: Alston (1967).
2  *Englische Studien*, X, 1887, 361–6.
3  Sweet (1899/1964: 81).
4  Kryazhev (1795: 72). The original is in Russian. He also used a semi-phonetic transcription not reproduced in the text. See Alston (1967), II, Plate CXLVI.
5  Miller (1797: 11).
6  Ibid.: 33.

# PART TWO

# On 'fixing' the language

Section 2
- mostly devoted to the
work of a representative sample
of writers + scholars from
each phase of growth + change
in ✓ dev't in Eng. L teaching
betw. 16th ↓ 18th C.

in order to illustrate the
various strands of dev't

(p. 81)

ch. 7 - John Hart + Richard Mulcaster
represent 2 sides of argument
re Orthographical reform in the
late 16th C.

Hart - innovator, seeking to replace
existing system with a specially
designed alternative
Mulcaster - conservative - trying to bring a
greater degree of order into
system with a minimum of dislocation

ch. 8   Description of English ("fixing" the lang.)
(Ben Johnson - relies on trad'l Latin framework
Contrast John Wallis - sets out to describe English
as an ind'l lang. with own characts
ch. 9 → Wilkins - creating a universal language
Roget - a thesaurus

ch. 10.

Dissenting tradition of ed'n

→ commitment to teachy of natural sciences + math, + practical skills like accounting, surveying + navigation.

- implied need for serious training in mother tongue literacy skills

(Baconian idea → modern scientific curriculum — essential trend'n was promotion of literacy in mother tongue

new "English" (not "Latin") schools needed grammars, sp. books, dictionaries for teachy of English. (vernacular system of ed'n gradually realized — needed tools)

- needed to augment + standardize the language.

- general demand for an

* authoritative work of reference (but not "imposed")

Elaboration of Standard English

N Bands of dictionary-makers

1) Samuel Johnson (1709-1784) — orthography, usage
2) John Walker (1732-1807) — The Critical pronouncing dictionary
3) Noah Webster (1758-1843) — informative + practical

+ Grammarians

P.116 like Robert Lowth + his fellows
-122 (1710-1787) (Murray, Cobbett
A Short Introduction to English grammar with critical of established usage notes (not trying to improve it)

# 6  Introduction

As English emerged from its medieval chrysalis in the sixteenth century, interest was naturally aroused in describing how it worked as a language, and in improving it where, as in the orthography, it was felt to be in need of attention. The Elizabethan posture of embattled national independence in a Protestant island fortress helped to create an intellectual climate, memorably articulated by Richard Mulcaster in 1582, in which English could seek to equal if not surpass the achievements of the prestigious Romance languages of Europe, particularly French. To reach the promised linguistic land, however, a great deal would have to be done. The erratic orthography would have to be stabilized, if not reformed altogether, a grammar would have to be written, and a national dictionary devised and created. Out of all this labour would emerge a standard ('fixed') language which would embody all that was best in English and would eradicate the blemishes. Such a language would then be a fit vehicle for a vernacular system of education and a strong vernacular literature which would inspire the nation at home and impress the foreigners abroad.

The most obvious starting-point for a programme of description and standardization was the English spelling system, believed by many of the reformers to be the chief stumbling-block both to the spread of literacy in England and to the learning of English as a foreign language. The Roman alphabet inherited from Latin did not match the sound system of English without the use of numerous idiosyncratic devices such as vowel digraphs, consonant digraphs, silent letters, and the like. To make matters worse, the introduction of printing in the late fifteenth century had disrupted the centrally-controlled royal scribal system which had been moving towards a disciplined standard orthography.[1] The absence of a fixed standard suggests the appealing thought that learners could not make 'spelling mistakes', but it was just as likely to mean that they did not know whether they had made a mistake or not. An unstable system does not necessarily imply a tolerant attitude, it can also encourage whims and fashions which no system of education could be expected to put up with for long.

The desire to reform the orthography prompted the first examples of what was to become one of the strongest and most productive traditions of enquiry in English linguistics, namely the description of speech and its practical applications to problems of everyday life. Most of the leading linguistic scholars in England between 1550 and 1700 were accomplished phoneticians in addition to their more traditional role as grammarians. Moreover, their work was, in general, motivated by the desire to improve and foster practical linguistic activities such as the teaching of English, both as a mother tongue and as a foreign language, spelling reform and the teaching of the deaf. Among the early contributors to this tradition was Sir Thomas Smith (1513–1577), a man of considerable eminence in the state who followed his influential work on the pronunciation of Greek with a study of English pronunciation and proposals for orthographical reform called *De recta et emendata linguae anglicae scriptione, Dialogus* (1568). Another contributor was William Bullokar (*c*.1531–1609), who was the author of a spelling reform scheme in his *Book at Large* (1580) and of the first grammar of English *Pamphlet for Grammar* (1586). Other leading figures included Richard Mulcaster (*c*.1530–1611) and the mysterious John Hart (*c*.1501–1574), both of whom are discussed in detail later in the book.

Orthographical reform continued as an important objective for linguistic scholarship well into the seventeenth century with significant contributions by Alexander Gill (*Logonomia Anglica*, 1619/1621), Charles Butler (*The English Grammar, or the Institution of Letters, Syllables, and Words, in the English Tongue*, 1633) and Richard Hodges (*The English Primrose*, 1644). As the century progressed, however, the principal centre of interest shifted from orthography to the description and teaching of grammar. Neverthless, the leading grammarians of the period like John Wallis (1616–1703) and Christopher Cooper (died 1698) were also skilled phoneticians committed to the serious study and teaching of spoken English.

While the emphasis on correct grammar was even more pronounced in the eighteenth century, the promotion of 'good speech' was another expression of the same passion for accuracy of expression and stylistic elegance. There was considerable popular enthusiasm for instruction in the arts of 'polite conversation', public speaking, and elocution. Out-of-work actors and others with similar gifts had a field-day among the socially ambitious upper-middle classes, particularly in cities anxious to impress the metropolis with their accomplishments. Thomas Sheridan (1719–88), for example, the father of the dramatist, was one of the more serious elocutionists and attracted no fewer than three hundred gentlemen to a month-long course of lectures four times a week in Edinburgh in 1761. He followed this up with a simpler course for ladies the next month which was equally popular, though not everyone was impressed, as the comment of a local journalist shows: 'Mr Sheridan's lectures are vastly too enthusiastic'.[2] Nevertheless, he drew equally large crowds three years later.

In spite of this interest in spoken language, it remained essentially 'extra-curricular' and made little impact on the basic education system. Prejudice perhaps played some part in this neglect, but there was a more serious, structural reason as well. The Renaissance had inherited a framework of linguistic description from the Middle Ages which, in its standard form, divided grammar into four components: Orthography, Etymology, Syntax, and Prosody (cf. the extract from Priestley on p. 5). There was no special category devoted exclusively to the study of speech, though Orthoëpy was occasionally proposed as a parallel study to Orthography. Of the 'big four', only Orthography and Prosody had anything to say about spoken language, but the former was mainly concerned with the teaching of spelling and the latter with the rules of versification. Johnson merged orthoëpy with both of them in his prefatory grammar to the 1755 *Dictionary*: 'In orthography I have supposed orthoëpy, or just utterance of words, to be included',[3] he says at one point and, later, 'prosody comprises orthoëpy, or the rules of pronunciation, and orthometry, or the laws of versification'.[4] Neither Etymology, which had a wider meaning than it does today and included the parts of speech and most of modern morphology, nor Syntax, which was preoccupied with the rules of concord and government, took any serious notice of the spoken language.

The neglect of speech is the most damaging of the criticisms that have been levelled against traditional grammars by contemporary linguists. There are, however, two further accusations which have been made often enough to require comment and study. The first is that grammarians in the past made arbitrary, 'prescriptive' judgements on what was 'correct' in grammar and usage which were not derived from observation of how the language was actually used. In a sense, this is a restatement of the earlier criticism that traditional grammars neglected speech. Their primary purpose was to establish a standard for the teaching of literacy and, as such, it was inevitable that they should be concerned with 'correct' English and, even more problematically, 'good' English. They were, in other words, normative in intention and didactic in purpose, but this does not necessarily mean that they were 'prescriptive' in the pejorative sense of inventing arbitrary rules.

Secondly, traditional grammars have been attacked for being 'Latin-based' and for imposing inappropriate categories of description on English and other living languages, thereby distorting the linguistic facts. While there is much justice in this view, it can be exaggerated. Some grammarians (Ben Jonson, for instance) certainly did little more than find English equivalents for Latin categories, but others (including John Wallis, for example, and Robert Lowth) were consciously aware of the need to devise descriptions of English that did not merely ape the grammars of the classical languages. Furthermore, we should not lose sight of the fact that until the nineteenth century schooling in particular and culture in general were dominated by the classics, and it could be argued that the original readers of traditional grammars were better placed to interpret them than we are today, coming as we do from a society in which classical studies are a minority specialist interest.

Some of the over-generalized criticism of traditional grammar has tended to create the impression that grammarians of the past lacked the perception and insight to realize that English and Latin were different languages with their own particular structural characteristics. On the contrary, many of them were uncomfortably aware that traditional etymology, for instance, with its techniques for establishing word-class paradigms based on inflections had very little to say about an uninflected language like English. Traditional syntax, which employed the inflectional paradigms as the basis for rules of government and concord, had even less to offer, as Johnson pointed out in a celebrated passage in his *Plan of a Dictionary* in 1747 where he claimed that English syntax was 'too inconstant to be reduced to rules' and depended on 'the distinct consideration of particular words as they are used by the best authors'.[5] Noting, for example, that in English you *die of wounds* but *perish with hunger*, Johnson concluded that syntax was essentially a problem for the dictionary rather than the grammar. Johnson's views, it should be added, were not typical of the time, and the high prestige accorded to the classical languages had a damaging influence on the teaching of English, not so much by distorting the facts as by over-emphasizing relatively minor linguistic details at the expense of more important features of the language.

Broadly speaking, the grammars, dictionaries, and other manuals of language in the seventeenth and eighteenth centuries took the form they did, and exhibited the priorities they did, because they were addressed to an audience that had practical need of them. The modern notion of an objective, scientific description of language as a self-justifying activity in its own right did not take root until the development of philological studies in the nineteenth century. What we may see as faults – the neglect of speech, the imposition of 'correct' norms, the influence of Latin, and so on – were positive virtues in the eyes of the customers for whom the grammars were intended. The emphasis on literate written English and the establishment of recognized standards provided the increasingly educated and affluent middle classes with the linguistic self-confidence they sought in their dealings with 'superiors', and the Latinate terminology was reassuringly familiar.

There were effectively four different groups of customers for grammars and dictionaries of English in the period to 1800: foreign students of the language, school pupils, private scholars, and a growing number of socially and professionally ambitious 'middle brow' learners. The expansion of this intermediate market during the eighteenth century helps to explain the large number of linguistic works that began to appear on the market from about 1720 onwards.

The majority of foreign students of English (as opposed to immigrants, exiles and others resident in Britain) were academics and scholars who wished to acquire a reading knowledge of the language. John Wallis, for example, describes the audience he had in mind for his *Grammatica Linguae Anglicanae* in 1653 very clearly:

> I have undertaken to write a grammar of this language (*i.e. English*) because there is clearly a great demand for it from foreigners, who want to be able to understand the various important works which are written in our tongue. For instance, there are many people, particularly foreign theologians whose great ambition is to study *Practical Theology* as it is normally taught in our tradition.[6]

There were a number of similar grammars written in Latin like Wallis's, of which the most notable was one by Christopher Cooper, also called *Grammatica Linguae Anglicanae* and published in 1685. Cooper was a schoolmaster from Bishop Stortford in Hertfordshire and some writers, notably Dobson,[7] have maintained that Cooper's reputation would have exceeded Wallis's if he had been better known to the great and the powerful. He made a translation of the first parts of his *Grammatica* and published them under the title *The English Teacher, or the Discovery of the Art of Teaching and Learning the English Tongue* in 1687. The work became an important elementary school textbook in its own right and, along with Elisha Coles, the author of *The Compleat English Schoolmaster* (1674), Cooper was one of the small number of native-speaking teachers of English as a foreign language of his time.

There is no doubt that Wallis's *Grammatica* stood out as the most influential and widely quoted grammar of the seventeenth century, and its 'anti-Latin' stance makes an interesting comparison with Ben Jonson's heavily Latinized *English Grammar* of 1640. Jonson's literary fame ensured his *Grammar* some attention, even though it is not very good. It also has the distinction of being the first grammar of English written in English using a traditional orthography. All the earlier grammars (for example, Bullokar (1586), Greaves (1594), Gill (1619/1621), Butler (1633)) were either in Latin or used reformed spelling.

Grammars for native speakers fell into three main categories, as we have said. First there were the elementary textbooks for young schoolchildren who, it was felt, would benefit from a basic course in English grammar before starting their Latin studies, instead of the other way round, as the usual practice dictated. The earliest handbook intended for this purpose was Joshua Pooles's *The English Accidence: or a Short, Plain and Easy way, for the more speedy attaining to the Latin tongue, by the help of the English* in 1646. Poole was followed later by other school grammars such as Jeremy Wharton's *English Grammar* (1654, also for 'strangers that desire to learn our language'), Joseph Aickin's *The English Grammar* (1693), Daniel Duncan's *A New English*

*Grammar* (1731), an anonymous *English Accidence* (1733) and, one of the best, Joseph Priestley's *Rudiments of English Grammar* in 1761.

At the other end of the intellectual scale were the grammars intended for scholars with an interest in the philosophy of grammar and its relationship to English. Among them were Michael Maittaire's *English Grammar, or, an Essay on the Art of Grammar, applied to and exemplified in the English Tongue* (1712), and the so-called *Brightland Grammar* of 1711, which is interesting for its radically different treatment of the parts of speech which are categorized notionally into four main groups: 1 Names, 2 Quantities, 3 Words of Affirmation, and 4 The Manner of Words, a system that derived from the Port Royal grammarians: a group of French scholars which flourished in the mid-seventeenth century whose work in grammar was influenced by the rationalist philosophy of Descartes. They proposed a system of linguistic categories based on logic and reason which were, in principle, applicable to all languages, hence the title of their *Grammaire générale et raisonée*, published in 1660.[8] Later in the 1660s the Port Royal schools were suppressed by Louis XIV for their religious unorthodoxy. John Fell's *Essay Towards an English Grammar* (1784) and possibly James Buchanan's *British Grammar* (1762) would also count as advanced works.

Most important of all, however, were the intermediate learners who included school pupils as well as adult students. These were the pupils of the English Schools, the 'brave boys' who, according to the unknown author of the 1733 *Accidence* looked forward to being 'Generals of armies by land, or Admirals of fleets at sea; to be Bishops in the church, or Lords Chief Justices and Judges of the people; to be Lord-Mayors, Aldermen, or one of the council of a city or town; to be eminent Merchants, Tradesmen or artificers, to be good Farmers; in a word, to be good subjects to your King and Country in any station, be it never so mean, never so great, high or low'.[9]

Many of these 'brave boys' would have required something rather more demanding than the 1733 *Accidence* if they were to achieve the exalted status planned out for them. There were several grammars to choose from: John Collyer's *General Principles of Grammar* (1735), James and John Gough's *Practical Grammar of the English Tongue* (1754), Daniel Fenning's *New Grammar of the English Language* (1771), and George Neville Ussher's *Elements of English Grammar* (1785) were typical examples. The most important, however, was Robert Lowth's *Short Introduction to English Grammar* (1762) which became the standard work of reference and the model for the school grammars of the early nineteenth century.

Schoolboys were not, of course, the only customers for these grammars. Some, like Lowth's, were intended for purely domestic use, aimed at those anxious to ensure acceptability in 'polite society'. Others were intended for adult learners who wanted to improve their written style, particularly in letter writing. Buchanan, for instance, discusses his teaching methods in this area in some detail in the Preface to his *British Grammar*. He was also concerned, along with many of his contemporaries, to improve the educational opportunities for girls:

> One Thing I would beg leave to recommend, which is, that every Boarding-School where there are young Ladies of Rank, proper Masters should attend at least three days in the Week; in order to teach them not only to read with an accurate pronunciation, and to acquire a natural, easy, and graceful Variation of the Voice, suitable to the Nature and Importance of the Subject, but to write their own Language grammatically, and to indite (*i.e. compose*) elegantly.[10]

In order to illustrate the various strands of development in English language teaching between the sixteenth and the eighteenth centuries, the remainder of this section is devoted to the work of a representative sample of writers and scholars from each phase of growth and change. John Hart and Richard Mulcaster represent two sides of the argument surrounding spelling reform in the late sixteenth century. Hart was the innovator seeking to replace the existing system with a specially designed alternative, while Mulcaster was the conservative trying to bring a greater degree of order into the system with the minimum of dislocation. Ben Jonson and John Wallis also make an interesting contrast in their differing approaches to the description of English for foreign learners, Jonson relying heavily on the traditional Latin framework and Wallis deliberately setting out to describe English as an independent language with its own characteristics. The final section concentrates on the work of dictionary-makers[11] like Samuel Johnson, John Walker, and Noah Webster, and grammarians like Robert Lowth and his followers, in the elaboration of Standard English.

## Notes

1 Scragg (1974: Chapter 5).
2 Law (1965: 158).
3 Maver (1809: xxxii). (All the quotations from Maver's reprint have been cross-checked with the 1755 Folio edition.)
4 Ibid.: xlvii.
5 Johnson (1747: 19).
6 Kemp (1972: 105).
7 Dobson (1957: 280).
8 Arnauld and Lancelot (1664/1753). See also Robins (1967: 124–7).
9 Anon. (1733: B1 verso).
10 Buchanan (1762: xxxi).

11  The earliest dictionary was Robert Cawdrey's *Table Alphabeticall*
    in 1604, followed by works by John Bullokar (William's son) and
    Henry Cockeram in 1616 and 1623 respectively.

# 7 Two proposals for orthographical reform in the sixteenth century

## The work of John Hart, Chester Herald

In spite of exhaustive enquiries by Jespersen, the first modern linguist to rescue John Hart from undeserved obscurity, and more recently by Danielsson in a painstaking account of his work, very little can be discovered about the man or his background.[1] The only clear fact we have about his life is that he was created Chester Herald in 1566, an honour that would only have been conferred on a man of some substance and standing. It is likely, however, that he was born near London and lived most of his life in the city. In Dobson's view there is no doubt that the model of spoken English which he described in his works was the accent of London and the Court, the 'received pronunciation' of mid-sixteenth century England.[2] Hart's father died in 1501 and there are reasons for believing Hart himself was born around the same time. He may have attended Cambridge University and he possibly came into contact with two of the other leading phoneticians and spelling reformers of the time, Sir John Cheke and Sir Thomas Smith, both with Cambridge backgrounds. Danielsson also suggests there may have been a connection between Hart and Sir William Cecil which involved intelligence work of some sort while Hart was travelling in Europe in the early 1560s.

In contrast to his life, Hart's work is well known. He wrote three studies all of which relate to the same project, his scheme for the reform of English spelling. The first, which was never printed, was called *The Opening of the Unreasonable Writing of Our English Tongue* written in 1551 and dedicated to King Edward VI. Shortly after this, history loses track of him until 1569 when his second, and most substantial, work was published. It was a re-working and expansion of the *Opening* called *An Orthography containing the due order and reason, how to write or paint the image of man's voice, most like to the life or nature* (1569). The *Orthography* contains a summary of Hart's reasons for embarking on the spelling reform project, the principles he adopted for his work and the objections which he expected to have to answer when it was published. It continues with a description of English pronunciation and criticizes the inability of contemporary orthography to represent the phonetic system of the language adequately. His own proposals for a small set of new letters (he adopted a minimalist position on this point) are presented and discussed in detail. The following year Hart brought out the primer he had promised in the *Opening* to exemplify the pedagogical advantages of his system. He called it, to use its full title, *A Method or comfortable beginning for all unlearned, whereby they may be taught to read English in a very short time, with pleasure* (1570).

In the 'prologue to his countrymen' in the 1551 *Opening* Hart announced his prime purpose in undertaking the scheme: 'I have undertaken this treatise of our English writing: wherein you may plainly see how far we are from the perfect order of writing, and painting of the Image unto the just proportion and liveliness of our pronunciation.'[3] This notion of letters being 'images' of sounds is continued in the statement of his basic principle: 'seeing then that letters are the Images of man's voice, ye are forced to grant that the writing should have so many Letters as the pronunciation needeth of voices, and no more, or less'.[4] One letter, one sound – a simple principle and indeed the fundamental principle of any alphabetic writing system. In English, however, the simple alphabetic principle had, in Hart's view, been abused by 'divers vices, and corruptions', including four main categories which he referred to as: (i) *diminution*, i.e. the absence in the orthography of letters to represent significant sound contrasts such as that between voiced and voiceless *th* (*this/thin*), (ii) *superfluity*, which is sub-divided into 'derivations' such as the retention of the *b* in *doubt* and 'differences' by which he meant the use of two letters to represent the same sound, for example, *u* and *o* in *sun/son*, (iii) *usurpation* where one letter 'usurps' the function of two as in the double value of *g* (*gem/gun*) or *c* (*cup/circle*) and finally, (iv) *misplacing* which he exemplified by saying that the *e* in *fable* and *circle* ought to come before and not after the *l* (i.e. *fabel, cirkel*).

Apart from minor quibbles, prejudices, and other 'small reasons', Hart anticipated three serious objections to a reformed spelling system. The first, and probably the most important, was 'use' or 'custom'. There was, he believed, no logical argument against the power of 'use' except to raise the counter-claim of 'reason'. 'Use should none otherwise take place than Experience proveth it to be reasonable and profitable'.[5] In the *Opening*, Hart used the religious argument that if use determined all human action, then 'we ought not to speak against the Bishop of Rome' but '(God be thanked) otherwise is come to us'.[6] This was omitted from the printed version in the 1569 *Orthography*. Perhaps he thought he needed all the help he could get, and there was little point in alienating potential Catholic spelling-reform enthusiasts.

Hart's other arguments are more technical and less emotive. First there was the argument of 'derivation'. It is a characteristic of English spelling, today as well as in Hart's time, to preserve the foreign appearance of loan words while anglicizing the pronunciation. (Modern examples would include words like *restaurant* and *café*.) Late sixteenth-century English borrowed a large number of words from various languages in the course of its expansion from a minor northern European dialect to a major national language. In Hart's view, there was no need to maintain the evidence of a foreign origin in the spelling of loan words, or to 'improve' the spelling of established English words by attempting to restore their visual association with other languages, particularly the prestigious classical languages. The best-known example of this 'false etymologizing' is the *s* in *island*, reinserted on the assumption that it was related to the Latin *isle* whereas it originated in fact from a Germanic source which does not contain *s*.

Hart's last point is one that has always caused problems for spelling reformers. He called it the argument of 'difference', and it refers to the fact that English spelling consistently distinguishes between homophones where the appropriate orthographical resources exist (*see/sea*, *meet/meat*, *horse/hoarse*, etc.), removing potentially confusing ambiguities. Hart did not accept that this argument was as strong as the claims that were, and still are, often made for it: 'If difference were so necessary as they say, it were much more needful in the speaking than in the writing, seeing the speech passeth quickly away, whereas the writing remaineth'.[7] This is quite a telling point, but it overlooks the importance of a shared context in spoken discourse. Secondly, if all homophones were represented as homographs, it would probably simplify the learning of spelling, but make the learning of reading more difficult.

Hart's policy on spelling reform was very moderate. He devised a few new letter-shapes and resuscitated others which had been allowed to lapse, the two letters representing the voiced and unvoiced *th*-sounds, for example, and the distinction between *u* and *v*. One of his new letters was invented to represent the *j*-sound in *jump* and distinguish it from 'i'. Eventually, *v* and *j* made their way into the standard English alphabet as separate letters. Dr. Johnson listed them in his *Dictionary* in 1755 as '*j*-consonant or *ja*' and '*v*-consonant or *va*' (*ja* and *va* should be read as rhyming with *k* (*kay*)). Johnson disapproved of *j*, calling it a 'letter useless except in etymology'[8] because it duplicated the 'soft *g*'. Notions of this kind may help to explain the delay in accepting *j*, but do not account for the failure to resolve the *u/v* problem, especially since the chancery scribes in the fifteenth century had been seeking to establish a visual distinction between the two letters.[9] It was not until the latter half of the eighteenth century, and particularly after the publication of Lowth's *Grammar* in 1762, that *j* and *v* were fully integrated into an alphabet of twenty-six letters. The long saga of *j* and *v* shows how slowly even the most uncontroversial and best-motivated orthographical changes come about.

Among Hart's other proposed modifications to the spelling system were the dropping of *j*, *w*, *y*, *c* and *q*, and the use of a small diacritic dot to indicate vowel length. This left him with an alphabet of twenty-five letters (five vowels and twenty consonants of which six were specially designed, see Figs. 15, 16), as the basic inventory for his reading primer.

Hart's *Method* is in its own way as remarkable as his orthographical system, but has received rather less attention. Dobson, for instance, has very little to say about it and suggests that Hart merely taught the 'names' of the letters.[10] This is not in fact the case. He expressly rejected the traditional practice of naming letters in the teaching of reading (he would have had to invent names for his new letters apart from anything else). He developed a carefully organized and graded system of 'phonic reading', as it would probably be called today. Unlike most of his contemporaries, he avoided the practice of merely listing words in alphabetical order or arranging them in groups by the number of syllables they contained. He introduced his letters in well-arranged tables of gradually increasing complexity, starting from a simple one consisting of two rows of five letters each, and moving to more elaborate ones later for practice purposes. Each letter was accompanied by a picture (a 'portraiture' as he called it) with a simple keyword underneath. At first sight this looks like the old 'L is for lion' technique, but his instructions are: 'you may not name the l. m. n. nor r. as you have been taught, calling them el, em, en, er: but give them the same sounds you do find in their portraitures, without sounding of any vowel before them, as may be thus: L-yon; M-oul; N-idl; R-ing'[11] (in modern spelling the words are *lion*, *mole*, *needle* and *ring*. Hart did not use different letter-shapes for capitals, but larger versions of the lower-case letters.)

His teaching material is beautifully laid out in eight short steps. First he introduces the five vowel letters (*a*, *e*, *i*, *o*, *u*) and five selected consonants (*l*, *m*, *n*, *r*, and *h*) chosen because they are easy to 'sound out' (Fig. 15). Step 2 introduces the remaining fifteen consonants, each with a picture and a keyword (Fig. 16). His pedagogical instructions are very precise, with useful hints on how to use the tables. For example, when the learner 'thinketh to know the letter alone, you may do well to hide the portraiture with your finger, or some paper fit to cover the five in the line you take level (*i.e. cover all five pictures in the same row*), to cause him to have the more regard to the shapes of the letters'.[12] Next there are two practice tables which drill the various contrasts from Steps 1 and 2. Step 4 introduces the vowel digraphs in a five-by-five table. There is more revision and practice (Step 5) before going on to syllables and exercises contrasting long and short vowels, and the important voiced/voiceless distinction. At the end of the book there are some phonic practice patterns, for example, *d-rum*, *dad*, *a-dd-er*, *did*, *la-dd-er*, *da-vid*, which carefully exemplify the sounds in different environments (initial, medial, and final). The manual closes with practice texts of familiar prayers and other religious pieces. Hart used the manual himself: 'I have of late experimented and proved the certainty and profit in the ease and readiness of the said new manner of teaching . . . and so the same is most profitable for such as cannot read, and are otherwise out of all hope ever to be able to attain to read'.[13] This trial of his materials, like his phonetic analysis, his orthographical system, and the design of his letter-shapes, reveals and emphasizes Hart's concern for perfection.

Unfortunately, perhaps, but not unexpectedly, his reformed spelling system was not adopted. Nor were any of the rival systems by his contemporaries and successors like Bullokar, Gill, and Hodges. The future did not lie with a new orthography, but with a more consistent version of the traditional one. The principal credit for this has to go to Richard Mulcaster, the most famous and influential pedagogue of his day.

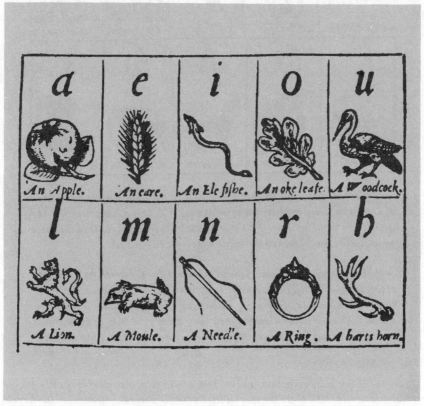

*Figure 15   John Hart's* Method *(1570). The first step, introducing the five basic vowels and a selection of five 'easy' consonants.*

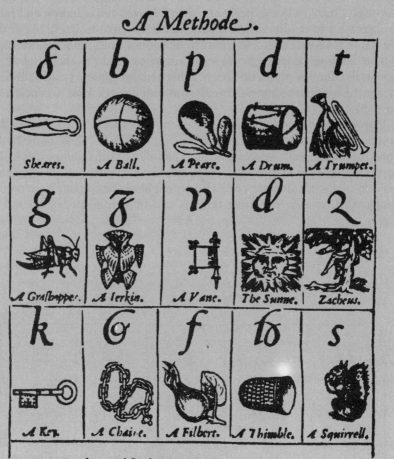

*Figure 16   John Hart's Method (1570). The second step, introducing the fifteen remaining consonants. Note the special letters for* sh *(shears),* j *(jerkin),* th (*different for* the *(sun)* and *thimble)* and ch *(chain). Note also the clear distinction between* v *(vane)* and *u (woodcock)* in Figure 15.

## Richard Mulcaster's *Elementarie*

Richard Mulcaster came from Cumbria in the north of England but was educated at Eton College. At about thirty he became the first headmaster of the newly-founded Merchant Taylors' School where he remained for the next twenty-five years. After a ten-year interlude as a clergyman, he returned to education in 1596 as High Master of St. Paul's School. He retired in 1608 aged 78.

It was during the last few years of his first headmastership that he wrote his two major works on education and the teaching of English. The first was a fairly short book called *Positions . . . for the Training Up of Children* (1581) which deals with general educational issues or, as he put it, 'those primitive circumstances . . . which are necessary for the training up of children, either for skill in their books or health in their body.'[14] The second is more substantial and better known. It is called *The First Part of the Elementarie* (1582) and was intended, as the title suggests, to be the first section of a large-scale work on the basic school curriculum which would transform education in England by replacing the traditional medieval structure of the trivium (grammar, rhetoric, and logic) and of the quadrivium (arithmetic, geometry, music, and astronomy) with a new system founded on vernacular literacy. It was, of course, far too ambitious ever to be completed.

*The First Part of the Elementarie* covers a great deal of ground, often rather turgidly, and outlines Mulcaster's 'five-branched' system of primary education, which comprised reading, writing, drawing, singing, and playing. But, as the title-page makes plain, it 'entreateth chiefly of the right writing of our English tongue'. He was in love with our English tongue and, at the end of the book, in a section called 'The Peroration', he was moved to an uncharacteristically lyrical affirmation of Elizabethan optimism and national self-confidence: 'I love Rome, but London better. I favour Italy, but England more. I honour the Latin, but I worship the English'.[15] Unfortunately, he did not always write like that, and much of the book is taken up with some very tedious accounts of 'ancient opinions' with quotations from Quintilian and others, a sixteenth-century version of 'reviewing the literature'. Like Florio, though with more obvious justification, he has often been cited as the possible original for Shakespeare's pedantic schoolmaster Holofernes in *Love's Labour's Lost*. However, Mulcaster was a serious and idealistic man who believed deeply in his mission to create for England an English education rooted in the use of the English language.

In the course of the *Elementarie* Mulcaster called for three great undertakings to prepare the language for its role in the education of the future: a grammar, a dictionary and, above all, a consistent orthography. 'Foreigners and strangers do wonder at us', he complained, 'both for the uncertainty in our writing and the inconstancy in our letters'.[16] An English grammar was essential in order to 'reduce our English tongue to some certain rule, for writing and reading, for words and speaking, for sentence and ornament, that men may know, when they write or speak right'.[17] In addition, a knowledge of grammar was a necessary preliminary to the study of foreign languages, 'where it serveth in the nature of an anatomy, for the resolving of the written speech'.[18] An authoritative national dictionary was no less important. 'It were a thing very praiseworthy in my opinion, and no less profitable than praise-worthy, if some one well-learned and as laborious a man, would gather all the words which we use in our English tongue, whether natural or incorporate, out of all professions, as well learned as not, into one dictionary'.[19] Eventually, the 'well-learned and laborious man' arrived in the imposing shape of Dr. Johnson, but not for nearly two hundred years. Mulcaster himself made an admirable start by compiling a lengthy word list which he called a General Table. It does not contain definitions since its principal purpose was to provide a check-list of regular spellings following his system of rules and conventions. This Table and the principles on which it was based were Mulcaster's chief contribution to the history of practical English teaching, and it is appropriate to spend the remainder of this section outlining how they worked.

It was not Mulcaster's intention to provide a new, phonetically consistent spelling system, but a stable one derived from tradition, or 'custom' as he called it, modified in the light of two further principles: 'reason' and 'sound'. 'Reason' should ensure consistency and regularity, and 'sound' implied a predictable relationship between sounds and spellings, though not necessarily on the 'one symbol, one sound' principle of John Hart. The outcome should be a publicly acceptable compromise between perfection and practicability. As Scragg points out, what the printing-houses wanted was a system of spelling that the customer would recognize as a public standard in printed books. With so many variants in use, there was always a danger that spellings would go in and out of fashion, which would be bad for business. Given a public standard, private spelling preferences could be tolerantly ignored. Scragg gives some interesting examples of manuscripts submitted to printers in one set of spelling conventions which emerge in print in a different one. Even the Queen herself spelt the same word in different ways in the same document if it suited her.[20] However, although the printers were pressing for public uniformity, they continued to reserve the right to use spelling variants where they were technologically convenient. If, for example, a word like *bad* could be spelt in a short form (*bad*) and a long one (*badde*), they would choose the former to avoid line-breaks and the latter to fill out a line to meet a right-hand margin.

Mulcaster's printer was a French Huguenot refugee called Thomas Vautrollier, who was also Bellot's printer for his *Familiar Dialogues* in

1586 (see Fig. 2). In 1587 his apprentice, Richard Field, took over the business and extended its high reputation for craftsmanship. Field was responsible for the 1609 edition of Holyband's *French Littleton* (see Fig. 3), and a comparison of the two textbooks shows how far spelling conventions had moved towards modern patterns in the twenty-three years between the two publications. Mulcaster's influence was import- ant in bringing these changes about, though, as we shall see, Field did not adopt all his suggestions.

The most substantial of Mulcaster's recommendations were that monosyllabic words with short vowels should not double the final consonant (*bed*, for example, not *bedde*), and secondly, that the silent final-*e* should be used to indicate long vowels when they were not already marked in some other way. So, for instance, *name* should retain the silent-*e* but *school* did not require one since the long vowel was already represented by the *oo* digraph. Both these conventions are standard in modern orthography, though the attempt to extend the principle to include *e* (*grene*, for example, in place of *green*) did not find favour. A further principle, that consonant doubling should be required in inflected forms such as *blotted* from *blot*, also became a standard procedure.

The Holyband text (Fig. 3) exemplifies Mulcaster's rules with forms such as *men*, *met*, *whip*, *did*, *quit*, and *rods* and inflections such as *whipped*, *chidden*, *spitted*, *blotted*, and *marred*. There is, however, less consistency with the silent-*e* rule. Field used *face*, *rise*, *home*, and *slide* (all Mulcastrian spellings), but retained the final-*e* unnecessarily in *schoole*, *beate*, *leape*, *turne*, and *speake*. He followed Mulcaster with *bene* on p. 20 but used *greene* elsewhere.

Among Mulcaster's less successful proposals was one to end words with *ie* rather than *y* (*cherrie* and *suretie* are two examples on p. 22 of the Holyband text). In this respect the earlier Bellot spellings *ready* and *always* are more 'modern'. However, Field did not follow Mulcaster in every case and included, for example, *say*, *way*, *pay* and *play*. Another failure was a recommendation to drop the *c* in words like *lack*, *duck*, and *quick*. Finally, Mulcaster did little to clear up the problems surrounding the use of *i* as both a vowel (*ink*) and a consonant (*iump*), and *v* as both a consonant (*vow*) and a vowel used in the place of *u* in initial position (*vntill*, *vpon*, etc.).

The formidable problems in the path of radical spelling reform meant that there was no practical alternative to the conservative argument for gradual standardization based on the three Mulcastrian principles of custom, reason, and sound. Enforcement of major orthographical change would have required the full weight of royal authority behind it to have had any chance of success, and there is no evidence that this was contemplated.

The intense interest in spelling reform in the late sixteenth century declined as a more stable public system emerged and the need for standardization became less acute. The normative processes continued for another century and a half until the Johnson *Dictionary* (1755) became accepted as the standard authority. From time to time new conventions emerged, notably the use of the apostrophe in past tense forms such as *disturb'd, rebuk'd,* and *provok'd,* ('manglings'[21] as Swift called them). However, the broad mass of English vocabulary had evolved a conventionalized spelling by the middle of the seventeeth century. Miège's lists in his 1688 *English Grammar,* for instance, contain examples of forms that were still in dispute, but they are not extensive and do not suggest any serious problems (see Fig. 8).

There is no doubt, however, that the system which finally emerged from 'custom, reason, and sound' is tiresomely complex. A further serious campaign to replace it was launched in the late nineteenth century by Henry Sweet (in an appendix to his *Handbook of Phonetics* (1877)) and his fellow phoneticians with support from liberal intellectuals such as George Bernard Shaw. Sweet maintained that the 'absolute necessity' for reform was 'universally recognized' and only 'prejudice and irrational conservatism' stood in the way.[22] Like others before and since, he too failed to appreciate the scale of the issue. 'Irrational conservatism' is a trivial argument when set beside the political power that would be required to implement spelling reform. It is not surprising that most of the successful reforms have been carried out by authoritarian political systems (Soviet Russia, for instance, or Atatürk's Turkey). The Tudor monarchy represents the nearest that England ever came to a system of centralized political power and, had Elizabeth I decided that orthographical reform was necessary for the health of the realm, she might just have succeeded in imposing it. English was little known abroad ('worth nothing past Dover' as Florio put it unkindly),[23] and literacy was restricted to a minority who would have been susceptible to political pressure from the top. Her father had imposed a Royal Grammar on the schools, and she might have followed suit with a Royal Spelling Book. However, for whatever reason, the opportunity passed for ever.

Once the printing houses had introduced a measure of discipline into the public system of orthography, intellectual attention turned towards more complex linguistic challenges and, in particular, the construction of a grammar of English. Until this had been achieved, any attempt to teach the language either to natives or foreigners was bound to be unsatisfactory. There was, moreover, a growing demand for English in Europe, among scholars and intellectuals attracted by the new ideas in theology and philosophy that were growing out of the work of thinkers like Francis Bacon and others. We turn now to two influential grammars of the first half of the seventeenth century which were specifically directed to this new market for English studies, Ben Jonson's

*English Grammar* of 1640 and John Wallis's *Grammatica Linguae Anglicanae* of 1653.

## Notes

1 Danielsson (1955). Also Jespersen (1907).
2 Dobson (1957: 64–5).
3 Hart (1551: 27), Danielsson (1955: 117).
4 Ibid.: 32 (118).
5 Ibid.: 44 (121).
6 Ibid.: 39 (120).
7 Ibid.: 73 (127).
8 Maver (1809: xxx).
9 Scragg (1974: 81).
10 Dobson (1957: 68–9).
11 Hart (1570: 2b), Danielsson (1955: 240).
12 Ibid.: 2a/b (240).
13 Ibid.: 11a/b (232).
14 Mulcaster (1581), title-page.
15 Mulcaster (1582: 254).
16 Ibid.: 87.
17 Ibid.: 450.
18 Ibid.: 50.
19 Ibid.: 166.
20 Scragg (1974: 68–9).
21 Scott (ed. 1907: 14).
22 Sweet (1877: 169).
23 Florio (1578: 50).

# 8 Early pedagogical grammars of English for foreign learners

## Ben Jonson's *English Grammar*

Ben Jonson's *English Grammar*—subtitled as being 'for the benefit of all strangers'—first appeared in an edition of his *Works* which was published posthumously in 1640. An earlier manuscript, probably written around 1623, was destroyed in a fire in 1625 that severely damaged Jonson's extensive library, and a second draft was completed some time in the early 1630s. The later years of Jonson's life were difficult and frustrating after the success he had experienced while he enjoyed the patronage of James I. The accession of Charles I, in the same year as the fire, led to a loss of favour at Court. He found great difficulty in publishing the second volume of his *Works* (the first, which contains the plays, had appeared in 1616, seven years before the First Folio of Shakespeare) and his health was poor. His decision to rewrite the *English Grammar* shows both his need to make a living in trying circumstances and also a serious commitment to the project.

Unlike Shakespeare, who was essentially a man of the theatre, Jonson was an intellectual and a scholar. His decision to print and publish his plays set him apart from his contemporaries, who saw their role merely as providing scripts for the actors in the theatre, and he was properly fussy about their accuracy and appearance in print. However, Jonson shared his fellow dramatists' deep love of language, but in a different sense from Marlowe's triumphant 'mighty lines' or Shakespeare's magical fluency. Jonson's texts are less accessible than theirs, and partly for this reason, his plays are less popular and less frequently performed. His syntax, for instance, is immensely complex, and some of his verbal extravagances, such as the alchemical arias in *The Alchemist*, are breathtaking. His parts are notoriously difficult for actors to memorize and, unlike Shakespeare, he has bequeathed few if any famous quotations which have gone into the language. While Shakespeare used the linguistic resources of English to their utmost, Jonson attempted, almost consciously, to push the language beyond itself. Although it would be unwise to press the contrast between divine inspiration and deliberate artistry too far, Shakespeare's genius would make him an unlikely author of a grammar. With Jonson, on the other hand, his love affair with the language never seems altogether spontaneous, and his decision to turn his hand to linguistics is not entirely unexpected. Whether he was wise to choose grammar as his subject rather than follow the example of his friend John Florio and attempt a dictionary of English instead is open to question.

In the early seventeenth century, there were two rival interpretations of general grammatical theory, and Jonson made use of both of them in his *Grammar*, which resulted in a number of inconsistencies. The first was the traditional theory derived from Aristotle through the Roman grammarians, Donatus (4th century) and Priscian (6th century), and the medieval scholars. This 'standard theory' was popularly represented in post-Renaissance England by 'Lily's Grammar', which every educated person knew by heart from school. The rival theory originated in the work of a French scholar Pierre de la Ramée (better-known as Petrus Ramus), who had pursued a brilliant and highly controversial academic career in France in the mid-sixteenth century. Some of his early writings, disputing the Aristotelian position on logic and dialectic, had been supressed by the academic establishment at the Sorbonne, but Ramus had some powerful friends, and he continued working in spite of this displeasure. His individualism later took him into more dangerous waters when he became a Protestant: he was murdered in the St. Bartholomew Massacre at the age of 57. Ramus's *Grammatica*, originally published in France in 1559, appeared in an English translation in 1585 along with an abridged version, called *Rudimenta Grammaticae*, set out in catechistic form for young learners. The Ramist belief in 'reason' rather than 'authority' appealed to the young intellectuals of late Elizabethan and Jacobean times, and inspired Jonson to attempt an application of the theory to the description of English. The Lilyan tradition was, however, too strong, and the Jonson *Grammar* suffers from the mixture of two conflicting approaches.

The *English Grammar* is a short work, only fifty folio-sized pages, and is divided into two sections: Part 1 is concerned with Etymology and Part 2 with Syntax. This two-part Ramist structure is one of the main differences between the ancient and modern approaches. 'Prosody and Orthography are not parts of Grammar', as Jonson put it, 'but diffus'd, like the blood and spirits, through the whole'.[1] Though Jonson describes 'letters and their powers' in the familiar letter-by-letter manner in his opening chapters, there is suprisingly little evidence of an interest in versification or the sounds of English in the work as a whole. In these early orthographical sections, Jonson uses the curious device of illustrating his comments on English pronunciation by giving examples in Latin and other languages. Presumably the reason for this was to communicate with his foreign learners who could be expected to know Latin fluently. The text itself is written, as we have said, in English, and anxiety on this score may help to account for the large number of Latin equivalences sprinkled throughout the book. Whatever the reason, they create the unfortunate impression that the principal task of an English grammarian is to discover forms in English which most nearly translate the familiar categories of Latin grammar. Jonson's treatment of the verb is a particularly conspicuous example:

> The futures are declared by the infinitive and the Verb, *shall*, or *will*: as *Amabo*: *I shall, or will love.*
> *Amavero* addeth thereunto *have*, taking the nature of two divers Times; that is, of the Future and the time Past:
> *I shall have loved*: or
> *I will have loved.*
>
> The Perfect times are expressed by the Verb *have*: as,
> *Amavi. Amaveram.*
> *I have loved. I had loved.*
>
> *Amaverim* and *Amavissem* add *might* unto the former Verb: as,
> *I might have loved.*[2]

Writing about twenty years after Jonson, Wallis simplified the problems of accounting for the structure of the English verb phrase by establishing a separate category of 'auxiliary' which he further subdivided into 'complete auxiliaries' (*have* and *be*) and 'defective auxiliaries' (*do, shall, will,* and the other modals), a framework of description which provides a reasonably satisfactory account of the facts of English.

As noted above, one of the characteristics of the Ramist model of grammar is a preference for binary distinctions, the twofold division of grammar into Etymology and Syntax being one example. Of particular importance is Ramus's treatment of the parts of speech where he makes a primary distinction between words that are marked for number and those which are not. Each of these categories further subdivides into two. Words which show number are either nouns or verbs, those which do not show number are either adverbs or conjunctions. Then there are more detailed sub-classes such as nouns substantive and nouns adjective. Prepositions and interjections are treated as sub-classes of adverbs. Jonson's application of the Ramist system to English is erratic. He begins his discussion of the parts of speech in a traditional 'Lilyan' fashion by listing the familiar eight ('we number the same parts with the Latins')[3], and sensibly adds the article as a ninth. He then introduces the Ramist notion of number as an afterthought. Later, he follows Ramus in treating prepositions as a sub-category of adverbs, in spite of having listed them separately at the beginning of the book as a part of speech in their own right.

One of the characteristics of Ramist grammar that has attracted the praise of twentieth-century linguists is the use of formal patterning as a device for determining linguistic distinctions. For example, Ramus defines the difference between masculine and feminine gender as follows:

D What is a noun of the masculine gender?
M It is a Noun before which *hic* may be set, as *hic magister*.
D What is a Noun of the feminine Gender?
M Before which *haec* may be set, as *haec musa*.[4]

This approach inevitably causes problems in a non-inflected language like English. In his description of the verb, Jonson proposes four conjugations, three of which are based on variations in the formation of 'irregular' preterites. The first conjugation is the 'regular' *love/loved* pattern. The second requires the modification of medial vowels (*shake/shook*), the third a similar modification of final diphthongs (*slay/slew*), and the fourth includes those verbs which require both vowel and consonant changes (*stand/stood, tell/told*, etc.). *Shall/should, will/would, can/could*, and *may/might* are listed as 'fourth conjugation verbs' alongside fully lexical verbs like *feel/felt* and *teach/taught*.[5] It is not really very satisfactory.

The description of case in English presents further difficulties for a grammar like Jonson's that relies heavily on 'endings' and other morphological markers to establish categories and paradigms. Having included case, along with gender and declension, as an 'accident' of the noun,[6] he omits any further reference to it, though it turns up briefly where he discusses the syntax of adverbs (of which, as we have seen, prepositions are a sub-set in his Ramist framework): 'the Preposition *of* hath the force of the Genitive; *to* of the Dative; *from, of, in, by*, and such like of the Ablative'.[7] Gender and declension were simpler to handle along traditional lines since gender classes co-occur with pronoun choices and declensions are realized by variations in the formation of the plural. Jonson followed Lily in setting up six gender classes: Masculine, Feminine, Neuter, Promiscuous (or Epicene) for words like *dog* which can be used to include both male dogs and bitches, Doubtful for words like *friend* and *neighbour* which can refer to either males or females, and Common of Three. The last class was required for adjectives which are, of course, indeclinable in English, and hence employ the same form for all three genders. Adjectives were, as we have seen, traditionally classified alongside substantives as a sub-class of nouns. The unfamiliar labels like Epicene were taken directly from Lily. Gender classes such as Promiscuous (a word which has acquired its sexual connotations only in the past hundred years or so) or Doubtful are not unmotivated in English. The social discomfort of not knowing whether to refer to a baby, for instance, as *he, she*, or *it*, is familiar enough to everyone. Jonson's final category was declension, and he identified two paradigms:

the first consisted of nouns with plurals ending in *(e)s*, and the second of nouns with *en* plurals.

Jonson's literary reputation has no doubt helped his work to survive, though sometimes as an 'Aunt Sally' for other writers. The syntax section is particularly incoherent, and perhaps deserved Dr. Johnson's acid comment that it contained 'petty observations as were better omitted'.[8] More generously, it might be said that if Jonson had been less famous, his *English Grammar* might have been judged less harshly.

## John Wallis's *Grammatica Linguae Anglicanae*

John Wallis (1616–1703) was born in Ashford, Kent, and educated at Emmanuel College, Cambridge. He took holy orders in 1640 and was appointed Savilian Professor of Geometry at Oxford in 1649. The first edition of his *Grammatica Linguae Anglicanae* appeared in 1653 and four further editions were published before the end of the century. There was one more edition, in 1765, but thereafter the work was neglected until J. A. Kemp's translation in 1972. All the quotations in this section derive from Kemp.

Sharing the general belief that the principal obstacle in the way of a foreigner learning English was the pronunciation and its complex relationship to the orthography, Wallis devoted more than half his book to these topics. Since the whole work is quite short (only 128 pages in the 1653 edition, though it was expanded later), the grammatical section does not pretend to be a comprehensive survey of the structure of the English language. It is severely pedagogical in its objectives and concentrates on those features of English which are most likely to strike the foreign learner as especially characteristic of English, and which he would not expect from his knowledge of Latin and other languages.

The grammar starts off in a very brisk style. The reader is informed that no attempt will be made to explain or define the parts of speech and other categories because 'they must be familiar to anyone having even the slightest acquaintance with the Latin language'.[9] It continues with a clear warning not to expect that everything in English will be exactly equivalent to something in Latin: 'Few people recognize this when describing our language and other modern languages, and, consequently, the task is usually made more complicated than it need be'.[10] This no-nonsense approach, which is underscored in the modern Kemp translation, also means that there is no attempt to apply either the Lilyan or the Ramist models rigorously, though Wallis draws on both traditions as and when they are required. There is no list of the parts of speech, for example, though the book is structured round the traditional categories (a fact that led some twentieth-century commentators to assume, wrongly, that it was 'Latin-based'). He also refuses to admit the standard Latin categories of gender and case: 'substantives in English do not have different genders or cases. This means that we escape much of the tedium which they give rise to in other languages, especially in Greek and Latin'.[11] He does, however, follow the Ramist principle of admitting number as a major contrast.

One of the interesting features of Wallis's grammar to many modern linguists is the clear association he makes between the notion of case and its realization in English through the use of prepositions, which he elevates to the status of a major category and which he decides to treat early in the text, rather than to follow tradition and leave them to the end: 'The English language, as I have already said, does not have a variety of different cases . . . Instead we use prepositions to convey all the meanings which in Greek and Latin are expressed partly by different cases and partly by prepositions'.[12]

There are two further issues which could be singled out as demonstrating Wallis's fresh and objective attitude to the description of English. One is his treatment of tense and the other of modal verbs or 'defective auxiliaries' (*auxiliaria mutila*) as he calls them. He uses 'tense' in the strict sense to refer to a morphologically marked contrast in the verb system (*love/loved, stand/stood, will/would, may/might*, etc.) and not in the loose sense of a characteristic 'pattern' of the verb phrase.[13] Thus, he identifies only two tenses in English, *present* and what he calls *imperfect past*. There is no 'future tense', 'conditional tense', or the like. Verb phrases such as *I shall love* or *I have loved* are treated not as tenses but as structures requiring the use of auxiliaries and verbal elements of different kinds. This approach allows him to describe the modal auxiliaries in notional terms, pointing out that *shall* and *will*, for instance, indicate futurity on many, but not all, occasions. He was among the first to notice that the modal implications of *shall* and *will* varied with the person of the verb, giving the 'futurity paradigm' *I shall, you/he will*, etc.,[14] with the contrasting paradigm *I will, you/he shall* indicating a range of meanings other than straightforward prediction. Wallis was criticized by some early modern descriptivists for inventing a prescriptive rule with respect to *shall* and *will*, but the charge is clearly unfair. It is interesting also that Miège (1688) draws attention to the same issue, but he restricts his comments to the 'marked' form *shall*.

Wallis's high reputation in intellectual circles and his membership of the Royal Society ensured a wide circulation for his *Grammatica*. It did not appear to suffer when he became involved in a serious dispute in the Society with William Holder over exactly who was responsible for 'curing' a deaf-mute called Alexander Popham. The details clearly demonstrate that Wallis, as Dobson put it, was 'a jealous guardian of his own reputation'.[15] Nevertheless, his reputation was well-deserved and outlived him. He is one of the few authorities consistently quoted in the eighteenth century and had his description been more complete it might have become the standard grammar of English.[16]

Wallis has been 're-discovered' lately, and sometimes the impression is given (though not, I should add, by Kemp) that he was the only grammarian of the past who was sensible enough to agree with the present. The others are seen as unrepentant prescriptivists. In this context, it is worth repeating Kemp's view that Wallis's desire to free the description of English from excessive Latin influences was shared by many later writers, including the much-maligned Robert Lowth.[17]

Certainly, Wallis's sharp originality owed much to his intellect and his scientific training (in contrast to Ben Jonson's literary interests). Nevertheless, it is equally important not to underestimate the significance of his practical objectives, and the role they played in focusing his *Grammar* on the essentials of English as a foreign language. Most modern teachers will recognize his priorities as theirs: tenses, the use of prepositions, modal auxiliaries and their meanings, etc. These are still central problems to the foreign learner, problems that have been increased since Wallis's time by the development of the continuous aspect which Wallis ignored (though, as we have seen, Miège picked up the beginnings of a trend towards it in his *Nouvelle Méthode*). The importance of a sense of audience as a device for organizing the grammarian's observations is sometimes underrated, and the foreigner provides a focus of objectivity that is not always evident in grammars for native speakers where considerations of dialectal variation and stylistic value play an important role. It is not, perhaps, entirely inappropriate that the best grammar of English in the seventeenth century should have been written with foreigners in mind, or that the best grammars of the twentieth century, including Jespersen's and the recent *Grammar of Contemporary English* by Randolph Quirk and his colleagues, should be rooted in the same soil.

## Notes

1 Jonson (1640: 35).
2 Ibid.: 79.
3 Ibid.: 56.
4 Ramus (1585: 7).
5 Jonson (1640: 66–7).
6 Ibid.: 57.
7 Ibid.: 81.
8 Maver (1809: xlvi).
9 Kemp (1972: 277).
10 Ibid.: 279.
11 Ibid.: 279.
12 Ibid.: 289.
13 Ibid.: 331.
14 Ibid.: 339.

15  Dobson (1957: 220).
16  He was also extensively plagiarized. See Kemp (1972: 67–9).
17  Kemp (1972: 69).

# 9 'Things, words and notions'

In recent years there has been a shift of interest among language planners, course writers and teachers away from differences of linguistic form which distinguish one language from another and towards the expression of meanings which they share. This shift has occurred for many reasons, ideological, theoretical, and practical. It is sometimes felt, for instance, that the moral purpose of language teaching in promoting international communication and understanding is better served by seeking what is universal rather than what is particular to a specific culture. The post-war role of English as a global *lingua franca* has intensified the need to search for categories of instructional organization that will reflect this generality and which could, in principle at least, provide the basis for teaching any language. The 'notional approach' has taken a number of different forms over the past decade and it is too early to say how it will eventually turn out. There is, however, an unavoidable problem at the end of the day, namely that people communicate through words rather than abstract conceptual systems. As Sweeny Agonistes says in T. S. Eliot's play: 'I gotta use words when I talk to you'.

For reasons which are not entirely dissimilar to those of today, there was considerable interest in the construction of a universal language in the late seventeenth century. The Protestant revolution had destroyed Latin as the international *lingua franca* and helped to promote a rivalry between the national languages of Europe. Its replacement by a new universal language without national or sectarian overtones was philosophically attractive. Among other things, it would serve the needs of missionaries for the reformed faith as well as facilitate expansion overseas. This last point was not lost on the promoters of the idea in the Royal Society. But it would be unfair to deny that it also excited interest as a scientific and philosophical project in its own right, and the Society commissioned one of its members, the then Dean of Ripon, John Wilkins, to draw up a scheme for further consideration and possible implementation. Wilkins called his report to the Society in 1668 *An Essay towards a Real Character and a Philosophical Language*. This immensely complex and impressive volume is not an 'essay' in the usual sense but a detailed analysis of the semantic categories, or 'notions' as Wilkins calls them, underlying all linguistic expression, along with the written symbols which were to realize these categories in his new universal language.

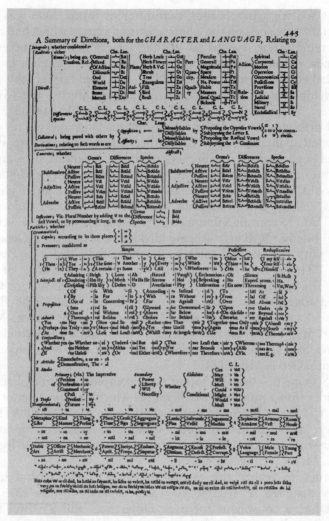

*Figure 17  John Wilkins' Summary of his scheme, illustrated above, is divided into three main tables with example texts at the foot. The top table gives the Genuses (General, Mixed, Of Action, etc.) with the letter-symbols for their Differences and Species underneath. Then there are two grammatical tables, one giving symbols for general categories like Substantives and Adjectives, and the other for individual items such as Pronouns. The two texts at the foot of the page are 'translations' of the Lord's Prayer, the upper one using the Real Character and the lower one in the Philosophical Language. The word for day is the sixth character from the right (disregarding the various small dots, etc.) and the third word from the right (poto) in the top line of the Philosophical Language text. Consulting the Genus table, the syllable po is given alongside Measure with the character in the adjacent column. The t is the fifth Difference and the o the fifth Species. Lists are provided elsewhere in the book for the actual items. For interest, the 'translation' of Father is coba, heaven is dad (it occurs twice in the top line) and Earth is dady.*

These written symbols took two different forms. One was a set of 'characters' modelled on the Chinese writing system which had attracted the attention of late seventeenth-century society along with other aspects of Chinese culture. It also reflected a long-standing English fascination for alphabets and writing systems which had been further stimulated by the development of secret codes and cyphers during the Civil War. However, Wilkins also required a pronounceable language with a normal orthography and this 'philosophical language', as he called it, was included in the *Essay*. Altogether the work comes to over five hundred pages with a large number of charts, diagrams, lists, and so on, and is one of the most astonishing linguistic enterprises ever undertaken.

It would be unrealistic here to give more than a brief glimpse of Wilkins' scheme and to urge the interested reader both to look at the original[1] and to consult Salmon's excellent papers on the project.[2]

Very briefly, Wilkins' scheme divided notions into General and Special with the General category further subdivided into Things and Words ('Things' in this context being abstract relations of various kinds). The Special notions break down into forty sub-sets, or Genuses, grouped together as 'Substances' such as the World, the Elements, Stones, Metals, Trees, etc. and 'Accidents' such as Space, Measure, Spiritual and Corporeal Actions, Civil and Military Relations, and so on. Thus, for example, the Special Notion DAY is to be found under the Accidental Genus MEASURE.

The Scheme is, however, rather more complex than this. Each Genus subdivides into a number of Differences which contain a set of Species. So, DAY is one of the Species of the Difference TIME (DURATION). In ordinary language this is quite straightforward. The notion DAY represents a measure of duration of time (others in the same list include HOUR, MONTH, YEAR, etc.).

In order to realize the categories in his 'philosophical language' Wilkins assigned a syllable to each Genus, in this case *po* for MEASURE, a consonant for each Difference, and a vowel for each Species according to a numbering system. In our example, this gives a *t* and an *o* respectively, making *poto* the word for *day* in the system. The word for *month* would be *poti* and the word for *morning poty*, etc. One of the features of the scheme which is of particular interest is the way in which the notions relate to each other. As *poto* means *day* as a specific measurement of the duration of time, so *pobo* means the numeral *five*, *pogo* means *pound* as a measurement of weight, and *popo* also means *pound* but as a measurement of money. Each of these letter and syllable symbols also has a special character associated with it into which it can be 'translated'. There are extra symbols to represent grammatical categories and structural items such as pronouns, prepositions, and so on (see Fig. 17).

Needless to say, the Wilkins scheme was not taken up by the

merchants, traders, and missionaries who, he hoped, might have profited by it. It had a certain, rather limited, influence on the development of general linguistic theory, notably on the grammar of Christopher Cooper, *Grammatica Linguae Anglicanae.*[3] It would, however, be quite wrong to assume that the ideas sank without trace. They eventually re-emerged in the nineteenth century in the famous *Thesaurus* of Peter Mark Roget (1779–1869).

Roget was educated at the University of Edinburgh where he took a degree in medicine in 1798. Later he moved to Manchester and then to London, and was active in the scientific community of his time. He became a Fellow of the Royal Society in 1815 and later its Secretary. It was not until after he retired from full-time medical and scientific work that he devoted himself entirely to the Thesaurus, and the completed work, the *Thesaurus of English Words and Phrases*, finally appeared in 1852 when Roget was seventy-three years of age. It was an immediate and enormous success, going through nearly thirty editions in Roget's own lifetime, and is now one of the standard works of reference.

As secretary to the Royal Society, Roget had almost certainly studied Wilkins' *Essay*, which was one of its first publications. He did not, however, acknowledge this directly in his Introduction to the first edition where he mentioned Wilkins only once, in order to point out that his work was 'abortive'. Nevertheless, the link was there, and perhaps it went deeper than we have been told. Roget's biographer[4] suggests, however, that the inspiration for the *Thesaurus* derived less from Roget's interest in language and linguistics than from his passion for classification and taxonomy construction. Given Roget's background and his academic work during his professional career, this seems a very reasonable view, and he joins that special group of eminent linguistic scholars who have come into the subject from the 'harder' sciences, a group that includes, for example, John Wallis (mathematics), Joseph Priestley (chemistry) and, nearer our own time, Franz Boas (geography), and Daniel Jones (mathematics).

## Notes

1 Reproduced in the Scolar facsimile series (No. 119).
2 Salmon (1979) includes two studies.
3 Ibid.: 203.
4 Emblen (1970).

# 10　The language 'fixed'

## Latin Schools and English Schools

The Restoration of the Stuart monarchy in 1660 was a pivotal event in the history of English education and therefore in the history of English language teaching. The Cromwellian Commonwealth of the previous decade had removed the control of education from the Anglican Church, thereby challenging the supremacy of the traditional Latin curriculum and opening the door to the nonconformist Baconian ideal of a modern scientific curriculum for which the essential foundation was the promotion of literacy in the mother tongue. The Restoration re-established the old order but failed to kill the reforming zeal of the non-conformist dissenters who continued to open their schools illegally in remote parts of the country. When the authorities caught up with them, they moved on to somewhere even more isolated and started again. This cat-and-mouse game continued for about twenty years but gradually petered out, particularly after the Protestant succession was confirmed in the 'Glorious Revolution' of 1688. Over the course of time, the sectarian overtones of the dissenting schools, or 'academies' as they were often called, became muted and, alongside the many non-denominational private schools that flourished as the reputation of the public grammar schools declined, they came to provide a focus for many of the more progressive ideas of eighteenth-century education.

The principal contribution of this dissenting tradition was, as we have said, its commitment to a curriculum in which prominence was given to the teaching of the natural sciences and mathematics as well as practical skills like accounting, surveying, and navigation. This implied a need for training of a fairly high order in mother tongue literacy skills and therefore the replacement of Latin as the basic educational discipline by English. Hans (1951), for example, in a study of twenty-eight private academies in the mid-eighteenth century found that English was taught in all twenty-eight, French in seventeen, and Latin in only fifteen.[1] While we should be careful not to oversimplify a complex pattern of provision in which different types of school followed different curricula, there was throughout the eighteenth century a clear contrast between 'English' and 'Latin' schools and the needs of the former provided the primary motivation for the production of grammars, spelling books, dictionaries, and other materials for the teaching of English.

The Latin Schools, on the other hand, remained faithful to the classical curriculum, starting with Latin grammar from the time the children entered school at the age of eight or nine. As we noted earlier, the educational absurdity of this practice had been criticized by Joshua Poole in his *English Accidence* (1646): 'I have often observed how children have been puzzled and confounded, by being set to the construing, parsing, and making of Latin, before they had the least knowledge of the Mother Tongue'.[2] The same complaint was made repeatedly over the next hundred years. Maittaire, for example, said in the Preface to his *English Grammar* in 1712: 'the Youths are forced to learn what they cannot understand; being hurried into Latin, before they are well able to read English'.[3] Twenty years later, an Islington teacher called Daniel Duncan reiterated the point even more forcibly: 'the learning of dead languages is a Yoke, that neither we nor our Fore-fathers could ever bear, when we were children. And I fancy the Loathsomeness of that dry Study comes for want of reasoning previously with them enough about the Nature of Words, and their Dependency on one another, in their own Mother Tongue. A Little Introduction of that Kind before they enter into Latin (I humbly conceive) would save them many a whipping bout, and the Master a vast deal of trouble'.[4] Even Robert Lowth himself in 1762 felt the need to stress yet again: 'If children were first taught the common principles of Grammar . . . they would have some notion of what they were going about, when they should enter into the Latin Grammar'.[5] Older learners who had been denied a serious training in the mother tongue at school through the preservation of this Latin tradition became a second audience for the many grammars and dictionaries of the time.

The eighteenth century was on the whole a time of relative calm after the religious and constitutional turbulence of the seventeenth. Social ambition and commercial enterprise began to take the place of intellectual controversy and religious disputation. The affluence and security of the landed aristocracy and the gentry encouraged investment in grand schemes of building and garden planning, for example, which provided a market for engineering talents and high-quality craft skills of many kinds for which the modern curriculum of the English Schools was an excellent preparation. Imperial trade and development, particularly in America, was also growing and provided opportunities for advancement. In such an atmosphere of stability it was natural that attention should be paid to the way in which language was used, partly to promote one's chances in life and partly to preserve the social order. Getting on in the world meant communicating in an effective and socially acceptable manner. Letter-writing became more important than composing tracts, and a polished style expressed in correctly spelt grammatical sentences became a sought-after accomplishment.

By 1700 the Mulcastrian dream of a vernacular system of education was on the way to realization, but English still lacked adequate means for fulfilling such ambitions. Joseph Aickin, for example, put the matter forthrightly in the Preface to his 1693 *English Grammar*:

> It were to be desired that all learning were to be taught in our Mother Tongue . . . But this good can never be expected till by your care and industry, English terms, proper for all Sciences be invented, till the vulgar prejudice of the difficulty of Learning it, be by your easy Methods taken away: till it be found that the English Tongue is copious enough of itself, to express every thing and notion; but more chiefly till people do see that it may be perfectly acquired, without being beholden to the Latin.[6]

There is more than a hint in this passage of the feelings of national linguistic pride and desire for improvement that characterize the language planning policies of those countries in the Third World at the present time which have elected to promote their national language in place of a European one inherited from a colonial past. The consequent need to augment and standardize the language is also echoed in Aickin's next remarks:

> The daily obstruction and difficulties, that occur in teaching and Learning our Mother Tongue, proceed from the want of an English Grammar, by Law establish'd, the Standard of education, as in other Tongues; for no Tongue can be acquired without Grammatical rules; since then all other Tongues, and Languages are taught by Grammar, why ought not the English Tongue to be taught so too. Imitation will never do it, under twenty years; I have known some Foreigners who have been longer in learning to speak English and yet are far from it: the not learning by Grammar, is the true cause. Hence it cometh, that Children go ten or eleven years or more to School, and yet do not attain the Perfection of the English Tongue . . . The want of such a Grammar, which ought to be the standard of the English Tongue, is the cause of all this.[7]

Aickin's own *Grammar* did not attain the status he sought, nor did any of the many grammars that were published over the next seventy years or so. When the 'standard grammar' did appear in the form of Lowth's *Short Introduction* in 1762, it was not, of course, established by Law but by Convention. The literate public recognized in Lowth what it had been looking for: clear, unambiguous guidance on what was good English and what was not.

Aickin's remark about the law echoes a controversy which had proceeded for some time on the advisability of setting up a body along the lines of the French and Italian Academies to regulate the English language. For example, a committee had been set up in 1664 by the Royal Society 'to improve the English Tongue' and it included such influential supporters as John Dryden and John Evelyn. In 1697 Daniel Defoe raised the question again in his *Essay upon Projects*. However, the proposal that came closest to realization was one put forward by Jonathan Swift in a letter to the Earl of Oxford in 1712 called *A Proposal for Correcting, Improving and Ascertaining the English Tongue* (in eighteenth-century usage *ascertaining* meant making certain or fixing).

## Swift's Proposal for a British Academy

'What I have most at heart', said Swift, 'is that some method should be thought on for ascertaining and fixing our language for ever, after such alterations are made in it as shall be thought requisite'.[8] As a mechanism for effecting this reform, he suggested that 'a free, judicious choice should be made of such persons, as are generally allowed to be best qualified for such a work, without any regard to quality, party or profession'. Having been properly selected, this embryonic academy should 'assemble at some appointed time and place, and fix on rules, by which they should design to proceed'.[9] Swift declined to go into any detail on how they should conduct their business.

For Swift the correct use of language was a moral issue and the social health of the nation was reflected in its attitude to the language and its literary achievements. He was sickened by the 'licentiousness which entered with the Restoration', and believed that 'from infecting our religion and our morals, it fell to corrupt our language'.[10] The English language was at the mercy of 'illiterate court fops, half-witted poets and university boys' with their 'manglings and abbreviations' (he particularly disliked the contemporary habit of using apostrophes in words like *drudg'd*, *rebuk'd*, and so on).[11] It was, as he saw it, a moral duty to stem the tide of corruption and degeneration in order to restore the old values, and preserve for ever the Golden Age of the English Language attained during the time of Elizabeth.

The proposal was immediately attacked by the opposition party in Parliament, the Whigs, who seem to have regarded it as some kind of Tory plot: 'The Arbitrary Government of an Ignorant and Tyrannical Faction',[12] as the Whig historian John Oldmixon put it in his *Reflections* on Swift published in the same year. After some heavy-handed sarcasm at Swift's expense, Oldmixon eventually came to the point: 'it will be in vain to pretend to ascertain Language, unless they had the Secret of setting Rules for Thinking, and could bring Thought to a Standard too'.[13] However, in spite of his reservations about the Academy, Oldmixon joined in the general demand for an authoritative work of reference, and made a special point of its importance for the learning of English as a foreign language: 'the want of a grammar and dictionary has long been complained of; and we cannot expect our tongue will ever spread abroad unless foreigners are put into a more regular method of learning it '.[14]

The enforcement of linguistic uniformity by the state did not appeal much to the British temperament. Dr. Johnson, for instance, whose *Dictionary of the English Language* effectively made Swift's proposal redundant, called it 'a petty treatise' and hoped that 'the spirit of English liberty (would) hinder or destroy' it.[15] In much the same vein, Joseph Priestley rejected it as both authoritarian and impractical: 'As to a public Academy, invested with authority to ascertain the use of words, which is a project that some persons are very sanguine in their expectations from, I think it not only unsuitable to the genius of a *free nation*, but in itself ill-calculated to reform and fix a language . . . (We should) wait the decisions of *Time*, which are slow and sure, (not) take those of *Synods*, which are often hasty and injudicious'.[16]

The idea of an Academy was not without its attractions, however, and the fact that it was still a topic of discussion fifty years later shows that the notion still had its adherents. Its immediate fate in 1712 depended on the maintenance of Tory supremacy at Court, and the death of Queen Anne in 1714 put an effective stop to plans, which had reached a fairly advanced stage of preparation, to implement the scheme. After the change of dynasty and the loss of Tory influence, Whig opposition made it politically impossible and interest subsided. Nevertheless, the fact that the proposal was made at all, and by a man of Swift's eminence, concentrated the minds of its opponents and possibly hastened the development of a more acceptable alternative. The public was in the mood to accept 'authority', and the time found the man in Dr. Samuel Johnson.

## Towards Standard English

*I. The dictionaries of Johnson, Walker, and Webster*
It is inevitable that the image of *Samuel Johnson (1709–1784)* which has passed into history should be that of an elderly man, deeply religious yet given to bouts of black depression and pessimism alternating with periods of ebullience and energy, an unpredictable genius, capable of great charm and wit who bestrode the narrow world of late eighteenth-century literary society like a Colossus. But the Johnson of the Boswell diaries was in many ways rather different from the Johnson of the *Dictionary*. For a start, Johnson was only in his mid-thirties when he undertook the project and forty-six when it was finally published in 1755. Yet the same stamina that saw him through his journey to the Hebrides in his old age was equally evident in the painstaking and repetitive research demanded by the *Dictionary*. As he reminds us at the close of the Preface: 'The *English Dictionary* was written with little assistance of the learned, and without any patronage of the great; not in

the soft obscurities of retirement, or under the shade of academic bowers, but amidst inconvenience and distraction, in sickness and in sorrow . . . If our language be not here fully displayed, I have only failed in an attempt which no human powers have hitherto completed'.[17]

The basic design of the work was published in his *Plan of a Dictionary of the English Language* (1747). In this he summed up his idea of the perfect English dictionary as one 'by which the pronunciation of our language may be fixed, and its attainment facilitated; by which its purity may be preserved, its use ascertained, and its duration lengthened'.[18] By the end of his labours the naïvety of such ambitions had been replaced by a more realistic assessment: 'When we see men grow old and die at a certain time one after another, from century to century, we laugh at the elixir that promises to prolong life to a thousand years; and with equal justice may the lexicographer be derided, who, being able to produce no example of a nation that has preserved their words and phrases from mutability, shall imagine that his dictionary can embalm his language, and secure it from corruption and decay'.[19]

Johnson's approach to dictionary writing was practical but at the same time didactic and conservative. 'It is not enough' he said at one point 'that a dictionary delights the critic, unless at the same time it instructs the learner'.[20] This led him to include, for example, words relating to specific professions or trades 'so far as they can be supposed useful in the occurrences of common life' as well as the words used by the great writers of the past who were his principal sources. Fully naturalized words of foreign origin would be included, but those still felt to be foreign would be printed in italics. 'Barbarous' words, on the other hand, would be excluded or 'branded with some note of infamy'.[21] Considerations of practicality also decided him against archaisms and no word used before the time of Sir Philip Sidney would be included unless it also appeared later. This decision had the added attraction of focusing attention on the Golden Age of Elizabethan English, a preference he shared with Swift.

Johnson's conservatism showed itself most strongly in his attitude to orthography. 'When a question of orthography is dubious, that practice has, in my opinion, a claim to preference, which . . . seems most to comply with the general custom of our language. But the chief rule I propose to follow, is to make no innovation without a reason sufficient to balance the inconvenience of change . . . All change is of itself an evil, which ought not to be hazarded but for evident advantage'.[22] Also, he resolved to 'admit no testimony of living authors' but relented 'when some performance of uncommon excellence excited my veneration'.[23]

Johnson included a grammar and comments on the pronunciation of English in the prefatory material of the *Dictionary*, but his heart was in neither of them. What captured his imagination was the way in which English was used, not of course in the everyday speech of the time since that, he believed, was capricious and ephemeral, but in the writings of great authors. We have to accept, therefore, that he provides us with a partial picture of English in the 1750s which concentrates attention on those features of mid-eighteenth century usage that preserved the traditions of the Golden Age. This is not so antiquarian as it sounds, particularly if we remind ourselves that the speech of Johnson's educated contemporaries could not have avoided the influence of the great Elizabethan and Jacobean texts, notably the King James Bible and the plays of Shakespeare which were studied, read, and listened to at home and in public until they were absorbed into the fabric of the language.

The outcome of Johnson's work can be seen, for example, in the famous entry for the word *oats* (Fig. 18). Alongside the headword he provides the minimal amount of grammatical information, classifying it as a noun substantive (n.s.) but neglecting to point out that it is usually used in the plural. There is no information on pronunciation, though polysyllabic words (for example *oatmalt*) are marked for stress. Then there is a brief historical comment and the basic definition which, in this case, has earned a place in the dictionaries of quotations. Finally, there is a set of historically organized 'special precedents' drawn from great writers.

Johnson did not 'fix' the language, and, as we have seen, he recognized the vanity of the aim for himself. However, in a different sense of the word, he provided a fixed point of reference against which future change could be set and assessed. He established a model for dictionary-making that was emulated and extended by later writers like Webster and the compilers of the great *Oxford English Dictionary* itself at the end of the following century. Also, without Johnson, the problems of educational expansion over the next hundred years would have proved more intractable than they were and, although someone else would doubtless have produced the standard dictionary, it is unlikely to have been anyone with the same humanity or the same grandeur.

For all its splendour the *Dictionary* did not realize all the ambitions set out in the *Plan*. The shortcomings of the disappointing introductory grammar were rectified in Lowth's *Short Introduction* a few years later. And Johnson's failure to take an interest in phonetics was compensated for in the work of his ardent admirer John Walker in his *Critical Pronouncing Dictionary* published in 1791.

*John Walker* (1732–1807), like Thomas Sheridan, had a background in the theatre and the teaching of elocution. However, when he came to write his pronouncing dictionary, he took a modern descriptive line that was quite different from Sheridan's archaism. He aimed to provide his readers with a description which would accurately represent the 'received pronunciation' of English in his own time.

Johnson's attitude to pronunciation had been dismissive, almost to

*Shakesp.*

OATH. n. f. [aith, Gothick ; að, Saxon.  The diftance between the noun *oath*, and the verb *fwear*, is very obfervable,
as it may fhew that our oldeft dialect is formed from different
languages.]  An affirmation, negation, or promife, corrobo-
rated by the atteftation of the Divine Being.

Read over Julia's heart, thy firft beft love,
For whofe dear fake thou then did'ft rend thy faith
Into a thoufand *oaths* ; and all thofe *oaths*
Defcended into perjury to love me.            *Shakefpeare.*
He that ftrikes the firft ftroke, I'll run him up to the
hilts as I am a foldier.
—An *oath* of mickle might ; and fury fhall abate.   *Sha.*
We have confultations, which inventions fhall be publifhed,
which not : and take an *oath* of fecrecy for the concealing of
thofe which we think fit to keep fecret.          *Bacon.*
Thofe called to any office of truft, are bound by an *oath*
to the faithful difcharge of it : but an *oath* is an appeal to
God, and therefore can have no influence, except upon thofe
who believe that he is.                          *Swift.*
OA'THABLE. adj. [from *oath*.  A word not ufed.]  Capable
of having an oath adminiftered.

You're not *oathable,*
Altho' I know you'll fwear
Into ftrong fhudders th' immortal gods.     *Shakefpeare.*
OATHBREA'KING. n. f. [*oath* and *break*.]  Perjury ; the vio-
lation of an oath.

His *oathbreaking* he mended thus,
By now forfwearing that he is forfworn.   *Shak. Hen.* IV.
OA'TMALT. n. f. [*oat* and *malt*.]  Malt made of oats.

In Kent they brew with one half *oatmalt*, and the other
half barleymalt.                       *Mortimer's Hufb.*
OA'TMEAL. n. f. [*oat* and *meal*.]  Flower made by grinding
oats.

*Oatmeal* and butter, outwardly applied, dry the fcab on the
head.                               *Arbuthnot on Aliment.*
Our neighbours tell me oft, in joking talk,
Of afhes, leather, *oatmeal*, bran, and chalk.     *Gay.*
OA'TMEAL. n. f.  An herb.                    *Ainfworth.*
OATS. n. f. [aten, Saxon.]  A grain, which in England is
generally given to horfes, but in Scotland fupports the people.

It is of the grafs leaved tribe ; the flowers have no petals,
and are difpofed in a loofe panicle : the grain is eatable.
The meal makes tolerable good bread.          *Miller.*
The *oats* have eaten the horfes.          *Shakefpeare.*
It is bare mechanifm, no otherwife produced than the
turning of a wild *oatbeard*, by the infinuation of the particles
of moifture.                               *Locke.*
For your lean cattle, fodder them with barley ftraw firft,
and the *oat* ftraw laft.               *Mortimer's Hufbandry.*
His horfe's allowance of *oats* and beans, was greater than
the journey required.                          *Swift.*
OA'TTHISTLE. n. f. [*oat* and *thiftle*.]  An herb.   *Ainf.*
OBAMBULA'TION. n. f. [*obambulatio*, from *obambulo*, Latin.]
• The act of walking about.                     *Dict.*

ŌAT, n.  [Sax. ate, oat or cockle, darnel ;
Russ. *oves* or *ovetzi*.]
A plant of the genus Avena, and more usually, the seed of the plant.  The word is
commonly used in the plural, *oats*.  This
plant flourishes best in cold latitudes, and
degenerates in the warm.  The meal of
this grain, *oatmeal*, forms a considerable
and very valuable article of food for man
in Scotland, and every where oats are excellent food for horses and cattle.
ŌATCAKE, n.  A cake made of the meal of
oats.                                        *Peacham.*
ŌATEN, a.  o'tn.  Made of oatmeal ; as, *oat-
en* cakes.
2. Consisting of an oat straw or stem ; as,
an *oaten* pipe.                             *Milton.*
ŌATH, n.  [Sax. ath ; Goth. *aiths* ; D. *eed* ;
G. *eid* ; Sw. *ed* ; Dan. *œed*.]
A solemn affirmation or declaration, made
with an appeal to God for the truth of
what is affirmed.  The appeal to God in
an oath, implies that the person imprecates
his vengeance and renounces his favor if
the declaration is false, or if the declaration
is a promise, the person invokes the vengeance of God if he should fail to fulfill it.
A false oath is called perjury.
ŌATHABLE, a.  Capable of having an oath
administered to. [*Not used.*]             *Shak.*
ŌATHBREAKING, n.  The violation of an
oath ; perjury.                            *Shak.*
ŌATMALT, n.  Malt made of oats.
                                          *Mortimer.*
ŌATMEAL, n.  Meal of oats produced by
grinding or pounding.                       *Gay.*
2. A plant. [*Not used.*]
ŌAT-THISTLE, n.  A plant. [*Not used.*]
                                         *Ainsworth.*
OB, a Latin preposition, signifies primarily,
in front, before, and hence against, towards ;
as in *objicio*, to object, that is, to throw
against.  It has also the force of *in* or *on* ;
as in *obtrude*.  In composition, the letter *b*
is often changed into the first letter of the
word to which it is prefixed ; as, in *occasion, offer, oppose.*
OBAM'BULATE, v. i.  [L. *obambulo*.]  To
walk about. [*Not used.*]                *Cockeram.*
OBAMBULATION, n.  A walking about.
[*Not used.*]                              *Dict.*

*Figure 18  Extracts from (left) Johnson's Dictionary of the English Language and
(right) Webster's American Dictionary of the English Language.  A comparison of the
two extracts clearly shows Webster's debt to Johnson.  Many definitions have been
copied virtually word-for-word (e.g. oathable, oathbreaking, oatmalt) and
Johnson's sources, though not his quotations, have been retained unchanged.
Cutting the quotations (though a few remained) allowed Webster to enlarge the
dictionary from 45,000 to 70,000 words, and expand the definitions of important
words.  Oath and oat(s) are good examples: where Johnson is stylishly laconic,
Webster is informative and practical.  Webster's diacritics (for example the 'long' o
and the 'hard' c) are helpful though he omits some indications of word stress.*

the point of contempt: 'In treating of the letters, I shall not enquire . . . into their formation and prolation by the organs of speech, as a mechanick, anatomist or physiologist . . . I suppose my reader already acquainted with the English language, and consequently able to pronounce the letters of which I teach the pronunciation'.[24] Nevertheless, Walker's respect was unbounded: 'a man whose friendship and advice I was honoured with, whose memory I love, and whose intellectual powers impress me with something like religious veneration and awe'.[25] However, even Dr. Johnson nodded: 'it may be asserted that in these observations (*i.e. Johnson's comments on pronunciation*) we do not perceive that justice and accuracy of thinking for which he is so remarkable'.[26] It was a fair point, tactfully put.

Johnson's prejudices were near the surface at times: 'language was at its beginning merely oral' and written language must not be permitted to 'comply with the corruptions of oral utterance'. 'For pronunciation' Johnson summed up, 'the best general rule is, to consider those as the most elegant speakers, who deviate least from the written words'.[27] Again, Walker tactfully disagreed: 'It would be doing great injustice (*to Johnson*) to suppose that he meant to exclude all possibility of conveying the actual pronunciation of many words that depart manifestly from their orthography, or of those that are written alike and pronounced differently: and inversely'.[28] One specific issue that concerned Walker was the distinction between stressed and unstressed vowels which is such a central feature of English pronunciation. 'The truth is, Dr. Johnson seems to have had a confused idea of the distinctness and indistinctness with which on solemn or familiar occasions, we sometimes pronounce the unaccented vowels'.[29]

The *Critical Pronouncing Dictionary* contains a wealth of information on the pronunciation of standard English as well as specially written sections providing detailed advice for Londoners, Irishmen, and Scotsmen on how to attain a standard English accent. There is also a brief note on 'Directions to Foreigners' which concentrates on the problems of English pronunciation for French-speaking learners and covers many of the same points as Miège: the *th* sounds, the diphthongs, and the problems of placing the stress in individual words. In general, Walker is the indispensable companion-piece to the Johnson *Dictionary* (his definitions, for example, are derived from Johnson), which can with some justice be said to have completed the great design originally sketched out in the *Plan* of 1747.

It is rather ironic that these determined attempts to fix the English language 'for ever' should have coincided with the secession of the American colonies and the establishment of an independent English-speaking nation which would inevitably seek to develop an alternative standard suited to its own purposes. The career of Noah Webster (1758–1843) reflects the shift in attitudes in America away from cultural dependence on London towards a separate American identity. He did his best, for example, to awaken national pride in the cause of a reformed system of spelling: 'Let us then seize the present moment, and establish a *national language* as well as a national government',[30] he wrote in 1789. He was by this time a household name as the author of *An American Spelling Book*, popularly known as the 'Bluebacked Speller' because of its distinctive blue paper covers. According to Warfel (1976),[31] the book sold one-and-a-half million copies by 1801 and around seventy-five million by 1875.

The 'Bluebacked Speller' started out in life as Part I of Webster's three-part *Grammatical Institute of the English Language*, first published in 1783. Renamed in 1787, it takes an orthodox view of spelling and precedes Webster's conversion to the cause of reform. In 1789, however, he published an essay on a reformed mode of spelling (quoted from above) as an appendix to a collection of papers called *Dissertations on the English Language*. Webster was a good popular communicator and, though the *Essay* does little more than rehearse the familiar reformist arguments, the basic principles come across very clearly. He recommended three major changes to the existing system. First, all superfluous and silent letters should be omitted, giving, for example, *hed* for *head*, *frend* for *friend*, etc. Secondly, alternative spellings for the same sound should be regularized. The 'long-*i*', for instance, should be spelt *ee*, giving *greef*, *kee*, *masheen*, and so on. He also recommended the use of diacritics and other marks to distinguish between different values of the same letter. The illustration (Fig.18) shows how this principle was used for 'hard' and 'soft' *c* in his *Dictionary*.

In 1804 he incorporated some of his ideas in a new edition of the 'Bluebacked Speller', dropping the final *k* from *-ick* endings in polysyllabic words like *energetic(k)*, and the *u* from *-our* endings to produce such characteristic American spellings as *labor* and *honor*. Two years later, he published the first of his major dictionaries, *A Compendious Dictionary of the English Language* (1806), in which he proposed a wide range of reformed spellings, not all of which have survived. They included two, however, which became standard American practice: the *-er* ending in words like *center*, and the regularization of consonant-doubling in *traveler*, for instance, and *leveling* where the final syllable of the root word does not carry the word stress.

The culmination of Webster's work was the publication of his *American Dictionary of the English Language* in 1828 in the belief that 'it is not only important, but in a degree necessary' that the American people should have their own national dictionary of English. He retained the spelling changes which had found popular favour and dropped, or compromised on, those which had not. He listed both *theatre* and *theater*, for example, but gave no alternative for *center*; he retained *crum* (*crumb* is not included), but gave the orthodox as well as the reformed spellings of *isle/ile*, *feather/fether*, *sponge/spunge*, and *aker/acre*. The *-or* and *-ic* reforms were preserved intact, as was the consonant-doubling principle.

Webster's success in imposing a measure of orthographical reform on the writing habits of 'a nation was no small achievement, and as a practical source of reference his *Dictionary* was in some ways more useful than Johnson's. His *oat* definition, for example (Fig.18) may lack Johnsonian style, but it is clearer and more informative to the average reader. He was a rather earnest man (Venezky calls him 'stern and humourless'),[32] and the decision to repeat Johnson's famous Scottish jibe in quite such leaden tones was probably a mistake. He could also be tendentious and even small-minded at times. His introductory 'Philosophical and Practical Grammar of the English Language', for instance, is preceded by a lengthy attack on Lindley Murray, whom he suspected of plagiarism, and the text is peppered with scornful comments on both predecessors and contemporaries. He also includes a long and rather unfortunate essay on the origins of language, tracing the European languages back to Hebrew and thence to Adam and Eve and, ultimately, God. At a time when the foundations of scientific historical philology were being laid by scholars like von Humboldt and the Grimm brothers, this anachronistic view is rather embarrassing. However, he succeeded in his basic aim: 'to furnish a standard of our vernacular tongue, which we shall not be ashamed to bequeath to three hundred millions of people, who are destined to occupy and, I hope, adorn the vast territory within our jurisdiction.'[33]

Webster was not the only American of the time to make an impact on practical English studies. In particular, there was the despised Lindley Murray, a Quaker from Pennsylvania who later settled in York, and even William Cobbett, archetypal Englishman though he was, had close associations with the United States ( not all of them entirely voluntary). Both these writers were popularizers who aimed to instruct the ordinary citizen in English grammar and both based their work on the most influential grammar of the eighteenth century, Robert Lowth's *Short Introduction to English Grammar*, to which we now turn.

II. *The grammars of Lowth, Murray, and Cobbett*
Robert Lowth (1710–1787) was a clergyman and a specialist in Hebrew poetry. He held a professorship of poetry at Oxford for three years between 1741 and 1744, and thereafter spent his life in the Church. His work did not bring him into direct contact with the schools, and his sole excursion into pedagogy, *A Short Introduction to English Grammar, with critical notes* (1762), was 'merely for a private and domestic use'. Four years after its publication, he was consecrated Bishop of Oxford and, eleven years later, moved to the capital as Bishop of London and

Dean of the Chapel Royal. He seems to have been a rather retiring man – he turned down the offer of the Archbishopric of Canterbury, for example – and may genuinely have sought anonymity when, like Lily, he omitted his name from the title-page of the *Short Introduction*. If that was indeed the case, it is rather ironic that the work should have made him the most famous and emulated grammarian of his time. Through his disciples, notably Murray and Cobbett, his influence extended through the nineteenth century to the fringe of modern times. This has served to make him a target for the 'descriptivist' philosophy in linguistics in our own century and his reputation can still arouse indignation today (see, for example, Aitchison 1981).

Lowth's basic aim was no different from that of other eighteenth-century grammarians: to provide a standard work of English grammar, and guide the learner to express himself 'with propriety' and 'judge of every phrase and form of construction, whether it be right or not'.[34] 'The plain way of doing this,' he states with characteristic clarity in his Preface, 'is to lay down rules, and to illustrate them by examples'.[35] This brisk tone and straightforward style is preserved throughout the main text of the book, and he is exceptionally liberal with worked examples. This last point helps to account for his commercial success, at least with learners studying on their own. None of his rivals went to the same trouble to ensure that each new point was exemplified in detail. Murray took the principle one step further by providing practice examples for the learners to do for themselves.

A second novel feature of Lowth's design was his use of footnotes. There was nothing new about footnotes as such, they had been used for a long time. But Lowth employed them for a deliberate pedagogical purpose. He believed that 'besides showing what is right, the matter may be further explained by pointing out what is wrong'[36] and he used his footnotes to discuss examples of 'bad English' in order to clarify his rules. As a teaching device, this form of 'error analysis' is a double-edged weapon. Although it helps to explain a new point, and possibly comforts the learner with the thought that other people also find English grammar difficult, it is rather alarming to discover that even authors with reputations as great as Pope, Swift, and Addison 'make mistakes'. Priestley had considered using the same technique in his *Rudiments of English Grammar* the previous year, but rejected it on the grounds that errors made 'so uncouth an appearance in print',[37] and, anyway, the teacher would have no difficulty in supplying examples for himself.

The other pedagogical advantage of the footnote device is that it creates a two-level course in a single book with the main text as the elementary material and footnotes as the more advanced commentary. Murray took this idea up and developed it systematically in his own work.

Lowth's approach is well-exemplified in the two extracts in Figs. 19

and 20. His section headings deliberately avoid technical terms like Orthography and Syntax in favour of simple ones like Letters, Words, and Sentences. His definitions could hardly be more straightforward and his treatment of the old *i/j*, *u/v* problem is admirably direct. Only seven years earlier, Johnson had entangled himself with 'j-consonant' and 'v-consonant'. Lowth's blunt statement that '*Jj* and *Vv* are consonants' must have been reassuring to many anxious learners.

After dealing with the spelling and pronunciation in a rather summary fashion (he was no more of a phonetician than Johnson), Lowth provides a traditional set of notional definitions of the parts of speech. A noun, for instance, is 'the name of anything conceived to subsist, or of which we have any notion', a verb signifies 'to be, to do, or to suffer',[38]

---

2    *A Short Introduction*

Grammar treats of Sentences, and the several parts of which they are compounded.

Sentences consist of Words; Words, of one or more Syllables; Syllables, of one or more Letters.

So that Letters, Syllables, Words, and Sentences, make up the whole subject of Grammar.

### LETTERS.

A Letter is the first Principle, or least part of a Word.

An Articulate Sound is the found of the human voice, formed by the organs of speech.

A Vowel is a simple articulate found, formed by the impulse of the voice, and by the opening only of the mouth in a particular manner.

A Consonant cannot be perfectly founded by itself; but joined with a vowel

*to English Grammar.*    3

a vowel forms a compound articulate found, by a particular motion or contact of the parts of the mouth.

A Diphthong, or Double Vowel, is the union of two or more vowels pronounced by a single impulse of the voice.

In English there are twenty-six Letters:

A, a; B, b; C, c; D, d; E, e; F, f; G, g; H, h; I, i; J, j; K, k; L, l; M, m; N, n; O, o; P, p; Q, q; R, r; S, s; T, t; U, u; V, v; W, w; X, x; Y, y; Z, z.

*J j*, and *V v*, are consonants; the former having the found of the soft *g*, and the latter that of a coarser *f*: they are therefore intirely different from the vowels *i* and *u*, and distinct letters of themselves; they ought also to be distinguished by a peculiar Name; the former may be called *ja*, and the latter *vee*.

B 2          Six

---

*Figure 19   Pages 2 and 3 from Robert Lowth's* Short Introduction to English Grammar, *published in 1762. Lowth's straightforward, confident style helped to make it the most influential grammar of its time. It was also the main source for later school grammars, notably the immensely popular work of Lindley Murray.*

and so on. It is evident from these definitions that Lowth presupposed a fairly high standard of general culture among his readers. Compare, for instance, Priestley's elementary definition in the *Rudiments*: 'A Noun (or as it is sometimes called a Substantive) is the name of any thing'.[39] Next the categories are exemplified in the parsing of a carefully constructed sample sentence that illustrates each part of speech (Lowth recognized nine) at least once. Finally, he works systematically through each part of speech in turn with more examples and detailed comments in the footnotes. There are a few observations on style at the end of the book. Altogether, Lowth's pedagogical design for the *Short Introduction* was meticulously planned, economical, and astute. Its success, in this respect

---

48   *A Short Introduction*

*have*, and *to be*, are thus varied according to Perſon, Number, Time, and Mode.

   Time is Preſent, Paſt, or Future.

To H A V E.
Indicative Mode.
Preſent Time.

| | Sing. | Plur. |
|---|---|---|
| 1. | I have, | We ⎫ |
| 2. | Thou haſt *, | Ye ⎬ have. |
| 3. | He hath, or has; | They ⎭ |

(Perſon)

Paſt

---

to *Engliſh Grammar.*   49

Paſt Time.

| | | | |
|---|---|---|---|
| 1. I had, | We | ⎫ | |
| 2. Thou hadſt, | Ye | ⎬ | had. |
| 3. He had; | They | ⎭ | |

Future Time.

| | | | |
|---|---|---|---|
| 1. I ſhall, or will, | ⎫ | We | ⎫ ſhall, |
| 2. Thou ſhalt, or wilt, | ⎬ have; | Ye | ⎬ or will, |
| 3. He ſhall, or will, | ⎭ | They | ⎭ have. |

Impe-

---

* *Thou*, in the Polite, and even in the Familiar Style, is diſuſed, and the Plural *You* is employed inſtead of it: we ſay *You have*, not *Thou haſt*. Tho' in this caſe we apply *You* to a ſingle Perſon, yet the Verb too muſt agree with it in the Plural Number: it muſt neceſſarily be *You have*, not *You haſt*. *You was*, the Second Perſon Plural of the Pronoun placed in agreement with the Firſt or Third Perſon Singular of the Verb, is an enormous Soleciſm: and yet Authors of the firſt rank have inadvertently fallen into it. " Knowing that *you was* my old maſter's good friend." Addiſon, Spect. N° 517. " Would to God *you*

*you was* within her reach." Lord Bolingbroke to Swift, Letter 46. " If *you was* here." Ditto, Letter 47. " I am juſt now as well, as when *you was* here." Pope to Swift, P. S. to Letter 56. On the contrary the Solemn Style admits not of *You* for a Single Perſon. This hath led Mr. Pope into a great impropriety in the beginning of his Meſſiah:

" O *Thou* my voice inſpire
Who *touch'd* Iſaiah's hallow'd lips with fire!"

The Solemnity of the Style would not admit of *You* for *Thou* in the Pronoun; nor the meaſure of the Verſe *touchedſt*, or *didſt touch*, in the Verb; as it indiſpenſably ought to be, in the one, or the other of theſe two forms: *You* who *touched*; or *Thou* who *touchedſt*, or *didſt touch*. Again:

" Juſt of *thy* word, in every thought ſincere,
Who *knew* no wiſh but what the world might
   hear."          Pope, Epitaph.

E          It

---

Figure 20   Pages 48–9 from Lowth's Short Introduction, *including the extensive footnotes in which he exemplified his rules by giving instances of infringements by famous writers. The extract shows both his concern for contemporary usage (for example 'Thou is disused') and his prescriptivism (for example he claims that* you was *'is an enormous Solecism', whereas in fact it was current in educated usage alongside* you were*).*

at least, was well-earned, and it was reprinted many times in Britain as well as appearing in a number of cities in America and elsewhere, including Germany where it was translated twice.

Some of Lowth's strengths and weaknesses are apparent from the illustrations reproduced in Figure 20. The main text presents the three tenses of *to have* in the traditional paradigmatic form. Given that 'Thou . . . is disused', one might question the need to include it at all, but that would be to overlook the ritualistic function of paradigms. They were hallowed by time (not, I suspect, by a desire to make English fit the rules of Latin) and persisted into modern times. Although *ye* was dropped fairly early, *thou* survived and was still being included in school grammars in the 1950s (see, for example, the 1954 reprint of J. C. Nesfield's *English Grammar Series*).

Lowth's reputation for 'prescriptivism' derives from his footnotes rather than his main text. The one in the illustration exemplifies quite well the distinction between a legitimately normative statement like 'We say *you have* and not *thou hast*', and an illegitimately prescriptive one like his treatment of *you was*. During the seventeenth and early eighteenth centuries the old four-term system of second-person pronouns (*thou/thee/ye/you*) had been replaced by the single term *you* in normal standard usage, leaving *thou/thee* as a feature of certain regional dialects and literary varieties. This shift, however, left a residual issue, namely the desire by some speakers and writers to preserve the singular-plural distinction by a contrast between *you was* and *you were*. This principle was restricted to the past tense of *be*: there was no hint of forms like *you is*, for example, or *you has*. *You was* had found favour with 'authors of the first rank', including Addison and Pope, for instance. The response of Lowth's contemporaries varied considerably. Buchanan (1762), for example, listed both *you was* and *you were*, as did Webster nearly seventy years later. Priestley (1761), on the other hand, was unhappy, and, rather reluctantly, condemned *you was* in typically tolerant terms: 'Many writers of no small reputation say *you was*, when speaking of a single person: but as the word *you* is confessedly *plural*, ought not the verb, agreeable to the analogy of all languages, to be plural too? Moreover, we always say *you are*.'[40] Lowth, however, pounced on the offending term as 'an enormous Solecism'. Adjudicating between two competing forms in an 'unstable' area of the language in this high-handed way is blatantly prescriptive. Nevertheless, it is important to recognize that Lowth was not trying to 'improve' established usage, as he has sometimes been accused of doing, through some idiosyncratic embellishment of his own.

In her recent book *Language Change: Progress or Decay?* Jean Aitchison launches a colourful attack on Lowth, accusing him of making idiosyncratic pronouncements as to what was 'right' and what was 'wrong',[41] as well as falling into the Latin Trap: 'Latin grammar was used as a model for the description of all other languages – however dissimilar – despite the fact that it was no longer anyone's native tongue'.[42] We shall come to the 'pronouncements' shortly, but the Latin comment is unfair on Lowth, who was quite sensitive to the specific characteristics of English that set it apart from the classical languages (see his Preface). Also, at one point he quite explicitly takes another commentator to task for 'forcing the English under the rules of a foreign language (*i.e. Latin*), with which it has little concern'.[43]

Aitchison gives three instances where Lowth's comments supposedly attempt to impose 'fixed and eccentric opinions' on his readers. Curiously, the *you was* example is not one of them. On examination, however, in all three cases Lowth was doing little more than repeating some very familiar points which had been made many times before. The first complaint is that 'contrary to general usage, he urged that prepositions at the ends of sentences should be avoided'.[44] In fact, Lowth accepted that prepositions at the ends of sentences suited 'very well with the familiar style of writing' though it was 'more graceful as well as more perspicuous' to place them earlier in the clause in more 'solemn and elevated' style.[45] Priestley makes exactly the same point in the *Rudiments*: 'It is often really diverting to see with what extreme caution words of such frequent occurrence as *of* and *to* are prevented from fixing themselves at the close of a sentence; though that be a situation they naturally incline to', and he concludes that 'nothing but the solemnity of an address from the pulpit' ought to dislodge them from their natural position at the end.[46] It is quite clear that people were worried about prepositions at the ends of sentences, but why they were, and where the anxiety came from, is a mystery. It certainly did not originate with Lowth or Priestley, who were both trying to clear the problem up.

Aitchison also accuses Lowth of 'insisting' that the pronoun *I* should be used in phrases such as *wiser than I*.[47] What he actually said was that the case of the pronoun after *than* depended on its presumed grammatical function in an elliptical second clause, giving, for example, *He is wiser than I (am)* and *You love him more than (you love) me*. This had been the standard analysis of *than*-phrases for a long time, and so cannot be dismissed as an 'eccentric opinion' of Dr. Lowth. The *wiser than I* pattern was hardly 'contrary to established usage' since it was used by, for example, Shakespeare ('I'll rant as well as thou', *Hamlet*, V/i), Marlowe ('Commend me to my son and bid him rule better than I', *Edward II*, V/i) and Jonson ('You talk as idly as they', *The Alchemist*, V/i).

The third criticism is a more interesting one. Aitchison suspects that Lowth 'may have been the first to argue that a double-negative is wrong'.[48] Disappointingly for anti-Lowthians, the self-cancelling effect of the double-negative had been pointed out much earlier, for example by Hugh Jones in his *Accidence to the English Tongue* in 1724: 'Two Negatives affirm, as, *you have not no money* is really *you have some money*'.[49] As an interesting postscript on this issue, double-negatives seem to have been a feature of 'foreigner talk' from at least the early eighteenth century. In Farquhar's *Beaux Stratagem* (1707) there is a character called Foigard whose 'mother tongue' is Flemish. At one point in the story he gets upset and swears 'I vill never spake English no more'.[50]

Lowth's *Short Introduction* marked a watershed in the development of pedagogical grammars of English. On the one hand, it was the culmination of the eighteenth-century search for a clear, reliable guide to the structure of the standard language. On the other, it established an authority for the next generation of grammars written to promote the expansion of literacy in the early industrializing decades of the nineteenth century.

Murray and Cobbett in particular represent the transition from the eighteenth century with its passion for linguistic propriety, elegance, and rhetorical stylishness to the more robust tradition of popular grammars of Victorian times. Both consciously based their work on Lowth and aimed to bring the advantages of correct English to a broader audience.

*Lindley Murray* (1745–1826) was born into a Quaker family in Pennsylvania and spent the first twenty years of his adult life as a lawyer, a profession which made him rich. In his late thirties, he emigrated to England and arrived in York in 1784. He began his second, and equally successful career as a school textbook writer in 1795 with the publication of his *English Grammar, adapted to the different classes of learners*, a work that earned him the title 'Father of English grammar'.

Murray's work was intended specifically for schools, an audience which, as we have seen, Lowth himself did not address. In making his adaptation of the *Short Introduction*, Murray established two new principles in the design of pedagogical grammars, both of them original at the time. The first was a deliberate system of grading (hence the reference to 'different classes of learners' in his subtitle). He took Lowth's device of distinguishing between the main text and the footnotes, and developed it into a system for organizing teaching materials for different levels of learners which were indicated by the use of different type sizes in the printed book.

Secondly, he pioneered the technique of providing practice exercises for classroom use (*English Exercises* (1797)). Like the exercises of the so-called 'grammar-translation method' in foreign language teaching, Murray's were based on sentences which illustrated the basic points in his textbook. His favourite technique was to get pupils to correct deliberate mistakes. He provided a simple rule – for example, that 'active verbs govern the objective case' – and listed a number of sentences in which the rule was broken which the pupils had to put right. For instance, *Who did they entertain so freely? He and they we know, but who are you? She that is idle and mischievous, reprove sharply* etc.[51] The moral tone of this last example is typical of the book and reflects Murray's close relationship with a Quaker school in York. Religion and ethics were his second major interest and he was deeply committed to philanthropic work in the local community. His own health was poor and in the last years of his life he became a recluse.

The fact that we associate 'doing grammar' so closely with 'doing exercises' is some measure of the influence that Murray's work exerted on the teaching of English in schools. His books sold in very large numbers for a great many years and established a pedagogical framework for the teaching of grammar which remained unchanged for over a century.

The second of Lowth's disciples was an altogether different personality. *William Cobbett* (1763–1835) was a man of enormous energies and enthusiasms acted out, for the most part, in the full glare of public attention. He came from a farming community in Surrey, but, bored with rural life, he ran away to sea. Through a chance meeting, he ended up not in Portsmouth but as an Army recruit in Chatham where he spent his spare time, usually at night, learning Lowth off by heart. His military career took him to North America but ended abruptly following a sedition charge, whereupon he took to journalism and teaching English to French emigré refugees in the United States. At this time his political attitudes were robustly anti-revolutionary, and his attacks on Tom Paine and others caused considerable hostility. Later he switched sides and became one of Paine's most ardent and vocal admirers. He spent some time in post-revolutionary France and wrote a grammar of the language. Later, during an (enforced) stay on Long Island in America, he wrote a series of letters to his fourteen-year-old son James Paul which provided the basis for his grammar, *A Grammar of the English Language, in a Series of Letters* (1819). The book was intended both for the use of 'schools and of young persons in general' and 'more especially for the use of soldiers, sailors, apprentices and ploughboys'.

The hint of political radicalism in this title-page announcement is developed in the book itself. Literacy founded on correct grammar was, in Cobbett's eyes, a political weapon that conferred power on those who knew how to use it, and undermined those who did not. Lowth had collected examples of 'errors' from great writers. Cobbett, in his turn, ransacked the speeches of politicians, generals, bishops, and even (cautiously) the King himself, to find the solecisms they had perpetrated and the stylistic barbarisms they had failed to amend. In acquiring a knowledge of grammar, he wrote in his Introduction, 'there is one motive which, though it ought at all times to be strongly felt, ought, at the present time, to be so felt in an extraordinary degree: I mean that desire which every man, and especially every young man, should entertain to be able to assert with effect the rights and liberties of his country'.[52]

Cobbett's philosophy provides an interesting contrast with modern views on the role of 'correct grammar' in a socially responsible system of education. Present-day egalitarianism encourages the notion that the standard language is merely one of a number of more or less 'equal' dialects – different but 'no better' than other varieties. In his comments on pronunciation, Cobbett echoed these sentiments: 'Children will pronounce as their fathers and mothers pronounce; and if . . . the matter be good and judiciously arranged, the facts clearly stated, the arguments conclusive, the words well-chosen and properly placed, hearers whose approbation is worth having will pay little attention to the accent'.[53] His views on grammar, however, were rather different. In order to achieve 'good and judiciously arranged arguments' and 'well-chosen words', and therefore the social and political power which they wield, a knowledge of grammar was essential. 'The actions of men proceed from their *thoughts*. In order to obtain the co-operation, the concurrence, or the consent, of others, we must communicate our thoughts to them. The means of this communication are *words*: and Grammar teaches us *how to make use of words*'.[54] Not only does this attitude have a harder cutting-edge than the modern desire for a co-operative condominium of dialects, it is also rather more realistic in its assessment of the workings of power.

## Notes

1 Hans (1951: 67).
2 Poole (1646: A2 recto/verso).
3 Maittaire (1712: A2 verso).
4 Duncan (1731: v).
5 Lowth (1762: xiii).
6 Aickin (1693: A3 recto).
7 Ibid.: A2 verso.
8 Scott (ed. 1907: 15).
9 Ibid.: 14.
10 Ibid.: 11.
11 Ibid.: 14.
12 Oldmixon (1712: 6–7).
13 Ibid.: 26–7.
14 Ibid.: 34.
15 Maver (1809: xxv).
16 Priestley (1761: vii).
17 Maver (1809: xxv).
18 Johnson (1747: 32).
19 Maver (1809: xxi).

20 Johnson (1747: 5).
21 Ibid.: 29.
22 Ibid.: 10.
23 Maver (1809: xvi).
24 Ibid.: xxviii.
25 Walker (1791/1856: viii).
26 Ibid.: viii.
27 Maver (1809: xxxii).
28 Walker (1791/1856: v).
29 Ibid.: v.
30 Webster (1789: 406).
31 Quoted in Venezky (1980: 13).
32 Ibid.: 13.
33 Webster (1828/32: viii):
34 Lowth (1762: xiii).
35/36 Ibid.: x.
37 Priestley (1761: xi).
38 Lowth (1762: 8).
39 Priestley (1761: 2).
40 Ibid.: 20–1.
41 Aitchison (1981: 23).
42 Ibid.: 22.
43 Lowth (1761: 107).
44 Aitchison (1981: 24).
45 Lowth (1762: 127).
46 Priestley (1761: 50–1).
47/48 Aitchison (1981: 24).
49 Jones (1724: 41). (See also Gough (1754: 14), Solecism X).
50 Act IV, scene ii.
51 Murray (1797/1813: 91).
52 Cobbett (1819/66: 11).
53 Ibid.: 17.
54 Ibid.: 11.

# PART THREE

# Language teaching in the nineteenth century

# Overview

The conventional picture of nineteenth-century language teaching is one where the grammar-translation method, after a long period of dominance, was finally challenged by the forces of reform at the end of the century and successfully humbled by a saner, more rational, and more practical approach. This is not an entirely unfair picture but it places rather too much emphasis on the teaching of languages in schools and ignores change and developments elsewhere. It also tends to give too much credit to intellectual arguments for reform and too little to the practical circumstances which made those arguments appear considerably more relevant to social and educational needs at the end of the century than they would have done earlier.

There are three major strands in the development of language teaching in the nineteenth century which twine together in the great controversies of the last two decades. The first is the most obvious and the best chronicled, namely the gradual integration of foreign language teaching into a modernized secondary school curriculum. In 1800 very few schools taught foreign languages except as optional 'extras' to the principal work of the school, the teaching of classical languages. By 1900 most secondary schools of what could generically be called 'the grammar school type' had incorporated one or more of the major European languages into their core curriculum. The process whereby modern languages 'infiltrated' the traditional preserves of the classics varied from one country to another but it was a tough struggle everywhere. Latin had dominated the school curriculum since the Middle Ages and had shared this pre-eminence with Greek since the Renaissance. They did not give in easily to the claims of living languages that 'anybody' could learn. It was conveniently forgotten that Latin had once been spoken by Roman navvies on the Appian Way and Greek by Athenian sandal-makers and theatre attendants.

The second strand is rather more difficult to describe because it is largely undocumented and unrecorded. This is the expansion of the market for utilitarian language learning related to practical needs and interests. It took place from about the middle of the century as the European nations came into closer and more frequent commercial contact with each other and with other countries throughout the world. The schools and universities took little if any interest; they were preoccupied with other things. In Germany, for instance, their principal priority was the training of an efficient and highly educated civil service. In Britain there was more concern for the social implications of a suitable education for 'gentlemen'. The utilitarian market existed, however, and it was growing. The most striking evidence for it was the enormous success of writers like Ahn and Ollendorff. Their books flooded on to the market in all the leading European languages. They were not used in schools, or not extensively anyway, because they were too easy and practical. The fact that they have come down to us as 'typical grammar-translation courses' is misleading. It is not how they were categorized at the time.

For various reasons, which we shall discuss later, the demand for utilitarian language teaching was more intense in Germany than elsewhere in Europe, which helps to account for the apparent dominance of textbooks and 'methods' by authors of German origin. There were, for example, no British counterparts to Ahn and Ollendorff. France produced one major author in the mid-nineteenth century called Karl (or Charles) Ploetz but he was not a 'popular' writer. He produced a lengthy series of textbooks for the teaching of French in schools and as the 'doyen' of the grammar-translation method, his work was prescribed for the French syllabus of the German *Gymnasien* (grammar schools) from about 1850 onwards.

The third strand in the story is the early history of reform. Throughout the century there were individuals with new ideas on how languages could be taught more efficiently and easily. France was particularly well represented here with writers like Jacotot, Marcel, and Gouin, and there was a very interesting Englishman called Prendergast whose ideas foreshadow many of the notions later developed in the twentieth century by men like Palmer and West. None of these early reformers attracted widespread support in their own time. The schools were unwilling to 'experiment' and the remainder of the market was composed of individual learners working largely on their own who required something familiar and recognizable. Also, it has to be added, some of the ideas, while interesting in themselves, were narrowly conceived. They lacked an adequate theoretical base and a professional context in which they could grow and develop. As a result they often seem very idiosyncratic. However, it has to be remembered that when the Reform Movement actually got under way in the 1880s it was not wholly without precedent.

# 11   The grammar-translation method

## Introduction

The grammar-translation method was devised and developed for use in secondary schools. It could even be called 'the grammar school method' since its strengths, weaknesses, and excesses reflected the requirements, aspirations, and ambitions of the nineteenth-century grammar school in its various guises in different countries. It began in Germany, or more accurately, Prussia, at the end of the eighteenth century and established an almost impregnable position as the favoured methodology of the Prussian *Gymnasien* after their expansion in the early years of the nineteenth century.

The 'grammar-translation' label is misleading in some respects. Coined by its opponents, it draws attention to two of the less significant features of the approach.[1] The origins of the method do not lie in an attempt to teach languages by grammar and translation, these were taken for granted anyway. The original motivation was reformist. The traditional scholastic approach among individual learners in the eighteenth century had been to acquire a reading knowledge of foreign languages by studying a grammar and applying this knowledge to the interpretation of texts with the use of a dictionary. Most of them were highly educated men and women who were trained in classical grammar and knew how to apply the familiar categories to new languages. (The fact that they did not always fit the new languages very well is another story.) However, scholastic methods of this kind were not well-suited to the capabilities of younger school pupils and, moreover, they were self-study methods which were inappropriate for group-teaching in classrooms. The grammar-translation method was an attempt to adapt these traditions to the circumstances and requirements of schools. It preserved the basic framework of grammar and translation because these were already familiar both to teachers and pupils from their classical studies. Its principal aim, ironically enough in view of what was to happen later, was to make language learning easier. The central feature was the replacement of the traditional texts by exemplificatory *sentences*. It was the special status accorded to the sentence at the expense of the text that attracted the most outspoken criticism of the reformers later in the century, not the use of grammar as such. It is perhaps appropriate to note here that the twentieth-century structuralist approach was also founded on the supremacy of the sentence and the two methodologies have much in common.

The earliest grammar-translation course for the teaching of English was written in 1793 by Johann Christian Fick (1763–1821) and published in Erlangen in south Germany. It was modelled on an earlier work for the teaching of French by the originator of the method Johann Valentin Meidinger (1756–1822), as the full title of Fick's book shows: *Praktische englische Sprachlehre für Deutsche beiderlei Geschlechts, nach der in Meidingers französische Grammatik befolgten Methode* (Practical English Course for Germans of both sexes, following the method of Meidinger's French Grammar).

One point to notice is the use of the word *practical* in the title. It appears time and again in nineteenth-century language courses and had an extra meaning it would not carry today. To us 'practical' is more or less a synonym for 'useful' but in the nineteenth century a practical course was also one which required *practice*. That is, it contained exercises of various kinds, typically sentences for translation into and out of the foreign language, which were another novel feature of the grammar-translation method. There is, of course, another reason for the emphasis on practice, namely the high priority attached to meticulous standards of accuracy which, as well as having an intrinsic moral value, was a prerequisite for passing the increasing number of formal written examinations that grew up during the century.

The grammar-translation sentences had a second purpose besides affording opportunities for practice work. They exemplified the grammar in a more concentrated and, it was hoped, clearer way than texts could do. Grammar-translation textbooks were graded, though not in the modern sense exactly, and presented new grammar points one-by-one in an organized sequence. Each step needed appropriate examples and specially devised sentences were simpler than samples from 'reputable authors' which contained extra difficulties for the pupils. This exemplificatory function was also taken over by the modern structuralists, though used to demonstrate a rather different kind of grammar.

The Meidinger-Fick approach was extended in the work of Johann Seidenstücker (1763–1817) and, as we have already seen, Karl Ploetz (1819–1881). We shall not be looking at either of these authors since they were both concerned with the teaching of French. We shall, however, discuss the popularized grammar-translation courses of Ahn and Ollendorff.

## The grammar-translation method and the schools: some Anglo-German contrasts

In order to understand how the grammar-translation method developed during the nineteenth century, and the pressures that led to the excesses of its later stages – the stress on accuracy, for example, the obsession with 'completeness', and the neglect of spoken language – it is important to relate foreign language teaching to a broader framework of educational and social change. The contrast between patterns of change in England and Germany is worth exploring in some detail, partly because Germany was considered the model of advanced educational thought at the time, and also because she was later to provide the cutting-edge of the Reform Movement.

In England the most significant development in middle-class education, and the device that levered modern languages on to the secondary school curriculum, was the establishment in the 1850s of a system of public examinations controlled by the universities. The 'washback effect' of these examinations had the inevitable result of determining both the content of the language teaching syllabus and the methodological principles of the teachers responsible for preparing children to take them. Though public examinations did not create the grammar-translation method, they fixed its priorities.

The system was devised principally as a means of bringing some semblance of order into the chaos of middle-class education (outside the ancient public schools)[1] by setting and maintaining academic standards. There were schools of every conceivable type, private, endowed, denominational, and so on, and it was clear that some structure was required to distinguish the serious schools from the charlatans and the heirs of Mr. Squeers. Some people looked with envy at the state-run system in Germany, but state involvement on anything like the Prussian model was unacceptable. The English answer lay in a different direction altogether and the solution that offered the best chance of success was to involve the universities. This would both avoid state interference and, it was hoped, minimize denominational dissension. Approaches were made to Oxford in 1857 and Cambridge shortly afterwards, both of which responded positively (and surprisingly quickly), and the system, known as the Oxford and Cambridge Local Examinations, got off the ground in the following year, 1858.

Attempts to amalgamate the two boards failed and they continued their separate ways. After a slower start, Cambridge took the lead in using the system to bring about far-reaching changes in English education, notably in the education of women. The establishment of the Overseas Examinations in the early 1860s eventually led to a famous world-wide service. They began in a small way in 1863 with ten candidates in Trinidad, 'the first of a mighty army'[2] as Roach put it in an admirable study called *Public Examinations in England 1850–1900*. There were obvious practical obstacles to the expansion of the overseas examinations, but by the 1890s the system was firmly entrenched and in 1898 there were 1,220 candidates, with a particularly large contingent from Jamaica.

The Locals, as the examinations were known, increased the status of both modern languages and English by including them on the curriculum alongside the classical languages. The unfortunate side-effect of this policy, however, was to allow the 'great' schools (Eton, Harrow, etc.), and those seeking to emulate them, to opt out on the grounds that they did not teach modern subjects. They later formalized the split by devising a 'special relationship' with the universities and a separate examinations board. In this way the academic status of the classics was enmeshed in the social pretensions of the public schools. Nor was this merely a matter of attitudes—there were tangible benefits in the form of scholarships, honours, and prizes traditionally linked to excellence in the classics, which were now to be considered as the 'specialist subjects' of the public schools. Modern languages and English lost academic prestige through their association with the Locals and social prestige by their exclusion from the 'best' schools. Hence, inevitably, they became 'soft options'. This was to have unfortunate results when the universities eventually, and reluctantly, came round to the notion of instituting modern language degrees (Cambridge in the 1880s and Oxford about twenty years later). The university involvement in determining the content of the secondary school curriculum effectively stifled the reform of language teaching in England at the end of the nineteenth century by requiring academic 'respectability' from the modern languages. The trend of reform towards the teaching of the spoken language was, of course, quite unacceptable ('travel courier' learning in the eyes of at least one Cambridge don)[3] and philology took its place.

There was at least one further reason for prejudice against the teaching of English and modern languages. Girls were good at them. The Locals admitted girls (amid considerable controversy and deep anxieties lest they should faint) in 1862 and from the outset they proved they were better than the boys at French, German, and the more 'expressive' aspects of English. The boys, on the other hand, excelled at classical languages and the more 'linguistic' side of English grammar. The girls, according to the Cambridge Syndicate Report of 1868 'appear to take a rational interest in the subject matter (*i.e. of French and German*) which to the large majority of the boys is evidently a matter of complete indifference'.[4]

Given this background, it is easier to understand why the late nineteeth-century reformers paid so much attention to the universities and the examination system. Sweet, for instance, in his seminal 1884 paper said quite openly, 'Reform must come from above – from that school of original investigation and experiment which can only be worked through some kind of university system'.[5] Widgery echoed him a little later in his pamphlet on modern language teaching in schools: 'Our present method needs a thorough reform. Who is to begin the change? What is the chief hindrance in our way? The change must come from the Universities: our hindrance lies in the exaggerated respect paid by the British public to examinations'.[6]

In practical terms, the fear of being labelled a 'soft option' forced modern language teachers and textbook writers to ape the methods of the classics. French had to be made as 'demanding' as Latin, and German as 'intellectually disciplined' as Greek. Textbooks had to be 'thorough' (i.e. exhaustive in their listing of exceptions and peculiarities) and based on selections from the 'best authors'. Spoken language was, at best, irrelevant and accuracy was elevated to the status of a moral imperative. In the Cambridge Report of 1868 already quoted above, the writer complains that '*parlez, parlé, parlais, parlaient*, etc. seem to be looked upon as convertible terms to be used with impartiality',[7] and recommends more regular written exercises. There was also 'a ludicrous ignorance of grammar', 'indifference as to spelling', and other inadequacies. Under pressure of this kind, who can blame the teachers for pushing the grammar-translation method even further in the direction of a tyrannical obsession with minutiae?

The 'unholy alliance' between the public examination system and educational privilege successfully blocked the reform of modern language teaching in the late nineteenth century by institutionalizing the special status of the classics and effectively, though unintentionally, guaranteeing for this country an unenviable reputation for being 'bad at languages'. At the same time, the energies of the Reform Movement were diverted into the teaching of English as a foreign language, but that is another story.

If this appears a rather harsh judgement, consider, for example, the fate of one of the central principles of the Reform Movement, namely the adoption of a basically monolingual teaching methodology through the use of the foreign language as the *normal* means of communication in the language classroom. (This never meant 'banning' the use of the mother tongue, except in the more extreme versions of the Direct Method.) In Britain, the monolingual principle is still a controversial issue in foreign language teaching, whereas in Germany, for instance, visitors to secondary schools a century ago[8] could witness monolingual foreign language lessons taking place, not as 'Direct Method experiments', but as a normal procedure in an ordinary school. For instance Klemm, an American visitor touring German schools in the 1880s, reported a reformed English lesson in a secondary school in Krefeld in the Rhineland that impressed him greatly. It consisted mainly of oral question-and-answer work on the text, following standard Reform Movement principles. But what struck him most was, with his own emphasis, 'Except where new rules had to be formulated, *English was the medium of instruction throughout*'.[9] Of course such lessons were not universal in Germany, or anywhere else in Europe, but their existence shows clearly that language teaching reform was taken seriously and, eventually, its influence spread through the system.

Germany was more open to reforming influences for a number of reasons, one of which was the structure of its state-run education system. The German system was rebuilt after the Napoleonic Wars on a Prussian model drawn up by Wilhelm von Humboldt (the author of *Über die Verschiedenheit des menschlichen Sprachbaues*, 1836). The secondary sector, where foreign languages were taught, was divided into two levels. First there was an upper-tier of *Gymnasien* with a ferociously academic curriculum based on the classical languages. French was included as a compulsory subject but English was optional and rarely taught. This was the academic hot-house of the grammar-translation method. As another contemporary American observer put it: 'The best that can be said for the modern-language teaching in the *Gymnasien* is that it is neither better nor worse than the corresponding work in American high schools. It is an open question which party is the most complimented by the comparison'.[10]

Below the *Gymnasien*, however, there was a second tier of so-called *Realschulen* which eventually developed a two-tier structure of their own, with the prestigiously-named *Realgymnasien* on top and the *Oberrealschulen* lower down. English was a compulsory subject in these schools from 1859 onwards, though it normally came after French and was introduced in Form III, i.e. about halfway up the school. The breakthrough in modern-language teaching reform in Germany came in the *Realgymnasien* which were prestigious enough to matter but sufficiently 'expendable' for change to be permitted. Viëtor himself was a *Realgymnasium* teacher in the early stages of his career, and the first experiments with the reformed method were carried out by Klinghardt in his *Realgymnasium* in Silesia in the mid-1880s These are reported in detail later.

Although the grammar-translation method started out as a simple approach to language learning for young schoolchildren, it was grossly distorted in the collision of interests between the classicists and their modern language rivals. Intrinsically, as we shall see later, the method is so ordinary that it is sometimes difficult to see what all the fuss was about. Each new lesson had one or two new grammar rules, a short vocabulary list, and some practice examples to translate. Boring, maybe, but hardly the horror story we are sometimes asked to believe. However, it also contained seeds which eventually grew into a jungle of obscure rules, endless lists of gender classes and gender-class exceptions, self-conscious 'literary' archaisms, snippets of philology, and a total loss of genuine feeling for living language. The really bad grammar-translation coursebooks were not those written by well-known names such as Ahn and Ollendorff, but those specially designed for use in secondary schools by ambitious schoolmasters. The two discussed below, by Tiarks and Weisse, are typical.

According to his publisher David Nutt, the Rev. J. G. Tiarks' German grammar books were 'the most extensively used series of elementary German books' in the 1860s – and Nutt also had Franz Ahn on his list. Certainly the facts are impressive: fifteen editions of his *Practical Grammar of German* by 1864 and eleven of his *Introductory Grammar* (1834). The Rev. Tiarks, Minister of the German Protestant Reformed Church in London, starts his Preface to the *Introductory Grammar* in uncompromising mood with an attack on the Hamilton System of interlinear translation, condemning it for providing 'nothing but a *smattering*' (Tiarks' own tight-lipped emphasis). He continues: 'the author has had the pleasure of practically convincing many of his pupils, that an accurate knowledge of languages like the German and Greek, with their numerous and various inflections, can be acquired in a much shorter time, and in a much safer way, by the method he adopts'.[11] Accuracy, the forelock-tugging link with the classics, the importance of 'endings' – it is all there and we know what to expect.

The book takes us through the parts of speech in German with their various declensions and conjugations. Then there is a set of short reading texts including some poems which will 'make a salutary impression, both moral and religious, on the mind of the young student' as well as being arranged 'in such a manner, that, whilst they inculcate the rules of grammar, they may, by being committed to memory, when corrected, be used instead of dialogues, and thus, at once, serve two important objects'.[12] The Rev. Tiarks' pomposity and humourlessness are rather exhausting. So, too, is his thoroughness. The need to prove one's philological credentials creeps into even the most elementary coursebook. The Third Declension of German nouns, we are told, 'originally contained all substantives of the masculine gender ending in *e*: but those given in Note 1 have lost the final *e*, and now end in a consonant'.[13] Note 1 dutifully lists forty-three *e*-less masculines, including useful words like those for *demagogue, ducat, herdsman, hussar, Jesuit, quadrant, theologian*, and *fool*. The grey obscurity of Tiarks' prose continues relentlessly throughout the book. In describing how to translate *a cup of tea* into German, we are informed that 'those words, the measure, weight, or number of which is expressed by the above-mentioned substantives, are not put in the genitive, unless a part of a certain quantity or quality is meant; but in the same case with the preceding word'.[14] At the end of the slog, the pupil is rewarded with the Reverend's selection of uplifting poems and a few edifying texts on cowherds and Frederick the Great.

The best that can be said for Tiarks' book is that it is only 172 pages long. The second of our grammar-translation schoolmasters, T. H. Weisse, produced a tome of over 500 pages. It was called (inevitably) *A Complete Practical Grammar of the German Language* and grew out of forty years' experience teaching 'large classes' in Edinburgh. It appeared in 1885 and came with a commendatory letter from the

Professor of Logic and Metaphysics at the University of Edinburgh who judged it 'in all respects satisfactory', adding, just to be on the safe side, 'when accompanied with your personal instructions'. A perceptive professor. The book is an organizational nightmare. Even the exercises are printed in unpredictable places, Exercise 1 being unaccountably on p. 333 and Exercise 15 on p. 43. The text is densely packed ('compendious' was the professor's word), crammed with facts, lists, cross-references to other parts of the book, and rules piled upon rules so that everything is as important as everything else, and nothing is important at all. His rules on the use of the article, for instance, contain the useful information that the definite article is used with the names of months, and, in the next sentence, the utterly useless information that is also used 'before the names of celestial bodies and constellations, so as to distinguish them from those of the mythological personages whose names they bear'.[15] So, now you can say *By Jupiter*, always assuming you can decide which of the two is being invoked.

Weisse's great joy in life is exception-hunting. Plurals in German provide excellent specimens, all laid out in neat lists: there are 37 feminine nouns on p. 177 that do not take *n* in the plural, 11 masculines on p. 180 that do not form their dative plurals regularly and an unbelievable list of 62 masculines on p. 186 which do not modify their vowels. This list contains some useful plurals like *dogs*, *shoes*, and *arms* but 'thoroughness' dictates that we should also know how to say *anvils*, *aeries*, *girths*, *capons*, *awls*, *ostriches*, *gluttons*, *scamps*, *haddocks*, *hoopoes*, and *hobgoblins*. Inter alia.

It is important to realize that Weisse's book is not a reference book but a textbook for use in class (though it contains a reference section). The children were expected to learn all this nonsense. Moreover, Weisse warns us in his Preface, 'teachers and examiners of schools will find in the examples here supplied the most efficient means for testing the student's knowledge of any grammatical point'.[16] The crowning insult is the inclusion of no fewer than 136 'directions for the proper use of Dr. F. Ahn's First Course' at the end of the book.[17] The whole point of Ahn's course was that it should be easy, practical, and short. His improvers ensured that it was difficult, scholastic, and long.

With hindsight, it might have been better if modern languages had not been brought on to the school curriculum. The books intended for the adult market may have had their faults, but they at least tried to keep their customers in mind.

## The grammar-translation method and adult language teaching: the 'practical approach' of Ahn and Ollendorff

Language, as a means of communication itself, is sensitive to changes elsewhere in the network of human communications, and, in particular, to developments in transport that encourage mobility, and bring people into face-to-face contact over long distances. The expansion of air travel in our own time, for instance, which has created a new role for English as a world auxiliary language, has repeated on an intercontinental scale the processes that bound the countries of the European continent together in a railway system during the nineteenth century. National rivalries, however, prevented the emergence of a generally accepted *lingua franca*, and, if people were to exploit the opportunities offered by the railways, they had to learn the languages spoken down at the end of the line.

One result was an increase in demand for travellers' phrasebooks like, for example, Bartels' *Modern Linguist* series in the 1850s. But there was also a need for textbooks that offered a more thorough grounding while at the same time keeping at least half-an-eye on the practical needs of the adult learner. The outcome was a growing market for 'methods': textbooks which established a basic design that was repeated from one language to the next.[18] Ahn was the first to exploit this market in 1834, followed by his rival Ollendorff a year later, and between them they dominated the scene for almost half a century, until the emergence of specialist language schools like Berlitz in the 1880s and 1890s.

Changes in patterns of transport were not restricted to the European continent as the new shipping lines carried people from one continent to another in increasingly large numbers. Emigration to the United States, for example, from virtually every country in Europe, swelled to enormous proportions as the century wore on, bringing with it a growing need for practical competence in English both among the immigrants themselves and among those left in Europe who wanted to keep in touch with relatives and friends. The full impact of these developments was not felt until later in the century, but the practical emphasis of Ahn and Ollendorff was a straw in the wind.

More generally, the industrialization of the second half of the nineteenth century created a new class of language learner, one that had not followed an academic 'grammar school' education and therefore could not be expected to learn foreign languages by traditional methods. A new approach was needed which would suit their particular circumstances and it eventually emerged in the form of 'direct' methods which required no knowledge of grammar at all. Ahn and Ollendorff were in some respects a 'halfway house'. Both included grammar rules in their courses, but they adopted a grading system that 'rationed' the learner to one or two new rules per lesson and generally tried to keep the detail of explanation under some control. Compared to the schoolbooks of Tiarks and Weisse, Ahn and Ollendorff have hardly any grammar in them, which explains why many teachers considered them lightweight and in need of 'improvement'.

*Franz Ahn* (1796–1865)

The grammar-translation method provoked such antagonism that the only way of considering it dispassionately is to look carefully at the work of the author who used it most consistently and self-effacingly. Unlike Ollendorff, Ahn was never idiosyncratic, had no 'bright ideas' about language teaching and never promised to teach a language in six months and, unlike his many imitators and 'improvers', his work was modest, compact, and useful. It was also immensely successful and it deserved to be. The public got what it was promised, a simple introduction to a foreign language, taught through a 'new, practical, and easy method'.

Franz Ahn was born in 1796. He came from the north-west of Germany and was a schoolmaster in Aachen on the German-Dutch border when he published his first textbook in 1827 at the age of thirty-one. It was a French reader for German learners and the first of a series of readers and conversation books (including one for English). Two years later he brought out a Dutch course for Germans called *Neue holländische Sprachlehre* (1829) which was published in Cologne. It went through six editions in the next fifteen years, no small achievement for a minority language textbook.

In 1834, at the age of 38, he published a French course, the first example of his famous *A New, Practical, and Easy Method* and courses appeared in German, English, Spanish, Italian, and Russian over the next twenty years. He also applied it to the two classical languages. His principal market was the private learner for whom a grammatical description and a bilingual approach were essential.

Ahn's method lives up to its title. It is both practical (in the sense discussed earlier) and easy. After a brief introduction to the pronunciation, the basic learning materials begin. They are arranged in short, consecutively numbered sections. Each odd-numbered section gives a grammatical summary, usually in the form of a paradigm, and about a dozen new vocabulary items, followed by a set of sentences to translate into the mother tongue. Each even-numbered section contains sentences to translate into the foreign language, and no new teaching points. In his First Course there are sixty-eight lessons in the space of only sixty-six pages, plus a set of twelve areas of vocabulary and twelve pages of 'easy dialogues' (phrases like 'Are you hungry?', 'It is foggy', 'What can I offer you?', and so on).

Ahn's grammar notes require only a minimum knowledge of grammatical terminology: singular, plural, masculine, feminine, etc. The vocabulary is useful, on the whole, and the practice sentences are short and easy to translate. They are also very dull. If a language textbook author may be known by his examples, then Franz Ahn was clearly a kind old gentleman, quiet, rather sentimental, a bit priggish but upright, moral, and eminently Victorian. His situations are domestic, and there are any number of minor crises to keep the interest up: 'our aunt has sold her scissors, Louisa has found her thimble, I have received this horse from my friend,' and plenty of little worries: 'How many physicians are there in this town? Has the shoemaker brought my boot? Have you had the kindness to give a glass of water to this poor man?'

The disconnected sentences of the grammar-translation approach are no sillier than the 'scientific' drills of the audiolingual method with which they share many features. Both are the inevitable outcome of two basic principles. The first is that a language teaching course can be based on a sequence of linguistic categories, and the second that these categories can be exemplified in sample sentences for intensive practice. We shall come back to both these principles when we discuss Ollendorff's work in the next section.

Ahn's textbooks follow a method that is largely the result of his intuitive feeling for simplicity; they proceed one step at a time, with not too many words in each lesson, plenty of practice, and so on. With Ollendorff, however, there is a much more deliberate approach to textbook planning and the organization of materials and practice activities. There are even the glimmerings of a theory.

### H.G.Ollendorff (1803–1865)

Heinrich Gottfried Ollendorff was born in 1803, which makes him seven years younger than Ahn. He was, however, less versatile, and having launched his *Method* in 1835, devoted all his energies to exploiting it.

The earliest examples of the Ollendorff Method, called *A New Method of Learning to Read, Write, and Speak, a Language in Six Months*, taught German to French and English speakers. Later he brought out courses 'adapted' to teach French (1843), Italian (1846), English (1848) and other languages. His books are massive, two-volume affairs and the Ollendorff industry must have been a large-scale international publishing operation. All the courses were originally published by Ollendorff himself in Paris, each copy being individually numbered and signed. Thereafter his work appeared in London, New York, Berlin, Frankfurt and, in authorized adaptations, in many other cities.

Ollendorff's courses have two original features of interest. The first is a curious and rather obscure theory of interaction on which he based all his exercises (and there a lot of exercises in an Ollendorff book). The other, which is more substantial, is his system of linguistic grading. The interaction theory is the more obvious at first sight: 'It is impossible to open the book without being struck by it'.[19] Indeed it is, as we shall see. Ollendorff continues, 'my system of acquiring a living language is founded on the principle, that each question contains nearly the answer

which one ought or which one wishes to make to it. The slight difference
between the question and the answer is always explained before the
question: so that the learner does not find it in the least difficult, either to
answer it, or to make similar questions for himself. Again, the question
being the same as the answer, as soon as the master pronounces it, it
strikes the pupil's ear, and is therefore easily reproduced by his speaking
organs'.[20]

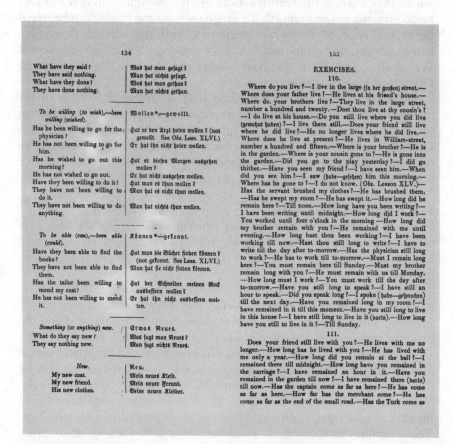

*Figure 21    Extract from Lesson 50 of Ollendorff's* New Method of Learning to
Read, Write, and Speak a Language in Six Months, *adapted to the German (2nd
edition, 1841, orig. publ. 1838). The lesson introduces locatives (not shown) and
ways of expressing modality (p. 154). Notice the absence of conventional rules
(though he did sometimes include them). Exercise examples in Ollendorff are always
given in the learner's mother tongue for translation into the foreign language. They
were intended to provide materials for 'conversations' between teacher and student.*

It is not easy to understand what Ollendorff meant by all this. What he may have had in mind was that the structure of declarative sentences ('answers') is closely related to the structure of interrogatives ('questions'). This does not, of course, have anything much to do with the answers that 'one ought or wishes to make'. His reference to the 'slight difference' between the question and the answer is particularly obscure. It sounds like a kind of 'cue' system, but how it worked is unclear.

The practical outcome of the 'interaction theory' is that Ollendorff's exercises consist of questions and answers in the mother tongue to be translated into the foreign language. There are no exercises in the other direction. Since these question-answer sequences are unnumbered, they merge together into a kind of manic interrogation. Here are a few examples. The full exercise (Number 110, Lesson 50) contains about four times as many:

> Where do you live? I live in the large street. Where does your father live? He lives at his friend's house. Where do your brothers live? They live in the large street, number a hundred and twenty. Dost thou live at thy cousin's? I do live at his house. Do you still live where you did live? I live there still. Does your friend still live where he did live? He no longer lives where he did live. Where does he live at present? He lives in William Street, number a hundred and fifteen, etc.[21]

The similarity between Ollendorffian grammar-translation courses and the structural approach is intensified if one looks at the linguistic organization of his materials. He was, as we saw earlier, the first language textbook writer to use a graded linguistic syllabus seriously. New points are introduced one-by-one and, unlike most of the other grammar-translation authors, he does not insist on covering the whole of a paradigm in one lesson. Below is the syllabus of his English course, in a version edited by J. U. Grönlund and published in Stockholm in 1885:

Lesson 1    The definite article.  Nom. *the*
                                   Gen. *of the*
                                   Dat. *to the*
                                   Acc. *the*
            *Have you . . . ?*
            *Yes sir, I have . . .*
            *my, your.*

Lesson 2    *It, not.*
            29 new vocabulary items.
            Example: *Have you the worsted stocking?*
                     *No, I have it not.*

**Lesson 3**    *Something, anything, nothing.*
*Are you (hungry)?*
*I am . . .*
*I am not . . .*
*This/that book.*
The Saxon genitive.

**Lesson 4**    Possessives (1) *mine, yours.*
*Which?*
*Neither . . . nor.*

(The rest of the possessives and the *wh*-words are introduced in Lessons 5–7.)

**Lesson 8**    Plurals, including exceptions, e.g. *mice, oxen, swine,* etc.
*Our(s), their(s).*

**Lesson 9**    *These/those.*

**Lesson 10**    *Some, any, no.*
*What?*
Example: *What bread has the baker?*
          *He has some good bread.*

**Lesson 11**    The indefinite article, *a/an.*
*One(s).*
*How much/many? Much, many, (a) little, too much/*
*many, enough, a few, a great deal of, a good many.*
Cardinal numbers.

The infinitive is introduced in Lesson 15 along with the gerund, which modern courses would not do. It is only in Lesson 21 that full lexical verbs appear for the first time.

Ollendorff's grading system is heavily influenced by convention and 'logic'. The present tense is introduced in both its progressive and simple aspects in the same lesson along with the *do*-transformation so that Ollendorff can use his interrogation exercises. The same happens with the past tense (Lesson 35). The imperative, formally the simplest of English verb forms, does not occur till Lesson 49, coming even after the passive voice.

Ollendorff uses a traditional parts of speech grammar. It is typical of such grammars that they concentrate their attention on the characteristics of word-classes and neglect the syntactic relationships between them. Syntax in a grammar-translation course is normally restricted to a few comments on 'word order' and a lot of fuss about 'local' problems such as making verbs agree with their nouns. Important regularities in complete sentence units are overlooked. An approach of this kind encourages the construction of sentences on a word-by-word basis, each word 'arithmetically' added to the one before. Henry Sweet christened this the 'arithmetical fallacy'[22], it is the main cause of the strangeness of grammar-translation examples like the infamous *pen of my aunt*. *Pen* is correct English, so is *my aunt* and so is *of*. So what is wrong with *pen of my aunt*? There was no way in which grammar-translation writers could distinguish between sentences that were 'grammatical' but at the same time unacceptable to a native speaker.

Sweet's 'arithmetical fallacy' is even more obvious if we consider the lexical structure, or more broadly the meaning, of sentences built up in this word-by-word fashion. Sweet's favourite example, which actually occurred in a Greek class at school, was the sentence *The philosopher pulled the lower jaw of the hen*.[23] None of the words on its own is in any way esoteric, but the utterance as a whole is surreal.

The impression that one derives from contemporary comments on both Ahn and Ollendorff is that their practical aims were appreciated, but a number of reviewers criticized them for their lack of profundity. A review of Ollendorff's German course in the *Foreign Quarterly Review* of 1845, for instance, summed the book up as 'in one word, the grammar put into a conversational shape',[24] but, having praised Ollendorff for achieving his aims, the critic concluded by saying 'a method exclusively and entirely conversational will never satisfy strong minds'.[25] Kroeh's later comments to the Modern Language Association of America in 1887 echoed these sentiments. Under the heading 'The Practical Method', he discussed both Ahn and Ollendorff, saying, 'Their leading idea is practice before theory, and although they have been subjected to much well-deserved ridicule for the puerility of their examples, they mark an important advance in the art of teaching languages . . . No grammatical aid is given except what may be gathered from an appendix and a few footnotes. The reaction against grammar was evidently too great. Sound instruction in language cannot be divorced entirely from grammar'.[26]

Kroeh's paper, an invaluable source of information on nineteenth-century language teaching, is generally very balanced and his views can probably be taken as representing informed professional opinion of the time. However, it is sad that, after all the excellent situational language teaching between the sixteenth and the eighteenth centuries, courses like Ahn's and Ollendorff's with their futile sentences should be thought of as 'practical' and 'conversational'. Academicism laid a heavy hand on the teaching of languages in the nineteenth century.

## Notes

1 'English public schools' in the modern sense (i.e. private schools, usually for boarding pupils) expanded during the nineteenth century, and many new schools joined the ancient foundations (Eton, Winchester, etc.). Their history gave them privileged access to the universities, and their exclusiveness was emphasized by the

formation of a separate association known as the Headmasters' Conference (1870).

2  Roach (1971: 146).

3  Leathes (1918: 6).

4  Roach (1971: 112).

5  Sweet (1884: 595).

6  Widgery (1888: 54).

7  Roach (1971: 158).

8  See Russell (1907) and Klemm (1903), both of whom describe tours in Germany undertaken in the 1880s.

9  Klemm (1903: 96).

10  Russell (1907: 274).

11  Tiarks (1864: iv), from the Preface to the second edition (1858).

12  Ibid.: iii.

13  Ibid.: 6.

14  Ibid.: 13.

15  Weisse (1888: 212).

16  Ibid.: viii.

17  Ibid.: 493–8.

18  Both Ahn and Ollendorff intended their books for use in schools, but their reputation as 'lightweight' courses, and the large sales of 'Keys', suggest that the private adult learner (with or without a tutor) was their principal market.

19/20  Ollendorff (1841: vii).

21  Ibid.: 155.

22  Sweet (1899/1964: 72–3).

23  Ibid.: 73.

24  *Foreign Quarterly Review*, XXXV, 1845, 185 (see Blackie 1845).

25  Ibid.: 186.

26  Kroeh (1887: 170–1).

# 12 Individual reformers

## Overview

Interest in improved methods of language teaching in the nineteenth century was not confined to the Reform Movement of its last two decades. It rose steadily as the practical need for foreign languages grew in importance, and the failure of the public education system to meet the challenge became more apparent. However, the work of the pre-Reform Movement writers is virtually unknown today. Their ideas were either ignored by the Reformers or condemned along with the traditional school methods as 'out of date'. Nevertheless, in spite of their shortcomings, they are worth discussing and four of them in particular – Jacotot, Marcel, Prendergast, and Gouin – had important, if sometimes rather limited, contributions to make to the field.

As Jespersen pointed out in his 1904 review of Reform Movement methods,[1] all the pre-Reform approaches were known by the names of their originators rather than by any intrinsic characteristic of the methods themselves. This individualism was a serious source of weakness that the Movement avoided. To be fair, however, it could hardly have been otherwise. There was no coherent foreign language teaching profession out of which new approaches could grow and to which they could relate. Training in the modern sense was unknown, and none of the modern networks of professional communication (conferences, journals, etc.) existed much before the last quarter of the century. Only the market-place was powerful, and the writers we know most about (Ahn, Ollendorff, etc.) are those whose books sold in large numbers. None of the authors discussed here made much of a commercial impact, with the possible exception of Gouin, who was, in any case, a contemporary of the Reform Movement.

All the early reformers were essentially 'loners'. Each of them produced a 'method', and each wrote a background thesis to justify the ideas which it represented. None of them, however, attracted a following or founded a school of thought with a potential for further development. Jacotot, Prendergast, and Gouin, in particular, devised teaching methods which were so tightly specified and constrained that they discouraged further exploration by other teachers. They were, in a sense, 'dead ends' that had to be accepted or rejected as they stood. The failure of Marcel, on the other hand, is more difficult to explain. His work ought to have become the principal point of reference for the serious discussion of language teaching methodology in the second half of the century, but, for some reason, it was ignored. Perhaps the simplest explanation for their isolation is that all of them, Marcel included, produced teaching methods and materials which implied a more radical change than the majority of ordinary language teachers were prepared to contemplate.

The first, *Jean Joseph Jacotot*, saw language teaching as one dimension of a philosophy of universal education (*enseignement universel*). In addition to his book on foreign language teaching, he also wrote companion pieces on the teaching of music and the mother tongue. He was a romantic idealist of the Revolution who believed in the equality of man and in the ability of each individual to attain any goal to which he aspired. His work drew attention to the ideological significance of education generally and of language teaching in particular.

While Jacotot was inspired by notions of universal brotherhood, his near contemporary *Claude Marcel* took a longer look at the role of language teaching in a general system of national education. Of the four writers, Marcel was intellectually the most impressive. He was the first to develop a coherent and educationally responsible methodology of language teaching derived from an analysis of the activity itself and its relationship to other branches of knowledge. His ideas were unjustly neglected, and had to be 're-discovered' in the twentieth century. Also, his reputation suffered because he promoted the teaching of reading only a decade or so before it was displaced in favour of the spoken language by the excitingly 'modern' claims of phonetics as a scientific discipline. However, Marcel had much more to say, and he is still worth attending to.

*Thomas Prendergast*, the only Englishman in the group, and one of the few Britons before Henry Sweet to show any serious interest in foreign language teaching, had a rather similar background to Marcel. They were both highly-educated men and both served in the overseas services of their respective countries, Marcel in the French consular service and Prendergast in the Indian Civil Service. Prendergast's 'Mastery' system was the first attempt to elaborate a psychological theory of child language acquisition and apply it to the teaching of foreign languages. Others had speculated on the success of children in learning their mother tongue, and drawn interesting conclusions at times. Prendergast, however, went further and observed what children were doing and the learning processes they appeared to be using. The teaching techniques he derived from these observations were radically different from anything suggested before, but on the surface they appeared to share many of the unfortunate characteristics of the traditional grammar-book methods. He used detached sentences as his basic learning data, for instance, which was anathema to the Reformers with their concern for texts, but his reasons for using them were not properly understood.

Prendergast and the last of our four innovators, *François Gouin*, also had much in common. They both studied the way in which children use language, Prendergast with a seriousness and objectivity that were alien to Gouin. Each of them achieved insights into the processes of language acquisition and development which have only become central to theoretical discussions of the subject in the last ten or fifteen years. To Prendergast, the crucial feature of language was the capacity of human beings to generate an infinite number of sentences from a finite set of means. He was not the first to conceive the generative principle, it is an ancient principle in the philosophy of language, but few had seen it in psycholinguistic terms before, and certainly nobody had tried to apply it to language teaching materials. In the case of Gouin, his emphasis on the importance of the structure of experience in the organization of language was, in the language teaching context at least, totally original. It was unfortunate, however, that his addiction to the belief that all experiential organization was sequential blinded him to the true significance of his insight, and its practical effect in the famous 'series' method was particularly disappointing, widely imitated though it may have been.

There were many other writers besides the four we shall look at in detail. The Scotsman, *James Hamilton* (1769–1829), for example, made a name for himself by reviving the old technique of interlinear translation, which was also used in an approach commonly referred to as the '*Toussaint-Langenscheidt Method*', a publishing venture rather than the effort of a single author. Toussaint-Langenscheidt also devised a system of 'phonetic' transcription to accompany their materials but it was excessively complicated. The success of materials-production devices like interlinear translation and transcription again underlines the great importance of self-instruction in nineteenth-century language learning. The schools failed to respond to the practical need for foreign languages in industrial and commercial life and it was left to publishing houses to try and fill the gap. Other names mentioned in surveys by Kroeh (1887) and Holmes (1903) include *T. Robertson*, the precursor of the Toussaint-Langenscheidt approach, *S. Rosenthal*, who adapted Prendergast into German as the 'Meisterschaft System', applying the ideas to the teaching of dialogues (with mixed results), and *J. D. Gaillard*, a Professor of French in New York, who devised a curious teaching technique based on the then fashionable theory of the association of ideas.[2] The pupils learnt a series of words and phrases by heart, for example *s'appeler – George d'Estainville – issu – famille – huguenots – exilés – au temps – persécution – protestants – Louis quatorze*. When they came to class, the teacher would supply the missing-links in the narrative.

**Teacher**   Notre héros . . .
**Pupil**       s'appelait George d'Estainville,
**Teacher**   Il était . . .
**Pupil**       issu . . .
**Teacher**   de l'une de ces nombreuses et honorables . . .
**Pupil**       familles de huguenot exilées au temps de la persécution
**Teacher**   de la persécution . . .
**Pupil**       des protestants.[3]

As Kroeh pointed out, 'too much must not be expected from the claim that the law of association has been followed'.[4]

The mid-nineteenth century did not lack ideas, all of them seriously intended and some of them worth exploring in detail. But like the 'Wonder Appliances' that proclaimed their magic from the cluttered walls of Victorian railway stations, these individualistic 'Methods' suffered from the over-zealous application of rather narrowly-conceived principles. The Reform Movement which succeeded them enjoyed a much firmer theoretical foundation, and hence a richer and more varied practical methodology.

### 'All is in all': Jean Joseph Jacotot

Jean Joseph Jacotot (1770–1840) became a language teacher by accident. A native of Dijon in central France, he became deeply involved in revolutionary politics in his teens and was a Professor of Latin briefly in 1789 at the age of nineteen. He organized a local youth movement in support of the revolution and, at twenty-two, was a captain in the army. In 1794 he returned home to Dijon to become Deputy Director of the newly established *Polytechnique* in the city. In 1815 the old order was restored after the defeat of Napoleon at Waterloo, and Jacotot was exiled to what is now Belgium, where he took up a post teaching French at the University of Louvain in the Flemish-speaking north of the country. He was not a Flemish-speaker and his students were beginners in French. Confronted by this challenge, he devised the earliest example of monolingual methods for the language classroom.

Jacotot's students were asked to acquire copies of Fénelon's *Aventures de Télémaque* along with a Flemish translation. Unable to translate or explain, Jacotot read the first sentence,[5] and then returned to the opening phrase and read it again: '*Calypso ne pouvoit . . .* '. He asked his students to hunt through the rest of the book for further examples of the words he had just read. *Ne*, of course, was common enough, *Calypso* turned up occasionally, and *pouvoit* (or something that looked like it) from time to time as well. Then Jacotot returned to the beginning of the text and added the next phrase: '*Calypso ne pouvoit se consoler . . .* '. The research activities were repeated, and the process continued: '*Calypso ne pouvoit se consoler du départ d'Ulysse*'. As the course proceeded, the students came to know the text by heart, and Jacotot supplemented the text-study with comprehension questions and other forms of linguistic work, insisting that the students should look for similarities and differences, generalize their observations, form and test hypotheses, and discover how the language worked.

What struck Jacotot most forcibly was the irrelevance of explanation. This, naturally enough, came as a complete surprise to him. How can you claim to be a language teacher if you cannot explain anything, had been his immediate thought on arriving at Louvain. He now realized that not only was explanation unnecessary, it was actually wrong. All his radical ideals were roused by this insight which he developed at some length in his *Enseignement universel, langue etrangère* (1830). Every individual had a God-given ability to instruct himself. The function of a teacher was to respond to the learner, not to direct and control him by explaining things in advance. This philosophy also chimed with his belief that everyone had equal intelligence, and that inherited differences in ability did not exist. His answer to the obvious counter-argument that some individuals achieve more than others was that, given sufficient strength of will and determination, these differences would disappear. This is not the 'environmentalist' argument that comparable egalitarian philosophies of education would put forward at the present time but has more in common with the 'self-help' tradition of writers like Samuel Smiles.

Jacotot's educational doctrines gained currency in England through the interest taken by the British educationalist Joseph Payne in a study of his work, published in the same year as Jacotot's return to France, called *A Compendious Exposition of the Principles and Practice of Professor Jacotot's Celebrated System of Education* (1830). The most famous of these doctrines was summarized in the motto 'All is in all', which was expanded into the more explicit advice, 'learn something thoroughly and relate everything else to it'. There is no doubt that the Louvain students learnt Fénelon thoroughly, but the technique of continually returning to the beginning of a text before adding a new phrase or sentence is one that few teachers, and even fewer learners, will tolerate for any length of time. Nevertheless, the basic principle of learning-by-heart and thoroughly 'mining' the text for all the information it can yield is one which deserves serious consideration. Whether it would have worked with pupils who were not university students is a more open question. Payne himself tried it with an eleven-year-old youngster learning Greek. In spite of his enthusiasm for Jacotot's educational ideas, he did not pursue the lessons for very long. However, he was able to claim that 'after twelve hours of lessons . . . he (the boy) will scarcely meet with fifty words in the remainder of the *Iliad* (*Book 1*), of which he does not know something'.[6]

It is difficult to avoid the conclusion that Jacotot failed to have much lasting influence on the development of language teaching methods. He is not mentioned by the reformers at the end of the century (except by Gouin, whose attitudes to most writers are unreliable). This failure is probably due to the almost unworkable classroom techniques which obscured his more general principles. Some of these—for example, his stress on the importance of text rather than isolated words and sentences—might otherwise have recommended him to the Reform Movement rather warmly.

## The Rational Method of Claude Marcel

In writing a history of language teaching, and, possibly, of many other human activities, it is always tempting to prick the balloon of contemporary self-satisfaction by demonstrating that what has been taken as evidence of progress in our time has, in fact, 'all been done before'. As a rule, this temptation has to be resisted in the interests of preserving the significant differences between the contexts out of which apparent parallels have emerged. With the work of Claude Marcel (1793–1876), however, the similarities are so striking that it becomes necessary to draw attention to them and, perhaps, to seek an explanation for their neglect.

If Marcel's work is known to us at all, it is because of his proposal to make the teaching of reading the first priority in foreign language teaching. This was unlikely to win him many friends among the phoneticians and spoken language enthusiasts of the Reform Movement, or among the Natural Method radicals. However, his 'reading-first' proposal derived from a complex and carefully thought-out methodology of language teaching which deserves to be better known. His principal work was a massive two-volume study of the role of language in education called *Language as a Means of Mental Culture and International Communication* published in 1853 when he was the French Consul in Cork in Ireland. Although he obviously had the French system of education in mind, the book goes much further than that. It attempts to define a role for the teaching of languages, native and foreign, modern and classical, in the context of a far-ranging study of the nature, purpose, and structure of education. The outcome of this analysis was an approach to language teaching methodology which is astonishingly modern in its general character and even in many of its details.

Marcel starts by making a primary distinction between what he calls *impression* and *expression* which together 'constitute the double object of language and mark the principal subdivision and order of study'.[7] Impression (or 'reception' as it would be called today) psychologically and pragmatically precedes expression ('production'). This 'principal subdivision' relates to a second subdivision between spoken and written language, giving rise to Marcel's 'four branches' of language study: hearing, speaking, reading, and writing, (the 'four skills' of modern times). Much of the book is taken up with the problem of ordering the priorities among the four 'branches' in the light of educational and pedagogical demands and constraints.

Having identified 'parents, teachers, and method' as 'the three great agents of education', he sets out to define the characteristics of 'a good method' and emerges at the end with twenty 'axiomatic truths of methodology', of which the first is the most important (and the most unexpected in view of his reputation for a 'reading-first' bias): 'The method of nature is the archetype of all methods, and especially of the method of learning languages'.[8] One of the crucial characteristics of the 'method of nature' is that 'the mind should be impressed with the idea before it takes cognizance of the sign that represents it' (Axiomatic Truth No. 8).[9] What Marcel is getting at here is something more complex than the general notion that comprehension precedes production. He means that the comprehension of meaning precedes the acquisition of the linguistic elements used in its communication. We do not, strictly speaking, understand what people say, we understand what they mean. When we learn the linguistic and other devices used to communicate meaning, we can take part ourselves and use the language expressively. Marcel's belief in the precedence of impression over expression implied the prior importance of the two impression 'branches' (reading and hearing) over the two expression 'branches' (speaking and writing) in his design for a 'Rational Method' of language teaching. His next task was to accommodate the contrast between written and spoken language.

The second strand in Marcel's argument rests on a distinction between *analytic* and *synthetic* methods of instruction (a distinction that has recently been revived by, for example, Wilkins, 1976). Analytic methods (i.e. 'methods of nature') start from example, practice, and experience, and then move on to general truths by a process of induction: 'The analytical method brings the learner in immediate contact with the objects of study; it presents to him models for decomposition and imitation. The synthetical method disregards example and imitation; it turns the attention of the learner to principles and rules, in order to lead him, by an indirect course, to the objects of study'.[10] The 'good method' will comprise both analysis and synthesis, but in different proportions depending on the characteristics of the learner and the relationship between the immediate learning task and the general aims of education.

The child learning its mother tongue is the obvious master-example of the 'method of nature', and the perennial question arises whether this provides a model for the foreign language classroom. Marcel believed that it did, provided the learners were under the age of twelve (though some older learners might benefit as well). He goes into considerable practical detail in describing lessons based on the Pestalozzian notion of 'object-lessons' in which he advocated the extensive use of pictures, for example, *This is a nice book, I open the book, I shut the book, there are pictures in this book, here is a picture, it is a nice picture*, etc.[11] His advice to the teacher is familiar: 'The instructor must frequently repeat the same expressions, and always accompany them with looks, tones, gestures, and actions which explain them. The language of action, thus used conformably to the process of nature, is, as an explanatory means, preferable to translation, which would create confusion by the mixture of the two idioms.'[12] The only unusual thing about this, apart from its mid-nineteenth-century diction, is the date it was written, 1853.

Analytical 'methods of nature' along Pestalozzian lines obviously determine the priority of spoken over written language and the hearing-speaking branches over the reading-writing ones. Marcel was not content, however, to leave the matter there and merely impose 'natural' methods on all language learners regardless of their relevance to wider educational values and aspirations. At this point, we can see how the cultural and practical demands of his time prompted Marcel to adjust his model in order to take them into account. In its final form, the two impression 'branches', reading and hearing, retain their place in the first rank followed by speaking and writing. However, since learning to read a foreign language was a more practical and useful objective in the 1850s than learning to speak, and, since it also offered a greater intrinsic reward in the form of access to knowledge and the literature of the foreign language, the first priority should be given to reading.

In working out the details of his 'reading-first' programme, Marcel encountered the obvious difficulties of attempting to teach four related activities as if they had nothing to do with each other. In its modern form, the four-skills model gave primary emphasis to the spoken-written contrast and aimed to teach the two oracy skills before the two literacy ones. Effectively, this meant attempting to teach literate learners as if they were illiterate in order to preserve the integrity of the model. Marcel's problem, as we have seen, was different. He attached greater importance to the impression-expression distinction and intended to teach the two receptive skills before the two productive ones, and reading before 'hearing'. In order to preserve the logic of his argument, he was forced to maintain that it did not matter what sound-values learners attached to the orthography of the foreign language in the initial stages of learning.

Not surprisingly, this last point caught the attention of the public since he appeared to be saying that 'pronunciation did not matter'. In fact, he thought it mattered a great deal but that it could—and should—be delayed until later in the course. 'When a learner has gained familiarity with the written words' he commented, 'he requires but little practice in hearing to be able to understand them when spoken'.[13] After extensive experience of listening, the correct pronunciation in spoken expression would come easily and naturally. The latter half of his argument would attract considerable support at the present time. The earlier part, however, would probably meet with strong disapproval, if indeed it were taken seriously at all. Giving special emphasis to reading in an integrated programme would cause little controversy, but 'giving special emphasis' is not what a 'four-skills' model is all about. If there are four separable skills, or branches, and they can be ordered pedagogically, then one of them must be taught first and the other three later. Marcel's choice of reading first meant that he required a theory of reading which would justify his decision.

Marcel's definition of the reading process is strikingly similar to modern definitions associated with the 'psycholinguistic approach to reading'. 'Reading', he said, 'is that operation of the mind by which ideas are attached to the written words as the eye glances over them'. And further: 'we have here nothing to do with the uttering of sounds previously known on perceiving the written words which represent them'.[14] In a more modern idiom, Marcel's main point is that reading is a cognitive process whereby meaning is imposed on written symbols, or, to quote Smith (1978) 'readers must bring meaning *to* print rather than expect to receive meaning *from* it'.[15] Both writers draw the same conclusion from the initial premise. Marcel: 'we have here nothing to do with the uttering of sounds', and Smith: 'we can read – in the sense of understanding print – without producing or imagining sounds'.[16] In Marcel's model, meaning was to be derived from a mother-tongue translation, which should be as literal as possible, and 'by means of these explanations (*i.e. the translation*), practice soon associates in the mind of the learner the foreign words with the native, so that a recurrence of the former will readily recall the latter; and thus will the power of comprehending the written language be rapidly acquired'.[17] In other words, the learner would move straight from meaning to print and *vice versa* without an intervening process of 'decoding to sound', to use Smith's well-known phrase.

It would be unjust to leave even this very brief sketch of Marcel's work without stressing again the greatness of his achievement in *Language as a Means of Mental Culture*. With the possible exception of Sweet's *Practical Study of Languages* in 1899, there is no single work in the history of language teaching to compare with it for the strength of intellect that holds it together over nearly 850 pages of closely-packed text, the breadth of scholarship with which it is informed, and the wealth of pedagogical detail on every aspect of language teaching and learning. It must also be admitted, however, that it never had the impact on contemporary or even subsequent opinion which it deserved. None of the Reform Movement writers in the latter part of the century refer to it, though there is much with which they would have agreed: the emphasis on text rather than sentences, for instance, and the inductive approach to the teaching of grammar. They would, however, have found Marcel's relegation of spoken language to a secondary role in the teaching of older learners quite unacceptable, overlooking the fact that he reversed these priorities in the teaching of languages to youngsters. Nor were any of the Natural Method pioneers of the 1860s and 1870s aware of work which in many ways looks forward to their own.

Perhaps part of the explanation for the neglect of Marcel is the sheer scale of his book and at times it can be heavy-going. While it is never clumsy, it tends to sprawl and can be repetitive. More likely, however, in the inevitable process of simplification that accompanies the spread of complex ideas, Marcel became tagged in the public mind as advocating a 'reading approach' that neglected everything else. If something of this kind did in fact happen, it was grossly unfair, but not entirely unreasonable. While Marcel, as one would expect, argues his case with skill and lucidity, he never gives the impression of being aware of the likely reaction that such an unusual proposal might provoke. His intellectual logic is stronger than his powers of persuasion. If he had met his reader halfway by admitting that there were relationships between the 'four branches' that were at least as important as the characteristics that persuaded him to keep them apart, he would have compromised the grand design of the Rational Method so severely that it might have collapsed. Its re-emergence a century later in the 'four skills' variant would have benefited from a closer knowledge and understanding of the original.

## Thomas Prendergast's 'Mastery System'

Thomas Prendergast (1806–1886) is the only Englishman among the earlier nineteenth-century reformers. He served in the Indian Civil Service in Madras, where he learnt Telugu and Hindustani. Returning to England in his mid-fifties, he wrote and published his 'Mastery System' for learning languages. The basic manual of the system, called *The Mastery of Languages, or the art of speaking foreign languages idiomatically*, appeared in 1864 and it was followed by a number of sample 'mastery' courses for French and German (both 1868), Spanish (1869), Latin (1872), and Hebrew (1871).

Prendergast fills the gap between the Ahn–Ollendorff era and the start of the Reform Movement in the eighties. His work was eventually engulfed by its successors and largely forgotten. Sweet, for instance, dismissed him along with Ahn and Ollendorff as having 'had his day'.[18] This judgement is a little harsh, and may probably owe more to Sweet's dislike of methods that did not make use of phonetics than to a close reading of what Prendergast actually had to say. It may also derive from the distrust on the part of all the reformers for teaching methods based on isolated sentences, which Prendergast's system undoubtedly is. However, in spite of changing fashions, or possibly because of them, his work deserves reappraisal since it contains much that was ahead of its time. Prendergast would have made an admirable associate of writers like Palmer and West in the thirties and one cannot help feeling that if he had had other professionals to talk to, he would not have become so narrowly concerned, almost obsessed, by a single teaching technique, the famous mastery sentences.

We shall come to the sentence-generating technique shortly. It is important first to look at the argument out of which it grew and which it was supposed to realize in practical terms. There is more logic and less inspired intuition about Prendergast than almost any other language teaching methodologist before Henry Sweet.

He started, like many from now on, with the example of language acquisition by young children. His account shows that he observed children carefully and did not come to them looking for confirmation of prejudices. He made a particularly telling point in his description right at the outset which many observers would have overlooked. He noticed that small infants interpret the meaning of language by making use of other information available to them in the wider context, what people do, how they look, their gestures and facial expressions, and so on. As he put it, 'the wonder is that they understand at the same time so much language, and so few words'.[19] His next point is equally perceptive, though his interpretation led him down the wrong path. Children, he noticed, learn ready-made 'chunks' of language, 'pre-fabs' as they have been called in recent times,[20] and weave them into their utterances: 'they employ sentences in which will be found many words which they do not thoroughly understand, and some common phrases, the precise meaning of which they do not, and need not, and perhaps never will comprehend, because they puzzle the grammarian himself'.[21] What impressed Prendergast most about these 'pre-fabs' was their fluency. They seemed so well-learnt that the only explanation he could offer was that they had been memorized as complete units. 'When they (i.e. the children) utter complete idiomatical sentences with fluency, with accurate pronunciation, and with decision, while they are still incapable of understanding any of the principles according to which they unconsciously combine their words in grammatical form, it is obvious that they must have learnt, retained, and reproduced them by dint of imitation and reiteration'.[22]

In other words, he saw the 'pre-fabs' as the products of a learning process that had worked perfectly. They were, he said, 'the rails on which the trains of thought travel swiftly and smoothly'.[23] The sentences the children produced for themselves, on the other hand, were indecisive, inaccurate, ill-learnt. At this point his argument turned the wrong corner. He had, in a sense, been misled by his own terminology. The 'pre-fabs' were not 'sentences', though they may have sounded like them. They were unanalysed chunks, 'words' rather than 'sentences', and represented the starting point or 'database' for the development of fluency rather than true fluency itself. His conclusion was that an efficient foreign language teaching system would consist entirely of memorized sentences, practised to the point of instant recall. This would avoid the inaccuracy and hesitancy of self-generated sentences altogether and lead to complete and fluent mastery. The obvious question was, which sentences are you going to use? Prendergast recognized as well as anybody else that you could not learn all the sentences of a language. His solution was essentially the same as the behaviourist–structuralist school in the twentieth century. You learn the sentences which contain the most frequently used items of the language. He actually went further than the structuralists by constructing sentences that would contain as many of the 'basic rules' of the language as possible in the compass of a single sentence. This reduced the number of sentences by increasing the number of rules each sentence exemplified.

Much of the later part of *The Mastery of Languages* is taken up by investigating the statistical properties of English in order to specify the linguistic content of the minimal set of sentences which would constitute 'mastery'. He drew up a list of 'the commonest English words',[24] and, although it is based entirely on his intuitions, it is remarkably similar to the frequency-based lists of the twentieth-century applied linguists. Altogether, out of a total of 214 words, 82 per cent are among the first 500 most frequent words on the Thorndike-Lorge (1944) list and another 14 per cent in the second 500. All his items, except two (*lest* and *procure*) are classified on Thorndike-Lorge either AA or A. There are, inevitably, unexpected omissions but his task was simplified by a decision to exclude nouns and adjectives since the learner would supply these himself from his own experience and interests. In modern times we have become used to thinking in terms of 'common words' and have spent years using teaching materials based on notions of lexical control. Prendergast had no such background and the general atmosphere of the time was if anything hostile to ideas such as simplicity or everydayness. The fact that his list is a great deal less idiosyncratic than might be expected derives from his own language learning experiences. For a European to learn Telugu or Hindustani properly (as a government official, he could not get away with informal bazaar-chat) requires a great deal of disciplined learning and an organized mind. These are characteristics very much to the fore in all Prendergast's work.

The 'mastery sentences' were, as we have noted, deliberately 'packed' with linguistic information. This gives them an unfortunate air of unreality. The following are typical:

*Why did you not ask him to come, with two or three of his friends, to see my brother's gardens?*

*When the man who brought this parcel for me yesterday evening calls again, give it back to him, and tell him that it is not what I ordered at the shop.*[25]

Having learnt a small set of these sentences to perfection, the learner is provided with the resources for generating hundreds more on the same models, another instance of the Jacotot motto, 'all is in all'. Towards the end of the book, Prendergast gives a diagram called 'The Labyrinth' which is a kind of gigantic substitution table. It demonstrates around two hundred and fifty of the possible sentences that can be generated from the two model sentences at the top of the diagram. He called these new sentences 'evolutions', and reckoned that the full set of possible 'evolutions' would require fifty more diagrams of the same size. The model sentences are numbered and the evolutions presented as formulae:

| 1 | 2 | 3 | 4 | 5. | 6 | 7 | 8 | 9 | 10 |

His servants saw your friend's new bag near our house.

---

| 11 | 12 | 13 | 14 | 15 | 16 | 17 | 18 | 19 | 20 |

Her cousins found my sister's little book in their carriage.

---

Among the possible 'evolutions' from these two models would be: 1.2.3.4.5.7. (*His servants saw your friend's bag*), 11.2.13.4.17.18.9.6.7. (*Her servants found your book in our new bag*), etc.

Prendergast's teaching method consisted of seven steps.[26] Step 1 required the memorization of five or six sentences making up about one hundred words altogether. The basic aim was a correct pronunciation and a fluent control of the model sentences. Lessons should be very short, but as frequent as possible. No books were permitted and the learner imitated the teacher. Meaning was taught by glossing the sentences in the mother tongue. All attempts at conscious analysis or 'grammar' were ruled out since the aim was unconscious mastery not 'understanding of structure'.

In Step 2 the learner moved on to the written language. Prendergast clearly had in mind the non-European learner who would have to learn the Roman alphabet and his very practical suggestions on how to teach it reflect his own learning of Indian languages.

Steps 3 and 4 are concerned with the manipulation of the model sentences ('evolutions') and the acquisition of further models. The last three steps deal with the development of reading and conversation skills. Prendergast made considerable use of translation but insisted that it should be 'cursory observation, not close study—habituation not

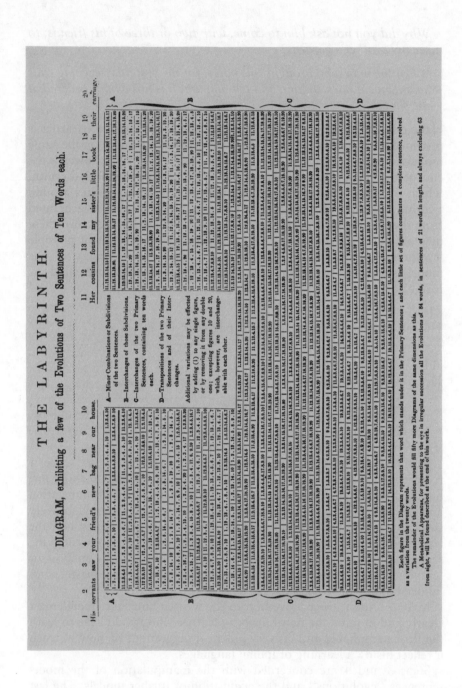

*Figure 22   'The Labyrinth' from Thomas Prendergast's* Mastery of Languages
*(1864). The numbered words in the two sample sentences could be combined
according to the formulae given in the chart.*

investigation'. 'Nothing', he says, 'can be more disheartening to a beginner, than to be checked at every second or third word, by cries of No, No, No from a pedagogue'.[27] The practice of translation has been condemned so strenuously for so long without any really convincing reasons that it is perhaps time the profession took another look at it. Was it really translation that the reformers objected to a hundred years ago, or, as Prendergast suggests, the way in which it was used?

Prendergast would have found the twenties and thirties in this century a much more congenial time for his particular gifts and talents than the 1860s. Like Michael West years later, he had worked in India, away from the over-heated intellectual squabbles that tend to clog European discussions on teaching methodology. He knew what learning a new language was really like when the language in question bore no resemblance to one's mother tongue. He came to the same basic conclusions as West—the need for simplicity, a small, carefully selected minimum vocabulary and a graded set of materials. He would also have had much in common with Palmer, particularly his belief in the possibility of creating a limited 'core', or 'microcosm' as Palmer was to call it, which could be thoroughly learnt and from which the rest could grow as experience with the new language increased. As it was, however, he allowed the technique of the sentences to overshadow the idea that lay behind them and he was linked in the minds of the reforming generation that was just around the corner with all the other mid-century textbook authors with 'funny sentences'. There may be a way of realizing Jacotot's maxim 'learn one thing thoroughly and relate everything else to it', but Prendergast's sentence system is probably not the right one.

## François Gouin and the 'Series'

François Gouin (1831–1896) was the last of the nineteenth-century individualists, which may help to explain why his name is better-known than Prendergast's or Marcel's, though the work they did was considerably more interesting. Gouin published his major work, *The Art of Teaching and Studying Languages*, in Paris in 1880 on the eve of the Reform Movement, but it had actually been written much earlier and printed privately in Geneva, where he owned a language school for a time. The English translation appeared in London in 1892.

The work of the contemporary Reform Movement attracted public attention to the inadequacy of traditional schoolroom methods of language teaching, and Gouin had a clear, easily understood and methodologically simple alternative to offer in the shape of the famous 'series' technique. He benefited from the 'new wave', but he did not directly contribute to it. The origins of the 'series' have passed into the folklore of language teaching and we shall return to them in a moment. First, however, the 'series' itself.

Gouin's central concept was that the structure of a language text reflected the structure of the experience it described. For reasons which we shall come to, he believed that sequentiality was the primary feature of experience and that all events could be described in terms of a 'series' of smaller component events, so that, for example, opening the door could be analysed into moving towards the door, turning the handle, opening it, holding it open, and so on. This sequential structure provided the framework for the associated language: *I am walking to the door, I am standing by the door, I am turning the handle*, etc., and the familiarity of happenings of this kind helped the learner to understand the new language and remember it more efficiently. Gouin also argued, less convincingly, that describing experiences of this kind was intrinsically motivating. Sweet, for one, was not impressed: 'some of the series, such as that which gives a detailed description of opening and shutting a door ... are as uninteresting as they are useless'.[28] Gouin's own example from his book is the celebrated log-chopping incident which, presumably, was intended to demonstrate how the most unassuming events of life could be put to useful service. He claimed four particular advantages for the exercise:

1   Each phrase expressing a detail, a new fact, the repetition of the same subjects and same complements, has not the character of an ordinary repetition, of a repetition pure and simple. Owing to this new detail, this step made in advance in each phrase, neither tediousness nor fatigue is to be feared.

2   This natural repetition of the same nouns, this constant and periodic return of the thought towards the same object, this reiterated effort of the representative or visualising faculty upon the same idea, is not all this the graver's tool which engraves the ideas and their expressions upon the memory?

3   This same repetition, this perpetual recurrence of the same sounds, is not this the essential condition, is not this the most sure and solid guarantee of a good pronunciation?

4   The listener, feeling himself safe in this repetition of subjects and complements, turns the principal effort of his attention quite naturally upon the verb. But the verb, which is the soul of the phrase, the most important and precious element of the sentence, is at the same time the most difficult to conquer and to keep. It is important, therefore, that the attention should be fixed entirely upon this term. Now, by means of the before-mentioned evolution, all the visual rays of the intelligence are verily concentrated upon a solitary fact, the action – upon a solitary word, the verb.[29]

After this enthusiastic introduction, we come to the exercise itself:

### The maid chops a log of wood

| | |
|---|---|
| The maid goes and seeks her hatchet, | *seeks* |
| the maid takes a log of wood, | *takes* |
| the maid draws near to the chopping-block, | *draws near* |
| the maid kneels down near this block, | *kneels down* |
| the maid places the' log of wood upright upon | |
| this block. | *places* |
| | |
| The maid raises her hatchet, | *raises* |
| the maid brings down her hatchet, | *brings down* |
| the hatchet cleaves the air, | *cleaves* |
| the blade strikes the wood, | *strikes* |
| the blade buries itself in the wood, | *buries itself* |
| the blade cleaves the wood, | *cleaves* |
| the two pieces fall to the ground. | *fall* |
| | |
| The maid picks up these pieces, | *picks up* |
| the maid chops them again and again to the | |
| size desired, | *chops again* |
| the maid stands up again, | *stands up* |
| the maid carries back the hatchet to its place[30] | *carries back* |

There are others to choose from: The Housewife Goes to the Wood-shed, The Cook Fetches Wood, The Housemaid Lays the Fire, and more.

Gouin defies easy interpretation. His book, from which I have deliberately quoted at length in order to allow the reader to judge independently, is repetitious and exhaustingly ebullient. Perhaps he was let down by his translators, but they cannot be held responsible for all the rhetorical questions or the repetitions. The log-chopping 'series' itself is weird, and 'the reiterated effort of the visualising faculty upon the same idea' is reminiscent of sequences in silent Russian films where sheer technique invests banal events with apocalyptic meanings. Nevertheless, in its own curious, almost 'hypnotic', way it works. Gouin has effectively extended the principle that comprehension is a function of the predictability of utterances in context to its logical, and some might say absurd, conclusion. The commonplaceness of the incidents themselves and the tenaciousness with which they have been dissected ('the hatchet cleaves the air, the blade strikes the wood, the blade cleaves the wood') leave little room for doubt as to the meaning of the new language. The repetition of the nouns, although anything but 'natural', does have the effect that he intended, namely to concentrate the learners' attention on the verbs, which, in representing the events of the situation, have an almost mystical significance as 'the soul of the phrase'. (In fairness to Gouin, it should be said that his translators' decision to retain the 'historic present' rather than transform the text into the more normal narrative past tense accounts for at least some of the oddness of the material.)

The most obvious practical drawback to Gouin's system is the over-abundance of third-person statements though he attempted to solve this problem by including a selection of everyday dialogue phrases. Here again, however, he offered a somewhat ornate theory that 'the third person includes within itself the entire conjugation' and 'like Nature we make this third person the basis of our operations'.[31] Part of the justification for this unusual view was his observation that young children frequently refer to themselves in the third person in the early stages of acquiring their mother tongue. Like Prendergast, Gouin based his teaching method on his observation of the way language was used by children. However, while Prendergast clearly listened to the speech of children closely and objectively, for Gouin it was a source of instant inspiration, a moment of truth on which he founded the whole methodology of his 'series'. The famous mill incident represented the climax of a much longer story and to understand it properly, we have to begin at the beginning. As an early commentator put it, 'it is almost as interesting as a novel'.[32]

When François Gouin was a young man, he set off from his home in Normandy to study philosophy at the University of Berlin in Germany. Not knowing any German, he stopped off in Hamburg to learn the language: 'my idea was there to conquer the foundation of the language, then to proceed to Berlin'.[33] Armed with a grammar and a dictionary, he set about his task. 'In ten days I had mastered the grammar of the German language,' he says, 'and hastened forthwith to the Academy . . . but alas! in vain did I strain my ears; in vain my eye strove to interpret the slightest movements of the lips of the professor; in vain I passed from the first class-room to the second; not a word, not a single word would penetrate to my understanding'.[34]

After this traumatic failure, he tried philology. Having memorized a thousand German 'roots' in four days (he is always very precise about these things) he went back to the Academy. 'Imagine then, if it be possible, the astonishment at first, then the stupefaction, then the degradation by which I was overtaken after the first quarter of an hour at the lecture I attended . . . it was a failure; nay, more than this, it was a defeat'.[35] So 'I sorrowfully wandered back to my lodgings, seeking the causes of my incapability, and unfortunately this time unable to give myself any explanation'.[36]

There were more disasters to come. His next idea was to 'pick the language up' by talking to his German host, who happened to be a hairdresser. He spent 'long hours' in the saloon attempting to engage the customers in conversation but 'I had an intense desire, an ardent thirst for order and logic, to which the scraps of ordinary conversation, more or less vapid and continually interrupted, corresponded but ill'.[37] In disgust at his failure, he went back to translation with the aid of a dictionary, but once again he was deceived. 'Translation is not merely a slow and painful process, but it leads to nothing and can lead to nothing'.[38]

His resolve undiminished, he took up Ollendorff. All went well at the beginning: 'Ollendorff's method was decidely based upon Nature; it was certainly a natural method. As such it could not fail'.[39] Needless to say, however, it did. After an heroic effort, he mastered the whole of Ollendorff in four weeks only to discover by the end that he had been deceived again: the book was lightweight, 'thousands of forms, thousands of words, forgotten or wilfully omitted by the author'. 'I was not to discover till much later the prodigious errors of the pedagogic art that had presided over this miserable compilation of words'.[40] He tried Jacotot ('quite as light as Ollendorff'), Robertson ('the same indictment'), and Ploetz who, he acknowledged, was 'upon the right track' in his vocabulary books.[41] Nothing, it seemed, would work and he was deeply depressed.

In despair he left Hamburg, 'sojourn of misfortune, witness of my many defeats', and went to Berlin. Dogged as ever, he went back to his lectures at the university, but 'I could distinguish neither the words, nor the sentences, nor the periods of the professor'. 'What was I to do next? Had I not tried everything? Was a Frenchman really a being incapable of learning any other language than his own?'[42]

'There still remained one last method . . . but one so strange, so extraordinary, so unusual—I might say, so heroic—that I hardly dared propose it to myself'.[43] He decided to learn the dictionary by heart. True to his instincts for order and logic, he divided the 30,000 words of the dictionary into 30 groups of 1,000 words each and resolved to learn one thousand-word group per day for a month. The effort sent him blind (temporarily) and he went back to France for a holiday.

The early stages of this extraordinary story are convincing enough and Gouin's determination to succeed in the face of repeated disappointments is even moving at times. However, as it goes on and he tries one textbook after another, discarding each of them in turn as useless, doubts begin to creep in, and one begins to lose patience with him. I hope I am not doing Gouin a terrible injustice, but, quite frankly, I do not believe him. I am quite prepared to accept that he found German difficult to learn and tried various approaches, but the systematic way in which he demolishes one method after another is very difficult to take, and in the dictionary episode, he goes over the top. What he gives us, in my opinion, is a 'fictionalized' review of the literature of language teaching methodology of his time, based to some extent on personal experience. There is no doubt that it got him into a certain amount of trouble at the time since his translators go to some lengths to defend him in their preface to the English version in 1892. They claim that only

French methods are attacked, which is both a curious defence and not strictly true, and secondly that 'methods not men are criticized'. This last remark is printed in capital letters and it highlights the dangers of Gouin's technique of presenting his opinions in autobiographical form.

All this is, however, merely an introduction to the incident at the mill, which, in contrast to the earlier fable, is totally convincing. He took his three-year-old nephew on an afternoon's outing to a local corn-mill in Normandy which the child greatly enjoyed and it clearly made a deep impression. Later, the boy reconstructed his visit with toys and other bits and pieces lying about the house, and simultaneously re-lived his experience by talking to himself. Naturally enough, since he had been watching an industrial process of grinding corn into flour, he organized his memories sequentially: first this happened, then that, then the next, etc. Gouin overheard him and – Eureka! – he had found the magic key to language: 'I wandered about,' he says, 'repeating to myself the words of the poet *I see, I hear, I know!*'.[44] Shorn of the rhapsodic rhetoric in which Gouin expresses all his comments, the insight he gained from observing the child's use of language was of great importance. The boy used language in order to understand and organize his experience, and he used his experience in order to control and explore the resources of his language. This dynamic relationship between language and cognition lies at the heart of linguistic development, and Gouin was justified in his recognition of its significance.

Nevertheless, Gouin's exaggerated enthusiasm ('a flash of light suddenly shot across my mind') blinded him to two serious flaws in his interpretation of the incident, both of which severely damaged the practical usefulness of his teaching materials. The first was his failure to realize that using language to structure experience (or 'ideationally' as Halliday[45] puts it) is only one of a number of functions for which it is employed. If he had listened to his nephew trying to talk about the mill-trip to somebody else, he would have come up with a different ('interpersonal') model, and instead of using descriptive texts in his teaching materials would have tried something else altogether. The second flaw resulted from mistaking the tokens ('events in sequence') for the type. If Gouin had reflected on his observation of the boy instead of exploding with excitement ('I have found it! Now I understand!'),[46] it would surely have occurred to him that there was a relationship between the sequences in the child's narrative and the sequences in the industrial grinding process. Other events must obviously be organized in their own particular ways. If he had taken the boy to the duck-pond the following weekend, he would have discovered something else, perhaps equally interesting: spatial organization maybe, or cause-and-effect, or the expression of delight. But he did not do any further research. From now on *everything* was a sequence.

He applied the 'series' notion to his German-learning problem and it disappeared. 'At the end of the week I began to comprehend ordinary conversations'.[47] He returned to the university shortly afterwards and started to take part in philosophy seminars on Descartes and Hegel in German. The series clearly suited him well. After leaving the university, he applied the idea in his own career as a language teacher which took him, briefly, to Romania and England before he founded his school in Geneva. Later he moved back to Elboef in Normandy and finished as the Director of the École Supérieure Arago in Paris. The Gouin system became famous, and institutions were specially set up to teach it in various places. One of its more illustrious students was the young Daniel Jones, who started his linguistic career by attending French classes at a Gouin school in London.

The Gouin series became a standard technique in direct method language teaching and most teachers have at one time or another done the door-routine if nothing else. As a self-contained method, however, it was too restricted to attract much enthusiasm, though it enjoyed a vogue for a time.[48] Sweet summed it up quite well in a remark which was, for him, unexpectedly restrained, given that Gouin did not use phonetics: 'the "series method" may in itself be a sound principle, but it is too limited in its application to form even the basis of a fully developed method'.[49]

## Notes

1  Jespersen (1904: 3).
2  Gaillard (1875), quoted in Kroeh (1887: 172–3).
3  Kroeh (1887: 172).
4  Ibid.: 173.
5  *Calypso ne pouvoit se consoler du départ d'Ulysse* (literally, Calypso could not console herself of (at) the departure of Ulysses), the first sentence of Fénelon's *Aventures du Télémaque* (Adventures of Telemachus).
6  Payne (1830: 55–6).
7  Marcel (1853, I: 335).
8  Ibid.: 216.
9  Ibid.: 217.
10  Ibid.: 209.
11  Ibid.: 330.
12  Ibid.: 331.
13  Ibid.: 338.
14  Ibid.: 337.
15  Smith (1978: 50).
16  Ibid.: 51.
17  Marcel (1853, II:93).
18  Sweet (1899/1964: 2).

19 Prendergast (1864: 7).
20 Hakuta (1974).
21 Prendergast (1864: 8–9).
22 Ibid.: 11.
23 Ibid.: 11.
24 Ibid.: 164.
25 Ibid.: 165.
26 Ibid.: Chapter 5.
27 Ibid.: 91.
28 Sweet (1899/1964: 113).
29 Gouin (1892: 82).
30 Ibid.: 69.
31 Ibid.: 208.
32 Ibid.: xii.
33 Ibid.: 9.
34 Ibid.: 11.
35/36 Ibid.: 14.
37 Ibid.: 15.
38 Ibid.: 17.
39 Ibid.: 19.
40 Ibid.: 21.
41 Ibid.: 23–5.
42/43 Ibid.: 26.
44 Ibid.: 38.
45 Halliday (1973).
46 Gouin (1892: 38).
47 Ibid.: 57. Gouin is uncharacteristically reticent about this crucial 'test case'. Perhaps coming back to German after his holiday convinced him he knew more than he realized before.
48 See Holmes (1903). Passy (1899: 20, footnote) also refers to the Gouin system as 'a vogue' which, it seems, owed a lot to a well-publicized success-story involving an eight-year-old child called Jack whose ability to understand French after a Gouin course was remarkable. On closer investigation it turned out that his powers of expression, however, were minimal.
49 Sweet (1899/1964: 3).

# 13   The Reform Movement

## Introduction

The late nineteenth-century Reform Movement is unique in language teaching history. For a period of about twenty years, not only did many of the leading phoneticians of the time co-operate towards a shared educational aim, but they also succeeded in attracting teachers and others in the field to the same common purpose. From 1882 onwards, there was a spate of publications, beginning with pamphlets and articles and, later, more substantial works like Sweet's *Practical Study of Languages* (1899). Professional associations and societies were formed, notably the International Phonetic Association (IPA), and there were new journals and periodicals, of which the best-known was the IPA's *Le Maître Phonétique*, first published under that title in 1889.

The Movement was a remarkable display of international and interdisciplinary co-operation in which the specialist phoneticians took as much interest in the classroom as the teachers did in the new science of phonetics. One of the reasons for this was the fact that three out of the four principal phoneticians – Viëtor in Germany, Passy in France, and Jespersen in Denmark – began their careers as schoolteachers, though they went on to other work later. The fourth, Henry Sweet, was the 'odd man out' in the sense that he remained a private scholar for most of his life and his teaching was limited to individual students. He continued to be respected, however, as the intellectual leader of the Movement.

On the teaching side, the principal figure was Klinghardt, a *Realgymnasium* teacher from Silesia, who followed up a review of Sweet's 1884 paper ('On the practical study of language')[1] with a carefully documented study of a year's work with the new methods which helped to increase the confidence of teachers in their practicality. Klinghardt's equivalent in Britain, W. H. Widgery, published an influential pamphlet called *The Teaching of Languages in Schools* in 1888, but he died before the full impact of his work could be felt. It seems he did not make personal contact with Sweet, and his description of Sweet's writing as 'curt and concise'[2] suggests that perhaps he did not seek to do so.

Among others attracted to the new ideas and the enthusiasm they generated, the most interesting was Franke, who also died at an early age. Had he lived, he might have become the theoretical psychologist of the Movement, expanding the ideas he explored in his remarkable pamphlet *Die praktische Spracherlernung* (Practical Language Acquisition) in 1884. His interest in the linguistic theories of von Humboldt might, if it had been developed further, have embedded the new methods more securely into an important tradition of the psychology of language which was revived in recent times by Chomsky and his colleagues in psycholinguistics.

Perhaps the simplest way of illustrating the scope of the Reform Movement is to outline a 'bird's-eye-view' of its achievements between 1882 when it first attracted attention, and 1904 when Jespersen summarized its practical implications for the classroom teacher in *How to Teach a Foreign Language*.

Unlike many examples of educational change, the Reform Movement began suddenly, with the publication of Viëtor's pamphlet *Der Sprachunterricht muss umkehren*! (Language teaching must start afresh!) under the pseudonym Quousque Tandem[3] in 1882. Its impact on the teaching profession at the time, and its later influence, make it one of the most significant documents in recent language teaching history. However, although it is often alluded to, its contents are less well-known, due, in part at least, to the absence of a published English translation. In an attempt to put this right, a translation (made in collaboration with David Abercrombie and Beat Buchmann) has been included as an Appendix to this book. In 1886 Viëtor finally acknowledged his authorship of *Der Sprachunterricht*, and a Quousque Tandem Society was formed in Scandinavia,[4] borrowing the famous but now discarded pseudonym. In the same year Passy set up the Phonetic Teachers' Association which was later to become the International Phonetic Association. Jespersen, then a young man of twenty-six, who had earlier formed a friendship by correspondence with Franke and had prepared a Danish translation of his pamphlet, became one of its first members.

The collaborative tradition of the Reform Movement was continued in 1887 when Klinghardt chose Sweet's *Elementarbuch* as the basic textbook for his trial of the new methods in his school in Silesia. The results were published in a pamphlet called *Ein Jahr Erfahrungen mit der neuen Methode* (A Year's Experiences with the New Method) in 1888 with a further study of the following three years' teaching (*Drei weitere Jahre Erfahrungen mit der imitativen Methode*) in 1892. Widgery's *Teaching of Languages in Schools* was another 1888 publication which brought together a series of articles he had previously written for the *Journal of Education*. Journals also played an important role in Germany, in particular *Englische Studien*, edited by Kölbing, which gave the Movement considerable support throughout the whole period by publishing articles, reviews, conference reports, and so on.

The 1890s were less rich in publication terms, but the Movement continued to expand and, at the turn of the century, reached its climax with the appearance of two works which together provide a definitive statement of its aims, principles and practical classroom methods. The first was Sweet's classic *The Practical Study of Languages* which, after nearly thirty years in preparation, was finally published in 1899. Impressive though Sweet's work is, it lacks a human dimension and, without its 'companion piece', Jespersen's *How to Teach a Foreign Language* (1904, originally published as *Sprogundervisning* in 1901), the Movement might have seemed rather cold and clinical.

Viëtor also played a role at the end as he had done at the beginning. He contributed directly by holding a series of summer schools, reported in *Die Methodik des neusprachlichen Unterrichts* in 1902, and indirectly through a language teaching institute in his home town of Marburg directed by a former colleague called William Tilly. Tilly, formerly Tilley, was an Australian who taught languages according to reformed principles and one of his summer students in 1900 was Daniel Jones, then a young man about to go up to Cambridge to study mathematics. Tilly ignited an interest in phonetics in Jones which was later followed up with a year's study under Passy in Paris. These somewhat fortuitous events forge the final link between *Der Sprachunterricht muss umkehren*! and the work of Jones, Palmer, and others at University College, London, out of which English as a foreign language emerged as an independent branch of practical language studies.

### The principles of reform

The Reform Movement was founded on three basic principles: the primacy of speech, the centrality of the connected text as the kernel of the teaching–learning process, and the absolute priority of an oral methodology in the classroom. Though these principles were variously interpreted by different writers, there were no serious disagreements about their basic objectives.

The Movement also drew strength from its broader educational aims. The subtitle to Viëtor's Quousque Tandem pamphlet ('Ein Beitrag zur Überbürdungsfrage'), for example, emphasized the point by associating the Movement with the controversial issue of overwork ('Überbürdung') in the schools and the consequent ill-health and mental stress. He sided with the reformist view that the demands made on children by the Prussian education system were excessive, and that language teaching bore a special responsibility since it dominated the curriculum. He was convinced that, if teachers adopted saner classroom methods based on the spoken language, not only would the children learn more effectively, but the Überbürdung problem would be solved by the abolition of written homework. Language study outside the classroom should, in his view, be restricted to the learning of rhymes, songs, and so on, by heart, and he published a collection of texts for this purpose in collaboration with Dörr called *Englisches Lesebuch* in 1887.

The primacy of the spoken language is Viëtor's leading theme in *Der Sprachunterricht*. In Part 1 he discusses the linguistic nonsense that had become endemic in the classroom through the neglect of speech. Sounds were confused with letters, and spelling with pronunciation. If speech was taught at all, it was badly done by teachers whose own pronunciation was inadequate. Partly as a result of the emphasis on writing, much of the grammatical information in the textbooks of the time was at best misleading, and the retention of Latin-based paradigms such as *house / Oh, house / of the house / by, with,* or *from the house* was absurd. 'There is an Augean stable of rules to cleanse', he exclaimed at one point.[5] Reform, he insisted, must begin with the provision of accurate descriptions of speech based on the science of phonetics, and there must be a properly trained language teaching profession. Quoting Sweet with approval, he said, 'If our wretched system of studying modern languages is ever to be reformed, it must be on the basis of a preliminary training in general phonetics'.[6]

To writers like Viëtor and Sweet, it was essential that the learner's pronunciation should be correct before moving on to texts, and that these texts should be printed in a scientifically accurate notation, not in the faulty traditional orthography, particularly for languages like English and French where the standard spelling is extremely misleading. Some Reform Movement phoneticians (especially Sweet) tended to exaggerate the pedagogical value of transcription and, as Klinghardt showed in his 1887 experiment, the transition to traditional orthography could take place quite early without a disastrous fall in the pupils' standards of pronunciation. Nevertheless, in many teachers' minds, modern methods of language teaching were synonymous with 'using phonetics', and 'phonetics' in turn meant learning a notation system. Some teachers claimed this imposed an extra learning burden, and most reformers found themselves having to defend its use at some time or another. With hindsight, the transcription issue ('that hobgoblin', as Jespersen put it),[7] may have done more harm than good, and distracted attention away from the broader aspects of reform.[8]

The principle of the connected text caused none of the dissension that arose over notation. The absurd example sentences of the grammar-translation method were an easy target, but the issue went deeper than this and raised significant questions concerning the psychology of language learning, and the role of language teaching in education. Though still an infant science, psychology had begun to emerge as a distinctive discipline in the 1880s and one of its central concepts was the notion of association. Disconnected words and sentences infringed the basic tenets of associationism, and they had to be replaced by texts in which the linguistic elements were correctly assembled so that the learner could make the necessary associations between one element and another. The use of translation was discouraged since it could lead to the formation of 'cross associations' and hinder the development of the foreign language.

From an educational point of view, connected texts on worthwhile topics were clearly preferable to the pointless sentences of traditional textbooks. This raised many problems in the selection and grading of suitable texts which in one form or another have continued till the present day.

The third implication of a text-based approach was an 'inductive' method of teaching grammar in which the language of the text provided the data for grammatical rules rather than being used to exemplify rules previously learnt out of context. As we have seen, many writers before the Reform Movement had proposed a post-text role for grammar (Holyband's *The French Littleton* was an early example), but some reformers intended a much closer relationship between text and grammar, even to the point of constructing texts specially to 'illustrate' the grammar—a technique Sweet, for example, strongly rejected.

The last major Reform Movement principle was the importance of oral methods in the classroom, especially in the early stages of learning. As Viëtor describes (see pp. 360–1), the text provided the starting point for question-and-answer work, retells, and so on, which required the learners to use the new language. The teacher was expected to speak the foreign language as the normal means of classroom communication, retaining the mother tongue only for glossing new words and explaining new grammar points. Most of the fuss about 'no translation' came from the Direct Method, particularly as interpreted by Berlitz, where the teachers were native speakers. The Reform Movement consisted of non-native teachers who accepted the basic sense of the monolingual principle, but did not see any advantage in an extremist view.

## The Klinghardt experiment

The next reform milestone after the Viëtor and Franke pamphlets and Sweet's 1884 address was the decision by Klinghardt to try out the new ideas in his *Realgymnasium* in Reichenbach in Silesia, using Sweet's *Elementarbuch des gesprochenen Englisch* (1885).

The experiment began in the spring of 1887 and continued until the March of the following year. The work was divided into two semesters, the first from mid-April to September with a summer break in July, and the second from October to March with a Christmas holiday. The pupils were fourteen-year-old boys in Form IIIB and all beginners in English, though they had done French for three years.

Klinghardt began his course with a two and a half week introduction to English pronunciation, including listening and speech exercises, during which he began to introduce the new phonetic notation. Ten hours of phonetics (they had four lessons a week) would not have satisfied Sweet, but such perfectionism would probably not have worked in a secondary school classroom. Klinghardt's instincts as a teacher told him that it was time to move on to the texts, and he began the first one in the third week of the course, writing it sentence-by-sentence on the blackboard because the boys had been unable to obtain the book for themselves.

In the early stages, writing the text on the board was no great hardship since the class spent four lessons on each new sentence. Later on in the year, however, when they were able to cope with longer passages, it became impossible and Klinghardt had to change their textbook. Working through a text at the rate of one sentence a week sounds extremely slow, but Sweet's sentences are (deliberately) complex and contain a lot to learn (see below). Pronunciation was of central importance, so the class listened while the teacher read the sentence aloud a couple of times, and repeated it until they could say it fluently. They also copied it down in the new notation. The meaning was glossed with an interlinear translation and, when it was thoroughly familiar, the new grammar point was discussed and taught. As the reader can see, Sweet's sentences contain a large number of potential 'grammar points', but only one was selected for teaching purposes. The remainder (for example, past tense forms in the example below) were treated as lexical items and left until a later part of the course. It was never Sweet's intention to restrict the language of his texts to grammar which had been 'introduced' earlier in the course, but to limit the amount that was taught in detail.

The new point in Lesson 1 is the contrast between the definite and indefinite articles before vowels (*the earth / an orange*) and consonants (*the sea / a ball*). (In the grammar-translation method the two values of *the* would probably never have been taught at all.) Below is the sentence, first in normal orthography (which the pupils did not see), then in transcription (a) reproduced from Klinghardt's book, and, finally, transcription (b) Sweet's Broad Romic:

'People used to think the earth was a kind of flat cake, with the sea all round it; but we know now that it's really round, like a ball — not quite round, but a little flattened, like an orange.'[9]

(a)[10]      *pí'pl 'ŭ*sttəþíŋkᾰi ắþªəzə kəindəv flắt kéik, *ĭđðə si'ŏl raŭndĭt; bʌlªí' noŭ naŭðətĭts rĭəli raŭnd, ləikə bŏl — nót kªəit raŭnd, bətəlĭtl flắtnd, ləikən órĭnᵹ.*

(b)[11]      -pijpl juwsttəþiŋkŏi əəþ wəzəkaindəv flæt keik`, -wiððə sijɔl raundit; bətwij nou nauðətits rĭəli ·raund`, :laikə bɔl`— not ˅kwait :raund, bətəlitl flætnd`, :laikən orinᵹ.

Sweet's transcription conventions replaced orthographical word boundaries by a system of division into speech units which tended to obscure linguistic patterns that are evident to the eye in normal orthography. Part of Klinghardt's classroom presentation work was to note the word boundaries by the use of commas so that he could provide his interlinear gloss.

None of the problems that a present-day teacher might foresee with material of this kind actually occurred. The pupils were kept busy doing oral work and listening exercises, and the notation had all the advantages of novelty. Moreover, they were actually *speaking* a foreign language from the beginning, which is more than they were doing in their French classes where they were struggling through Ploetz's grammar book. Once they knew the text well (in effect by heart, though this was not the intention), Klinghardt began to 'induce' the grammar patterns. All the necessary material was in the text and it was one of the cardinal principles of the method never to go outside it (no long lists of exceptions, 'special uses of the article', etc., only the basic point, simply illustrated).

After the first month, Klinghardt began to teach the children how to ask and answer comprehension questions on the text and also how to extend them to topics in their own lives and experience. It is at this point that the Reform Method really begins to take off with question-and-answer work, discussion, retelling the story, and so on, all of it conducted in English.

Klinghardt made the transition to traditional orthography at the beginning of the second semester when he switched from the *Elementarbuch* to a reader by Gesenius. The texts were longer, and included such perennial favourites as The Story of Robin Hood. The class was introduced to writing for the first time: copying, writing answers to questions, doing simple retells, and so on. By the end of the first year, they had made good progress in their knowledge of the language, even measured in traditional terms of 'how much grammar they had got through', but the really remarkable difference was the confidence with which they used the spoken language. The controversial early work with the transcribed texts paid dividends in the end.

Sweet himself did not comment on the Klinghardt experiment in *The Practical Study of Languages*, though it is difficult to believe he did not know about it. He was not a man who compromised easily and some of Klinghardt's decisions, especially the short introductory phonetics course and the early discarding of transcription, would not have pleased him.

## The role of phonetics

The Reform Movement offered language teaching something it could hardly refuse – a scientific approach. Science had become to the public mind of the nineteenth century what Reason had been to the eighteenth-century Enlightenment, the indispensable basis of achievement and progress. To the man in the street its magic was evident in the new technologies that created the great industries and fed the nineteenth-century passion for gadgetry. Here now was the opportunity for science to enter what had hitherto been regarded as the inner sanctum of the humanities, the study and teaching of language.

The scientific impulse expressed itself in a number of different ways, some profound and academically rigorous, others more popular and keener for practical results. On the more academic side, there was a rich tradition of historical and comparative philology pursued by German scholars such as Bopp and Schleicher in the earlier part of the century and, later, the group of so-called 'neo-grammarians' ('Junggrammatiker') clustered round Osthoff, Brugmann and Paul, the author of the standard work on the subject *Die Prinzipien der Sprachgeschichte* (1880).[12] Secondly, there were important developments in research in the physiology of speech, much of it also undertaken in Germany, and made known in Britain through publications such as Max Müller's *Lectures on Language* (1864). Both these traditions exerted an influence on the thinking and practice of the Reform Movement, the latter more directly than the former.

The more popular side was represented by, for example, the appearance in 1837 of Isaac Pitman's new system of shorthand in a booklet called *Stenographic Soundhand*, later renamed *Manual of Phonography* (1842).[13] There was also a growing interest in dialect studies which chimed to some extent with the 'back-to-our-roots' romanticism of the time, and a revival of pressure for spelling reform, partly in response to the expansion of universal education, which was accepted in principle if not immediately in practice in the Education Act of 1870. Finally, there were the ever-popular arts of elocution and public verse-speaking that had stimulated the work of actor-phoneticians like Sheridan and Walker in the eighteenth century and which continued to attract audiences.

The Scottish family of the Bells provides a good example of how applied phonetics produced ideas which later were to exert a considerable influence on language teaching. Grandfather Alexander Bell had been an orthoëpist ('no charge until impediment removed')[14] and an elocution teacher with a system of Simultaneous Reading 'adapted for classes of five hundred or one thousand pupils'. Both his sons took up the family business and became university lecturers in the subject: David Charles Bell rose to be Professor of Elocution at Dublin and his better-known younger brother, Alexander Melville Bell, lectured at the University of Edinburgh for twenty-two years (1843–65) and later at London. In 1870 Alexander Melville took his even more famous son, Alexander Graham Bell, to Canada and then to the United States. He was a prolific writer on speech and elocution, but his most significant achievement was the invention of a notation system called 'Visible Speech', published in *Visible Speech, the Science of Universal Alphabetics* (1867), a work that greatly impressed Henry Sweet: 'Bell has in this work done more for phonetics than all his predecessors put together',[15] he said in the preface to his *Handbook* (1877). Visible speech itself was impractical for general use since it did not use the Roman alphabet, but it provided Sweet with a model from which, ultimately, he developed his Broad Romic transcription system. This in turn influenced the final shape of the International Phonetic Alphabet.

By the 1880s the popular 'image' of phonetics was a mixture of advanced technology (the telephone of grandson Bell, the phonograph, and so on) and of pure philological science. It was not unlike the image of applied linguistics in the early sixties with its language laboratories backed by modern structural linguistics and scientific analyses of behaviour. However, the language teaching classroom of the Reform Movement was not a 'guinea-pig' research-bed for the new science (experimentalism on the twentieth-century model would have had little appeal). The leaders of the Movement were more concerned with the educational implications of the appalling teaching methods of the time, and phonetics offered both a scientific foundation for their reformist zeal and a practical technique for bringing about the improvements in the classroom that they were looking for. The reform of language teaching was a moral issue for all the members of the Reform Movement, but in particular for Passy, a devout Christian and a dedicated teacher.

Paul Passy came from a family in which ethical conviction and moral commitment were matters of profound importance. His father, Frédéric Passy, was the first holder of the Nobel Peace Prize, and similar pacifist beliefs led Paul to enter teaching as an optional alternative to military service. In 1878 he became a Christian, a faith that he later expressed in his attachment to the Christian Socialist movement. He was educated at home and learnt English, German, and Italian in his youth. Later he attended the École des Hautes Études in Paris where he studied Sanskrit and Gothic. Most of his work as a teacher was concerned with English and this, coupled with his later role as Daniel Jones's phonetics teacher, makes him a particularly significant figure in the history of English language teaching.

During his early years as a teacher, Passy devised a private phonetic alphabet and, impressed by its usefulness in the classroom, drew together a small group of other like-minded language teachers to discuss how such ideas could be expanded for the general good. The group comprised nine Frenchmen in addition to himself and his brother Jean, and a Belgian. Calling themselves the Phonetic Teachers' Association, they quickly attracted new members: Jespersen joined in May 1886 only a few months after its formation, Viëtor in July, and Sweet in September. The first issue of their journal, *The Phonetic Teacher*, appeared in May and continued to appear under that title for three years when it was re-named *Le Maître Phonétique* (1889). In 1897 the Association took its final title, the International Phonetic Association (IPA.).

Passy's views on transcription drew on his experience with young children and were influential in moulding the attitudes of the IPA. They were characteristically very simple. In the first place, transcription for classroom use should be as broad as possible (scientific research was another matter), and, secondly, the number of symbols should be as small as possible. Breadth and economy may seem obvious notions now but, without them, the excitement of a new technique, rivalries between competing systems, and the glitter of 'science' could well have betrayed the needs of the classroom teacher as the specialists continued to pursue 'completeness', 'accuracy', 'scientific rigour', and so on. Something of the kind was to happen in the early years of the structuralist movement in America in the forties and fifties.

The IPA is a fitting memorial to Passy's philosophical principles as well as his linguistic and educational interests, and his publications show the extent of his concern for different aspects of the subject. His work in descriptive and applied phonetics includes the influential *Les sons du français* (1887, with seven editions before 1914),[16] a dictionary (*Dictionnaire phonétique de la langue française* (1897)), and a general study (*La phonétique et ses applications* (1929)). His teaching materials included works for French as a mother tongue and as a foreign language, as well as for English and German (see the Biographical Note). He may also have been the first writer to use the term 'direct method' in a published work in a pamphlet called *De la méthode directe dans l'enseignement des langues vivantes* in 1899, but for him the label carried Reform Movement connotations rather than the 'conversational' overtones associated with, for example, Berlitz.

What, in the longer term, did phonetics accomplish? The answer depends to some extent on how the term is understood. We have already seen that 'using phonetics' popularly meant teaching a transcription system to learners, and this narrow interpretation became engrained and difficult to eradicate. Abercrombie, for instance, writing in 1949, pointed to 'this common misconception' and stressed again that 'phonetics is *not* identical with phonetic transcription'.[17] At the time of the Reform Movement itself, attitudes towards this issue varied somewhat, though the basic principle was never at issue. Sweet, for instance, believed that transcription should be used almost indefinitely in the teaching of orthographically irregular languages like English and French, and transition to the standard (or 'nomic' as he called it) should be made only when the learner started to read original literature.[18] Palmer took a similar hard line in 1917 and called for 'a minimum of two years'.[19] Others like, for instance, Rippmann (or Ripman) were less demanding: 'for the first term at least, employ the phonetic transcription only',[20] he wrote in an appendix to his English version of Viëtor's *Kleine Phonetik*. Widgery and Jespersen came somewhere in between. 'Phonetical transcription should be used for as long as possible',[21] was Jespersen's tolerant view. By the thirties, Rippmann's suggestion seems to have become standard practice, as a schools inspector of the time noted: 'most people keep on phonetics for a term, a few enthusiasts for a year'.[22] It was used sparingly by the textbook writers of the forties and fifties such as Hornby and Eckersley, and today it rarely appears in materials intended for student use. Its value in teachers' manuals, reference materials, and so on has, of course, never been in doubt.

Phonetics is, however, much more than a system of transcription. As Abercrombie put it, 'the language teacher ... will inevitably be a phonetician'.[23] The important question is the amount of training that is required and the quality of that training. In his emphasis on the role of phonetics in the professional preparation of teachers, Abercrombie echoes Sweet's eloquent demand (1884) for a scientifically trained profession whose members would know the sound-system of their own language as well as that of the foreign language they were responsible for teaching. They would also understand how sounds were produced physiologically, and they would be proficient performers themselves. In the end, Sweet's ambitions were realized in spite of disappointments in his own lifetime, and it would be rare today to find any (non-native) language teacher who had not undergone some training in phonetics.

## The work of Henry Sweet: an applied linguistic approach

Henry Sweet was born in London in 1845 and lived in or near the city for most of his life before moving to Oxford in his later years. After completing his secondary school education at King's College School, he spent a short time studying in Heidelberg and then returned to England to take up an office job with a trading company in London. Five years later, at the age of twenty-four, he entered Balliol College, Oxford, winning a scholarship in German. In 1873 he graduated with a fourth-class degree in *literae humaniores*. He was by that time nearly thirty years of age.

The apparent aimlessness and the failure of Sweet's early career is deceptive. It was the outward and public manifestation of his single-minded pursuit of excellence in his private studies, the first recognition of which came in his first year at Oxford (1869) with the publication of a paper on Old English by the prestigious Philological Society. He later became President of the Society, and was closely involved in the early history of the *Oxford English Dictionary*. After abortive discussions with Macmillans, Sweet wrote to the Delegates of the Oxford University Press offering them, as he put it, 'a share in what promises to be a very safe and remunerative (undertaking)'.[24] This first approach was made in 1877 but it was not until February 1879 that the final agreement was ratified by the Society and, in the meantime, Sweet had fallen out with the Press. Not for the last time, Sweet and Oxford had crossed swords, though the Press was to publish most of his major works, except, as it happens, *The Practical Study of Languages*.

*Figure 23    Henry Sweet (1845–1912). Henry Sweet's reputation as the man who 'taught phonetics to Europe' has long been secure. However, his role as the prime originator of an applied linguistic approach to the teaching of languages has been less widely acknowledged. His classic work in this field,* The Practical Study of Languages, *was published in 1899 after nearly thirty years in preparation.*

During the 1870s Sweet's professional reputation rose with each of his published works, culminating in 1877 with the appearance of the *Handbook of Phonetics, including a Popular Exposition of the Principles of Spelling Reform*, completed while Sweet was in Norway visiting Johan Storm, who, he was later to acknowledge,[25] had provided the 'main impulse' for his interest in the reform of language teaching methodology. As Wrenn commented: 'This book (i.e. the *Handbook*), as has often been remarked, taught phonetics to Europe and made England the birthplace of the modern science'.[26] This famous phrase about 'teaching phonetics to Europe' derives from Onions's entry on Sweet in the *Dictionary of National Biography, 1912–1921*.[27] It does not in fact refer to the *Handbook* but to Sweet's textbook for teaching English as a foreign language to German learners, the *Elementarbuch des gesprochenen Englisch* (1885) which has already been discussed. Not only does Onions misinterpret the purpose of the *Elementarbuch*, he also omits any reference to *The Practical Study of Languages* and hence to Sweet's contribution to the development and reform of language teaching. Wrenn, it is true, does praise *The Practical Study*, but it is only a brief comment in a long paper.[28] In *The Indispensable Foundation* (1971), a collection of Sweet's writings, Henderson concentrates entirely on Sweet's work as a phonetician. It is not, of course, the fault of phoneticians that applied linguists have failed to recognize their founding genius, but it is a fact nonetheless.

As we have said, *The Practical Study* grew out of a paper with almost the same title, 'On the practical study of language', delivered to the Philological Society on the occasion of the Presidential Address by James Murray, the first editor of the *Oxford English Dictionary*, in May 1884 and we shall return to it in detail below. In the following year, Sweet's career suffered a blow which crippled his relationships with colleagues and fellow professionals for the rest of his life. He was passed over for the Chair of English Language and Literature at Merton College, Oxford. It was not the first time he had been turned down for a professorship, nor was it to be the last, but it was the failure that mattered most to him. According to Wrenn, Sweet had been so sure that he would be selected that he had omitted to canvass even his closest colleagues, who were therefore unaware of his interest and voted for another candidate.[29] This lethal mixture of presumption and shyness, coupled with what Wrenn refers to many times as his 'candour', made him a difficult man to like. After the Merton fiasco, he nursed what Shaw described as a 'Satanic contempt for all academic dignitaries and persons in general who thought more of Greek than of phonetics'.[30]

It is well-known that Sweet was the starting-point for Shaw's Henry Higgins in *Pygmalion*, which conjures up a picture in the mind of the modern reader of a debonair mysogynist with a lot of upper-class panache. But although the original *Pygmalion* Higgins is closer to Sweet than the *My Fair Lady* version, Shaw himself insisted that he was 'not a portrait'. There were, however, 'touches of Sweet' in the character, most particularly one suspects in the perfectionist pronunciation teacher of the earlier part of the play.

Academically, the second half of Sweet's career after the 1885 disaster was as distinguished as the first. *A Primer of Spoken English* (an English version of the *Elementarbuch*) appeared in 1890, in the same year as his *Primer of Phonetics*, which became a standard introductory text on the subject. In the last twenty years of his life, he published four major works: *A New English Grammar* (1892 and 1898), *The Practical Study of Languages* (1899), *The History of Language* (1900) and his final contribution to phonetics, *The Sounds of English* (1908). After 1901 he was employed by Oxford University as a Reader in Phonetics, a consolation prize for another failure to secure a Chair. Shaw's comment on this not unexpected defeat probably expressed the thoughts of most people, including Sweet's admirers, as Shaw himself certainly was: 'I do not blame Oxford, because I think Oxford is quite right in demanding a certain social amenity from its nurslings (heaven knows it is not exorbitant in its requirements!)'.[31]

There were two passions in Sweet's life: phonetics and England. He was an intensely patriotic man in a style that the modern world cannot easily respond to. Many people have the same difficulty in finding sympathy with the poetry of Kipling, for instance, or some of the early music of Elgar. Sweet died before such attitudes were tested to destruction in Flanders and perhaps those events would have had the same impact on him as they did on Elgar himself. We cannot know. Both these passions were expressed in a passage towards the end of his 1884 paper on the reform of language teaching which is of great significance in the history of the subject since it articulates for the first time the partnership between the science of language and the science of learning which acts as the corner-stone of applied linguistics:

> The general result we have arrived at is the recognition of a science of *living*, as opposed to dead, or antiquarian philology, based on phonology[32] and psychology. This science in its practical application is the indispensable foundation of the study of our own and foreign languages, of dialectology, and of historical and comparative philology. It is of the greatest importance to England.[33]

Part of Sweet's motivation in writing the last sentence was his conviction that, given the proper training rooted in the study and the practice of phonetics, native Englishmen could teach foreign languages as well, if not better, than the 'swarms of foreigners, most of them very indifferently prepared for their task'[34] that dominated the profession at the time. He was a committed believer in the non-native-speaking teacher of languages: 'For teaching Germans English, a phonetically trained German is far superior to an untrained Englishman, the latter being quite unable to communicate his knowledge; and this principle applies, of course, with equal force to the teaching of foreign languages in England'.[35] He expressed the point less emotively in his 1899 book, but repeated the substance of the issue, believing it to be part of his life's work to found a strong national language teaching profession.[36]

Sweet's overall aim in *The Practical Study of Languages* was to devise, in a phrase he used many times, 'a rationally progressive method'[37] of practical language study which included the teaching and learning of foreign languages in schools, but it was also intended as a 'comprehensive general view of the whole field'. The plan of the book makes it clear what he had in mind. It is divided into three main sections. The first (Chapters 2–7) deals in detail with the teaching of phonetics and its practical application in pronunciation teaching and the use of transcription, culminating in a statement of his fundamental principle: 'start with the spoken language'. The next seven chapters contain a superbly sustained and coolly logical exploration of methodological principles and practices covering the five major areas of practical language learning: grammar, vocabulary, the study of texts, translation, and conversation. It is unsurpassed in the literature of linguistic pedagogy. The book closes with a series of essays on specific topics such as the study of a foreign literature, the learning of classical and what he calls 'remoter' languages, and the original investigation of unwritten languages. The techniques he proposes for such 'original investigation' are strikingly similar to those suggested later by Bloomfield in his influential 1942 pamphlet with a title that must be a deliberate echo of Sweet, *An Outline Guide for the Practical Study of Foreign Languages*. More by accident than by design, this document was to provide the blueprint for the 'structural approach' of the American applied linguists in the forties and fifties.

*The Practical Study* has little to say about education or the place of language teaching in the curriculum and Sweet's attempts to cover the topic in the final chapter of the book are rather perfunctory. However, this is consistent with his basic aim announced in the opening pages: 'I am not much concerned with such questions as, Why do we learn languages? . . . Our first business is to find out the most efficient and economical way of learning them'.[38] This bias has, until very recently, been a recurrent feature of applied linguistic approaches to language teaching.

The *Study* begins with the uncompromising statement that 'all study of language must be based on phonetics'[39] and then goes on to outline what this means in practice. Phonetics provides an analytic framework and a practical methodolgy for the acquistion of an accurate pronunciation. Secondly, it offers a more reliable system of sound-notation than traditional orthography, and, finally, it serves as the scientific discipline on which a principled approach to the training of language teachers can be built.

The importance Sweet attached to accurate pronunciation as the foundation of successful language learning made it imperative for the learner to acquire a knowledge of phonetics himself. It was, he believed, a 'popular fallacy' ('fallacy' is Sweet's favourite term of disapproval), to believe that a good pronunciation could be achieved by imitation alone. This was not the view of all the reformers, it should be added, particularly those with more experience of teaching in schools. Jespersen, for example, had a much more moderate attitude: 'Phonetics is not a new study that we want to add to the school curriculum; we only want to take as much of the science as will really be a positive help in learning something which has to be learnt *anyway*'.[40] Widgery, while he shared the general view that children should learn how their vocal organs worked in producing sounds, treated the topic very informally with his pupils. For example, in determining the place in the mouth where the different consonants are produced, 'the class must not be helped too much, but left to think for itself. At first the answers will be very wild, but by pitting boys with the most divergent fancies against one another, clearness comes in time'.[41]

The second 'popular fallacy' that interfered with good pronunciation teaching was the notion that it did not matter very much. 'Experience shows', Sweet retorted, 'that even the slightest distinctions of sound cannot be disregarded without the danger of unintelligibility'.[42] This is not in fact as extremist as it sounds. What Sweet had in mind were the basic phonemic contrasts in the language, as his examples, *man/men*, *head/had*, show quite clearly. The term 'phoneme' was not in general use in the 1890s (Firth traced it back to an essay by a student of Baudouin de Courtenay called Kruszewski in 1879),[43] so Sweet's remarks about 'the slightest distinctions' or 'minute distinctions'[44] make him sound more finicky than he actually was. Alongside this introduction to pronunciation, the learner was expected to learn phonetic notation, to which Sweet devotes a lengthy section of the first part of the book.

From Chapter 7 onwards, however, Sweet moves away from his specialist interests and begins to weave them into a broader pattern of linguistic pedagogy. At this point *The Practical Study* moves to an altogether different and higher plane of achievement. Though there had been flashes of insight in the work of earlier writers like Prendergast and, particularly, Marcel, no one before Sweet had explored the intellectual foundations of practical methodology with a comparable economy of expression or acuity of mind. At the heart of his approach was the partnership between linguistics and psychology that he had announced at the close of his 1884 paper.

Sweet adopted the theory of psychology which was dominant at the end of the nineteenth century, namely *associationism*. Following the associationist principle meant that the learner's central task was to form and maintain correct associations both between linguistic elements within the language, and between these elements and the outside world. Fluency in the spoken language implied the establishment of well-practised associations along the stream of speech in the production of smooth and intelligible utterances, and the avoidance of 'cross-associations' through, for instance, the misuse of translation. Sweet's system of transcription, which we have already seen in the Klinghardt experiment (see p. 174), is a good example of the principle in practice. Orthographically distinct words are assimilated into speech-units in transcription, giving, for instance, **aksebo** for the French *ah, que c'est beau*.[45]

Forster's 'only connect' might have been the slogan of the Reform Movement. Lists of disconnected words were rejected ('stones for bread' as Jespersen puts it rather memorably),[46] so too were isolated sentences strung together in incongruous sequences ('the arithmetical fallacy').[47] Both offended against the principle of association. Only a connected, coherent text allowed the learner to form and strengthen the correct associations, and only after it had been thoroughly studied and assimilated should the teacher draw out of it such generalizations, grammar points and vocabulary items as he felt the need to teach.

The isolated sentence had a specific role to play in the new methods. Instead of being the vehicle for the presentation of new linguistic information, it became 'the real bridge across the gulf between texts and grammar'.[48] This is what Sweet meant by the 'inductive' teaching of grammar. What he did *not* mean was a process of 'discovery' on the part of the learner, or, as this notion was called at the time, 'invention'. He foresaw this danger and, in a very interesting passage in the book, warned teachers against 'inventional methods':

> There is certainly something plausible in the idea of making the learner's progress consist in finding out by himself the solution of a series of problems of progressive difficulty . . . but although these inventional methods excite great interest at first in the minds of the more gifted pupils, those who are less original and slower in mind instinctively rebel against them, and all, sooner or later, get tired of their sham originality.[49]

In exposing the 'inventional fallacy', Sweet pointed to the dilemma it posed for the average learner:

> If the work really requires much thought or originality of mind, it will be too difficult for them, or, at any rate, will cause them to make so many mistakes that the labour of establishing correct associations will be far greater than it is worth; if, on the other hand, the work is so

easy as not to tax the intellectual powers of the pupils, it will cease to excite their interest.[50]

The inductive approach meant in practice that teachers should collect examples of the new grammar from the text, demonstrate and explain how they worked, and help pupils to draw the appropriate conclusions. But 'there will be no harm in varying the course . . . by an occasional application of the inventive method'.[51]

Given the role of texts in the success of the reformed method, their selection and grading were obviously important. Sweet believed in using natural texts, and would probably have approved of the modern 'authentic text' movement. 'If we try to make our texts embody certain definite grammatical categories, the texts cease to be natural: they become either trivial, tedious, and long-winded, or else they become more or less monstrosities'.[52] On the other hand, he was aware that 'if the texts are perfectly free and natural, they cannot be brought into any definite relation to the grammar'.[53] His solution to this dilemma was to rely on the skill of the textbook writer to produce natural texts which were simple enough to be comprehensible to the elementary learner but would not distort the language by forcing it into pre-determined grammatical categories. There was no reason why any teacher should have to deal with 'everything' in a text, and, therefore, no need to straitjacket the texts inside a grammatical syllabus. This is a fairly sophisticated solution to the problem. Unfortunately, it was discarded later and textbooks reverted to presenting 'one thing at a time', with the result that the early lessons offer a rather meagre diet of language while later ones constantly re-use a narrow range of grammatical points that have already been 'introduced'.

Sweet's system of grading was based on a functional typology of texts, starting from descriptive ones, which he believed were the simplest linguistically, moving to narratives and, finally, dialogues. Descriptions fulfilled his four criteria for good teaching texts: they were direct, clear, simple, and familiar.[54] They also permitted a wide range of factual subject-matter, which he preferred to anecdotes and dialogues. His *Elementarbuch* texts, for instance, were adapted from works on physiography, anthropology, and other sciences and social sciences, for example:

> Nature: the earth, the sea, the River Thames, the sun, the seasons, the months, the days of the week, light, colours.
> Man: different races of men, tools and weapons, food, houses, clothes, language.[55]

Factual texts of this kind had the linguistic advantage of requiring simple verb phrases. Most of the verbs were in the present tense, for instance, and there was little need for variation. Other tense forms would arise naturally out of the narrative texts later: past tenses obviously, and certain uses of the perfect aspect. The story-line itself would also help to hold the text together as a connected whole. Contrary to modern opinion, however, Sweet believed that dialogues presented the most difficult linguistic problems: modal verbs, question-and-answer forms, and so on. They were also the most difficult to write, and should never be attempted by non-native speakers.

It is clear from this order of priorities that when Sweet talked about teaching the spoken language first, he did not mean what would be meant today. Spoken interaction, or conversation, was the end-point of classroom instruction, not its point of departure. He had little time for 'natural methods' based on conversation in the classroom. The process of learning one's mother tongue was, he believed, 'carried on under peculiarly favourable circumstances, which cannot even be approximately reproduced in the later study of foreign languages'.[56] Moreover, older learners possessed advantages of maturity which were unavailable to infants. 'The fundamental objection to the natural method' was that 'it puts the adult into the position of an infant, which he is no longer capable of utilizing, and, at the same time, does not allow him to make use of his own special advantages ... the power of analysis and generalization – in short, the power of using a grammar and dictionary'.[57]

New vocabulary should be firmly controlled in a rational method, even if this conflicted with the intrinsic interest of the text, and he reckoned that 3,000 common words would probably suffice[58] for all except specialist purposes. He was also severely practical in his selection of words: objects in the house, articles of clothing, food and drink, etc. These were important items to know, even if they were not very exciting. 'Be dull and commonplace', he said at one point,[59] adding carefully, 'but not too much so.' He had the somewhat puritanical belief that interesting materials distracted the learner from the language being learnt. There is, nevertheless, something in what he says. Interest derives from lessons, not from textbooks. Also, interest can be fickle, and he was particularly scathing about Gouin's claim that 'interest' was the basis for the success of the 'series' method: 'We may be sure that if a year afterwards Gouin's nephew had to go through the same mill-series in a foreign language, the old interest would not have been forthcoming, and the youth would perhaps have declined to take part in any series in which tin soldiers and a pop-gun did not figure'.[60]

Sweet drew the threads of his methodology together in a graded curriculum consisting of five stages. First, there was the *Mechanical Stage* during which the learner concentrated on acquiring a good pronunciation and becoming familiar with phonetic transcription. How long this was to last is unclear (Sweet never commits himself on questions of this kind), but the answer appears to be 'as long as necessary': 'In the case of immature or slow minds the first stage may be indefinitely prolonged'.[61] One cannot help feeling that he might have modified this attitude if he had been faced with 'immature or slow minds' more often in a classroom.

The second, *Grammatical Stage*, was described in detail in the Klinghardt experiment. The learner began to work on the texts, gradually building up his knowledge of the grammar and acquiring a basic vocabulary. The third, *Idiomatic Stage* dealt almost exclusively with the learner's lexical development. This completed the basic course, while Stages Four and Five (*Literary* and *Archaic* respectively) were university-level studies devoted to literature and philology. Only at Stage Four could the transition to the standard orthography be made without risking a deterioration in the learner's pronunciation. As we have seen, Klinghardt made the change during Stage Two without, it seems, much difficulty.

In modern eyes, Sweet's curriculum seems excessively linguistic. It also presupposes a learner rather like himself: assiduous, systematic, and deeply absorbed in the subject for its own sake. However, with Sweet the learner is never sharply in focus. At times he appears to be the grammar-school pupil that the other reformers had in mind, but at others, he is the kind of educated adult student of English that came to Sweet for private lessons at his house in Reigate. Sweet's learner is an abstraction rather than a real person with likes and dislikes, capacities and limitations, whose progress varies from lesson to lesson, the sort of individual that emerges, for example, in the writing of Jespersen. There is no doubt that Sweet's concern for his learner is genuine enough, but in the end it is rather lonely, the perfect teacher with the perfect learner in an entirely rational world.

Given the purpose of this book, the emphasis has naturally been on those aspects of *The Practical Study* most closely concerned with language teaching methodology. Even in this area, however, much of interest has had to be omitted: Sweet's detailed suggestions for the teaching of grammar, for example, his proposals for a 'logical dictionary' along Rogetian lines, his comments on translation, his advice to learners studying on their own, and many other things. It would be wrong, however, to leave the reader with the impression that Sweet intended 'the practical study of language' to refer *only* to the teaching and learning of languages. He had a wider purpose in mind, namely the establishment of a new science which could be applied to all forms of practical linguistic activity including dialectology, the investigation of hitherto unwritten languages, problems in historical philology, and so on, as well as language teaching. Unfortunately, however, he did not give his new field of study a name, which brings me to the final point.

In the key passage from the 1884 paper already quoted,[62] Sweet talks about the application of 'living' as opposed to 'antiquarian' philology, and uses the expression 'living philology' regularly throughout the book in a sense which essentially corresponds to the modern interpretation of 'linguistics'. By neglecting to label the activity of 'applying living philology to the practical study of languages', he left a semantic gap which was later filled by the term 'applied linguistics' in America in the 1940s.

Sweet came tantalizingly close to calling his subject 'practical philology'. Although he used the term, he did not pursue it.[63] Had he done so, we might now be in the fortunate position of being able to distinguish between 'practical linguistics' as the term for activities associated with language teaching and other practical matters, and 'applied linguistics' as a more appropriate label for activities more closely dependent on theoretical studies such as, for example, devising linguistic descriptions. Nomenclature apart, Sweet's work established an applied linguistic tradition in language teaching which has continued uninterruptedly to the present day.

## Notes

1 *Englische Studien*, X, 1887, 48–80.
2 Widgery (1888: 20).
3 Quousque Tandem informally translated means 'How long is all this going to go on for?' It is the opening challenge in Cicero's address to the Senate on the Catiline conspiracy.
4 Jespersen was a founder member.
5 Viëtor (1886 edition: 16), see Appendix in this volume.
6 Ibid.: 27, see Appendix in this volume.
7 Jespersen (1904: 143).
8 cf. Abercrombie (1949a).
9/10 Klinghardt (1888: 14). The notation (modified from Sweet's original) was italicized by Klinghardt's printer.
11 From the third improved edition of the *Elementarbuch* (1904).
12 The neo-grammarian emphasis on the rigorous study of genuine language data exerted considerable influence on the intellectual development of the Reform Movement. (See Robins 1967: 182–92.) I am indebted to John Trim for drawing my attention to the importance of this link.
13 See Kelly (1981).
14 Firth (1946/1957a: 116–9), a useful source of information about the Bell family, in spite of Firth's double-edged motivation for including it.
15 Sweet (1877: vii).
16 Translated as *The Sounds of the French Language* and published by Oxford University Press in 1907.
17 Abercrombie (1949a: 114).

18  Sweet (1899/1964: 121).
19  Palmer (1917/1968: 130).
20  Rippmann (1910: 142).
21  Jespersen (1904: 173).
22  Brereton (1930: 50).
23  Abercrombie (1949a: 115).
24  Murray (1977: 342).
25  Sweet (1884: 578).
26  From Wrenn's Presidential Address to the Philological Society in 1946 to mark the (slightly delayed) centenary of Sweet's birth. Wrenn (1946: 182).
27  *Dictionary of National Biography, 1912–1921*: 519.
28  Wrenn (1946: 191).
29  Ibid.: 9.
30  Preface to *Pygmalion*, Penguin edition (1967: 6).
31  Ibid.: 9.
32  In an almost identical quotation in *The Practical Study of Languages* (p.1), Sweet uses *phonetics* rather than *phonology*. His use of the two terms seems to have changed over time. In his Presidential Address to the Philological Society in 1877, they appear to be synonymous. In his *History of Language* (1900), *phonology* refers to 'the whole science of speech sounds'. Later it changed again, (see Henderson (1971: 26–8)).
33  Sweet (1884: 593).
34  Ibid.: 594.
35  Ibid.: 583.
36  Sweet (1899/1964: 47).
37  Ibid.: 116.
38  Ibid.: 5.
39  Ibid.: 4.
40  Jespersen (1904: 143).
41  Widgery (1888: 23).
42  Sweet (1899/1964: 6).
43  Firth (1934/1957a: 1).
44  Sweet (1899/1964: 5). He also used the term *significant sound-distinctions* (p.18), which is even closer to the phoneme notion.
45  Ibid.: 9.
46  Jespersen (1904: 11).
47  Sweet (1899/1964: 24).
48  Ibid.: 191.
49/50  Ibid.: 115.
51  Ibid.: 116.
52  Ibid.: 190–1.
53  Ibid.: 190.
54  Ibid.: 163.

55  Ibid.: 165.
56  Ibid.: 74.
57  Ibid.: 75.
58  Ibid.: 172.
59  Ibid.: 113.
60  Ibid.: 112–13.
61  Ibid.: 118.
62  Ibid.: 1.
63  Sweet (1884: 594).

# 14  Natural methods of language teaching from Montaigne to Berlitz

The communicative language teaching methods which have attracted a great deal of interest over the last ten years are the most recent manifestation of ideas that have appealed to the imagination of teachers for a very long time, and which were last revived about a hundred and twenty years ago by native-speaking immigrant teachers in America. These ideas have been known by a variety of labels (Natural Method, Conversation Method, Direct Method, Communicative Approach, and so on), and the classroom techniques associated with them have also changed from time to time. But the underlying philosophy has remained constant. Learning how to speak a new language, it is held, is not a rational process which can be organized in a step-by-step manner following graded syllabuses of new points to learn, exercises and explanations. It is an intuitive process for which human beings have a natural capacity that can be awakened provided only that the proper conditions exist. Put simply, there are three such conditions: someone to talk to, something to talk about, and a desire to understand and make yourself understood. *Interaction* is at the heart of natural language acquisition, or *conversation* as Lambert Sauveur called it when he initiated the revival of interest that led eventually to the Direct Method.

The most celebrated early example of natural foreign language teaching was the story of Michel de Montaigne in the sixteenth century, and Sauveur never ceased using his famous compatriot as the model learner. It is a very well-known story, but an essential component in the folklore of language teaching.

Montaigne's father was determined that his son should have every possible advantage in life, and in particular a perfect education. This led him to the idea of bringing the boy up as a native speaker of Latin, an experience that Montaigne himself described later in his *Essay on the Education of Children* (1580):

> While I was at nurse and before the first loosing of my tongue, he put me in charge of a German, totally ignorant of our language and very well versed in Latin . . . (This man) carried me around constantly; and with him he had two others less learned to look after me and relieve him. None of them spoke to me in any language but Latin. As for the

rest of the house, it was an inviolable rule that neither my father nor my mother, nor any manservant nor maid, should utter in my presence anything but such Latin words as each of them had learnt in order to chat with me. It was wonderful how much they all profited by this.[1]

Montaigne's wry comment that everybody else got more out of the experiment than he did himself was justified, in his eyes at least, by the fact that when he went to school at the age of seven or so:

> My Latin immediately grew corrupt, and through lack of practice I have since lost all use of it. The only service that this new method of education did me was to let me skip the lower classes at the beginning. For when I left school at thirteen, I had finished the course – as they call it – and really without any benefit that I can now note in its favour.[2]

In view of his later achievements in scholarship and literature, he may have been a little unfair on his father. In some ways the most interesting feature of this story is not that he learnt Latin as an infant – it would have been difficult not to have done so – but that he became one of the great masters of the French language which, it seems, he did not encounter until he was seven years old. Montaigne usefully pricks the mystical bubble surrounding the 'deep significance of the mother tongue'. But that is another story.

Natural language learning, though not on the Montaigne model, was commonplace before 1800 because of the preference among those who could afford it of having children educated at home. Many of the Huguenot refugees found employment as tutors of French in the houses of the well-to-do and taught the children French by talking to them. It was not necessary to be a member of the aristocracy to have such ambitions for one's family. Edward Clarke, for instance, the addressee of John Locke's celebrated 'open letter' *Some Thoughts Concerning Education* (1693) was a Somerset gentleman. As Locke put it:

> Men learn languages for the ordinary intercourse of Society and Communication of thoughts in common Life without any further design in their use of them. And for this purpose, the Original way of Learning a Language by Conversation, not only serves well enough, but is to be prefer'd as the most Expedite, Proper and Natural.[3]

Locke goes on to explain that, while there are special categories of learner for whom a detailed knowledge of grammar is essential, the 'natural' approach is the fundamental one, applicable to all in the early stages:

> As soon as he can speak *English*, 'tis time for him to learn some other Language: this no body doubts of, when *French* is proposed. And the

Reason is, because People are accustomed to the right way of teaching that Language, which is by talking it into Children in constant Conversation and not by Grammatical Rules. The *Latin* tongue would easily be taught the same way if his Tutor, being constantly with him, would talk nothing else to him, and make him answer still in the same Language.[4]

Both the Montaigne experiment and Locke's advice to his friend were concerned with the private education of individual children working with tutors at home. The application of 'natural methods' to the teaching of larger groups and school classes presents different problems. J. S. Blackie, a nineteenth-century Scots professor of Latin and Greek, included the following account of an early sixteenth-century 'direct method' lesson in an article he wrote for the *Foreign Quarterly Review* in 1845. The description came originally from a work called *Polyhistor* (1688),[5] an encyclopaedia of contemporary knowledge, by the German historian Morhof. It depicts the Latin lessons of a teacher called Nicholas Clenard[6] who gathered together 'a multitude of the most motley description: there were some boys scarcely five years old; there were clergymen; negro servants; and some very old men.' Parents came along too and 'yielded obedience to the master as pointedly as the youngest tyro.' Once this extraordinary bunch had congregated together, Clenard began to teach them:

> I commenced immediately talking nothing but Latin, and by constant practice, succeeded to such a degree, that within a few months they all understood whatever I said, and the smallest boys babbled Latin fluently after their fashion, when they scarcely knew their alphabet. For I did not vex their tender brains prematurely with things too hard for them, but whatever they knew I taught them in sport, so that my school became a *ludus*, in the original sense of that word, not in name only but in deed.[7]

Unfortunately, Clenard says little about his older learners. In this extract he describes his method in more detail:

> I endeavoured by every possible means, as merchants learn the idioms of various foreign countries by intercourse with the natives, to cause the ears of my pupils, in every corner, to be assailed by Latin words, and Latin words only . . . If in the course of our talking, any sentiment or adage presented itself, comprised in a few words, it was immediately set into circulation through the whole class, and as hand rubs hand, communicated from one to another, while I stood by as they were talking, and made the thing more evident by gesticulations.[8]

The central section of Blackie's article, which leads, eventually, to a review of new textbooks by Ollendorff and others, is remarkable for a detailed natural-method teaching syllabus in eighteen steps beginning with object lessons and closing with a carefully organized reading development programme. It follows a vividly expressed denunciation not only of existing methods but also of public attitudes towards foreign language teaching and the appalling state of the teaching profession. Denunciations were common enough, even if few were expressed as entertainingly as Blackie's (he was trained as an advocate and skilled in expansive rhetoric), and the article would not be worth discussing were it not for the teaching syllabus. Blackie begins by re-asserting the basic philosophy of all 'natural methods':

> All persons being normal and healthy specimens of the genus *homo*, can speak; and by the same natural capability that they do speak one language, they could speak two, three, four and half-a-dozen, if only external circumstances were favourable for such a result.[9]

External circumstances in mid-nineteenth-century Britain were, however, extremely unfavourable. The teachers themselves were partly to blame ('the masters have been bunglers').[10] But they had to contend with 'the culpable indifference and neglect of the British people to the interests of education generally.'[11] Nor does Blackie exonerate his native Scotland 'where they long delighted themselves to make loud boasts of their "parochial schools"' in which 'the "dominie" was and in great measure is, the lean and meagre product which the neglect of a money-making population, the shabbiness of a "game-preserving aristocracy", and the jealousy of a half-educated church, have starved out of all fellowship with living society, and banished from every possible contact with politeness'.[12] Things were no better elsewhere. The teachers of classical languages had proved themselves 'heavy and unproductive hulks', and the teachers of modern languages were, if anything, even worse. Public neglect had meant that languages were taught by 'any poor Polish refugee, German baron, or Italian marchese, that can find nothing better to do'.[13] Blackie's final target is the textbook writers, 'the swarms of superficial quacks and empirics of all kinds, who perambulate the country and the booksellers' shops, big with their own praises, and fertile every one in his own infallible method to master the most difficult language of Europe in six weeks, or it may be six days'.[14] This last piece of barbed invective was directed specifically at Ollendorff with his claim to teach a language in six months. After all this, Sweet's complaint about 'swarms of foreigners' dominating the teaching profession in England sounds positively restrained (see Chapter 13).

What was needed was a systematic method for teaching languages which was neither pedantic nor promised more than it could hope to deliver. The obvious basis for such a method was Nature:

> The more near a method approaches to the method employed by Nature the more near does that method approach to perfection . . .

What then are the elements of this natural method? 'Tis a simple affair. First: there is a direct appeal to the ear, the natural organs by which the language is acquired. Secondly: this appeal is made in circumstances where there is a direct relation, *ipso facto*, established between the sound and the thing signified . . . Thirdly: the same living appeal to the ear is continuously and for a considerable length of time repeated. Fourthly: the appeal is made under circumstances which cannot fail strongly to excite the attention, and to engage the sympathies of the hearer. In these four points, lies the whole plain mystery of Nature's method.[15]

Blackie's four points sum up everything that has been said about natural or direct methods of language teaching (he even uses the adjective *direct* twice in the above quotation). Teach the spoken language first, relate the words of the new language directly to their referents in the outside world, practise, and work as hard as possible to gain and keep the learner's interest.

Having pointed out where existing methods fall down on each of the four points, Blackie outlines his eighteen-step syllabus for 'a well-ordered system of linguistical study'.[16]

Steps 1–4   The teacher should start with objects, 'baptizing them audibly with their several designations', and get the learner to repeat them. The new words should then be written on the blackboard, and practised along with 'a few turns and variations' introduced 'ever and anon'.

Step 5   Writing should be introduced, 'offering its tangible body as a sort of test to examine the more vague and fleeting element of speech'.

Step 6   Here Blackie suggests something very interesting, extended listening practice in the form of 'short and easy lectures' on 'any object of natural history, a picture, a map, or any thing that admits of being described in few and simple sentences'. Harold Palmer was to press for the same thing in a technique he called 'subconscious comprehension'.[17]

Step 7   'Grammar may now be introduced, or rather deduced out of the preceding practice'. A remarkable statement for its time, but, as we have already seen, the 'inductive approach to grammar teaching' was not invented by the Reform Movement, though their use of it was more consistent.

Steps 8–18  The second phase of Blackie's programme consists of a graded reading scheme starting with simple materials 'suited to the stage of linguistical progress where the pupil stands' and, interesting for him to read. 'It is on this point that we see learned and excellent persons most apt to err', he warns.

We have to remind ourselves that Blackie's article is a review of Ollendorff's first published textbook. Marcel was not to publish his great work for another eight years and the horrors of late grammar-translation methodology had not been perpetrated. Blackie's 'direct method' curriculum fell to the bottom of the well like a stone. A generation later, the same ideas and the same practical suggestions surfaced again, only this time attached to names that have survived rather better than his.

The true roots of natural language teaching methods lie deep in the art of teaching itself. They may owe something to organized pedagogy, but not a great deal, even less to psychology and virtually nothing to linguistics. In this sense they represent the 'alter ego' or 'mirror image' of rational teaching methods such as those put forward by the Reform Movement. Fittingly, the modern tradition of natural approaches originated in the work and example of a teacher of genius, Johann Heinrich Pestalozzi (1746–1827).

Pestalozzi is even more difficult to characterize than Comenius (see Chapter 3). They both had a Pied Piper quality of magic that fascinated children. Pestalozzi could hold the attention of his class for hours at a time simply by talking to them but, unlike Comenius, he found it impossible to explain the secret of this remarkable gift to anyone else. He liked to express his ideas on education obliquely through the medium of novels which were both powerful and obscure, the product of a deeply-felt sympathy for the poor of rural Switzerland and an emotional attachment to the simplicity of life in daily contact with the elements and the processes of nature. But he was not a good administrator, his attempts to found a school failed, and his practical classroom techniques, in so far as they were made explicit in his writings, often seem dull and commonplace. To put it crudely, it was not what Pestalozzi did that mattered, it was the way he did it.

For many people the famous 'object lessons' represented the Pestalozzian 'method', which was scarcely what he had in mind, but it was at least a concrete idea that could be used. Applied to language teaching, they provided a workable system for elementary classes (*This is a book. It is red. It is on the table*, etc.) but it was difficult to know what to do once the objects failed to provide sufficiently complex stimuli for linguistic activities. As we have seen (Chapter 12), Marcel was attracted to the notion, but considered it suitable only for younger pupils, and the Direct Method itself peters out in a fog somewhere around the intermediate level. One of the most valuable contributions of modern communicative methodology has been to provide a framework for the development of more advanced linguistic activities, to pick up where the Direct Method leaves off.

One of Pestalozzi's disciples in Germany was a schoolteacher called Gottlieb Heness who applied the object-lesson technique to the teaching of standard German (*Hochdeutsch*) to his dialect-speaking pupils in south Germany. His success encouraged him to think of broadening the method to the teaching of German as a foreign language, and an opportunity to experiment along these lines came while he was on a trip to America in 1865. He offered to teach German for nine months to a group of children of the staff of Yale University where he was working. As often happens with informal experiments of this kind, it was an outstanding success and Heness decided to extend the idea even further and set up a language school of his own. For commercial reasons, however, he needed to offer French as well as German and looked around for a native-speaking Frenchman to join him in the venture. He eventually found him in the person of an extraordinary man called Lambert Sauveur (1826–1907).

Sauveur had emigrated to the United States some time in the late 1860s and came across Heness in New Haven, Connecticut. He ran a French course along Heness's lines for faculty members at Yale which seems to have gone well. At all events, Sauveur was enthusiastic: 'After this time they were almost as French as I, and I have afterwards passed with them more than one evening without hearing a word of English pronounced'.[18] Like most of the Heness-Sauveur courses it consisted of a hundred hours of intensive instruction, two hours a day, five days a week, for four and a half months.

Sauveur and Heness moved to Boston in 1869 and opened a School of Modern Languages in the city. It prospered, and five years later they described their ideas and experiences in two related publications, one by Sauveur for French and the other an adaptation for German by Heness. It is Sauveur's work, *An Introduction to the Teaching of Living Languages without Grammar or Dictionary* (1874), that has survived and we shall concentrate on it for the rest of this section.

Sauveur's *Introduction* was originally intended as a kind of 'teacher's manual' to accompany his 'coursebook' *Causeries avec mes élèves* (also 1874). But *Causeries* (Conversations) was not what we would now understand by a textbook. It consists of a series of idealized conversations such as might have taken place in Sauveur's classroom during the course of a lesson. To give an impression of the work, here is an extract (with a translation) from Chapter 10 called *Les Oreilles – Les Écouteurs* (literally, *Ears – Listeners*). The material is laid out in the continuous dialogue form shown below:

> Revenons aux parties du corps.
> Nous avons deux oreilles, une de chaque côté de la tête. L'oreille est l'organe de l'ouïe. Entendez-vous? – Oui, j'entends. – C'est un grand bonheur d'entendre. Le sourd n'entend pas, il est misérable. Est-il malheureux? – Je ne sais pas. – C'est bien. Les misérables ne sont pas nécessairement malheureux. – Le vieillard entend-il? – Oui, plus ou moins; il y a des vieillards qui sont presque sourds. Il y en qui sont tout-à-fait sourds.[19]

> (Let us return to the parts of the body.
> We have two ears, one on each side of the head. The ear is the organ of hearing. Can you hear? Yes, I can hear. We are very fortunate to be able to hear. The deaf cannot hear, they are unfortunate. Are they unhappy? I don't know. Right, the unfortunate are not necessarily unhappy. Can old people hear? Yes, more or less: some old people are almost deaf. Others are completely deaf.)

Sauveur's students did not start the book until they had spent at least a month entirely on intensive oral work in class. In a sense the *Causeries* texts function as a written reminder of the classwork rather than as the starting-point of a lesson. With material as unfamiliar as this, it is not surprising that the teachers Sauveur was training on his summer schools demanded a more explicit guide to the new methods, and the *Introduction* was the outcome.

Sauveur was, above all, a gifted and immensely enthusiastic language teacher, utterly committed to his vocation and possessed with boundless energy. The first chapter of the *Introduction* conveys the spirit of his work admirably. He begins with 'The First Lesson':

> The most beautiful lesson that I can imagine of any kind, and assuredly the most interesting that there can be, is the first lesson given to a class learning a language without grammar. There is no orator, were it even Demosthenes, who can hold a public more attentive, more eagerly expectant of every word, than the professor who is giving his first lesson. Not one of his movements is lost. His word, his eye, his gesture, his whole person, speaks; and he is in possession of the undivided mind of those who are before him. During two or three hours, neither they nor he have had a single distraction, even for a second.
>
> Is it astonishing, think you? And is there a work more interesting than this, or a greater?[20]

Sauveur conveys better than any other writer what it is that makes teaching magical. It is a gift that not many people possess and it is also very difficult to translate into concrete terms. There is little doubt that his trainees would either have left his courses brimming over with enthusiasm or would have packed it in on the first day, there are no half-measures with men like Sauveur. But whether they would know what to do in the classroom is another matter. However, Sauveur does try:

> What is then, this lesson? It is a conversation during two hours *in the French language* with twenty persons who know nothing of this language. After five minutes only, I am carrying on a dialogue with them, and this dialogue does not cease. It continues the following days, and ends only the last day of the year. Not a word of English is pronounced, and every thing is understood, and all talk. (I have never seen a single pupil who did not understand and talk from this first hour).[21]

His boundless self-confidence obviously communicated itself to his learners. He *expected* them to understand, so they did. Also, he never 'corrected' them. He certainly picked up linguistic points and discussed them, but they were 'investigations' not offences against French.

Next Sauveur tries to clarify his classroom technique by providing a 'transcription' of a 'typical lesson'. It reads rather like the extract from the *Causeries*:

> Here is the finger. Look. Here is the forefinger, here is the middle finger, here is the ring-finger, here is the little finger, and here is the thumb. Do you see the finger, madame? Yes, you see the finger and I see the finger. Do you see the finger, monsieur? – Yes, I see the finger. – Do you see the forefinger, madame? – Yes, I see the forefinger. – And you, monsieur? etc.[22]

He claimed that this first lesson contained 120–130 words, all of which were assimilated during the two-hour class period. 'It is a serious acquisition', as he said. The first five lessons are on parts of the body and obviously he made considerable use of gesture in conveying meaning. He does not appear to have used pictures much. What he was able to do easily, and most people find difficult, was to talk to his students in such a way that they did not fail to understand what he was getting at, even if perhaps they did not understand 'every word'. He had an intuitive knowledge of his students' 'internalized competence' and succeeded in organizing and controlling his own discourse in such a way that it 'matched' the interpretive capacities of his learners.

He was not unaware of what he was doing, and the most interesting sections of the *Introduction* relate to his advice on how to talk to learners. This is, I believe, the heart of all 'natural methods' and cannot be replaced by 'oral techniques in the classroom'. He followed two basic principles. The first was only to ask what he called 'earnest questions'. What he meant was genuine questions, not in the sense that he was seeking information he did not possess, but in the sense that he was genuinely looking for an answer. There is a view at the present time that the only genuine classroom questions are ones to which the teacher does not already know the answer, like 'What's the time, please?' when he has forgotten his watch or it has stopped or something of the kind. The argument is that all other 'questions' are merely code-practising devices. This is not, it seems to me, necessarily the case. If, for instance, a teacher holds up four fingers and asks 'How many fingers am I holding up?', it may not be a 'real' question, but it is a genuine one provided the teacher takes the answer seriously.

Sauveur's second principle of linguistic organization in the use of classroom language was *coherence*: 'to connect scrupulously the questions in such a manner that one may give rise to another'.[23] This principle probably explains his success in communicating with his students better than anything else. They understood what he was talking about because they were able to predict the course of the conversation. A great many 'direct method' courses break the rule that human learners are able to 'learn from the context' because they switch incoherently from one topic to another: 'this is a house, it is big', 'this is a book, it is green', and so on.

The Sauveur-Heness School of Modern Languages caused a great deal of interest, locally at first and then nationally. In the early days, they had a visit from 'an eminent minister of the city' who was clearly sceptical of the voluble Frenchman's claims. The class were on Lesson 10 (about 25 hours into the course) and the eminent visitor was asked what he wanted the class to discuss. 'God' came the breath-taking reply. No problem. 'I talked for an hour with my pupils without a single answer being refused me'. The minister relented: 'It is admirable', said he, 'I see the thing: it is done; how, I cannot imagine!'[24]

Within a decade or so the Natural Method, as the Sauveur approach was known, had become the most seriously considered new development in language teaching in America. Kroeh (1887) in his review of methods for the Modern Language Association devotes more than five pages of his article to Sauveur's work and ends: 'I conclude from these considerations that the 'Natural Method' furnishes the most philosophical introduction to the study of languages which has ever been proposed for the classroom'.[25]

The issue that Kroeh dwells on at greatest length is one that continues to exercise language teachers: is learning a second language the same as learning the mother tongue? In the *Introduction* Sauveur implies that he thinks the two processes are comparable, but argument is not one of his strong points and it is difficult to be sure. He does, however, discuss Montaigne a number of times in different contexts and presumably the Montaigne experiment was at the back of his mind. Kroeh examines the first/second language question more coherently and clearly sides with the view that 'the conditions will never again be the same as those under which (the learner) learnt his mother tongue . . . The new language has not the same chance of success as the first. It has a habit to overcome'.[26] This does not, however, lead him to condemn the Natural Method because 'the "natural method" is not the process by which children learn from their mothers. It is, or ought to be, a great deal better than that, though based upon it. It is natural in its basis; but highly artificial in its development'.[27]

Kroeh makes two further points in his perceptive review, both of which were to influence many people's attitudes to the development and wider application of 'natural methods'. The first is the common complaint that 'the conversation necessarily turns upon trivial subjects'.[28] Kroeh is very fair to Sauveur on this point. While agreeing that the objection is a serious one, he draws on his own language teaching experience to stress that 'many of my adult pupils even find great difficulties in these very commonplaces' and concludes that they are 'a necessary evil' but 'fortunately only a brief one'.[29] Professional anxiety about 'trivialization' continued to gnaw away at direct methods and it helps to explain their relative failure in schools in the early years of the present century. What was needed was a stronger theoretical foundation than Sauveur was able to provide, and it is quite possible that without the underpinning provided by the Reform Movement, all 'modern methods' would have been dismissed as 'just another fad'.

Kroeh's second point is that 'the teacher is required to do a disproportionate share of the work'.[30] This, in the long run, was a more serious objection, not merely because teachers were required to work hard, though they were, but because learners came to rely too heavily on the teacher's lead and were discouraged from taking the initiative themselves. They learnt how to answer questions very skilfully, but could not ask them. Student interaction is the most significant feature of modern versions of 'natural methods', but it took a long time to become accepted.

'Natural methods' had started well and attracted professional interest and support. What they needed now was a vehicle which would bring them to the customers.

The ordinary schools of America, or anywhere else at the time, would never have adopted 'natural methods'. The teachers would not have known what to do, and parents would have been horrified at the loss of prestige that 'ordinary conversation' implied. Natural methods required schools of their own and someone with the feel for business to see and grasp the opportunity that was on offer. Immigrants were pouring into the United States speaking virtually every language in Europe and all of them needed to learn the language of their adopted country. But they were not an educated élite with years of the *Gymnasium*, the *lycée*, or whatever behind them. They were ordinary people, the poor, the dispossessed that passed under the Statue of Liberty in the steamships from Genoa and Hamburg. Like the Huguenots in sixteenth-century England, they needed to survive in their new environment and to cope with the problems of everyday life in a new language. They also brought with them their own natural skills as native speakers of their various languages. Someone who could put these two sets of needs and talents

*Figure 24   Maximilian D. Berlitz (1852–1921). Berlitz opened his first language school in Providence, Rhode Island, in 1878, and his textbooks started to appear four years later. Though he did not invent the Direct Method, he made it available to large numbers of language learners in Europe and America through his system of schools. His success was at its height in the decade before the First World War, and by 1914 he had nearly 200 schools, the largest number (63) being in Germany. There were 27 in Britain.*

together in a system of language teaching that made no appeal to traditional scholastic knowledge but concentrated on what was actually wanted, would make his fortune. The moment found the man, in the shape of Maximilian Berlitz, appropriately enough an immigrant himself. Without Sauveur, the Direct Method would not have happened when it did; without Berlitz, very few people would have benefited from it.

In some respects Sauveur and Berlitz shared a common background. They were both immigrants, though Sauveur had arrived in the United States about ten years earlier. They were both in the teaching profession – Berlitz came from a family of teachers in south Germany – and they both ran language schools within a few miles of each other on the New England coast.

According to the 'Official History of the Berlitz Organization' published in 1978 to mark its centenary year, Maximilian Berlitz decided as a young immigrant (he was only in his late twenties) that the most promising future he could carve for himself in America was to use his skills as a teacher and his status as a native speaker of German and open a school of his own in Providence, Rhode Island. He then advertised for an assistant who could speak French. (The parallel with the Heness-Sauveur story is very close.) The man who answered the advertisement was a young Frenchman, also a recent immigrant who had not yet learnt English, called Nicholas Joly. The Official History then tells us that Berlitz, overworked by the exertion of getting the school going, fell ill and left the students to the mercies of the 'untried' Joly. Returning a month or so later, and expecting to find his customers in a very dissatisfied frame of mind, Berlitz discovered to his amazement that young Joly was getting on very well and talking to them in French. The Direct Method had, it seems, been discovered twice in ten years in virtually the same place, once in Yale and the second time in Providence. This raises a rather interesting question. There is no reason to doubt the Berlitz story as it stands, but what, if anything, did Joly know of Sauveur's work in Boston? Had he perhaps talked to teachers who had attended a Sauveur summer-school, or even been present at one himself? It would be interesting to know more about him.

During the next thirty years, Berlitz built up a network of language schools, first in America and then back in Europe. The first school he opened after Providence was in Sauveur's home town of Boston, then in New York, and then Washington. By the end of the century he had sixteen American schools and another thirty in Europe, more than half of them in his native Germany. There were five in England: in London, Leeds, Bradford, Manchester, and Newcastle-upon-Tyne, all large industrial cities with strong commercial links abroad. His textbooks provided a framework within which the teachers he employed in his schools could work according to a predictable routine which would ensure, as far as possible, that all Berlitz Schools followed the same basic course patterns. He began with French and German ( both in 1882), and English as a foreign language followed shortly afterwards. Thereafter Spanish and Italian appeared in the early 1890s and Russian, Dutch, Danish, Czech, and Hungarian had all been added by 1910 along with Swedish, Polish, Portuguese, and Japanese. The Berlitz industry was a bigger version of the Ahn-Ollendorff enterprises in the 1850s.

Berlitz was not an academic methodologist, but he was an excellent systematizer of basic language teaching materials organized on 'direct method' lines. His biggest sellers run to two coursebooks, but none of them is really an advanced course, or even a high-intermediate one. Berlitz catered for beginners and provided them with a useful grounding in the language. All his books contain the same directions to the teacher, but this is as far as his methodological interests went. He never, for example, wrote a manual like Sauveur's *Introduction*. The teacher's directions are very clear and straightforward: no translation under any circumstances ('teachers are cautioned against the slightest compromise on this point')[31], a strong emphasis on oral work, avoidance of grammatical explanations until late in the course, and the maximum use of question-and-answer techniques. His teachers were all native speakers, a cardinal Berlitz principle, and this meant in practice that most of them were young and there was inevitably a high turnover of staff. Training could not go very deep, nor did Berlitz put many resources into it. The routinized methodology contained in the teacher's directions, and the layout and content of the textbooks, were the basic means of exerting control over standards and aims. It was a matter of some professional pride in the Berlitz organization, according to Pakscher (1895), that a student leaving a course in New York could pick it up again at the same lesson in London, and then in Dresden, Paris, or Berlin.[32]

As far as many of the teachers were concerned, the Berlitz schools were a splendid device for keeping body and soul together while exploring Europe and 'finding themselves'. Some of them, like Harold Palmer for instance, ended up in the profession. Most used the system for a time and then moved onto other things. Except in rare circumstances, it was not a career in itself and neither the teachers nor the schools treated it as one. The Berlitz system was intended to be a 'teacher proof' system for relatively inexperienced, and not always very highly motivated, teachers. It could, on the other hand, be a stimulating and, for a time, a rewarding experience.

One teacher who was typical of many was the poet Wilfred Owen. Owen worked at the Berlitz School in Bordeaux just before the outbreak of the First World War and, though overworked and underpaid, enjoyed his time there as his letters home showed. This extract is from one to his sister written in February 1914: 'I wonder whether you are doing anything at French? My serious advice to you is not – to work hard; but to *leave it entirely*! Time spent on Grammars and Translations under the direction of an English Teacher is wasted. Such is the conclusion I have come to! . . . The majority of English Teachers have an execrable Accent, and what is worse, no notion of the *Direct Method*. If only I could give you a few lessons à la Berlitz! But I will, too, before long! We will form a French course in the dining-room every night. I guarantee I would have you *all* talking good French in three months! At least, there are dozens of pupils who have learnt English in that time'.[33] Owen started preliminary negotiations towards opening a school of his own in Angers, but nothing came of it in the end. He was not yet twenty-one years of age.

The best account of the Berlitz approach and the important role it played in late nineteenth-century adult education is contained in an article written by Pakscher for *Englische Studien* (1895). Pakscher was the Director of the Dresden School, a post he had hesitated to take up as the popular view of Berlitz schools was that they taught languages in a 'mechanical and superficial' manner. This is the same 'trivialization' point that Kroeh mentioned in his survey. After a trial period, he became convinced of its value and took the job on full-time.

He describes the early Berlitz English course in great detail. It was in two parts, each subdivided into two sections. The opening section of Part I began with the objects in the classroom followed by *to be* and the most common adjectives (*big, small, thin, thick*, etc.). Other vocabulary items that could be taught ostensively (parts of the body, clothing, etc.) were introduced next as well as prepositional relationships. Lexical verbs appeared from Lesson 5 onwards but the alphabet was withheld until Lesson 8, a very unfamiliar procedure for a nineteenth-century language course. The second section of Part I introduced simple texts, which were continued, along with everyday dialogues, in Part 2. Most of the classwork consisted of question-and-answer activities, always, of course, in the foreign language. Berlitz wrote a number of short reference grammars to accompany his most popular courses. Compared with Sauveur's intuitive style, the Berlitz Method was simple, systematic, ordered, and replicable.

The most interesting feature of Pakscher's article is his description of the typical Berlitz students of the time. Some were schoolchildren who could not keep up with their lessons at school, others were rather idiosyncratic private students like the Swedish cavalry captain who was doing English and French at the same time and coping well 'despite his advanced age'. The most important group, however, were the evening-class students. We can see in Pakscher's rather moving account of these students the true role of the Berlitz schools at the time. Anyone who has taught in similar circumstances will recognize it as a standard situation, but in the 1890s it was happening more or less for the first time.

'The most astonishing successes, however, are with our evening classes. We run special further education courses for young sales assistants from 8 – 9 o'clock and even occasionally 9 – 10 o'clock in the evening. This is the most unpromising material one could imagine. Everyone is exhausted in the evenings and much less inclined to learn something new than during the day. These young people have, however, been working hard all day, most have no knowledge of English at all, and many have never even studied a foreign language before, and therefore, have no notion of grammar. It is extremely satisfying to see the interest with which they take part in the class, and the attention and understanding with which they follow each new activity the teacher presents. It is possible, therefore, even in these classes which only meet twice a week for an hour, where homework cannot be expected, to get through the first Berlitz book in three to four months, an achievement which would take two years at school. When one of these young people unexpectedly gets the chance to travel to England or America – and it happens quite often – they will never be at a loss for words in the hotel, on the train or in the street, and they will probably make much better progress in the foreign language while they are abroad than those who never learnt to understand an Englishman when they were at school.'[34]

This extract really says it all, a new language learning customer with no formal linguistic training from school who needed English in order to keep in touch with friends and relatives who had emigrated to the United States, or who perhaps wanted to emigrate there themselves. Others may have had personal links with England, or their business had English-speaking clients. The *Gymnasium* teachers scarcely knew such a world existed, and even the Viëtor-Sweet reformers were a long way from seeing language in this straightforward, utilitarian light.

Before leaving this section on 'natural methods', there is one final point which an historical study might have been expected to clarify, namely the origin of the term Direct Method, but there seems to be no simple answer. There is little doubt that it was associated in the public mind with Berlitz, and, as we have seen, Berlitz teachers like Wilfred Owen used it to describe their work. Nevertheless, Berlitz himself did not, but preferred to stick to his own 'brand name', The Berlitz Method, in all his textbooks. Kroeh's 1887 survey does not mention it at all, which is fairly strong evidence that it was not current before the 1890s, at the earliest.[35] Nor does Sweet use it in *The Practical Study* in 1899.[36] Passy, on the other hand, writing in the same year, called his pamphlet *De la méthode directe dans l'enseignement des langues vivantes*. At first sight, this publication seems to settle the issue, but it does not account for the popular association of the term with 'conversational' methods which were alien to the Reform Movement and do not feature in Passy's work.

The most reasonable explanation of the mystery is the obvious one that nobody invented the term, but that it 'emerged' (rather like our contemporary 'Communicative Approach') as a useful generic label to refer to all methods of language teaching which adopted the monolingual principle as a cornerstone of their beliefs.

## Notes

1 Cohen (ed. 1958: 81–2).
2 Ibid.: 83–4.
3 Axtell (ed. 1968: 277–8).
4 Ibid.: 266.
5 *Polyhistor* (1688–1707), ii, 10. ('De curriculo scholastico') by David Georg Morhof (1639–1691).
6 Nicholas Clenard (1495–1542). Flemish grammarian and language teacher. He wrote the definitive Renaissance grammar of Greek. His educational writings include the posthumous *De modo docendi pueros analphabeticos* (On teaching illiterate boys), from which, presumably, the extract originates.
7 Blackie (1845: 174–5).
8 Ibid.: 175.
9 Ibid.: 170.
10/11 Ibid.: 171.
12 Ibid.: 172.
13/14 Ibid.: 173.
15 Ibid.: 176–7.
16 Ibid.: 180–3.
17 Palmer (1917/1968: 90ff.).
18 Sauveur (1874a: 44).
19 Ibid.: 48.
20 Ibid.: 7.
21 Ibid.: 8.
22 Ibid.: 10.
23 Ibid.: 28.
24 Ibid.: 8.
25 Kroeh (1887: 182–3).
26 Ibid.: 179–80.
27–30 Ibid.: 180.
31 Berlitz (1907: 7).
32 Pakscher (1895: 311).
33 Owen and Bell (eds 1967: 232), Owen's emphasis.
34 Pakscher (1895: 317), my translation.
35 Kroeh (1887). It should be remembered that Kroeh was addressing an American audience. It is possible that the term was in use in Europe, but it is unlikely.
36 Sweet (1899/1964: 74–5).

PART FOUR
# The making of a profession

# Overview of English Language Teaching since 1900

# 15 The teaching of English as a foreign or second language since 1900: a survey

During the first half of the present century, the teaching of English as a foreign language emerged as an autonomous profession. In the course of time it spawned further distinct specialisms, notably the teaching of English as a second language, at first in the Empire, later the Commonwealth, and more recently in Britain itself. The intellectual foundations for this autonomy rested on the fusion of the two reforming traditions inherited from the previous century: the applied linguistic approach of the Reform Movement and the monolingual methodology of the Direct Method. The catalyst was the work of Harold Palmer in the Department of Phonetics at University College, London, between 1915 and 1922, underpinned by the research in theoretical and applied English phonetics of his Head of Department, Daniel Jones.

The second strand in the development of English language teaching (ELT) in the modern sense derived from a reinterpretation of the role of English in the Empire. During the nineteenth century there was a largely unquestioned assumption that English should be taught in colonial schools in essentially the same way as in the mother country. The basic educational aim was the assimilation of British culture through the medium of English literature. There was no provision for language work specially designed to help the non-native learner, and school grammars like those of the prolific J. C. Nesfield, which were originally written to get British youngsters through the Oxford and Cambridge Local Examinations, were exported in large numbers to the colonies. By the twenties, the notion that English was a second language with a utilitarian function in the communication of knowledge had begun to emerge,[1] though it was not until the fifties that the modern distinction between English as a 'foreign' and a 'second' language (EFL and ESL) became widespread.

The promotion and maintenance of a monolingual approach to language teaching has characterized both sides of the profession, though perhaps for different reasons, and it became the hallmark which set ELT apart from foreign language teaching in Britain. It was also relatively uncontroversial, with none of the heart-searchings that are evident in the literature of modern language teaching.[2] Instead, there was a general consensus that translation should be avoided as far as possible, but that it was helpful from time to time. On the other hand, the grammar half of the grammar-translation formula excited rather more concern and Nesfield and his successors continued in business for some time. Although the study of texts devised to illustrate 'sentence patterns', or 'constructions' as they were often called ('structures' came later), was the appropriate way of introducing English grammar to beginners, such methods needed the support of more traditional descriptions at a later stage. The contrast between the early success of monolingual methods in English as a foreign language and the persistence of grammar-translation in British schools (at least until very recent times) helps to explain why the Direct Method retained the image of 'modernity' for so long. It was continually 're-discovered' as succeeding generations of grammar-school-educated recruits came into the ELT profession.

A distinctive intellectual framework of basic principle is a necessary condition for an autonomous profession, but not a sufficient one. There must also be a sense of coherence and stability reinforced by the establishment of institutions with various functions: the regulation of entry, for example, the maintenance of standards, the provision of initial and higher-level training, career structures, communication through journals, associations, conferences, and so on. Finally, there must be some commitment to research and development for the future. The ELT profession took a very long time to acknowledge its own existence— most of the developments referred to above have only occurred in the past twenty years or so. It is not easy to explain this lack of self-confidence, if that is what it was, but perhaps the simplest explanation is that ELT is a scattered profession by definition, and it was only after 1960 with the sudden growth of EFL and ESL activity in Britain itself that a sense of unity began to emerge.

In the next few pages, I shall attempt to trace four phases of professional development since 1900: a foundation phase ending with Palmer's departure for Japan in 1922, a research and development phase between the wars, a phase of consolidation from immediately after the Second World War until around 1960, and a final one in which the principal characteristics have been variation and adaptation to rapid changes of circumstance. Following this survey, I shall discuss a selection of specific topics in greater detail.

## Laying the foundations (1900 – 1922)

The first steps towards the new profession were taken in 1906 when Daniel Jones, having returned from his studies with Passy in Paris, persuaded the University of London (the principal if not the sole centre of university-level activity in the field for the next half century) to permit him to give a series of public lectures on the phonetics of French. The lectures, delivered in the spring term of 1907, proved so successful with local school teachers and others that a further course was arranged for the following year, with an additional one in the phonetics of English. Courses specifically for overseas students of English started next and, in 1910, the programme was expanded to include Spoken English Grammar. This was the course Harold Palmer was invited to take over in 1915. During these years, Daniel Jones published the series of works which have since served as indispensable source-books for every English language teacher: *The Pronunciation of English* (1909), the *English Pronouncing Dictionary* (1917), which built on an earlier publication called *A Phonetic Dictionary of the English Language* (1913), and the *Outline of English Phonetics* (1918).

1917 was a particularly productive year. Not only did it see the first edition of the *EPD*, but also the publication of Palmer's first major work, *The Scientific Study and Teaching of Languages*. Palmer had started his career at London University with a series of lectures to local school teachers on language teaching methodology, the content of which formed the basis for the *Scientific Study*. Before leaving London, he had added a short summary of his approach called *The Oral Method of Teaching Languages* (1921) and his definitive *Principles of Language-Study* (1921). The Jones-Palmer association effectively ensured that one of the 'ground rules' of English as a foreign language was an applied linguistic philosophy, the amalgamation of Jones's extension of the Sweet-Viëtor tradition in phonetics and Palmer's experience as a Direct Method teacher and materials writer in Belgium.

### Research and development (1922–1939)

In very broad terms, the twenties were a decade of research, the thirties of development. Palmer, for example, spent most of his first seven years in Japan working towards two complementary objectives. The first was the realization of the principles of the Oral Method in a concrete form which would work in a Japanese school classroom. He devised various types of oral drills and exercises which he tried out with the help of his daughter Dorothée and published through the Institute for Research in English Teaching (IRET) of which he was Director. The best-known of these works is *English Through Actions* (1925) written with Dorothée Palmer, but there were many others: *Sequence Series: Questions, Sequence Series: Answers* (1923), *Systematic Exercises in English Sentence Building, Substitution Tables* (1924–5), *English for Children* (1927), *English Through Questions and Answers* (1930), and *The Technique of Question Answering* (1931).[3] The question-answer techniques of the Direct Method are evident from these titles. At the same time, Palmer was working on his vocabulary research, which is discussed in detail in the next section, and a steady stream of background papers, reports and word-lists appeared from the late twenties onwards.

Vocabulary research was also the principal objective of Michael West, who was working in Bengal in India, though his interests were different. In the early twenties, West, in his capacity as an official in the Indian Education Service, carried out the most extensive study of English language needs yet undertaken, the results of which were published in a lengthy report, *Bilingualism, with special reference to Bengal*, in 1926. His conclusion was that the most pressing need was for simple reading materials written within a controlled vocabulary, and the early New Method materials were piloted as part of the bilingualism study. (It is interesting to note West's choice of title for his report and his consistent use of the term 'second language' to refer to English.)

Palmer and West joined forces to produce the so-called 'Carnegie Report' on vocabulary selection in 1936 and, thereafter, there was a spate of publications. West's *New Method English Dictionary* (with Endicott) had appeared in 1935, Palmer published his *Thousand-Word English* (with Hornby) in 1937 and his *Grammar of English Words* in 1938. Palmer also made a significant contribution to West's ambitious New Method scheme published by Longmans, Green from the late thirties onwards: *The New Method Grammar* (1938), *The New Method English Practice Books* (three vols.) (1939), *The New Method English Course for West Africa* (1942), and a number of *New Method Readers*.

Though Palmer and West dominated the inter-war period, there were others whose work, while less prolific, was equally important. The first was a teacher and textbook writer called Lawrence Faucett, whose career followed a similar pattern to Palmer's. Faucett taught English as a foreign language in a number of countries overseas including, in particular, China. He collaborated with Itsu Maki on a study of word-frequency counts for English which was published in Tokyo in 1932 under the title *A Study of English Word-Values*. At the same time, in the late twenties, he developed the first large-scale direct-method course for English as a foreign language, which was published by Oxford University Press as *The Oxford English Course* (1933). It established a pattern which was widely copied later, the course 'package'. The materials consisted of Language Books, Reading Books, and Supplementary Readers, each divided into four levels corresponding to vocabulary counts (500 words, 1,000 words, etc.) plus a set of Reading Cards and a Direct Method Picture Dictionary of 200 words.

On his return from overseas, Faucett joined the staff of the Institute of Education at London University and, in 1932, the year in which the Institute was constituted under that name, he started the first training course for teachers of English as a foreign language. The Institute played an historically important role three years later by hosting the London meeting of the Carnegie Conference, Faucett himself being one of the principal contributors, along with West, Palmer, and Thorndike.

Even better known was C. E. Eckersley (1893–1967), originally a schoolteacher at the Polytechnic Boys' School in Regent Street in London who came into English as a foreign language as a part-time evening-class teacher at the associated Polytechnic Institute. He began his publishing career with a literary anthology (*England and the English* (1932)) and a grammar (*A Concise English Grammar for Foreign Students* (1933)), but his reputation rests on the course he began in the late thirties, *Essential English for Foreign Students*, Book 1 of which appeared in 1938, followed by Books 2–4 between 1940 and 1942. His success with *Essential Engish* encouraged him to leave schoolteaching in 1943 and devote himself full-time to materials writing.[4]

Eckersley represented a branch of the profession, which is more numerous today than in the twenties, engaged in the teaching of English to foreigners resident in Britain or visiting the country temporarily. His classes were in the main multilingual groups of European adults who needed English for a variety of utilitarian purposes. His students provided Eckersley with the central situation round which *Essential English* was constructed, a class (Pedro, Olaf, Jan, Lucille, Freda, and Hob) who discuss their linguistic worries and problems with their kind and imperturbable teacher, Mr Priestley. This simple, but original device allowed Eckersley to combine samples of everyday dialogue with the language needed to talk about English, and it offered a more relaxed and livelier atmosphere than the severely pedagogical texts of some of the rival courses.

In the thirties the grim political developments brought a growing stream of refugees from countries in central Europe. A large number of them were well-educated, literate adults who needed the practical spoken language of everyday life in England which was not reflected in the simple reading materials of the New Method or in the vocabulary research that underlay them. While *Essential English*, in common with most courses of the time, was organized in terms of vocabulary levels (500 words at each of the four stages of the course), the choice of words was not restricted to the Carnegie list, but included everyday items which it ignores (*bacon, beef, cabbage*, and *luggage* are four of Eckersley's examples.)[5]

*Essential English* in various editions stood the test of time and remained one of the leading EFL courses for around thirty years, when it was overtaken by more overtly situational courses like L. G. Alexander's *First Things First* (1967). There is an interesting historical parallel between authors like Eckersley and the refugee textbook writers of the sixteenth and seventeenth centuries. Both were attempting to help learners in similar unfortunate circumstances, and Eckersley's return to the neglected dialogue format shows a similar approach to the problem, while not 'situational' in the modern sense.

The final example of a writer whose research in the twenties was developed and extended in the following decade was C. K. Ogden, whose principal publication in the field, *Basic English*, appeared in 1930. It provoked a storm of controversy which did little to enhance the reputation of those involved. The *Basic* affair is of interest if only because it was, in a sense, a litmus-test of the existence of an English Language Teaching profession. The darker side of professions is revealed when they are threatened and members tend to close ranks against outsiders. The nineteenth century would have tolerated Ogden as it tolerated the other individualists with interesting, if idiosyncratic, ideas. The twentieth century, however, did not. Basic English failed primarily because the profession and its burgeoning institutions rejected it.

By the time war broke out in 1939, the first steps towards a professional organization in English as a foreign language had been taken. The existence of a training course at the Institute in London has already been mentioned. Of rather wider significance, however, was the establishment in 1934 of The British Committee for Relations with Other Countries, re-named the British Council the following year. In 1940, mainly through the commitment of its influential third chairman, Lord Lloyd, the Council was incorporated by Royal Charter. The existence of the Council and its network of British Institutes and other centres overseas provided at the very least a professional sheet-anchor and at best a career structure. In particular, it acted as a focus of continuity through the war years, and played an important role in re-establishing a sense of purpose and direction after 1945.

## Consolidation (1945–1960)

One of the first actions of the British Council after the war was to found a long-overdue professional journal. The first issue appeared in October 1946 under the title *English Language Teaching, a Periodical devoted to the Teaching of English as a Foreign Language*. For the first five years it was published no fewer than eight times a year under the editorship of A. S. Hornby, who had joined the Council after his return from Japan in 1942. Hornby was succeeded by R. T. Butlin in November 1950 but remained on the editorial board. The journal became a quarterly from Volume VI (Autumn 1951) onwards and in 1961 the responsibility for publication was shared with Oxford University Press, an arrangement which has continued to the present day. Since 1972 it has been published under the slightly different title of *English Language Teaching Journal* (*ELTJ*). To anyone entering the profession as a young teacher twenty or so years ago, before the establishment of associations and other groups, *ELT* provided a comforting feeling of community and continuity, strengthened by the long editorship of W. R. Lee between 1961 and 1981.[6]

The post-war years, a difficult period for the British Council, were referred to by its official historian and second Secretary-General A. J. S. White as the 'Years of Retrenchment'. Eventually, however, the Council found a new friend at court in the person of Dr. Charles Hill, the former 'Radio Doctor' then a member of the government, who, after a review of the Council's work in 1957, promoted a White Paper which expressed considerable confidence in its future, and extra funds were made available to continue and expand its activities. 'The Government attach the highest importance', it said, 'to the care of students who come to this country from the Commonwealth and from foreign countries, and to the teaching of English'.[7]

With its future assured, the Council was able to play a more active role, including the provision of advanced training both for its own personnel and for sponsored students from overseas. To this end, it assisted in the setting up of a School of Applied Linguistics at the University of Edinburgh under the Directorship of J. C. Catford and with the close involvement of David Abercrombie of the Department of Phonetics (both of whom had been teachers of English abroad and regular contributors to *ELT*). The Edinburgh example was later followed at Leeds University under the leadership of Peter Strevens, a former colleague of Abercrombie, and S. Pit Corder, who later succeeded Catford at Edinburgh. Thereafter, many other universities followed suit in the late sixties, including Essex, Lancaster, Reading, and London.

On the materials side, the post-war years saw the fruition of work that had begun in the thirties. The innovative initiative, however, passed to the United States, in particular to Fries's English Language Institute at Michigan University, but the impact of American thinking was not felt in Britain till the late fifties. In the meantime, West picked up the threads of the Carnegie project and published his *General Service List of English Words* in 1953 while continuing the New Method scheme with courses adapted for various parts of the world. Palmer died in 1949, but his tradition (see Chapter 16) was carried on by Hornby with an impressive string of publications, including the famous *Advanced Learner's Dictionary*, which are discussed in detail later (see Chapter 18).

Though the general mood of the period in Britain was one of consolidation and consensus, there were straws in the wind of the changes which would hit the profession in the sixties. There was, for example, the notion that adult learners with specific purposes in learning English would benefit from courses written specially for them. The 'special purpose' idea itself was familiar enough from the many 'commercial English' manuals that had been a feature of the language teaching scene since the nineteenth century. Now, however, the principle was to be taken further, for example, into technical English[8] and other specialisms. Mackin and Weinberger's course for Spanish-speaking doctors *El Inglés para Médicos y Estudiantes de Medicina* (1949) was an early example. Though the emphasis was on the linguistic characteristics of medical texts rather than on the use of language for professional purposes, which is the current focus in English for specific purposes (ESP), a start had been made.

In addition, there was technology. The gramophone had played a role in language teaching for some time (for example, Palmer's experiments in Japan in the twenties), but the old 78 r.p.m. system was clumsy and unwieldy. The arrival of long-playing records in the early fifties solved some of the problems, but it was still impossible for learners to record and listen to their own work. The more enthusiastic establishments invested in wire-recorders but it was not until they were replaced by tape recorders in the mid-fifties that any extensive use of recording in class became practical. The language laboratory itself did not arrive in Britain till the next decade, but the pioneer work had been carried out in America long before that. Kiddle, for example, writing in *Language Learning* in 1949, described a laboratory he had supervised for the United States Navy during the war in 1943 and another for the Peruvians in 1945. By 1949 he had developed a laboratory at Michigan in which six students could work together, each using two machines, one for listening and the other for personal recording. By the end of the decade, laboratories were sufficiently common in America for Edward M. Stack to publish his immensely influential manual on the subject, *The Language Laboratory and Modern Language Teaching* (1960), and three years later A. S. Hayes prepared a technical report for the United States government called *Language Laboratory Facilities* (1963). The stage was set for a major attack on the equipment budgets of countless unsuspecting education authorities.

A start had also been made in other areas of communications technology. *English by Radio*, for instance, had been set up during the war with short five-minute lessons that began transmission in 1943.[9] It expanded into an important service in the years that followed. Of the audio-visual systems, only film offered anything substantial—the television era was a decade away—but it was expensive and there were considerable practical difficulties in arranging for its use in schools. It never really 'caught on', despite some enthusiastic support from Roger Manvell and others in a series of *ELT* articles in the late forties.[10] The real breakthrough in language teaching technology came from France with the development of the audio-visual courses at CREDIF[11] such as *Voix et Images de France* (1961) and *Bonjour Line* (1963) which married the tape recorder and the filmstrip in a system that required a minimum of classroom disruption.

Finally, beneath the surface of consensus that had settled on the Palmerian tradition was an undercurrent of theoretical challenge which eventually broke through and engulfed the sixties in controversy. The absence in Britain of professional associations and journals other than *ELT* (which fostered rather than questioned the prevailing mood) meant that new ideas in linguistics, applied linguistics, the psychology of learning, and so on, were relatively unknown outside specialist circles. American developments were reported in the Michigan-based journal *Language Learning*, but its British circulation was limited, and they were largely ignored in *ELT*. This lack of interest was reciprocated across the Atlantic, to nobody's benefit. One or two of the more influential publications of the Michigan school, notably Fries's *The Structure of English* (1952) and Lado's *Linguistics Across Cultures* (1957), made a mark. However, the absence of institutionalized channels of communication before the establishment of advanced training in applied linguistics meant that a 'backlog' of ideas such as pattern practice, the structural syllabus, the language laboratory, and programmed learning—all pioneered in America in the fifties—was suddenly unloaded in Britain in the sixties. It was exciting, if a little indigestible.

## Change and variation since 1960

Far-reaching political, economic, and technological changes affecting the relationship between Britain and the rest of the world began to gather momentum from the late fifties onwards, bringing a radical shift in priorities for English language teaching, and forcing the development of an increasingly varied range of professional specialisms. Of the greatest importance was the transformation of English from the language of imperial power and administration to a new role which was simultaneously more localized and more pervasive. Each newly independent state was obliged to work out for itself the status which the former colonial language would be accorded in the new nation in the light of both its own aspirations and the practical realities of global communication. The resulting pattern is too complex to summarize briefly, but the basic contrast between learning English as a foreign language for external communication and as a second language for specialized internal functions, became sharper. The crucial decision was whether to retain English as the medium of secondary and higher education: some countries such as Nigeria maintained an English-medium policy, typically for reasons of national cohesion, while others such as Malaysia pursued a national language policy.

The second outcome of post-colonial change in the Third World was the emigration to Britain of a substantial number of people attracted by the opportunities offered in the former mother country or, in some cases, to escape the political consequences of independence at home. The impact of settlement in Britain by non-English-speaking families presented a formidable challenge to the adaptability and resourcefulness of the English teaching profession, and to the willingness of the authorities to respond positively. An important step was taken in 1966 with the decision to set up a materials development project at the University of Leeds Institute of Education to design and pilot a programme of English for immigrant primary school children.[12] Later, the project, funded by the Schools Council, was extended to cover children of secondary school age. The resulting materials, called *Scope* (see Chapter 18), pioneered new ideas in the integration of language teaching with the broader purposes of educational development, and foreshadowed many of the activity-based techniques later associated with the communicative approach. The same could also be said of a second Schools Council project intended to help immigrant children with their use of English called *Concept 7–9* (also described in more detail in Chapter 18). Located in the University of Birmingham, it continued for five years from 1967 to 1972.

Projects like *Scope* and *Concept 7–9* set the teaching of English as a second language (TESL) along a path which was quite distinct from that of English as a foreign language (TEFL). The distinctive features were even more marked in adult teaching which, in the case of TEFL, typically took place in colleges of further education and in the growing private sector. TESL teaching, on the other hand, owed more to the informal contexts of community or adult basic education, and required materials and training programmes which reflected a less intensive and more flexible teaching and learning style (see Chapter 18). By the late seventies, TESL had formed a National Association for the Teaching of ESL to Adults (NATESLA 1978), and had promoted its own training programme with a specialized certificate administered by the Royal Society of Arts in 1979 to run in parallel with Society's work in TEFL training. In Scotland, separate associations (SATEFL and SATESL) were set up in 1980 with a joint annual conference and, in 1983, co-sponsorship of a Scottish branch of TESOL.

In the Third World, the post-imperial redefinition of English in the Commonwealth, and the expansion of English as a world auxiliary language required, among other things, a more precise definition of those aspects of English language education which impinged on the expression of national cultural identity, and those which linked the individual country to the international English-using community. As Ogden and others had recognized forty years earlier, English was the *lingua franca* of modern science and technology. By 1970 it was also the language of transnational commerce, finance, and practical communication generally. The developmental aspirations of the Third World could only be met in an acceptable span of time by a programme of higher-level training overseas. With the assistance of sponsoring bodies such as the British Council, the path was smoothed for both Commonwealth and non-Commonwealth students to gain advanced specialist qualifications, particularly in fields of direct relevance to economic and practical welfare problems at home: for example, science, engineering, human and veterinary medicine, agriculture, and English teaching. While English remained the medium of instruction at home, the language-related problems of overseas students in Britain were minimal. When, however, there was a marked increase in students for whom that was not the case, specialized courses of English were required which would relate closely to their particular needs and aspirations. This led to the rapid development in the seventies of English for Special, more recently Specific, Purposes (ESP).

ESP in the modern sense could be said to have begun in 1969 with the publication of a conference report called *Languages for Special Purposes*,[13] but the groundwork had been laid at both the theoretical and the practical levels during the previous decade. As far as coursebooks were concerned, the familiar commercial correspondence courses and technical English readers were being replaced by materials which took a fresh look at the subject. Mackin's book for doctors has already been mentioned. He also edited a set of special-purpose text anthologies with exercises, called The English Studies Series, from 1964 onwards.[14] There were others, among them *A Modern Course in Business English* (1963/66) by Howatt, Webb, and Knight, the first published course to use authentic listening materials,[15] Close's *The English We Use for Science* (1965),[16] the BBC's project *The Scientist Speaks* (1967) and Ewer and Latorre's influential *Course in Basic Scientific English* (1969).[17] On the theoretical side, Firth's early work on 'restricted languages' (1959) had been developed by Halliday and his colleagues into a specialized technique of descriptive linguistics known as 'register analysis' within the wider field of language varieties, which also included dialect studies and stylistic analysis.[18] *Sentence and Clause in Scientific English* (1968) by Huddleston and others was a particularly important publication representing this school of thought.[19] There were also a few contributions to methodology, including an article by Widdowson on integrating the teaching of English and science (1968).[20]

The generally accepted view around 1970 was essentially a linguistic one: there were different varieties of English, the distinctive features of which could be described and taught through the use of appropriately selected texts, and carefully devised practice exercises. In some respects John Swales' *Writing Scientific English* (1971)[21] reflects many of the concerns of this period, though it also contains features which look forward to the approaching communicative movement.

The communicative philosophy of the seventies encouraged three rather different approaches to ESP, though they shared many common principles. One emphasized a functionalist interpretation of 'the way English is used' which made extensive use of syllabus categories drawn from discourse analysis (definition, explanation, and other rhetorical acts). Allen and Widdowson's *English in Focus* series is a well-known example (see p. 278). The second, exemplified by the more elementary Bates and Dudley-Evans' series *Nucleus* drew on the notional rather than the functional strand in the new approach with categories such as dimension, measurement, and so on.[22] The third type took a different starting-point, not in language use but rather in the communicative activities and skills, which the learner would have to perform in his studies, his work, or whatever he was preparing for. This approach stressed the importance of training useful communicative strategies (for reading, listening to lectures, etc.) rather than analysing the detailed linguistic features of representative texts. The work of Candlin and what might be called 'The Lancaster school of ESP' has concentrated on this interpretation of the subject.[23]

Cutting across the different pedagogical approaches was a growing refinement of definition within ESP.[24] Strevens (1977/8), for example, offers a diagram which makes a basic distinction between occupational and educational purposes in studying English. The former, often referred to as EOP (English for Occupational Purposes), comprises most of what is informally referred to as 'technical English' or 'commercial English' as well as courses for more specialized groups such as air-hostesses, for example, bankers, or diplomats. Often such courses are too specialized to reach the market in the normal way, and many private-sector EFL establishments have made a positive feature of their willingness to design once-off courses, for example, The English Language Teaching Development Unit (ELTDU) attached for many years to the Colchester English Study Centre.[25] On the educational side, usually referred to prestigiously as EAP (English for Academic Purposes), there has been rather more publication, some of which has already been discussed above (see also Chapter 18). EST (English for Science and Technology) is another common acronym but it is really subsumed in the other two. Although ESP has been largely a British initiative, there has also been interesting work in America, notably by Trimble and Selinker in the occupational purposes field.[26]

Finally, the publication in 1978 of John Munby's influential *Communicative Syllabus Design*, which offers 'a sociolinguistic model for defining the content of purpose-specific language programmes', drew many of the categories already noted into a detailed inventory which has proved useful for a number of administrative purposes, in particular the specification of an ESP-oriented test for intending overseas students developed by the English Language Testing Services department of the British Council.

One effect of the specialization and diversification of professional activity discussed above has been an increased demand for higher-level training in applied linguistics, which has grown at a rather faster pace than provision for initial training. Post-experience courses at diploma or Master's level are available at many universities and colleges, but basic training is more difficult to come by. Since 1967 the gap has been filled by the *Certificate in the Teaching of English as a Foreign Language to Adults* offered by the Royal Society of Arts. Although the 'RSA Certificate', as it is usually called, has become the standard professional qualification, it was originally designed for in-service training and requires previous experience. The new *Preparatory Certificate* promises to fill the initial training need.

Before the RSA Certificate was set up, and on an increasing scale since, much of the basic work in initial training has been done by the private sector, either for serving employees or more widely for the general public. The earliest, and perhaps the best-known, scheme was one pioneered from the late fifties onwards by Anthony Abrahams, Ian Dunlop, Michael Knight, and others in Stockholm for the British Centre, and later expanded by Abrahams into Germany, Malaysia, Morocco, and elsewhere through the (initially related) Centre for British Teachers (CBT). The Centre's work in furthering the cause of a trained profession, particularly in the early sixties when it was virtually alone in the field, was important in ensuring that there was a foundation of experience on which to build when TEFL expanded rapidly in the seventies. The Centre has not, however, been alone and other private institutions, notably International House directed by John Haycraft which began publicly available courses in 1962, have also played an important role.

Associations, information centres, and the like are further markers of professional cohesion and a number of important ones were set up in the late sixties. The Association of Teachers of English as a Foreign Language (ATEFL) was founded in 1967, and internationalized as IATEFL in 1971, with W. R. Lee, then Editor of *ELT*, as Chairman. Apart from providing a much-needed focus for activity at home, IATEFL broke new ground in 1974 by holding (in Budapest) the first of a series of annual conferences abroad. It publishes a *Newsletter* with detailed reports of conference proceedings, reviews, etc.[27] In 1967 the British Association for Applied Linguistics (BAAL) held its first meeting and the increasingly influential American-based association TESOL (Teachers of English to Speakers of Other Languages) was formed. The private sector set up a self-regulatory professional body called ARELS (Association of Recognized English Language Schools) in 1960. The British Council's English Teaching Information Centre (ETIC, 1961), and the independent Centre for Information on Language Teaching (and Research) (CILT, 1966),[22] with their important source journal

*Language Teaching and Linguistics: Abstracts*, were additional indicators of a growing professional self-confidence.

To return to the 'mainstream' of ELT development, the sixties introduced two principal innovations. Both originated abroad, but neither can be said to have provoked any radical departure from the basic Palmer-Hornby tradition in Britain. One was situational language teaching as represented in the audiovisual courses of CREDIF such as *Voix et Images de France* (1961) and *Bonjour Line* (1963), which presented situations via a filmstrip with the related dialogue played on a synchronized tape recorder. A British attempt to emulate them called *The Turners* (1969) came too late since, by that time, a simpler adaptation, which used pictures in the textbook, had been popularized by L. G. Alexander in his widely used elementary course *First Things First* (1967). This is a straightforward book in which the new structural patterns are presented in dialogues with visual 'cartoon strips' beside them, and then practised in the second half of each unit. Unlike the French courses, it could be handled by a relatively inexperienced teacher. The situational approach was also evident in a successful course of the mid-seventies called *Access to English* (1974 onwards), though this contains more cultural information and a story-line.[29] Even courses with a functional rather than a structural syllabus, for example the *Strategies* series, *Communicate*, and *Approaches*, retain a strong situational element in their design.[30]

The second innovation was the American audiolingual method derived from the structural approach developed by Fries at Michigan (see Chapter 18). It followed the orthodox 'four skills' model (listening, speaking, reading, writing) (cf. Marcel in Chapter 12), but more rigorously than other methods, and required a considerable amount of aural-oral drill work based on the structures selected from a graded syllabus. There was usually a minimal context (for example a short dialogue) but it was unimportant. In many audiolingual programmes the language laboratory was a central feature, and much of the work, though worthy in intention, was very dull. In British eyes the audiolingual approach seemed little more than a rather 'tighter' and less varied version of the Palmer-Hornby materials. The all-important connected text inherited from the Reform Movement was missing, however, and, in general, the approach had relatively little impact. Broughton's *Success with English* (1968)[31] shows some audiolingual influence but it is still recognizably a Hornby-type course. Out-and-out audiolingual materials like *English 900*[32] were not much used. However, structure drills were added to most courses as the language laboratory spread around the country but only as a supplementary component, or, as in the British Council's ambitious *English Language Units* project,[33] as a library resource.

The communicative movement of the seventies is traced in some detail in Chapter 18 and need not be rehearsed here. The first signs of the notional/functional approach came in 1972 with Wilkins' Council of Europe paper and were reinforced by the appearance of the *Threshold Level* in 1975. Widdowson's early papers on teaching the use of English as communication also date from 1972. Large-scale ESP series like *English in Focus* and *Nucleus* came out from the middle of the decade onwards, and, by 1980, virtually every publishing house had promoted new courses which adopted a communicative element of one kind or another. Nevertheless, more traditional work still found a market, notably the perennially useful *Kernel* series by O'Neill and others.[34] Among other materials, readers have improved in appearance and in choice; they are no longer rather dreary little books with standardized covers, but have emulated the presentation techniques of the paperback market with considerable success. Audio-tapes have benefited greatly from the cassette revolution, though, so far, video has not caught up. In general, the range of new ideas for practice books, games, simulations, group activities, and project work has been impressively wide and the effort and investment of publishers in improving the attractiveness of materials has been one of the most noticeable features of the decade.

Methodology in a more systematic sense has been less in evidence since 1970 ( no one speaks of the 'communicative method', for instance), though publication in the methods field (for example Brumfit) has often been of a high order.[35] So-called 'fringe' methods like Gattegno's Silent Way, first proposed in the early sixties,[36] counselling learning, and Community Language Learning have caused increased interest[37] and are likely to attract more 'official' support in the eighties.

Finally, if there is one single source which has been responsible for stimulating innovation and activity, it is (in one or another of its various guises) applied linguistics. It has not performed miracles, but as a focus of enquiry, critical self-examination, and new ideas, it has enriched the profession at least as much as it has irritated it.

## Notes

1 See, for example, West (1926).
2 Cf. HMSO (1918), Brereton (1930).
3 For a full list of Palmer's works, see Mackin's edition of Palmer and Redman (1969: 133–66).
4 See Quinault (1967).
5 Eckersley (1955: 13).
6 See Strevens (1981).
7 White (1965: 136).
8 West, assisted by W. E. Flood, added a *Word List for the Writing of Popular Science and Technology* to his 1953 *General Service List*.
9 Quinault (1947).

10 For example, Bell (*ELT* I/1: 1946), Travis (*ELT* I/6: 1946), Manvell (ELT IV/3: 1949, and *ELT* IV/4: 1950).
11 CREDIF: Centre de Recherche et d'Étude pour la Diffusion du Français, a research centre at the École Normale Supérieure de St. Cloud, near Paris.
12 The Schools Council was set up in 1964 to promote curriculum development and new initiatives in education. The *Scope* project was funded from 1966 (see Chapter 18).
13 CILT Reports and Papers No 1, edited by George Perren, CILT.
14 Published by Oxford University Press.
15 First published by Folkuniversitets Förlag, Stockholm, 1963. Later by Oxford University Press, 1966, second edition, 1975.
16 Published by Longman.
17 Published by Longman.
18 See, for example, Halliday, McIntosh and Strevens (1964), Chapter 4, 'The users and uses of English'.
19 By R. D. Huddleston, R. A. Hudson, E. O. Winter and A. Henrici. The Communication Research Centre, Dept of General Linguistics, University of London.
20 See Dakin *et al.* (1968).
21 See Chapter 18.
22 Edited by Martin Bates and Tony Dudley-Evans, published by Longman, 1976 onwards. The series originated from a project in Tabriz in Iran.
23 C. N. Candlin and his colleagues at Lancaster University have produced numerous reports, papers, and teaching materials that lay stress on the recording of authentic data and its use in developing study-skills courses, for example Candlin, Kirkwood, and Moore, *Study Skills in English*, 1976 (course materials with a supporting article by the same authors in Mackay and Mountford (eds. 1978: 190–219); Candlin, Bruton, Leather, and Woods, *Doctor-Patient Communication Skills* (undated) (course materials); Candlin and Murphy, *Engineering discourse and listening comprehension*, 1976 (report). All published by the University of Lancaster.
24 See Robinson (1980), an informative account of ESP with an excellent bibliography. Also Strevens (1980).
25 ELTDU (originally directed by John Webb) was set up by Oxford University Press to develop special-purpose courses. Projects included *English for Business* with the BBC. It is now an independent company in Bicester.
26 For example Selinker, Trimble, and Vroman: (i) *Working Papers in English for Science and Technology*, Seattle: University of Washington, 1972; (ii) 'Presupposition and technical rhetoric' *ELTJ* 29/1: 1974.
27 See Spencer(1982) for a history of the Association.

28 Directed first by George Perren, now by J. L. M. Trim. The CILT acronym remained unchanged when 'and Research' was added to the title later.

29 A four-volume course by Michael Coles and Basil Lord, published by Oxford University Press.

30 See Note 55 on p. 292.

31 A three-volume course by Geoffrey Broughton, published by Penguin.

32 A six-volume course prepared by English Language Services, Inc. and published by Collier-Macmillan in New York in 1964. A British edition was prepared by Peter Strevens in 1968.

33 Edited by C. E. Nuttall and published by Longman from 1968 onwards.

34 *Kernel Lessons Intermediate* by R. O'Neill, Roy Kingsbury and Tony Yeadon (1971), *Kernel Lessons Plus* (1973), *Kernel One* (1978), *Kernel Two* (1982), all by O'Neill and published by Longman.

35 See, for example, Brumfit's contributions to Brumfit and Johnson (eds. 1979) and Brumfit (1980).

36 Gattegno (1963).

37 Stevick (1980).

# SECTION 2
# Essays in the history of English language teaching since 1900

# 16 Harold E. Palmer

## Palmer's life and work

When Harold Palmer (1877–1949) first began as a teacher of English as a foreign language at the Berlitz School in Verviers in 1902, the main attraction of the job was that it allowed him to live abroad in a French-speaking country. In all likelihood he would eventually come back home in a few years and 'settle down', like many others before and since. Palmer, however, stayed on, opened his own school, and began to think seriously about the work he was doing and how it could be improved. When he died forty-five years later, English language teaching was well on its way to a professionhood which he, more than any other single individual, had helped to bring about.

Palmer's career falls into two, quite distinct, phases. The first, which ended with his departure for Japan in 1922, was primarily concerned with general principles of language teaching method and course design rather than the specific problems of English language teaching. This period culminated in the publication of *The Scientific Study and Teaching of Languages* in 1917, based on his lectures to modern language teachers in London, and two methodological studies, *The Oral Method of Teaching Languages* and *The Principles of Language-Study* both published in 1921. The second phase of his life was almost exclusively devoted to English as a foreign language. He became Linguistic Adviser to the Japanese Ministry of Education in 1922 and the following year he was appointed Director of a specialized institute set up by the Ministry called the Institute for Research in English Teaching (IRET). It eventually became a focus of world attention and attracted a large number of interested teachers, both native-speaking British and Americans, and Japanese. Among them was A. S. Hornby, who arrived in Tokyo in the late twenties and collaborated closely with Palmer on a number of projects.

While he was at IRET Palmer pursued both the professional aims which engaged his attention and energies throughout his life. The first was the development of practical classroom materials following the Oral Method he had established in his earlier theoretical studies. *English Through Actions*, for example, was published in 1925, but it was only one of a long list of similar works to help the teacher in the classroom. His second ambition was to extend the applied linguistic work he began during his time with Daniel Jones between 1915 and 1922. His pedagogical grammar (*A Grammar of Spoken English*) appeared in 1924, for example, and his interest in vocabulary control continued throughout his professional life. He was also an accomplished phonetician and a gifted practical linguist.

*Figure 25   Harold E. Palmer (1877–1949). In combining the direct methods of Berlitz with the applied linguistic approach of Sweet and the Reform Movement, Palmer created a solid intellectual and practical foundation for the development of ELT as an autonomous profession.*

Palmer's later years, after his return to Britain in 1936, were largely spent in writing and he contributed extensively to the New Method Series of Michael West, with whom he had come into contact in the early thirties. He also lectured and advised on English language teaching for the British Council and, in 1944, undertook a tour of South America. His health, however, was poor by this time and he could not complete it. He died, suddenly, in 1949 at the age of seventy-two.

To return to the beginning of Palmer's career after this brief 'bird's-eye-view', his early years in Verviers between 1902 and the outbreak of the First World War were very productive. He developed many new ideas for language teaching materials and already had an impressive list of publications behind him when he escaped to England with his young family in 1914.[1] On returning to London, he made contact with Daniel Jones with whom he had been corresponding for many years and whom he had once met by chance on a cross-channel steamer. Jones offered him a job as a lecturer in spoken English and the following year, 1916, Palmer began giving the lectures on language teaching methodology to local foreign language teachers which formed the basis for his first major work, *The Scientific Study and Teaching of Languages*, published only one year later. To make the transition from refugee English language teacher to the authorship of a classic text in the field inside three years was a phenomenal achievement. Obviously, it would not have been possible if he had not thought deeply about the issues while working in his school in Belgium, or without the stimulus of his contacts with Daniel Jones and his colleagues in the Phonetics Department at University College.

*The Scientific Study* was followed in 1921 by the shorter and more 'orderly' *The Principles of Language-Study*, and both works will be discussed in detail in the next section of this chapter. They form a well-balanced pair in the sense that on their own the former might have sunk under its own weight, while the latter might have seemed rather bland. Taken together, however, they provided a statement of intellectual principle on which the English language teaching profession was to build for the next half century. Having laid the foundations, as it were, Palmer left Britain and began the second phase of his career in Japan.

Accounts of how Palmer came to be offered the Japanese job differ. According to his friend Sir Vere Redman,[2] the initiative came from a wealthy business man, Kojiro Matsukata who, disturbed by the commercial implications of poor standards of spoken English among his compatriots, persuaded the Ministry to hire Palmer as Linguistic Adviser by offering to pay all the expenses. Japanese sources, on the other hand, give the Ministry the credit for the idea.[3] Either way, however, Matsukata paid the bills.

Within a year of arriving in Tokyo, Palmer was made Director of IRET, where he was given a small staff and a larger Board of

Administration, including 'a number of educationists of repute' as the 1931 Prospectus put it.[4] Among them were an American and an Englishman as the project was conceived from the start as a joint Anglo-American venture. Members were accepted for a small subscription, and by 1931 there were about 700, of whom a quarter or so were Japanese. IRET's main commitment was to hold an Annual Conference of English Teachers, an event that attracted a regular following of about three hundred. It also published a *Bulletin* ten times a year. It was not financed by the government, but had to meet its expenses out of membership fees, royalties, and 'occasional donations'.[5]

There was a hidden motive behind the Ministry's enthusiasm for IRET. As a Ministry official, Palmer was a threat to established vested interests, whereas in IRET he could do little harm. The 'politics' of his appointment surfaced very early in his career in Tokyo when he was asked by a prominent official with some influence in Tokyo what he thought was the most useful reform he could propose to improve English teaching in Japan. His reply – a controlled vocabulary of 3,000 words – clearly implied a completely new set of basic schoolbooks. He had said the wrong thing. Japanese schoolchildren, he was told, needed 'full' English, and Palmer was obliged to put his lexical research interests aside for a number of years.[6] The official turned up eight years later as the Japanese agent for Ogden's Basic English programme, having, it seems, had second thoughts about 'full English'. Palmer wrote to Ogden offering to try Basic out in Tokyo in 1931, but Ogden wrote back saying 'Take care, or our lawyers will be prosecuting you for infringement of copyright'.[7] Since this happened three years before Palmer's support for West in his conflict over Basic, it is not very easy to understand.

Basic was a headache for the future. Palmer's immediate aim on becoming Director of IRET was to establish contact with the teachers in the schools and launch his campaign for oral methods of language teaching. This phase of his work was very productive in terms of publication including, in particular, *A Grammar of Spoken English* in 1924 and *English Through Actions* (1925) which he wrote with his daughter Dorothée who had been helping him by trying out the ideas in a school in Osaka. The latter, a comprehensive collection of oral drills and exercises for the classroom, has stood the test of time and was published again in 1959.

It seems, however, that his enthusiasm for oral methods did not always suit the established patterns of relationships in Japanese classrooms. To work properly, oral activities require both linguistic self-confidence and a certain amount of histrionic gusto. As a native speaker, Palmer did not have to worry about the former, and as a keen amateur actor he no doubt exhibited plenty of the latter. His Japanese customers, however, preferred reading and 'felt that the oral method was valid only when a native English speaker conducted the class'.[8]

*English Through Actions* was 'a little bit difficult' and underlined Palmer's reputation for being 'fond of novelty'.[9] Nevertheless, they continued to attend both his lectures and the IRET Conferences where his 'typical southern English charmed the audience'.[10] When he finally left the country in 1936, he received an honorary D.Litt. from the Imperial University in Tokyo in recognition of his services.

Why did Palmer fail to convince his Japanese hosts – as he clearly did, in spite of making some enthusiastic converts? The fault, if there is one, lies on both sides. By putting him in an annexe to 'do research', the Ministry absolved itself of any responsibility for supporting his campaign. If it had actually worked, they would have been in trouble with demands for new materials, such as recordings (Palmer had explored the use of records in which he had developed a 'pause' system which was to become a standard feature of language laboratory tapes in the future).[11] There would also have been requests to change the all-important assessment system, and, possibly more alarming in its implications, a need for massive teacher re-training, including trips abroad. Basically, the Japanese did not want radical notions such as the Oral Method. They simply wanted their pupils to have a better pronunciation.

Palmer's perception of his task may also have been misjudged. He was evidently an excellent direct-method teacher of adults, but he had less experience of schoolteaching. The Direct Method, as we have seen, originated in a desire to do something that the schools of the time were not doing, and probably could not do, namely to teach foreign languages as practical skills for everyday purposes of social survival. Questions of educational value and 'worthwhileness' were irrelevant, what mattered was the ability to communicate effectively in ordinary ('trivial') life. The students were typically working adults, equals with whom it was possible to strike up a friendship. In a Japanese school, however, with complex traditions of behaviour quite unlike European schools, and with teachers who had little confidence in their spoken fluency, it was unrealistic to hope that the validity of the method would overcome the bruising of sensitivities that would accompany an attempt to implement it.

Once he was firmly established at IRET, Palmer revived his interest in vocabulary selection. The early thirties were a particularly fertile period for his work. He presented the first draft of a 3,000-word vocabulary for the middle-schools to the Seventh Annual Conference of English Teachers at IRET in 1930. It was laid out in the form of 'radii', one of the terms used by the vocabulary-control specialists, which suggested a 'dartsboard' image with the absolute minimum vocabulary in the 'bull's-eye', surrounded by concentric rings at radii of 1,000 words, 2,000 words and so on moving out towards the edge. In the following year he offered the Conference a revised version of the 3,000-word radius along with proposals for two smaller radius lists, *The First and Second 500 Most Frequently Used Words.*

In 1931 Palmer set off on a world tour starting with a visit to the Soviet Union, and then on to London, where he met Michael West for the first time, and also had a brief and rather unsatisfactory interview with Ogden. He continued to the United States, spending some weeks in New York, though he did not at this time meet Thorndike himself. He renewed his acquaintance with Sapir before moving on to Chicago and California. His main purpose in America was to learn at first hand about the statistical procedures used in most American work on vocabulary control, though he was not a supporter of the so-called 'objective' approach himself. He returned to Tokyo after a trip lasting eight months altogether and began the serious work of writing and adapting English texts within the radius of the vocabulary accepted at the 1931 Teachers' Conference. His efforts were described in an IRET pamphlet called *The Grading and Simplifying of Literary Material* (1932).

At this point his partnership with Hornby began in earnest and together they devised the *IRET 600-word Vocabulary for Story-telling Purposes* (1932) and adapted and enlarged it into the first draft of *Thousand-Word English* (1937), already referred to. It was this draft that Palmer took along with him to the first meeting in 1934 of the Carnegie Conference in New York and its follow-up meeting the following year in London.

Palmer was a true representative of the long tradition of practical English linguistics which stretches back to the Renaissance. He was a brilliant phonetician (his *English Intonation* in 1922, for example, has long been recognized as an important contribution to the subject) and absorbed by lexicography and the study of words. In grammar, however, his contribution is less easy to assess.

He wrote two grammars, *The Grammar of Spoken English, on a strictly phonetic basis* in 1924 and *The New Method Grammar* in 1938. The latter is a brave, but not entirely successful, attempt to teach grammar to younger learners through an analogy with railway networks. There are 'direct-object stations', 'prepositional branch-lines', and so on, ideas which he tried out in a real-life model in the garden of his home in Surrey.[12] It is a 'collector's piece' really, but an original approach to a difficult problem.

*A Grammar of Spoken English*, on the other hand, is a major work aimed at the more advanced learner and at teachers. It is the first large-scale attempt to provide a detailed description of standard spoken English for pedagogical purposes. His treatment of intonation is particularly impressive. He identified four tone-groups which he related to functionally distinct variants of basic sentence types: statements, questions, commands, and so on. Of special interest at the present time, however, is the fact that he devoted Part Four ('Logical Categories') to the relationship between grammatical forms and their notional meanings. Palmer's *Grammar* stands firmly in the great line of English grammars written since the end of the nineteenth century which aim to be both comprehensive as sources of reference and instructive to the serious student of the language. These grammars deserve more than the following list (in chronological order): Henry Sweet, *A New English Grammar* (two volumes) (1892,1898), Otto Jespersen, *A Modern English Grammar* (seven volumes) (1909–49) and *Essentials of English Grammar* (1933), H. Poutsma, *A Grammar of Late Modern English* (four volumes) (1904–26), H. E. Palmer, *A Grammar of Spoken English* (1924), R. W. Zandvoort, *A Handbook of English Grammar* (1945/57), A. S. Hornby, *A Guide to Patterns and Usage in English* (1954) and Randolph Quirk, Sidney Greenbaum, Geoffrey Leech, and Jan Svartvik, *A Grammar of Contemporary English* (1972). Though these grammars are very different in many ways, some are more scholarly, others more pedagogical, they belong to a tradition that has run in parallel to more theoretically adventurous but less accessible linguistic descriptions.[13]

Unfortunately, Palmer never wrote a full-scale English course, except for *An International English Course*, but its (unexpected) bilingual methodology made it difficult to publish, and it never became widely known.[14] The Spanish version, *Curso Internacional de Inglés*, was reissued in the Language and Language Learning Series of Oxford University Press in the sixties along with the *Scientific Study* and the *Principles of Language-Study*.[15]

Palmer was a prolific writer – the bibliography in Mackin's 1969 edition of *This Language-Learning Business* (1932) lists over 120 items, some of them consisting of more than one volume. However, even if the full corpus of his work were readily available (and much of it is not), it would be difficult to resist the conclusion that the full realization of the programme he envisaged in his pioneering work at University College required more than one lifetime to complete, and that his partnership with Hornby forged in the thirties was essential to its fulfilment.

## Palmer's methodology

Both of Palmer's major books on language teaching methodology were written before 1922. We know, therefore, a great deal about his ideas as they had developed during the years he spent running his school in Verviers, but rather less about how those ideas matured at IRET or later when he was the 'grand old man' of English language teaching. Like West, he did his most interesting and thought-provoking work before he became famous and therefore in constant demand.

He was forty when he wrote *The Scientific Study and Teaching of*

*Languages*. It is a unique book, creative, sprawling, and infectiously (Sweet) enthusiastic. It is not a good book in the sense that *The Principles of Language-Study* is good. It is not thought-through, distilled, and authoritative. It is organized in thirty-eight consecutively numbered sections and, although perfectly coherent and logical, has a breathless quality, as though dictated in a sustained rush of inspiration. One can understand why the lectures on which it was based were so popular and stimulating.

The central concern of the *Study* is language and how it should be taught and learnt. In 1917 Palmer was still the heir of Henry Sweet. His ambition was to rejuvenate the teaching of foreign languages in Britain by calling on his experience of teaching his own language abroad. As with Sweet, his chosen vehicle was a general methodology of language-study: 'our survey of the problems must be on a most comprehensive basis; we must not be content with stating formulae for the teaching of French to English children; our outlook must embrace the study of any aspect of any foreign language by students of all ages and nationalities'.[16]

In the opening chapters, he creates a private system of linguistic description with its own terminology. Starting from the question that had haunted him as a teacher, 'What is a word?', he constructs a descriptive apparatus that distinguishes between form and function in an astonishingly modern way. His form-classes are called miologs (morphemes), monologs (word forms), and polylogs (collocations or phrases). These form-classes enter into functional, or, as he calls them, *ergonic* relationships with each other to create sentences. At the end of the book he provides an 'ergonic chart' for French which, he says, 'teaches us (1) to classify the units of a given language according to their function in the sentence (and) (2) to build up original (i.e. unknown) units from the smaller known units of which they are composed'.[17]

The learner's task is to acquire these 'known units' (or 'primary matter') as the data-base from which an infinite set of sentences ('secondary matter') can be generated. If this sounds 'Chomskyan', consider Palmer's own summary of his approach: 'the number of sentences, being infinite, resource must be had to the study of their mechanism in order that, from the relatively limited number of lesser ergons, an infinite number of sentences may be composed at will'.[18] Palmer called his data-base 'The Microcosm' and it was in some ways a restatement of Prendergast's 'mastery' system from the 1860s, though it is not clear how well Palmer knew the earlier work, if at all. The notion of an irreducible minimum or 'kernel' as it has been called (following Chomsky's use of the term in an early model of transformational grammar), or 'common core' to use the contemporary equivalent, is a powerful one. Whether it can be expressed in linguistic terms such as Palmer's primary sentence patterns or West's 'minimum adequate vocabulary' would be open to question at the present time. There would be voices raised in favour of a different approach entirely, some form of 'minimal communication system', for example.

Palmer's functional grammar (ergonic system) consists of three types of structural unit: (i) minimal (m) groups, (ii) product (p) groups and (iii) sum (s) groups. M-groups are essentially word-classes (nouns, pronouns, adjectives, and so on). They combine together to form p-groups (phrase-structures of various kinds, with the exception of P1 which is the sentence itself). In his chart for French, he identified seventy-eight m-groups which combined to form sixty-eight p-groups. In addition, there were twenty-five s-groups. To exemplify the system in English, the phrase *my dog* would be a p-group consisting of two m-groups (possessive adjectives and nouns). The s-groups account for the fact that more than one m-group can have the same functional relationship to other m-groups. For instance, *my*, *this*, and *the* would make an s-group since all three can co-occur with nouns: *my dog*, *this dog*, *the dog*. Essentially, p-groups account for syntagmatic (chain) relations between m-groups, while s-groups cover the paradigmatic choices that can be made among members of an m-group. Palmer identified a very large number of m-groups, partly because he was anxious to include collocations like *tomorrow morning* as single items.

The ergonic system has been likened to an early transformational grammar,[19] but this is not really the case. It is a form of item-and-arrangement surface structure grammar, but with the important characteristic that, unlike the grammars used in language teaching at the time, it lays particular stress on the functional relationships between elements of sentence structure. Palmer did not use the ergonic terminology explicitly in his published work or teaching materials. It provided, however, the intellectual framework for the notion of the 'sentence pattern' which was to dominate the teaching of English as a foreign language for the next forty years or more.

Unfortunately, the 'sentence pattern' also destroyed one of the cardinal principles of the Reform Movement, namely the central importance of the connected text. In this sense, it was a retrograde step, back to the sentence-based methodology of the nineteenth century, though it avoided Sweet's 'arithmetical fallacy' by treating sentences as complete units rather than the outcome of stringing words together. Also, the new approach rejected a bilingual teaching method and therefore condemned the teaching of grammar 'rules' in the mother tongue. In order to stay within the confines of a monolingual methodology, the 'sentence patterns' had to be presented to the learner in the form of example sentences, sometimes laid out in substitution tables, and sometimes illustrated in specially constructed teaching texts. In inexpert hands, these 'illustrative' texts became so over-crammed with examples of the new 'pattern' that, as Sweet had predicted, they turned into 'monstrosities'.

Why, one wonders, did Palmer overturn the principle of the connected text so readily, almost one feels without noticing that he had done so? Perhaps the explanation lies in his experience as a direct method language teacher. When Berlitz and others systematized Sauveur's conversational methods, they simplified the language used in the lessons and pared it down to a few utterances which were easy to demonstrate in class. Inevitably, the distinction between a communicative utterance and a grammatical sentence disappeared altogether: *This is a book. It is big. It is on the table. Can you see it?* etc. Instead of talking to the students in a simple way so that they would understand (Sauveur's principle), the Direct Method taught the language system by using simple sentences (which is not at all the same thing).

The heart of the *Scientific Study* is the organization of the curriculum or syllabus, 'the Ideal Standard Programme' as Palmer called it. He proposed three stages over a four-year school period. First there should be a short *Introductory Stage* lasting about one school term during which the pupils would learn how to learn a foreign language, and follow a detailed programme of pronunciation teaching. He also had the very interesting notion of starting learners off with what he called 'subconscious comprehension'. This was not listening practice in the ordinary sense, but a form of interaction without any pressure for reciprocity. If the learners wanted to participate, they could, but there was no need to do so. This 'incubation' period deserves very careful consideration, and appropriate support materials. Palmer's own ideas were a first stab at the problem, but did not arouse much interest at the time. The recent revival of interest in 'input models' shows yet again how advanced much of Palmer's thinking was.

Stage Two, which he called *Intermediate*, began with the memorization ('catenization' as he labelled it) of the basic 'primary matter' in the form of oral exercises, drills, and Direct Method speechwork activities. As soon as these primary speech patterns were assimilated, the learners were encouraged to derive further examples ('secondary matter') on the same models. Accuracy was essential in this habit-formation process and there was little room for the private use of language.

Stage Three, *Advanced*, was devoted to the use of language in reading, composition, conversation, and other practical skills. Literature came on to the syllabus at this point, and the students made the transition from phonetic transcription to traditional orthography.

Although the central idea of habitualized speech patterns derived from the Direct Method, many of Palmer's other views were closer to the Reform Movement. His support for phonetic transcription is a case in point. So, too, was his attitude to translation. He did not follow the Berlitz line of 'never translate' but took the moderate view that the whole question was a pragmatic one. His audience for the *Scientific Study* was composed of British secondary-school teachers of modern languages, not native-speaking English teachers. If, as in this case, the teacher knew the student's mother tongue, there was no reason why he should not use it to gloss the meanings of new items, particularly if this made comprehension more accurate. 'Let us recognize frankly', he said,[20] 'that the withholding of an "official" or authentic translation does not prevent the student from forming faulty associations, but that, on the contrary, such withholding may often engender them'. In view of this comment, his decision to write a bilingual course himself, *The International English Course* (1944), is not as surprising as it seems at first sight.

Habit-formation was, as we have seen, Palmer's core methodological principle. If it was derived from anywhere – and he does not make his sources very clear – one possible candidate is William James's *Principles of Psychology* published in 1890, an immensely influential work which stands, as it were, on the dividing line between speculative and scientific psychology. He was also influenced by Bloomfield's *Introduction to the Study of Language* (1914), an early work which drew on the theories of Wilhelm Wundt (1832–1920), a German physiologist who aimed to give his psychological studies a scientific basis through the controlled use of introspective techniques, a procedure rejected outright by the behaviourists. The founding paper of behaviourism appeared in 1913, 'Psychology as the Behaviorist Views It' by John B. Watson, in which Watson defined his subject as 'a purely objective, experimental branch of science which needs introspection as little as do the sciences of chemistry and physics'.[21] In the same year, E. L. Thorndike published his important book *The Psychology of Learning* in which he put forward his trial-and-error concepts for the first time. However, the bulk of the research into habit-formation conducted by the leading behaviourist psychologists of the twenties and thirties had not been conducted when Palmer wrote *The Principles of Language-Study* in 1921. Strictly speaking, therefore, to call Palmer a 'behaviourist', as is sometimes done, is anachronistic though in all probability it is a label he would have accepted without much of a struggle.

In *The Principles of Language-Study* Palmer put forward nine fundamental principles of good language teaching and learning, of which habit-formation is the first and the most important. These principles are not a random list, but derive from a model of some present-day interest. Palmer took as his point of departure the distinction between language learning in real-life and learning in the classroom. Having noted the success of the former, particularly among infants, of course, he attributed the relative failure of the latter to a misunderstanding of the nature of the language learning process. There was, he insisted, a basic difference between the *spontaneous capacities* of the human being to acquire language naturally and unconsciously on the one hand, and, on the other, the trained or *'studial' capacities* of the classroom learner which allow him to organize his learning and apply his conscious knowledge to the task in hand. Palmer then made the interesting point that spontaneous capacities are brought into play in the acquisition of spoken language whereas studial capacities are required in the development of literacy. The spontaneous/studial distinction has recently found an echo in the acquisition/learning distinction underlying Krashen's 'Monitor Model',[22] which, interestingly enough, also makes considerable use of a concept of a 'silent period' in language acquisition closely akin to Palmer's notion of 'subconscious assimilation' already referred to above. It has to be said, however, that Palmer's association of spontaneous/studial learning with the contrast between speech and writing has more far-reaching implications than Krashen's distinction between the acquisition of an 'internalized grammar' and the learning of grammatical rules. The function of literacy teaching in creating an awareness of linguistic form has received insufficient attention in the argument over whether learning a second language by post-literate learners is 'the same as' learning the mother tongue by pre-literate infants. (This point is touched on again in the Epilogue.) However, Palmer did not pursue his distinction in any depth, but concentrated his attention on what, to him, was the crucial feature of spontaneity, namely the habitualization of foreign language speech patterns.

Of his eight remaining principles, three relate to habit-formation (*accuracy, interest,* and the importance of *initial preparation*), while the other five have more to do with course design and classroom teaching. *Initial preparation* is obviously of basic importance if good speech habits are to be established early in the course, and *accuracy* must be maintained for the same reason. Palmer had no time for the kind of hypothesis-testing notions which are influential at the present time, as the following extract makes clear: 'there seems to be a real danger in the misapplication of such terms as "trial and error", "the selection of the successful and the rejection of the unsuccessful efforts", "practice makes perfect", etc. Misunderstanding on this point has caused many teachers to encourage, and many students to acquire, pidgin-speech, and to consider it as the inevitable or even indispensable prelude to normal speech'.[23] This is an interesting passage in view of the modern comparison between the development of language in the individual learner and the social development of pidgin and creole languages. Although Palmer is clearly using the term 'pidgin' in a non-technical, and indeed pejorative sense, the thought is there.

Today we would probably call the *interest* principle 'motivation'. Palmer made four points, each of which has as much relevance now as in 1921. The first is the essential importance of progress. Only if progress can be perceived and maintained is there a real chance for long-term success. This point was also stressed in a Report in 1974 on modern language teaching in England and Wales,[24] and is the prime objective behind the development of graded materials for use in the classroom. Secondly, the learner ought to understand what is happening in a language class. This may seem obvious enough, but bewilderment may be more common than is generally supposed, particularly when a monolingual methodology is adopted. The other two points are the importance of a good relationship beween teacher and learner (an issue that has been explored in some detail in recent years), and the value of games and a variety of classroom activities.

Palmer's five course-design and teaching principles (*gradation, concreteness, proportion, the multiple line of approach,* and *a rational order of progression*) follow logically from his earlier analysis of the learning process. *Gradation* was later to become a major preoccupation of language textbook writers, applied linguists, and others. In *The Principles of Language-Study*, however, Palmer restricts his discussion to a few general guidelines. Having pointed out that 'gradation means passing from the known to the unknown by easy stages', an uncontroversial Comenian concept, he then makes what to many people must be a very unexpected point: 'In the ideally graded course the student first assimilates a relatively small but exceedingly important vocabulary.'[25] Only later on does he combine the words into sentences and longer stretches of language. The 'standard' view of grading that has come down to us from the structuralist tradition is that it is almost exclusively a matter of ordering the grammatical and phonological features of the foreign language. To Palmer, however, and, as it happens, to Bloomfield as well, the starting point in acquiring a new language was lexical and not grammatical.

His principle of *concreteness* was a restatement of the direct method notion of giving examples rather than rules, and trying to teach a foreign language as far as possible through experience as opposed to intellectual discussion – 'teach the language not about the language' as a later slogan (not Palmer's) had it.

*Proportion* and the *multiple line of approach* imply a balanced eclecticism but not merely in the sense of choosing a bit of this and a bit of that. A good method deliberately sets out to combine alternative strategies which may on the face of things appear to be in conflict with each other. Both intensive and extensive reading are needed, for example, both drills and free work, and so on, for different purposes at different times.

Palmer's *rational order of progression* is a good place to end this review of *The Principles of Language-Study* since it provides an excellent summary of his course design proposals. It bears, as we have said, a remarkable similarity to the work of Prendergast (see Chapter 12) though Palmer would probably not have approved of his predecessor's technique of 'packing' sentences with as much grammar as possible. However, the following quotation could have come from the work of either man: 'the most successful linguists have attained their proficiency by memorizing sentences they could not analyse'.[26] Here is the *rational order*:

1 Become proficient in recognizing and in producing foreign sounds and tones, both isolated and in combinations.
2 Memorize (without analysis or synthesis) a large number of complete sentences chosen specifically for this purpose by the teacher or by the composer of the course.
3 Learn to build up all types of sentences (both regular and irregular) from 'working sentence-units' (i.e. ergons) chosen specifically for this purpose by the teacher or by the composer of the course.
4 Learn how to convert 'dictionary words' (i.e. etymons) into 'working sentence-units' (i.e. ergons).[27]

At the end of the day, it was Palmer's early experience as a native-speaking direct method teacher that provided the strongest elements in his methodology, in spite of his modified views on the role of translation. His abandonment of the Reform Movement principle of the connected text in favour of sentence patterns introduced and practised orally by the teacher in the classroom meant, as he discovered in Japan, an additional burden on the non-native teacher. However, he inherited from the Reformers a serious concern for the teaching of spoken language based on the science of phonetics and a desire to develop a methodology of language teaching that was theoretically well-grounded, intellectually ordered and practically workable. He was also a follower of Sweet in one further respect. He isolated the teaching of languages from the rest of the education process and treated it as a separate almost 'technical' task that required no further justification than its own successful completion. Sweet said 'I am not much concerned with such questions as, why do we learn languages?'[28] Such questions did not much concern Palmer, either. They did, however, concern Palmer's younger contemporary, Michael West, as we shall see in the next chapter.

## Notes

1 For example, *Cartes Palmer A/B* (1906/7); *Cours éleméntaire de correspondance anglaise* (1912); *Manual d'anglais parlé. Méthode Palmer* (1913). All published in Verviers.
2 Redman (1967: 12).
3 Yamamoto (1978: 151).
4 Bongers (1947: 41).
5 Ibid.: 42.
6 Ibid.: 77–8.

7  Ibid.: 80, footnote.
8  Yamamoto (1978: 158).
9  Ibid.: 159, quote.
10  Ibid.: 152, quote.
11  Redman (1967: 14).
12  See Dorothée Anderson (formerly Palmer) (1969: 158–9). Also Tickoo (1982a: 115).
13  See Strevens (1978: 103–16), where a useful distinction is made between 'descriptivist' grammars, for example, Sweet and Palmer, and 'linguistic' grammars, for example, Fries.
14  Published by Evans Bros., London. Editions were prepared in Italian, French, Dutch, Spanish, Polish and Czech.
15  *The Scientific Study and Teaching of Languages*, edited by D. Harper, 1968; *The Principles of Language-Study*, 1964, *Curso Internacional de Inglés*, 1965, and *This Language-Learning Business*, 1969, all edited by R. Mackin.
16  Palmer (1917/1968: 4).
17  Ibid.: 226.
18  Ibid.: 22.
19  Barrutia (1965).
20  Palmer (1917/1968: 65).
21  Watson (1913: 176).
22  See, for example, Krashen (1981).
23  Palmer (1921/1964: 42).
24  Burstall *et al.* (1974).
25  Palmer (1921/1964: 68).
26  Ibid.: 50.
27  Ibid.: 106.
28  Sweet (1899/1964: 2).

# 17 Choosing the right words

## Michael West and the New Method

The *New Method Readers* by Michael West (1888–1973) are the first language teaching materials to have emerged from an experimental project. The project itself was written up in a report called *Bilingualism (with special reference to Bengal)* published by the Indian Bureau of Education in 1926 and also provided the data for West's D. Phil. awarded by the University of Oxford in 1927 under the title: 'The Position of English in a National System of Education for Bengal'.

The Bengal project report ought to be better known. It contains a great deal which is of current interest in the teaching of reading and many ideas which were not pursued very far at the time, but which have become more important since. One of the most significant was West's concept of 'surrender value' (a term he invented). The imperial education system had, up until the First World War, pursued an educational policy known as 'filtering', that is, trying to ensure that the best students were 'filtered' through the system to end up, preferably with a British university degree, in government employment of some appropriate kind. West challenged this concept by pointing to the enormous educational wastage it entailed. He quotes some relevant figures for 1919 in his report: 32 per cent of Class 3 pupils (eight-year-olds) never even reached Class 4 and as many as 82 per cent had dropped out before the end of school in Class 10. What this meant to West was that each year in school had to be treated as a separate educational experience in its own right, not merely as preparation for the next year that large numbers of the children would never reach. He defined 'surrender value' as 'the proportionate amount of benefit which will be derived by any pupil from an incompleted course of instruction'.[1] In his view, training in spoken English took far too long to have any useful surrender value for the majority of school-leavers. Basic literacy skills in English, on the other hand, could be acquired much more rapidly, particularly if the children were already literate in their mother tongue (though this sometimes turned out not to be the case). They could, moreover, be used in later life whereas spoken English was a useless skill for most Bengalis away from the major centres of imperial influence.

In order to investigate his concept of surrender value in more depth,

West completed a needs-analysis survey ('An analysis of the Bengali's
need of English', Chapter 5 of the report) stressing his interest in 'all
Bengalis, not merely a few selected individuals of the upper classes'.[2] If
this all sounds unexpectedly modern, one might ask why the West model
was not followed more often. Perhaps it has been, and, like the Bengali
project, been forgotten.

The number of Bengali speakers of English in 1919 (the year to which
most of his data relates) was only 1 in 2407. Teaching spoken English
along Palmerian lines was not likely to bring much benefit unless the
majority of children stayed at school long enough to gain from an
English-medium secondary education, and West knew this was not
going to happen. Reading was the obvious alternative, and he
investigated the notion which was popular at the time, that translation
into Bengali would ultimately solve the problem of access to information
rather than a reading programme in English.

Concentrating on informative texts, he discovered that during the
twelve and a half years to 1919 the proportion of informative
publications in Bengali and English were: for science, 9 Bengali to 434
English; for technology, 3 to 686; for agriculture 4 to 228; and for
business 1 to 139. In 1919 book production in technical subjects in the
English language, taking both the United States and Britain together,
was running at forty-eight times the Bengali level. Clearly Bengali would
never catch up. 'The outlook is not hopeful' as he put it, 'human activity
and human knowledge are becoming every year more complex and more
specialized, and the average man desires and is required more and more
to keep in touch with new developments in his occupation or profession.
One hundred years ago the promoters of education in Bengal might
reasonably have hoped by vigorous translation within a conceivable
period to bring Bengal level with the knowledge of the rest of the world.
The situation is now immensely changed.'[3]

Faced with this evidence of the importance of practical informative
reading and the need to provide worthwhile learning at each stage of the
school, West decided that the teaching of reading must have first
priority, even if this meant the relative neglect of the spoken language.
His research also accorded with his own experience of working as an
educationalist in Bengal over a fairly long period of time. He had gone to
India in 1912 after leaving Christ Church College, Oxford, and became
the Principal of the Teachers' Training College in Dacca as well as
Principal Inspector of Schools for Chittagong and Calcutta. He was also
an Honorary Reader in Education at Dacca University and had
published in the field as well. Both his experience and his knowledge of
the Bengali education system had prepared him for the experiment in
materials development which he undertook in 1923–5.

As a pilot experiment West tried his ideas out with a class of
eight-year-olds whose knowledge of English on the standard tests he

used was virtually zero. At this stage the reading materials were locally produced primers and elementary readers. Each new text was introduced by the teacher who selected what he thought were the new words, glossed them and practised them on the blackboard. Comprehension questions were set, to be answered in the vernacular. The results of this first trial were disappointing and the procedures were changed so that the children were actively encouraged to tell the teacher which words they did not understand. But there were still a great many difficulties, and progress was slow.

It seemed to West that there were two main ways in which the reading texts could be improved in order to help the children to achieve more. The first was to simplify the vocabulary by replacing old-fashioned literary words by more common modern equivalents. For example, West discovered words like *plight, mode, isle, nought, ere* and *groom* and substituted more frequent items such as *state, way, island, nothing, before,* and *servant* instead. This principle, which could be called a *lexical selection* principle (though West did not use the term), was to become a dominant one during the next twenty years. It also echoed the ideas of Palmer, with whom West was eventually to work closely. It is not entirely clear, however, how using 'common words' makes reading easier for children for whom *all* the words are unfamiliar anyway. And on the surrender value theory, it could be argued that if words like *plight* were common in locally-produced texts then they should have been retained in the teaching materials. What West was getting at ultimately was, as we have seen, access to 'international English', particularly in the shape of informative texts. Most of the texts he actually used, however, were stories and other literary pieces.

West's second and perhaps more important principle of readability could be called a *lexical distribution* principle. Not only were there too many new words overall, but they were packed too closely together. Almost every sentence contained a new item, with the result that both teacher and pupils became frustrated and none of the new words was ever properly practised. In the table below, which is summarized from a longer one in the Bengal Report, West compared his 'New Method' materials with four readers in current use at both Primer and First Reading Book levels, the type of materials he had used in his abortive early experiments. It can be seen that, in the new texts that West wrote or adapted, the overall number of new words dropped from an average of just under 450 to 208 in the Primers, and from an average of 420 down to 236 in the First Reading Books. At the same time he increased the total number of words of running-text from a mean length of 3,269 words to 9,296 in the Primers and from a mean of 5,926 to 13,217 in the First Reading Books. The key statistic is in the bottom row of the table which shows the average rate at which new words were introduced. West increased this from a mean of 1 in 7.4 to no less than 1 in 44.7. This meant, in effect, that instead of meeting a new word in every sentence, the children would have five or six sentences of practice material between each new word. The comparable figures for the First Reading Book level show a slightly less striking pattern, but the difference is still substantial at a mean of 1 in 15.1 ('old') to 1 in 56.0 ('new').

West's lexical distribution patterns meant that, in theory at least, the children ought to be able to cover very much more material in the time available. He calculated that, on the assumption that the children had two lessons per week and spent forty per cent of their time reading, they should be able to get through 60,000 words of text, even at their slow reading speed of 50 words per minute. The textbook they were using contained only 5,000 words and was used as a 'composite' manual for all teaching purposes, oral work, reading, writing, etc. The children did not read enough, he believed, and what they did read, they did not understand.

| | Primers | | | | | First reading-books | | | | |
|---|---|---|---|---|---|---|---|---|---|---|
| | New Method | 1 | 2 | 3 | 4 | New Method | 1 | 2 | 3 | 4 |
| Number of new words | 208 | 353 | 327 | 313 | 844 | 236 | 429 | 572 | 292 | 377 |
| Length of running text | 9296 | 2358 | 1797 | 3415 | 5506 | 13217 | 8371 | 4639 | 5853 | 4842 |
| Running words per new word | 44.7 | 6.7 | 5.5 | 10.9 | 6.5 | 56.0 | 19.5 | 8.1 | 20.0 | 12.8 |

*Figure 26   West's lexical distribution patterns. Adapted from West (1926), p. 275.*

West's first experiment with the New Method materials compared the children in Class 2 of a severely disadvantaged school with one of the best schools in the province. On entry the disadvantaged children knew an average of 9.5 letters of the English alphabet and 0.4 words. In seventeen and a half weeks they had gained the equivalent of two and a half years and were comparable to good Class IV children in the better school, who were still using the old materials. The second experiment was more impressive with a gain of two and a half years in only ten weeks. The starting-point here was higher, and all the children were literate in Bengali, which had not been the case in the first school. Research of this kind is full of uncontrolled variables of one sort or another. Nevertheless, the main point was clear enough. The children made better progress in reading with texts that did not introduce too many new words too quickly.

There was also a second lesson to be learnt from the project which derived from working closely with the teachers and varying the procedures of text presentation in the classroom. Neither the old system of relying completely on the teacher's intuition or memory as to which words were new and which were not, nor the system of depending on the children to volunteer information, and thus confess their ignorance, worked particularly well. What the teachers needed was a clear, unambiguous indication of the new words, properly marked in the text so that the children would also be alerted to them. A controlled vocabulary with each new item explicitly indicated on the printed page, provided the model for the *New Method Reader Scheme* which began to appear from Longmans in Calcutta from 1927 onwards.[4] Later they were published for the world market in London along with other *New Method* series such as *New Method Conversation* (1933), *New Method Composition* (1938), and, of course, the *New Method Dictionary* (1935), written jointly by West and J. G. Endicott. In addition, as we have already seen, Harold Palmer contributed the *New Method Grammar* (1938) and also wrote a series of *New Method English Practice* books published in the same year.

There seems to have been a 'meeting of minds' between Palmer and West in the 1930s, mainly as a result of the events surrounding the Carnegie Conference and the 'Basic English Affair' which are dealt with elsewhere. While there is no doubt that West respected Palmer's work, and in particular the *Principles of Language-Study*, he was unsure of the value of starting from an oral approach when the needs for reading were more important for the children for whom he was responsible. The strengths of the two men complemented each other, Palmer in the spoken language and West in the written, with professionally beneficial results. However, West's departure from India after the Bengal Report and his emergence as one of the world leaders of English language teaching, meant that his specialist interests in the teaching of reading did not develop in the way he had planned while he was writing the Report.

West's scheme for a full-scale reading development programme is of particular interest as it envisaged the training of three distinct types of reading strategy. The first stage, represented by the Bengal work, was a vocabulary stage in which each new word was introduced carefully and deliberately up to a maximum of about 1,500 words, the figure he decided on for the *New Method Dictionary* which defines the meanings of 24,000 entries within a vocabulary of 1,490 words. The second stage was to concentrate on the development of skills, holding the vocabulary level more or less constant. At the third stage the student would move on to strategic reading, in particular the use of skimming and scanning techniques. (West preferred the American term *scanning* since it did not carry the pejorative overtones of *skimming*.) Strategic skills did not fit very readily into the 'nitty-gritty' intellectual atmosphere of the mid-twentieth century with its (almost obsessive) concern for the detail of vocabulary selection, structural organization and grading. So the plan as a whole never matured as West seems to have intended in 1926.

It is also disappointing that West's 'reading first' philosophy was later swamped in the general oral consensus that grew up after the war among the methodologists of the forties and fifties who saw themselves as the vanguard of a new approach to the science of language as applied to the teaching of languages. American linguistics, in particular, stressed the primacy of speech and drew on its origins in anthropological research to create a radically different set of descriptive linguistic procedures that owed nothing at all to a literate tradition. 'Reading first' sounded old-fashioned and 'literary' in a world of phonemics and speech-sound analyses. It also has to be said that West himself rather lost sight of the early emphasis on practical, informative reading with which he started out in Bengal. There are more stories like *Robinson Crusoe* and *Black Beauty* in the reader-scheme than 'How to mend a bike' or 'The economics of farming'.

Aside from the *New Method Readers* Michael West's most substantial and permanent contribution to the development of English language teaching was the *General Service List of English Words*, which eventually came out in 1953, after almost twenty years in the making since the first draft at the second Carnegie Conference in London in 1935. However, before moving to Carnegie, it is necessary to fill in the background in rather more detail by a brief account of the 'cause célèbre' of the thirties, Basic English.

### The Basic issue

'Basic English is English made simple by limiting the number of its words to 850, and by cutting down the rules for using them to the smallest necessary number for the clear statement of ideas. And this is done without change in the normal order and behaviour of these words in everyday English. This is the first point to make clear. Basic English, though it has only 850 words, is still normal English. It is limited in its words and its rules, but it keeps to the regular forms of English. And though it is designed to give the learner as little trouble as possible, it is no more strange to the eyes of my readers than these lines, which are in fact in Basic English'.[5]

I. A. Richards, whose defence of Basic English in 1943 (*Basic English and its Uses*) is quoted above, had worked with the founder of the 'language', C. K. Ogden, in 1923 on *The Meaning of Meaning*, an influential text in theoretical semantics. Richards himself was the most important of Ogden's supporters while the controversy surrounding Basic English was at its height during the thirties and up to the end of the Second World War. He was also the co-author, with Christine Gibson, of the one application of Basic that has survived in general use. It was originally called *A Pocket Book of Basic English* (1945) but is known to large numbers of people throughout the world as *English Through Pictures*, the first of a series of 'Through Pictures' spin-offs. Richards' decision to modify Basic for the book led to a split with Ogden, who disassociated himself from the publication. Ogden always believed that the thought and research that had gone into Basic before its appearance in 1930 was sufficiently thorough and extensive to guarantee its integrity, and that 'improvements' would only damage its credibility. From a distance this attitude may seem intransigent, but to Ogden himself it was a matter both of conviction and commonsense. Other attempts to construct auxiliary languages had suffered badly from the well-intentioned intervention of 'improvers'.

BASIC stands for British American Scientific International Commercial. It is not merely a simplified form of English but a language in its own right, a rival to Esperanto or Jespersen's Novial or any of the other artificial languages which were proposed as a means of international communication in a divided world, and which attracted the idealism of the post-war generation with particular strength. Basic consists of 850 words, as the Richards' quote says, and a small number of standard grammar rules. Ogden claimed that it could be learnt in a week or 'at worst' in a month, and once acquired, could be used to express any meaning that could also be expressed in normal English. He was, however, careful to add that specialist topics would require additional vocabularies. All 850 items could be written 'on one side of a sheet of notepaper', and were always printed on a detachable paper which every Basic publication included as an insert.

There is no doubt that, in the hands of an expert like Richards or Ogden himself, Basic can sound quite normal and translations were made of a number of standard texts like *Treasure Island* or *Arms and the Man* to prove the point. More usefully, original texts for the teaching of elementary science were also written by Basic enthusiasts like A. P. Rossiter and H. S. Hatfield. Perhaps if this application of Basic had been pursued more single-mindedly and resulted in an extensive list of simple science and technology texts, the system might have had a much greater chance of long-term survival. It would not have met all the problems that it inevitably encountered as Ogden's enthusiasm drove it towards a role as a 'replacement' for ordinary standard English. Essentially, it is a reasonably good system for writing simple texts, but it is not an appropriate medium for everyday social interaction in the spoken language. Nor, to be fair, was it intended to be.

The 850 Basic words are composed of 150 items representing Qualities, 600 representing Things, and 100 representing Operations. The Qualities and Things (200 of which were deliberately chosen because they could easily be illustrated) are, effectively, adjectives and nouns respectively. The Operations, on the other hand, are difficult to characterize. They appear at first sight to be a mixed bag of verbs, prepositions, conjunctions, articles, and demonstratives. However, the notion of 'operations' goes deeper than this, and represents the core of Ogden's theoretical work underlying Basic.

Ogden was a Cambridge philosopher and logician who had made a reputation as an authority on the works of Jeremy Bentham and had taken a particular interest in Bentham's 'Theory of Fictions'. 'Fictions' are not, of course, untruths or imaginary tales, but they characterize the propensity of natural language to 'hide' true meanings behind linguistic representations. This notion is somewhat akin to the Chomskyan contrast between the 'surface' appearance of language and its 'deep' structure. For example, the 'true meaning' of *ask* is *put a question*, *want* really means *have a desire for*, and so on. Notions like *put* and *have* represent Operations that relate the Things named by the nouns on either side of them. Looked at in this way, there are very few basic operations 'hiding' behind the very large number of verbs in the normal standard language. Not only can most of the so-called verbs in the language be circumlocuted by phrases such as *have a desire for* and *put a question*, but such circumlocutions represent a 'truer' meaning than the 'fictions' ( *want*, *ask*) which they replace. This insight prompted Ogden into devising a kind of 'notional grammar' of English in which everything could be expressed by translating it into terms of relationships between Things (with or without modifying Qualities) and Operations. The principal practical benefit was to reduce the number of lexical verbs to a small handful of operational items. In the end he decided on only fourteen (*come, get, give, go, keep, let, make, put, seem, take, do, say, see*, and *send*) plus two auxiliaries (*be* and *have*) and two modals (*will* and *may*). The propositional content of any statement can be expressed in a sentence containing only these operators. This allows the total number of items to be learnt to be reduced to 850. Or so it would seem.

However, Ogden permits a rule whereby any nouns on the list of 850 may take the endings *-ing* or *-ed* (not all of them do, of course). The 600 Things include items such as *act*, *end*, and *sleep*, for instance. His *-ing* or *-ed* rule therefore allows him to produce *acting, ending, sleeping, acted*, and *ended*, and some verb phrases which can be constructed with them (*He is acting as the manager, the play was acted*, etc.). Suddenly, there is a large reservoir of 'verbs' to be drawn on (though Basic does not permit the ending *-s*, so *he acts* or *it ends* would be 'ungrammatical'). This puts the claim that Basic consists of 'only 850 words' in a new light. In a sense, the 600 Things are not 'nouns', though some of them (*servant*, for instance, or *owner*) cannot be anything else. They are 'entities' which can be nominalized or verbalized as occasion dictates. Secondly, Ogden permits his Operator verbs to collocate with his Operator prepositions to form compounds such as *get in/on/off*, etc. opening up another source of 'verbs'. This is a much more serious teaching point than the *act/acting/acted* issue. There may perhaps be a sense in which *come* and *across* in *He came across the river in a boat* are 'the same' as in *He came across a Roman coin in a field*, but the argument would be an abstract one of some complexity. For the average learner of English there is little doubt that they represent two different 'things to learn'.

The publication of *Basic English* in 1930 led to an increasingly bitter controversy between Ogden and, in particular, Michael West, though Palmer lent his support as well. In the early thirties neither West nor Palmer were yet in a position to exploit their research work in the production of language teaching materials on a wide scale. Suddenly, it looked as though a Cambridge academic with little if any relevant experience of teaching English as a foreign language had made a pre-emptive bid for both the leadership and the market. West, in collaboration with Elaine Swenson and others, and with Palmer's public approval, published a powerful attack on Basic in a paper called 'A Critical Examination of Basic English' which came out in 1934 in the form of a Bulletin from the Ontario College of Education at the University of Toronto (West *et al.* 1934).[6] Ogden lost his temper and replied with a book nearly four times the length of West's paper called *Counter-Offensive* (1935). With hindsight this was rather unwise. His passionate and over-elaborate defence of his system contrasts rather badly with West's heavily studied restraint. It was a case of 'protesting too much', at least to a reader long after the events which provoked it have passed into history. His sense of grievance was not, however, entirely unjustified. Only a year before the Bulletin appeared, West had written: 'It (Basic) takes a very elastic vocabulary and gets the last inch of stretch out of it, and so makes it a system ideally suited to adult learning.'[7] Now here was West pulling the system to pieces. Ogden ascribed purely mercenary motives to the change of heart and accused both Palmer and West of 'ganging up' on him. It was all very unpleasant, and many of the issues were absurdly trivial. There were others, however, which were more serious, in particular the claim that Basic was easy to learn because it contained 850 words and, secondly, the vexed question about 'natural' English.

Ogden's repeated claim that Basic could be learnt 'in a week or at worst a month' was, to put it mildly, disingenuous. What he meant, of course, was that a learner could memorize the 850 words and the list of rules in the stipulated period of time. This is not the same as learning Basic or any other language. The Basic system depends on the principle of reducing the number of different dictionary items to a minimum and extending their use to a maximum. Learning how to map a small number of words on to a large number of meanings is not likely to be easy. One language learning problem, the number of new words, has been exchanged for another one, the multiplicity of meanings that each new word is required to carry. The overall learning load has remained more or less the same, except perhaps for those learners whose native language mirrors English in the construction of compounds like *get in*, *come across*, and so on. For the others, the net result might well be an increase in learning difficulty. There is a further problem. Ogden's insistence that Basic was a self-contained language meant that teachers had to learn it. There were obviously no 'native speakers' of Basic, which meant that teachers, and in particular native-speaking teachers of English, would have to be retrained. Also, it is rare to find language teachers who actually stick to the syllabus of their teaching course, even in a tightly-graded structural programme, when the need arises for direct communication with their students. In theory at least, such conversations would have to be in Basic rather than in normal English. This suggests that the most effective teachers of Basic would be those who did not know normal English, which is a rather curious state of affairs. Perhaps in practice these problems did not arise.

The strongest argument against Basic by English language teachers was that it produced 'unnatural' English. You cannot say *Good-bye* in Basic or *Good evening* or *Thank you*. You cannot use some of the commonest words in the English language such as *like*, *big*, *never*, *sit*, *understand*, *can*, or *want*. Ogden's answer to this was, of course, that you can express the same notions in a different way and the final outcome is just as 'natural' as it would be in normal English. This was profoundly unsatisfactory, at least in the eyes of many teachers of English as a foreign language who felt that if courses were offered which claimed to teach Basic English, they should in fact teach basic English.

Ultimately, the issue is insoluble, with both sides arguing from different premises. Basic was a separate language into which English had to be translated whereas the teachers were developing a grading system based on a selection of common words in standard English.

Basic itself survived and expanded its activities, but it did not explore the possibilities of professional co-operation. Ogden preferred to work entirely through his own centre, the Orthological Institute, and his own contacts overseas. Towards the end of the war, the rivalry between the two contrasting views of 'simple English' reached a climax. Basic had come to the attention of the Prime Minister, Winston Churchill, and muttered speculations about the role of (British) English in the post-war world filtered down the corridors of power. Eventually, in March 1944, the issue surfaced in the House of Commons, in the form of a prepared answer by the Prime Minister himself.[8] In his statement Churchill disavowed any concern on the part of His Majesty's Government for the methodology of English language teaching, but expressed an interest in the claims of Basic English to be an auxiliary language with a strong potential for international communication. He thought, for instance, that its use might be encouraged in the publications of colonial governments. But the Churchill statement meant the effective end of Basic since the entire question was to be left in the hands of the British Council, who undertook to promote Basic 'where practicable'. The Council, however, insisted that it 'had always preserved an attitude of strict neutrality among the competing systems of English teaching'[9], and, without its active support, Ogden's system could not survive except as a minority enthusiasm. In 1950 Catford published an eloquent defence of Basic in *ELT* but it has been quiescent since then.

Essentially, Basic dissipated its energies by seeking to replace English, a task it could not hope to accomplish. It might have been wiser to try and carve out a specialist role as an auxiliary language for the production of written texts, particularly of a scientific or informative nature. Basic is a literate code well-suited to the purpose for which it was devised, namely the expression of propositional content. This does not mean it cannot be spoken, clearly it can, but it does mean that it is ill-suited to the role of mediating social interaction. A lost code looking for a speech community. It is somewhat ironic that Malinowski's paper outlining the concept of 'context of situation' ('The problem of meaning in primitive languages') should have appeared in tandem with Ogden's first major work in semantics in 1923. In that paper Malinowski summarized his views by saying that 'language in its primitive function and original form has an essentially pragmatic character; it is a mode of behaviour, an indispensable element of concerted human action. And negatively: to regard it as a means for the embodiment or expression of thought is to take a one-sided view of one of its most derivative and specialized functions'.[10] Basic was a work of intellectual art, 'magnifique – mais ce n'est pas la parole'.

## Carnegie and after

As we have already seen, a great deal of groundwork had been done on vocabulary selection in the twenties and early thirties, but it was mainly unco-ordinated private enterprise. In addition, there was the established American work in statistical word frequency led by E. L. Thorndike. The time had come for some resolution of the issues surrounding vocabulary selection and, if possible, a definitive list for pedagogical purposes. On West's initiative, and with a grant from the Carnegie Corporation, a conference of specialists in the field was held in New York in 1934. The participants included Thorndike and other American workers as well as West, Palmer, and Faucett. Ogden was invited but, not surprisingly, he did not attend. The result of the New York discussions was a decision to a set up a sub-committee of the three Britons, with Thorndike as a consultant, which would meet in London the following year. This second meeting was held under the auspices of the Institute of Education at London University with the remit to prepare a report on vocabulary selection procedures and criteria, and draw up a draft list of words. The outcome was the *Interim Report on Vocabulary Selection for English as a Foreign Language* (1936), usually referred to as 'The Carnegie Report', which eventually became the *General Service List of English Words* compiled and edited by Michael West and published by Longmans, Green in 1953.

The first decision of the sub-committee was to produce a general service list rather than one for any specific set of purposes. However, it is impossible to draw up lists without some purpose in mind, and the aim which was most consistent with the needs of the participants was a lexical guide for the production of simple reading materials. The Carnegie *General Service List (GSL)* suits its basic purposes very well but it is less appropriate for other purposes such as the words needed by visitors to England or new residents, for example, for use in everyday situations.

In its final published form the *GSL* contained frequency statistics, but these were added later. The initial choice of words made at the London meeting of the committee in 1935 was based mainly on intuition and experience guided by the contents of earlier lists [11] and an agreed set of criteria.

1  Word frequency
2  Structural value (all structure words included)
3  Universality (words likely to cause offence locally excluded)
4  Subject range (no specialist items)
5  Definition words (for dictionary-making, etc.)
6  Word-building capability
7  Style ('colloquial' or slang words excluded).

The final list amounted to around 2,000 headwords sub-classified according to their grammatical status (*right*, for example, is listed separately as a noun, an adjective, and an adverb) and their semantic meanings (*cry* meaning *shout*, for instance, as distinct from *cry* meaning *weep*). These sub-categories were a major advance on previous word lists and greatly increased the pedagogical value of the work.

The *GSL* is not a frequency list as is sometimes supposed, though the presence of Thorndike as a consultant to the committee ensured that the evidence from frequency statistics was available to the team. He was the leading figure among word-frequency statisticians in America and had published an influential word count called *The Teacher's Word Book* in 1921. Ten years later it was enlarged to reappear as *The Teacher's Word Book of 20,000 Words* (1932) and further expanded, in co-operation with Irving Lorge, into *The Teacher's Word Book of 30,000 Words* (1944). It was Lorge who did most of the research work on the *GSL* after the London meeting in order to provide frequency figures for the 2,000 headwords and for their semantic sub-categories. This *Semantic*

*Count of English Words* appeared in 1938, but the project was shelved during the war, and, by the time West took it up again, Lorge had produced a more detailed study called *A Semantic Count of the 570 Commonest Words* (1949). The final work included a supplement of scientific and technical terms prepared by West and Flood.

Word frequency had interested people since the first astonishing count made in the 1890s by Kaeding to help in the training of sten-ographers. It was on a huge scale for a manual count, eleven million words of running text were subjected to analysis by an army of research assistants under the supervision of the Prussian Bureau of Statistics, and the results published in *Häufigkeitswörterbuch der deutschen Sprache* (1898).[12] The central fact that the pedagogical word lists were trying to capture was that a small number of individual words do a great deal of work. Palmer reckoned, for instance, that the items on his 3,000-word list would account for 95 per cent of running-text, a point that Bongers investigated with a number of literary texts including Shaw's *Doctor's Dilemma* (96.1 per cent) and Arnold Bennett's *The Card* (95.2 per cent). Reducing the list to a mere 1,000 items would still cover 85 per cent of running-text.

The more words that were included in the study (and even in pre-computer days it ran into millions) the higher the total frequency of the common words, and the longer the 'tail' of uncommon words. The amount of information gained from massive counts was, therefore, disproportionate to the effort required to do them. Also, it is doubtful whether all the results were really worth having from a practical point of view. Once you have obtained your high-frequency list, there is little point in knowing that obviously unusual words like *blithesome*, *mugwump*, *epistolatory*, and *oubliette* are as frequent ('once in 4 million' (Thorndike-Lorge 1944)) as everyday words like *barman*, *hostel*, *raincoat*, and *bike*. Clearly, what must be defined are the criteria for selecting the texts for inclusion in the count since the statistics are a reflection of that original choice.

Criticisms of this kind were familiar to the Carnegie sub-committee, which explains their insistence on multiple and, for the most part, subjective criteria in finalizing the GSL.[13] Nevertheless, the title of the Report (and of West's 1953 book) tends to mask the limitations of the original objective, namely to provide a practical research tool for the preparation of basic literacy materials in English as a foreign language. The addition of Lorge's statistics further emphasizes the suggestion that the GSL is a lexical study of 'English as a whole'. This ambiguity was noted fairly early by Eckersley when he came to prepare his *Essential English* course (see Chapter 15) and became evident later as the need to teach colloquial spoken English (which the GSL ignores) increased.

The practical application of word-frequency counts to the production of language teaching materials rested on the assumption that common words must also be useful words. Up to a point, this is true: the really high-frequency items are indispensable. However, words are not useful in some abstract sense, but useful for someone or some purpose. This idea was developed further in France in the fifties during the research to establish 'basic French', *le français fondamental*.[14] In order to supplement their frequency-based vocabulary, the researchers proposed a concept they called *disponibilité* (usually translated as *availability*) in order to account for the words which ought to be 'available' in specific contexts, like *pint* in a pub or *petrol* in a garage, for instance, though neither of them would come very high on a frequency-count of 'the language as a whole'. The results were used in the preparation of the CREDIF audio-visual courses.

Much the same approach has been used more recently to establish the lexical content of the Council of Europe's *Threshold Level* (Van Ek 1975), though on a more intuitive basis. By specifying the contexts, settings, and so on in which the new language is likely to be needed, the materials writing team can, it is hoped, predict the words that the learners will want outside the specified T-level 'core'.

Statistical approaches to lexical selection have been under a cloud in recent times. However, modern computer-based techniques ought to permit interesting insights into linguistic patterning (particularly in the field of collocational relationships that Palmer tried to investigate) to the eventual benefit of language teaching materials.

## Notes

1 West (1926: 112).
2 Ibid.: 91.
3 Ibid.: 107.
4 It seems that the Readers did not make a lasting impression in Bengal. Cf. Mackin's comment: 'His (i.e. West's) influence has been slight. This, I think, is a strange thing . . . It may be that if you go away from a country . . . the whole thing just disintegrates' (Center for Applied Linguistics 1959: 145).
5 Richards (1943: 20).
6 West later withdrew the paper and destroyed the remaining copies.
7 Quoted in Ogden (1935: 22).
8 Hansard, 9th March 1944, 397, 2187.
9 White (1965: 47).
10 Malinowski (1923: 316).
11 The lists included Faucett-Maki (1932), Palmer (1930–31), Thorndike (1921, 1932), West-Endicott (1935) and Horn (1926). See Hornby (1953: 19) and Bongers (1947: 218).
12 See H. Bongers' study, *The History and Principles of Vocabulary Control* (1947), a valuable source of information on every aspect of

the subject, and in particular on the work of Harold Palmer.
13 'Subjective' in the sense that decisions were reached by consensus among the committee members.
14 Ministère de l'Education nationale (1954), Gougenheim *et al.* (1956).

# 18 Old patterns and new directions

## A. S. Hornby and the post-war consensus

In keeping with the mood of the time, the post-war years in English language teaching were a constructive period in which earlier initiatives were consolidated in an atmosphere of methodological consensus. The battles over 'grammar' and 'translation' were over, the dust had settled, and the most useful thing to do was develop a modified 'direct method' approach which teachers could handle with confidence and learners could assimilate with ease. This uncontroversial aim was consistently reflected in the contributions to *English Language Teaching* (*ELT*), founded in 1946, for example in a series of short articles called 'Linguistic pedagogy' written by its first editor A. S. Hornby in 1946–7.

The traditional British interest in pedagogical phonetics was also strongly represented with regular articles by leading phoneticians such as Daniel Jones, David Abercrombie, Roger Kingdon, Peter McCarthy, and others. Rather a different note, however, was struck in some of Abercrombie's early papers such as 'The social basis of language' (1948), and 'Some first principles' (1949) which look towards closer links between language teaching and linguistic theory. J. C. Catford's contributions on 'Intelligibility' (1950a) and 'The background and origins of Basic English' (1950b) were straws in the same wind. We shall return to these new directions later.

In the meantime, A. S. Hornby (or ASH as he liked to be called) brought the work of the inter-war years to fruition in four major publications between 1948 and 1959, and a host of minor ones, which helped to make this a particularly productive period. There may not have been much in the way of innovation, but there was a great deal of solid foundation work. When Japan entered the war in 1941, Hornby returned to England and joined the British Council. He worked in the University of Teheran until 1945 and was then appointed Linguistic Adviser to the Council in London. In 1946, he took on the editorship of *ELT* and modelled his policy on the *IRET Bulletin*, which he had taken over from Palmer in 1936. Under his leadership, *ELT* strengthened the ties between the various branches of the growing profession: the Council itself, the Institute of Education at London University, which established a Chair with responsibilities for English as a foreign language in 1948, other British universities, notably Leeds and Edinburgh, and many individuals with experience and expertise in the field.

In 1950, Hornby resigned the editorship to devote himself to full-time materials writing. His famous dictionary, which had appeared in 1948 under the title *A Learner's Dictionary of Current English* was re-issued

*Figure 27* A. S. Hornby (1898–1978). *Hornby's work in the forties and fifties represented the culmination of the tradition begun by Sweet and Palmer. His* Advanced Learner's Dictionary of Current English, *which first appeared under a slightly different title in 1948, is accepted as one of the great works in ELT in the present century.*

with its more familiar name, *An Advanced-Learner's Dictionary of Current English*, in 1952. Further editions were to appear in 1963, with the co-operation of the original Japanese publishers Kaitakusha, and in 1974 when *Oxford* was added to the title, with echoes of the *OED* itself. The *Advanced Learner's* now has some worthy rivals, notably the *Longman Dictionary of Contemporary English* (1978), but for a long time it held the field alone, and won a definitive status informally bestowed by the profession. One might say that, just as Johnson 'fixed' the English of the eighteenth century, Hornby 'fixed' English as a foreign language, and later works have built on the foundations he laid. It became the standard work of reference, not only in traditional dictionary terms, but in a broader sense, by developing the principle that a work for learners of English should demonstrate how the language is used, and show the collocational contexts in which the words normally occur. This close relationship between grammar and lexis was underpinned by the pedagogical grammar of English sentence patterns contained in the second of Hornby's main publications, the *Guide to Patterns and Usage in English* in 1954.

The *Guide* was the climax of the approach originally explored by Palmer in his ergonic analysis of 1917, and his *Grammar of Spoken English* in 1924. It also draws heavily on the traditional pedagogical grammars of writers like Jespersen and Zandvoort. It is set out in a clear, systematic, and thoroughly accessible form. The tabular presentation inherited from Palmer emphasizes the sentence pattern rather than the word-class as the primary unit of description. Like his dictionary, Hornby's *Guide* was intended for advanced learners, though its value for teachers and course writers is equally evident. Few coursebooks after 1954 have been written without at least half-an-eye on the Hornby pattern lists, however superficially different they may appear.

Hornby himself published the model 'sentence-pattern course', his *Oxford Progressive English for Adult Learners*, in the same year as the *Guide*, 1954. More memorably known as 'the Hornby Course', it fused the Palmer tradition of the Oral Method with the older Sweet-Jespersen tradition of the connected text in a remarkably subtle way. After a few 'Direct Method' lessons, the materials settle down to a text-based approach in which the new patterns are embedded in the texts without any sense of strain, and the subsequent 'For Study' sections realize the Reform Movement principle of 'inductive grammar'. 'Hornby' is in many ways a rather austere course, even superficially dull in places, with few concessions to humour or entertainment. Hornby himself, however, was quite different, a warm and very humane man with a great sense of humour who made friends easily and impressed teachers with his professional integrity and personal charm. This apparent 'lack of fit' was once pointed out to him at a small teachers' conference I attended in Germany in the early sixties. He accepted the point immediately:

materials in his view should not seek to entertain because no course writer can know the circumstances under which they will be used. Language lessons can, indeed should, be fun, but that is a matter for the students and the teacher not for the materials. Looking at Hornby's coursebooks now, when a great deal is spent on presentation, it may be difficult to see why they were so popular and successful. Part of the explanation lies in the fact that the interesting oral classwork is not contained in the textbooks. It formed a sort of 'sub-text', as it were, originating from the teacher.

Hornby christened his method 'The Situational Approach'.[1] The term has a different meaning today, but to Hornby it meant that each new pattern or lexical item should be introduced to the class in advance of the work with the text. This may be standard practice now, but it was not always so. The oral techniques required were worked out in great detail in his last large-scale publication, *The Teaching of Structural Words and Sentence Patterns*, a set of four manuals which appeared from 1959 onwards.

These four books are the closest Hornby came to a handbook of language teaching method or a teacher-training manual. He more than anyone else could have been to the Palmerian tradition what Jespersen had been to the Reform Movement in *How to Teach a Foreign Language*. No one can do everything, and Hornby did more than most, but it is sad none the less that his experience was never distilled into a guide for young teachers. Such a proposal must have been put to him many times, and one assumes that his reasons for declining must have been deeply held. Like all lexicographers, he was a man for whom precision was a cardinal virtue, and precision in classroom matters meant either working closely with familiar materials, or with individual teachers whose problems could be explored co-operatively and in detail. Methods and techniques interested him greatly, as the Teacher's Handbooks for his course show quite clearly, but methodology in a broader sense inevitably implied the imprecision of making generalizations, a mode of thinking and working with which he was uncomfortable.

Towards the end of his life, he expressed his concern for the future of the profession in an original and characteristically generous manner. He established the Hornby Educational Trust, to support individual students and teachers, and to promote professional innovation and development. To date, the Trust's work has included, for example, library grants in Singapore and Outer Mongolia, support for organizations such as Voluntary Services Overseas (VSO), as well as numerous scholarships and study grants awarded to individuals all over the world. Shortly before his death in 1978, a volume in his honour was presented to him to mark his eightieth birthday with contributions from many distinguished members of the profession which he and Harold Palmer did more than anyone else to create.[2]

Hornby was not, of course, alone. There were many others, foremost among whom were established writers like West and Eckersley, whose *Essential English* was given a new lease of life in a revised edition in 1955. Other course writers in the same mould included Hornby's collaborator on the *Dictionary*, E. V. Gatenby, who wrote a *Direct Method English Course* in 1952, and another British Council officer, David Hicks (*Foundations of English* (1956)). The Daniel Jones tradition produced a valuable series of studies in the teaching of pronunciation, including McCarthy's *English Pronunciation, a practical handbook for the foreign learner* (1944), Christophersen's *English Phonetics Course* (1956) and Kingdon's two *Groundwork* books on stress and intonation (1958). W. Stannard Allen's *Living English Speech* (1954) belongs to the same stable, but he is better-known for his earlier *Living English Structure* (1947) with its immortalization of Maisie and Cyril. With a rather broader aim, Abercrombie's *Problems and Principles* (1956) was one of the most influential publications of the period, leading up to Gimson's re-statement of the Jones tradition in *An Introduction to the Pronunciation of English* in 1962.

Books on teaching methods were, for the most part, practical and quietly uncontroversial. Gurrey's *Teaching English as a Foreign Language* (1955) was a typical example, as was Gauntlett's book with the same title in 1957, and Frisby's *Teaching English, Notes and Comments on Teaching English Overseas* (1957). West's *Teaching English in Difficult Circumstances* (1960) and Billows' *Techniques of Language Teaching* (1961) belong in a sense to the same period, though the latter, with its interest in situational methods, marks a clear shift of emphasis and style. It deservedly became the basic training handbook of the sixties.

The concerns of the Hornby era – the careful selection and grading of language patterns and vocabulary, the emphasis on pronunciation, and the importance of text – were in some ways more in tune with Sweet than anyone else: rational, civilized and, above all, literate. At first sight, 'literate' (not, of course, 'literary') may seem a strange adjective to use about an oral approach to language teaching which emphasized the importance of the spoken language. But, on reflection, it is not so inappropriate. Oral work in the classroom certainly gave students a fair command of spoken English, but the language being taught conformed closely to literate norms: well-formed, Standard English sentences, which were, so to speak, 'translated into speech' by the teacher. The patterns on which the materials were based were arrived at by a process of idealization from the flow of common talk, and it was important that they should be learnt accurately.

Natural oracy, on the other hand, is of a different order altogether. It emerges out of the experience of interacting with other members of the speech community, and does not always conform to standardized notions of well-formedness. This was the reality that Sauveur had attempted to capture for the classroom back in 1870, but it is not easily tameable. Classrooms, except those designed for very young children, do not provide much opportunity for action. It is assumed, in fact, that they will act as the unobtrusive setting for the use of language in learning, not for the original acquisition of language. Nor is it easy to see how natural oracy processes can be promoted when the ratio of native sources to non-native learners is one-to-many, instead of the other way round, as it is in real life. The evolution of Sauveurian principles into the procedures of the Direct Method recognized both the constraints of the classroom and the literate experience of the learners. By the middle of the twentieth century, the results had achieved a high level of sophistication, but they were to be challenged again, in terms not at all dissimilar from those used by Sauveur, in the communicative approach which was only a few years ahead.

## The impact of applied linguistics

Applied linguistics is not the recent development that is sometimes supposed,[3] but derives from the involvement of linguists in America, particularly Leonard Bloomfield and Charles C. Fries, in specialized language-teaching programmes during and immediately after the Second World War. The first public use of the term was, to the best of my knowledge, in the subtitle of the journal *Language Learning – A Quarterly Journal of Applied Linguistics* first published in 1948. It had been founded by Fries and other colleagues, including Kenneth L. Pike and W. Freeman Twaddell, in order to bring the ideas developed at Fries's English Language Institute at the University of Michigan to the attention of a wider public and to development subject generally.

The origins of Fries's work lie in the American tradition of descriptivist linguistics pioneered since the beginning of the century by linguists like Franz Boas, Edward Sapir and, most importantly from our point of view, Bloomfield himself. Of all the leading linguists of his time, Bloomfield was perhaps the most committed to the idea that his discipline should find a useful role in the community. An early work of his, *Introduction to the Study of Language* (1914), had already influenced Palmer's views, and his classic *Language* (1933) ends with a chapter called 'Applications and Outlook' in which he sets out a programme of practical uses of linguistics in education, the creation of a universal language, and other activities. He was himself especially interested in the development of a more efficient approach to the teaching of reading to young children.

Since the beginning of the century, American linguistics had been motivated by the need to record indigenous Indian languages before they became extinct, and, as an extension of this work in the thirties, the Linguistic Society of America sponsored a project called the Intensive Language Program. Bloomfield, a past-President of the Society, was invited to contribute a short paper outlining the practical fieldwork techniques required to elicit and record previously unwritten languages. He produced the handbook in the form of a sixteen-page pamphlet called *An Outline Guide for the Practical Study of Foreign Languages*, which the Society published in 1942.

As a source of instruction on elementary linguistic fieldwork, the *Guide* is simple, clear, and practical. However, the title, with its echo of Sweet, and the inclusion of some informal advice on language learning, seems to have given the impression that it was intended as a general methodology of language teaching which could be applied in any instructional context. Rather unexpectedly, it became the model for a major programme of foreign language teaching to the American armed services known as the Army Specialized Training Program (ASTP).[4] It was a set text which the teaching staff were required to study, along with Bloch and Trager's *Outline of Linguistic Analysis*, also published by the Linguistic Society in 1942.

This decision is difficult to understand since Bloomfield says quite explicitly in the *Guide* that it was intended to 'help the reader to shift for himself', which is not what happens in a teaching programme run on military lines for thousands of service personnel. Secondly, it was designed to train fieldworkers to elicit linguistic data from informants by careful questioning and observation, after which the material had to be systematically recorded and learnt. Following the model in the *Guide*, native speakers of the languages included in the Program were hired as 'informants'. The students, however, could not be expected to 'discover' the language they were learning for themselves, a task that presupposes considerable training and expertise. A mediator was needed, trained in linguistics, who would do the 'applied linguistic' work in analysing the target language and providing appropriate teaching materials. As a result, Senior Instructors were appointed with, it was hoped, sufficient training in linguistics to prepare materials from scratch in languages such as Japanese which had rarely been taught before in America. (Even the familiar languages like French and German posed problems since there were no materials suitable for the oral approach adopted by the ASTP.)

Both the senior instructors and the informants acted as classroom teachers. The former introduced the new material with any necessary explanations and then left the native speakers to drill the patterns by a simple method of imitation and repetition. This became known as the 'mim-mem' method (mimicry and memorization), and is the obvious forerunner of the audiolingual approach and the early language laboratory techniques.

The ASTP ran for approximately nine months from April 1943 and involved about 15,000 servicemen (carefully selected ex-college students) following courses in twenty-seven different languages. Separate establishments called Civil Affairs Training Schools (CATS) were set up to provide language instruction for the officers, a project that proved particularly fruitful. It led, for example, to the production of a set of language courses called 'The Spoken Language Series' which included *Spoken Dutch* and *Spoken Russian* (both by Bloomfield himself), *Spoken Japanese* (Bloch), *Spoken Norwegian* (Haugen) and *Spoken Chinese* (Hockett). After the war, the work came under the general direction of the American Council of Learned Societies to which, it should be recorded, the eminent authors of the Series donated their royalties in support of linguistic research.

The 'G.I. Method' as the ASTP was irreverently called, caused great interest among language teachers generally. However, as Moulton (1961) noted, their perceptions of the value of the new approach were different from those of the applied linguists. 'To most language teachers, what was "new" about the new method was its intensive nature and its primary emphasis on speaking; all talk about instruction being based on "sound linguistic principles" and being supervised by a "trained linguist" struck them as professional exaggeration, not to say arrogance, on the part of the linguists'.[5] To Fries and his colleagues, however, 'sound linguistic principles' were to be taken seriously.

Fries's model of applied linguistics, as outlined for example in his paper 'As we see it' written for the first issue of *Language Learning* in 1948, is a hierarchical one. The descriptive linguist, at the 'top' has the responsibility of producing the basic, scientific descriptions of the source and target languages. The applied linguist then takes over in a dual role. He has to select and grade the structures taken from the original description to suit the relevant pedagogical purposes, and prepare a contrastive description of source and target languages in order to pinpoint areas of potential difficulty. Secondly, he has to write teaching materials which will illustrate the patterns of the new language and provide special practice on difficult points. The materials are then passed on to the teacher for use in class. The authority of the approach resided in the materials themselves, not in the lessons given by the teacher using them, a philosophy which paved the way for the replacement of teachers by machines such as language laboratories.

This cult of materials was not balanced by an equally serious concern for teaching method. The Michigan Oral Approach is often credited with having applied behaviourist psychology to language teaching, but this is a rather doubtful claim. Fries himself, for example, does not mention psychology in the early papers which established the Approach, and Bloomfield's attitude to language learning is strictly commonsensical: 'practise everything until it becomes second nature',[6] and 'language learning is overlearning; anything else is of no use'.[7] This sounds rather like behaviourist advice, but in reality, behaviourism was rather more complex. Skinner, for example, aimed to develop new repertoires of behaviour by a process he referred to as 'shaping', which became the starting-point of programmed learning in the late fifties and sixties. Simplistic habit formation of the Michigan variety does not need a theory of learning, and none was offered. Fries's great achievement in applied linguistics was the elaboration of a new approach to pedagogical grammar, not a new language teaching method.[8]

In many ways Fries's Oral Approach is very similar to Palmer's Oral Method. Both writers stressed the importance of training good foreign-language speech-habits in the early stages of learning. Both adopted a sentence-based approach to the teaching of grammar, and both emphasized practice as essential for progress. Palmer, however, was an experienced teacher with an instinctive feel for what would work in a classroom. His notions of grading, for instance, were based on his intuitions about what learners would find difficult. Fries, on the other hand, had the linguistic training that Palmer lacked and preferred to trust in the findings of contrastive analysis. In his influential book *The Structure of English* in 1952, he produced the definitive study of 'sentence-pattern grammar' that Palmer had been aiming at in his ergonic analysis back in 1917.

The teaching of English as a foreign language in America before 1940 was a minority activity[9] and Fries's application of the Michigan model to English in his monograph *Teaching and Learning English as a Foreign Language* in 1945 was a major contribution to the field. His programme was a tough one. The students followed a detailed course of speech-habit training before moving to an equally spare programme of structure drills and pattern exercises. Vocabulary was kept to a minimum (Fries always stressed this strongly), and the emphasis was on the intensive habitualization of the essentials of English structure. None of this work was intended to last more than three months, a point that is often overlooked by Fries's critics.

The Structural Approach, as it became known, attracted high-level institutional support throughout the forties and fifties. The Army, for instance, developed the method at their Language School in Monterey and by 1960 employed over 450 teachers teaching nearly thirty languages. In 1946 the Foreign Service Institute of the United States State Department sponsored a Language Training Program for foreign service personnel which employed substantial numbers of young linguists and resulted in publications such as Trager and Smith's *Outline of English Structure* (1951). The *Outline* provided what was known as the 'General Form', a structural analysis of English which could be adapted for use by learners of different language backgrounds. Between 1953 and 1956, ten courses had appeared for speakers of Burmese,

Mandarin, Greek, Indonesian, Korean, Persian, Serbo-Croatian, Thai, Turkish, and Vietnamese.[10] This impressive list shows again the concern for the expansion of English language instruction in hitherto neglected contexts. More cynically, it also shows the generosity of patronage for the application of linguistics to languages of strategic importance to United States foreign policy, and the employment opportunities for experts in contrastive linguistics.

The launching of the Sputnik provided an immense boost to language teaching in America by provoking the National Defense Education Act of 1958. Among other things, this led to twelve summer institutes for foreign language teachers in 1959 on courses which included 'instruction in linguistic analysis and its application in language teaching', a government contract with the Modern Language Association for the preparation of tests relating to further teacher qualifications, and another with the newly established Center for Applied Linguistics in Washington to produce contrastive studies of English and the main European languages. These would, it was hoped, 'constitute a major step in bringing the results of modern linguistic science to bear on the teaching of foreign languages'.[11]

The stimulus of the Michigan Institute directly or indirectly prompted the publication of many significant descriptive and applied linguistic studies including, for example, Pike's *Intonation of American English* (1946) and *Phonemics* (1947), Nida's *Morphology* (1946/9) and more popular works such as *Linguistics Across Cultures* by Robert Lado, Fries's successor as Director of the Institute. There were also many articles and papers in *Language Learning* and elsewhere by writers like Sapir, Hill, Twaddell, Marckwardt, and many others.

The teaching of English overseas also expanded, supported by the Ford Foundation, the Fulbright Program, and so on. Fries himself, for example, followed in the footsteps of Palmer and Hornby in helping to develop the teaching of English as a foreign language in Japan as part of the Fulbright initiative. Ford helped to finance the Center for Applied Linguistics, and Rockefeller had been involved from the start, having supported work at Cornell in 1946 and the Foreign Language Program of the Modern Language Association (1952 onwards). This activity did not go unnoticed in Britain.

In 1955 the British Council had sponsored a conference on English language teaching at Oxford which included participation by the United States Information Agency (USIA) and four years later the invitation was reciprocated. Under USIA auspices, and officially opened by its Director George V. Allen, the 1959 Washington Conference on English Teaching Abroad attracted high-level interest in both governmental and professional circles. Among the American contributors were Charles A. Ferguson, Director of the Center for Applied Linguistics (a co-sponsor of the Conference), Albert H. Marckwardt from Michigan, A. A. Hill,

Earl W. Stevick, and many others. British opinion was energetically represented by Ronald Mackin from the newly-founded School of Applied Linguistics at Edinburgh. During the course of discussion it became clear that, while there was much in common between them, the British interpretation of applied linguistics in language teaching diverged from the Michigan model on a number of key points. The absolute priority accorded to the training of speech-habits, for example, did not accord with the growing British interest in situational approaches fostered by the ideas of the Firthian school of linguistics. The contrastive approach was even more strongly resisted as being 'of doubtful validity (and) in any case not practical'.[12] With hindsight, this agreement to disagree was probably more significant than it might have appeared at the time. From now on 'sound linguistic principles' had more than one possible interpretation, and there was no mechanism in the Michigan model for choosing between them. They could imply either neo-Bloomfieldian structuralist language teaching based on pattern practice or, with equal logic, neo-Firthian situational methods based on a social model of language use. Over the next decade the two approaches came much closer together, though the route was somewhat circuitous.

Well before the Washington Conference the Bloomfield-Fries tradition in descriptive linguistics had been challenged by the publication, in 1957, of Noam Chomsky's *Syntactic Structures* which offered a radically different approach based on a theory of transformational-generative (TG) grammar. In addition to his revolutionary proposals for making linguistic descriptions, which replaced procedures for establishing 'patterns' by systems of rules for generating sentences, Chomsky pursued the theoretical implications of generative grammar into other areas of linguistic enquiry, notably the psychology of language, which was dominated at the time by the behaviourism of writers like Skinner. Chomsky's assault on behaviourism, most forcefully in a review of Skinner's *Verbal Behaviour* in 1959, stimulated the growth of alternative theoretical models which reinstated the importance of cognition in accounting for human language activity. This dual interest in linguistics and what became known as psycholinguistics was expressed most memorably and influentially in the opening chapter of *Aspects of the Theory of Syntax* in 1965: 'By a generative grammar I mean simply a system of rules that in some explicit and well-defined way assigns structural descriptions to sentences. Obviously, every speaker of a language has mastered and internalized a generative grammar that expresses his knowledge of his language'.[13] This knowledge Chomsky labelled 'competence' in contrast to 'the actual use of language in concrete situations' which he called 'performance',[14] reinterpreting in a psychological context the comparable sociological distinction that de Saussure had drawn between *langue* and *parole* in his *Cours de linguistique générale* published posthumously in 1916.

In a narrow technical sense, the influence of transformational-generative grammar on language teaching, for example on the preparation of teaching materials, was limited. In a broader sense, however, the impact of Chomsky's work on the thinking of the profession was very considerable indeed. For example, his reintroduction of a distinction between the surface forms of sentences and their underlying or 'deep' structure implied a thorough-going revision of the language teacher's assumptions about 'patterns' which had held sway over the construction of teaching syllabuses, texts and exercises for a long time. If, to use Chomsky's famous example, *John is easy to please* and *John is eager to please* have two quite different deep structures despite their surface similarity, the orthodox teaching devices of substitution tables, drills, and so on which 'matched like with like' would have to be rethought. So too would the assumption that these surface structure patterns constituted the basic 'habits' of perfomance in the new language. More significantly, however, than the details of linguistic description, Chomsky's whole approach to the study of language forced a reappraisal of what 'sound linguistic principles' in language teaching meant. He himself caused something of a stir at the North East Conference of language teachers in 1966 when he confessed to being 'rather sceptical' about the value of 'such insights and understanding as have been attained in linguistics and pyschology' for the teaching of languages.[15] He went on to exhort the profession to take a more positive view of its own work, and treat outside 'experts' with greater caution. After twenty years of evaluating language teaching activities in terms of their fidelity to specific theoretical models in both linguistics and psychology, Chomsky's advice would take some time to assimilate.

In the longer term, the most far-reaching effect of Chomsky's work on the whole spectrum of language teaching derived indirectly from the competence-performance distinction in *Aspects*. In the autumn of its publication year (1965), a small group of linguists, anthropologists, sociologists, and others, including Joshua Fishman, John Gumperz, and Dell Hymes, held a seminar to formulate possible guidelines for the United States Office of Education for research on the relationship between language and success by children at school. Among the outcomes of this meeting was a theoretical statement by Hymes which was read to a conference at Yeshiva University the following year.[16] Hymes chose to adopt Chomsky's notion of competence as his starting-point and build from it a broader framework for the description of language use to which he gave the name 'communicative competence'. Believing that what was crucial was 'not so much a better understanding of how language is structured, but a better understanding of how language is used',[17] Hymes and his colleagues sounded a new note in American linguistic studies which found an echo in many of the practical problems and issues confronting workers in language education in the United States in the late sixties and early seventies. It was also consonant with many of the ideas and aims of contemporary British research in general and applied linguistics which had grown out of the Firthian tradition during the previous decade. After 1970 British and American work shared common themes, to which we shall return in the final chapter. Nevertheless, there were different emphases deriving in part from the concept of 'situation' which had played a central role in the thinking of Firth and the so-called London School of linguistics, to which we should now turn.

John Rupert Firth (1890–1960) began his professional career as a teacher with the Indian Education Service and, after war service in various places, was appointed Professor of English at the University of the Punjab in 1920. During his Indian service he became one of the leading authorities on the Hindustani language. He returned to Britain in 1928 and, after four years in Daniel Jones's department, became a part-time lecturer in the School of Oriental and African studies (SOAS), where in 1944 he was appointed to the first Chair of General Linguistics in Britain.

The School of Oriental Studies as SOAS was originally called (the full name dates from 1939) was founded in 1916, the fruition of many years' planning and discussion.[18] It represented and furthered a long tradition of British scholarly interest in the culture and languages of the orient (particularly India) stretching back to the late eighteenth century and the work of Sir William Jones. Jones's Third Anniversary Discourse to the Bengal Asiatic Society in 1786 drew attention for the first time to linguistic links between Sanskrit and the European languages, and became one of the major documents in the history of linguistics.

While working at the School, Firth came into contact with the anthropologist Bronislaw Malinowski, from whom he derived a central strut in his framework of linguistic analysis, the concept of 'context of situation'[19] which says, in very rough terms, that the meaning of an utterance is a function of the cultural and situational context in which it occurs. In developing this notion, Firth proposed a rather abstract formulation based on three major categories in terms of which language events could be described. First, there was the verbal and non-verbal action of the participants in the event, then what he called the 'relevant objects' and finally the observable effect of the verbal action.[20] While the details may be a little unclear, there is no mistaking the emphasis Firth places on the unity of language and social activity. Among the practical applications that Firth found for his situational approach to meaning was in the preparation of a 'special purpose' course of Japanese for RAF pilots during the Second World War, a service for which he was awarded the OBE in 1946. His interest in the practical purposes that might be found for his subject continued to grow. His Presidential Address to the Philological Society in 1957, for example, carried the title

'Applications of General Linguistics',[21] and one of the ideas he was working on towards the end of his life was the existence of what he called 'restricted languages', specialized varieties of language related to particular social roles, professional interests, working activities, etc.[22] This line of thought was later to develop into so-called 'register studies', and, more widely, into the study of language variation which proved an important stimulus to the development of special purpose language teaching in the seventies.

In general linguistics itself, Firth's principal work was in phonology and it was left to his students, notably Halliday, to extend his principles into detailed proposals for the description of grammar and lexis. Halliday's first contribution was a paper called 'Categories of the theory of grammar' in 1961, an early model that was known as 'scale-and-category grammar'. It was considerably expanded and developed later in the decade into a sophisticated instrument for relating linguistic forms to language functions through a network of systems and choices of various kinds, and was rechristened 'systemic grammar'. The chief strength of the Hallidayan approach in an applied context has been its consistent concern, which is Firthian in origin, to preserve the unity of language and language use, no matter how complicated the analytical procedures required to relate them. Firth liked the metaphor of the spectrum[23] which disperses the component parts of light into colour-bands for detailed inspection and analysis but returns them, so to speak, to their original 'white' form undistorted. Linguistic analysis, he believed, should attempt something similar by 'dispersing' language into a set of related levels of analysis. For example, he firmly rejected dichotomies such as de Saussure's *langue* and *parole* and, following the same tradition, Halliday declined to adopt the term 'communicative competence', though he was working a seam in linguistic studies very close to that of Hymes and his associates in America.[24] By 1970 'sociolinguistics' had become an accepted umbrella term to cover those types of linguistic enquiry in which the use of language was accorded at least equal status to its formal features.[25] This emphasis had far-reaching implications for language in education.

## The notion of communication

In the past, the diffusion of new ideas into the teaching profession from contributory theoretical disciplines such as linguistics had been relatively slow. However, the expansion of university-level courses from the mid-sixties onwards in response to a growing demand for professional qualifications, meant that change and development accelerated noticeably after about 1970. Moreover, the growth of national investment in education[26] encouraged a substantial flow of research funding from both independent and state sources, a due proportion of which found its way into projects related to language and language teaching. When the ultimate source of this relative affluence (cheap energy) was abruptly cut off in 1974, it discouraged home-financed activities, but at the same time opened up opportunities in other fields. The appearance of large numbers of overseas students fuelled an expansion of language teaching institutions in Britain itself, as well as hastening the development of English-teaching operations in the students' countries of origin. Furthermore, the generally weak pound of 1974–77 attracted customers into British EFL classrooms and tempted publishers into expansionist investment policies. While the optimistic project-funding of the earlier period tended to favour home-based language teaching initiatives in, for example, mother-tongue teaching, modern languages and the growing field of English as a second language (ESL), the later swing in world economics brought greater benefits to EFL, particularly in the rather expensive market for tailor-made specific-purpose courses.

Though economic factors facilitate investment in educational development, they do not motivate it, or determine which direction it will take. In addition to its affluence, or, some might argue, because of it, the decade before the oil-price-rise was a period of social and cultural reappraisal and reorientation on an ambitious scale. The results may sometimes have been more ephemeral, or less radical, than they seemed at first, but, all in all, the educational changes which took place during the period were significant and lasting. The groundwork was laid in a series of reports in the early sixties affecting every sector of the educational system.[27] The expansion of higher education following the Robbins Report (1963), for example, has already been mentioned as a factor in bringing linguistics and ELT together. But the really radical changes were in the secondary sector where the abolition of selection at eleven-plus opened the way to a fully comprehensive system of education up to the age of sixteen. The philosophy of social equality which powered structural changes of this kind also motivated decisions in research and development, both in determining priorities and in setting objectives. The evident importance of language in an educational programme with a reformist ideology ensured a sympathetic hearing for ideas and proposals which shared the same basic aims, with the practical result that a number of projects were established both to research specific problems in language teaching and to produce useful classroom materials.

The first in the field was a major project funded by the Nuffield Foundation to extend the teaching of foreign languages, hitherto the special preserve of the grammar schools, to all sections of the community.[28] It was an ambitious aim initiated in 1963 before the comprehensivization programme had really got started. For this and for other reasons, the decision was made to introduce the teaching of French into the (non-selective) primary schools in the hope that this would promote the language 'across the board' at secondary level. It was also hoped that languages other than French would benefit by attracting secondary school beginners who wanted to add a second language or, possibly, switch to a different one. It cannot really be said that the Nuffield Project, as it was usually known, succeeded in its more far-reaching aims. What it did achieve, however, was to make the teaching of foreign languages in Britain a matter of public concern after fifty years of stagnation in the grammar schools, and to bring together and train a pool of professional expertise which has directly or indirectly fed the language teaching profession (including the teaching of English) since the Project came to an end in 1974.[29] Moreover, it had the resources to explore new ideas in the production and presentation of teaching materials. Basically, *En Avant* and its sister courses in German, Spanish, and Russian,[30] follow a situational approach using audio-visual techniques, but, particularly in the later stages, as the project teams gathered experience, the range of ideas for language practice and development became freer and more varied. Earlier team projects like Michigan, for example, tended to work to a model. Nuffield encouraged diversity, though within the discipline and accountability of the team.

Following Nuffield, and for a time also working at Leeds University, was a group funded by the Schools Council to produce a course of English for immigrant children of primary school age. It began work in 1966 and the materials, *Scope, Stage 1*, were published in 1969, with two further stages appearing in 1972. *Scope* broke new ground in English language teaching by bringing together the EFL tradition of the linguistically organized syllabus (structural patterns, controlled vocabulary, etc.) and the primary school tradition of activity methods which required the children to use the new language co-operatively to make puppets, charts, models of various kinds, and so on. By tying the language work closely into activities and small projects with an educational value in their own right, as well as taking into account the children's needs for English both in and out of school, *Scope* created a new philosophy for English as a second language which has since matured into a branch of the profession with a distinctive voice.

In its concern to integrate language and language use, *Scope* foreshadowed one of the principal themes of the communicative approach as it developed during the next decade. The composition of the project team,[31] which included both sociologists and linguists, and the important emphasis given to the social and cultural background of the children in the teachers' support materials,[32] make *Scope* the first attempt to sketch out a sociolinguistic model of language teaching as opposed to a purely linguistic one. Much theoretical groundwork remained to be done, however, before the *Scope* technique of 'matching' linguistic patterns with useful classroom activities could develop into a more coherent view of the functional relationship between linguistic systems and their communicative values.

One approach to this issue was being explored in a third project also funded by the Nuffield Foundation (1964–67) and the Schools Council (1967–71) which ran concurrently with *Scope* and the modern languages project. This was the Programme in Linguistics and English Teaching directed by M. A. K. Halliday and located in the Communication Research Centre linked to his Department of General Linguistics at London University. As its title suggests, the programme looked both towards linguistics and towards the practical relevance of linguistic studies for classroom materials. It was the most theoretically minded of the three projects we have discussed, though the associated teaching materials, *Breakthrough to Literacy* (1970),[33] for example, and *Language in Use* (1971),[34] were important contributions to the practical teaching of English as a mother tongue. In addition to teaching materials, the programme produced a long series of papers, many of which were valuable additions to the subject in their own right, and one became particularly influential when it was published in an expanded form in the mid-seventies. This was Ruqaiya Hasan's *Grammatical cohesion in spoken and written English, part one*, originally written in 1968, which eventually appeared as the first three chapters of *Cohesion in English*, a collaborative publication with Halliday in 1976. It has since become a standard work of reference on the linguistic aspects of text construction for writers of teaching materials for advanced learners and for university-level students of English.

Halliday and Hasan define cohesion by saying: 'where the interpretation of any item in the discourse requires making reference to some other item in the discourse, there is cohesion'.[35] Such items would include, for example, pronouns, adverbial sequences such as *firstly, secondly, finally*, elliptical utterances like *Yes, I can*, and lexical sets where different items are used to refer to the same object or person (for example *Hamlet, the Prince of Denmark, royal cousin*, etc.). Cohesion is one dimension of the general Hallidayan aim of devising principled methods of relating elements of grammatical structure to their use in discourse. In this sense, Halliday's interests are complementary to those of the American sociolinguists whose work was mentioned briefly earlier. Hymes, for example, in 'On communicative competence' speaks of 'rules of use without which the rules of grammar would be useless',[36] and continues by characterizing, in very general terms, what form such 'rules of use' might have. Labov makes much the same point when he says 'The rules we need will show how things are done with words and how one interprets these utterances as actions'.[37] Language, in other words, plays a role in a broader theory of communication. The starting-point is sociological, the roles people adopt, their rights and obligations, and the unspoken contracts they enter into to preserve communication.

In a long series of papers and articles culminating in a book, *Teaching Language as Communication* (1978), which sums up many of the influential ideas of the seventies, H. G. Widdowson drew on both traditions to develop a distinction between the cohesion of texts as linguistic objects and the coherence of discourse as communication.[38] Believing that the latter was unjustifiably ignored, Widdowson placed considerable emphasis on it in his early papers 'in order to restore the balance for language teaching'.[39] Writing in *ELT* in 1972, for example, he insisted that 'it (was) a radical mistake to suppose that a knowledge of how sentences are put to use in communication follows automatically from a knowledge of how sentences are composed and what significa-tion they have as linguistic units. Learners have to be taught what values they may have as predictions, qualifications, reports, descriptions, and so on'.[40] He therefore proposed a different type of teaching syllabus built around a graded selection of rhetorical (or communicative) acts which the learner would have to perform in using English for his particular purposes. The scientist, for instance, would necessarily make extensive use of such acts as definition, classification, deduction, and so on. Other learners would need to communicate in more ordinary, everyday situations where greetings, making social arrangements, and exchanging personal information would be more important.

The switch of attention from teaching the language system to teaching the language as communication highlighted a potentially difficult problem in organizing syllabuses, materials, and other forms of classroom activity. The range of possible uses of language is as extensive as the range of possible purposes and intentions that people have for using it. Some principled way of making generalizations about types of language use is essential if the concept is not to disintegrate into an endless list of tokens, all apparently of equal value. 'Register analysis' offered one solution (for example, 'scientific English'), but registers do not illuminate the functional use of language. A more promising approach was to develop a system of discourse analysis which would focus attention on the way English is used in texts which are held to be typical of a particular subject-matter (for example, academic texts in science) and identify the learners as professional consumers of such texts. The third possibility, which is more appropriate to the spoken language, would be to concentrate on the users themselves, an emphasis which is evident, for example, in the approach to discourse adopted by Sinclair, Coulthard, and others in *The English Used by Teachers and Pupils* (1972).[41]

In his teaching materials, written in collaboration with J. P. B. Allen, Widdowson chose the second of the three solutions, and built his course round texts specifically constructed to illustrate the selected rhetorical acts (definition, classification, etc.) in use. Allen and Widdowson's series title, *English in Focus*, and the individual volumes (for example, *English in Physical Science*, *English in Education*, etc.)[42] reinforce their primary stress on language rather than, for instance, the characteristics of any particular group of language users. Moreover the stress on written English (including some very interesting work with non-verbal printed material such as diagrams, charts, etc.) has the advantage, assuming it is one, of further standardizing the purposes of the 'typical' learner.

Widdowson's second venture in the materials field is a counter-argument to the criticism that discourse-based approaches to language teaching throw away the pedagogical advantages of systematic organization and grading which the structural approach emphasized. He acted as Associate Editor with John Moore on a series called *Reading and Thinking in English*,[43] a highly systematic attempt to organize a course for intermediate-advanced learners built on the principle of semantic rather than structural grading. It begins with the way in which English is used to express specific concepts and moves on to the functional values of longer stretches of language, ending with the communicative processes of discourse itself. Like *Focus* it is concerned with written and not spoken English and, also like *Focus*, it makes considerable use, at least in the early stages, of specially constructed texts in order to clarify the teaching points being made in a lesson. The latter point, in particular, is one which has caused some controversy during the last ten years or so. Widdowson's view is quite clear: learners need specially written texts to bring them to the point when they can handle 'authentic' material for themselves. The teacher's 'central problem' is 'how to prepare material in such a way as to guide the learners to an awareness of the communicative conventions operating in the kind of discourse they will be concerned with'.[44]

Widdowson's literacy model of discourse allows him to maintain that constructed texts are valid since *all* written texts are constructed. They vary with their audience, but they are deliberately fashioned. Other writers in the applied discourse analysis field, such as Candlin, for example, or Sinclair, have adopted an interactive, oracy model of discourse in which the spontaneous use of spoken language makes the issue of authenticity more acute. The psycholinguistics of reading would not be greatly disturbed, if at all, by texts specially written for learners (assuming they are well written). The comprehension processes involved in making sense of spontaneous speech, on the other hand, are quite different from those employed in, say, following a tape-recorded textbook dialogue. Also, there is a sense in which 'using language in order to communicate' sounds rather strange with reference to spontaneous speech. People do not consciously 'use' language; they communicate and language gets used in the process, which is not quite the same thing. The focus shifts away from the language and towards the user, emphasizing the effectiveness with which the communication takes place and the skills which the user can muster in order to maintain and promote it.

In this interpretation of communicative language teaching, the heart of the language lesson is the communicative activity itself, and a communicative syllabus would presumably consist of a series of such activities organized round some central principle. Hitherto, the language teaching profession has responded to these rather powerful ideas with a mixture of enthusiasm and caution. It has been enthusiastic in adopting the communicative activity as an exercise type, and most modern courses of English as foreign or second language contain suggestions for 'information-gap' activities, role-plays, simulations, language games of various kinds, and so on. Building a course syllabus round interactive communication is, however, more problematical. So far the most successful applications have, again, been those where the communicative purposes of the learners can be specified with some degree of accuracy in advance, and Candlin's work in devising study-skill development programmes for overseas students is a good example.[45]

There is, in a sense, a 'strong' version of the communicative approach and a 'weak' version. The weak version, which has become more or less standard practice in the last ten years, stresses the importance of providing learners with opportunities to use their English for communicative purposes and, characteristically, attempts to integrate such activities into a wider programme of language teaching. In order to avoid the charge that communicative activities are merely side-shows, efforts are made to ensure that they relate to the purposes of the course as specified in the syllabus, hence the importance of proposals to include semantic as well as purely structural features in a syllabus design, a point we shall return to shortly. The 'strong' version of communicative teaching, on the other hand, advances the claim that language is acquired through communication, so that it is not merely a question of activating an existing but inert knowledge of the language, but of stimulating the development of the language system itself. If the former could be described as 'learning to use' English, the latter entails 'using English to learn it'.

One of the first examples of a 'using to learn' strategy was pioneered in the project at Birmingham referred to earlier called *Concept 7–9.* (1972).[46] The origins of the scheme lay in a concern at the apparent failure of many children in inner-city communities, particularly those with a West Indian background, to cope as adequately as they should with the demands of school learning. There was a current view that such children suffered from some kind of 'language deficit' which could be compensated for by a 'richer' linguistic environment. The Birmingham team, directed by John Sinclair, took the alternative view that it was not the children's knowledge of English that was 'restricted' but rather their experience of using it to explore the more abstract concepts and relationships required in school learning. The outcome was a 'kit' of problem solving tasks[47] which demanded the ideational use of English to communicate information about notions such as space relations, size, direction, shape, and so on. Informal, socialized conversation was discouraged by the use of screens so that the full weight of communication should fall on the precise use of information-carrying language for which the children would have to develop workable strategies.

A similar approach is evident in Sinclair's later work on the teaching of academic study skills in a programme originally developed by a team under his direction in Malaysia and published in Britain as *Skills for Learning* (1980).[48]

Much of what has been said so far has concerned more advanced learners, overseas students, for example, wishing to improve their knowledge of English before attending university or college. For such students the need to breathe communicative life into a bookish knowledge of English acquired, possibly some time ago, at school, is a fairly obvious aim, and their purposes in learning are clear enough to allow courses to be designed which bear some relationship to their needs. Nothing so far has been said about the general purpose learner who simply 'wants to learn English' and who knows little if anything of the language already. The adoption of a communicative approach in the design of general purpose materials coincided with the discourse-based developments we have already looked at, but originated from rather different roots.

By the end of the sixties it was clear that the situational approach as understood in, for example, the audio-visual method, had run its course. There was no future in continuing to pursue the chimera of predicting language on the basis of situational events. What was required was a closer study of the language itself and a return to the traditional concept that utterances carried meaning in themselves and expressed the intentions of the speakers and writers who created them. Language is not just a set of structure-habits, nor a collection of situationally sensitive phrases like *Can I help you?* or *How do you do*. It is a vehicle for the comprehension and expression of meanings, or 'notions' as Jespersen called them in 1924, and as they were to be called in the new model of syllabus construction being devised in the early seventies.

'We are led to recognize', Jespersen said in his exposition of notional categories in *The Philosophy of Grammar*, 'that beside, or above, or behind, the syntactic categories which depend on the structure of each language as it is actually found, there are some extralingual categories which are independent of the more or less accidental facts of existing languages; they are universal in so far as they are applicable to all languages, though rarely expressed in them in a clear and unmistakable way'.[49]

After a generation in which orthodox opinion proclaimed that 'all languages are different', here was a reminder that there existed a level of semantic generalization which brought different languages into contact with each other as varying manifestations of 'the same' notions. The potential of this insight for a programme of language teaching across linguistic frontiers provided one of the strands in an ambitious project initiated by the Council of Europe[50] in 1971 which has since become popularly known as 'The Threshold Level' or 'T-Level'.

The T-level effectively began at a symposium at Rüschlikon near Zürich in 1971 as a result of which three position papers were commissioned. The first set out a model of the archetypal adult learner of foreign languages in Europe in terms of an analysis of communicative needs. It appeared the following year as *A model for the definition of language needs of adults* by René Richterich. In a sense, this is the key document of the whole project since it set the parameters within which all the other elements were designed to work. It is divided into two sections, language needs and learning needs, for each of which Richterich provides a detailed taxonomy of the situations in which a learner might have to use the foreign language, the roles he might have to play, and the types of communicative activity he might have to take part in. The Richterich model later provided the starting-point for a more elaborate version by John Munby in *Communicative Syllabus Design* in 1978.

The second and third papers, by J. A. Van Ek and D. A. Wilkins, both address themselves to the same basic issue: the specification of a syllabus for the fundamental 'common core' which all learners would be expected to acquire before moving to their specific professional or other interests. Van Ek's *The 'Threshold Level' in a unit/credit system* (1973) concentrates on the problems of setting limits to the notion of 'common core' while Wilkins' *Linguistic and situational content of the common core in a unit/credit system* (1972)[51] is essentially an applied linguistic statement on how the core should be specified. Throughout the remainder of the decade, the project worked to realize the objectives summarized in these initial documents, and T-level specifications have appeared for English (1975), French (1976), Spanish (1979), German (1980) and Italian (1981).[52] The rationale for the scheme was eloquently articulated by J. L. M. Trim in 1973: 'The major developments of the last thirty years have progressively weakened the self-sufficiency of national cultures, even in day-to-day living. Mass travel for business and pleasure over continental motorway networks and air routes, electronic media, mass movements of immigrant labour and at managerial level in multinational corporations, supranational economic, cultural and political institutions, interdependence of imports/exports in an increasingly unified market, all conspire to render hard national frontiers . . . increasingly obsolete'.[53]

Wilkins' approach to his rather daunting task of specifying a syllabus for Europe began, as we saw earlier, from Jespersen's notional categories which 'are universal in so far as they are applicable to all languages'.[54] Wilkins recognizes three different types of notional category in the expanded version of his paper, published as *Notional Syllabuses* in 1976: (i) semantico-grammatical categories such as past, future, location, etc., (ii) categories of modality such as possibility, necessity, obligation, etc., and (iii) categories of communicative function, which include asking questions, making requests, expressing agreement and disagreement, and so on. In the 1975 *Threshold Level* inventory itself, Van Ek collapses (i) and (ii) into 'General Notions', and adds a category of 'Specific Notions' which represent word-meanings. 'Language Functions' are listed separately, and the approach as a whole has become known informally as the 'notional/functional approach'.

The slight uneasiness about terminology has been reflected in the response of the profession. While 'notions' seemed rather abstract for practical use, the value of 'functions' was recognized immediately as a means of organizing classroom activities and materials. They provided, in particular, a way of exploiting the situational dialogues inherited from the past, by demonstrating that the same function (for example, 'asking for things') occurred in many different situations. More generally, the use of functional labels for language lessons provided teachers with a means of communicating with learners which was both concrete and clearly related to their reasons for learning the language. 'Today we are going to practise asking for things in shops' makes much more obvious sense than 'practising question-forms', which is too abstract, or role-playing a dialogue such as 'At the florist's', which is too arbitrary. By the late seventies, most new courses in English had incorporated a functional dimension to their syllabus design. Typically, the familiar structural patterns remained, but they were ordered differently, and organized around functional headings which served to hold the individual lesson units together.[55]

While functional language teaching provided EFL with a more realistic, and probably more motivating, approach, it offered ESL something more fundamental, a central principle on which the new specialism could be based, and from which it could grow. The starting-point of functionalist teaching, the needs of learners and their purposes in learning English, both reflected the philosophy of community education in which much of ESL provision is located, and provided an explicit procedure for linking language forms and their use in everyday life which made practical sense to both learners and teachers. The informal adult basic education models adopted for most ESL teaching outside schools do not work effectively with highly structured, and often intensive, courses designed on the EFL pattern. They require a looser, more flexible approach in which a small number of guiding principles can be adapted to the specific needs of individual students, or small groups, by the teachers themselves who are, therefore, responsible for devising appropriate activities and materials. A particularly imaginative handbook designed for such purposes called *Industrial English*, by T. C. Jupp and Susan Hodlin,[56] was published in 1975, and similar materials have appeared since. It combines a specific example of a course in workplace English taught along functionalist lines with a well-exemplified discussion of basic ideas that could be adapted to other circumstances.

Where, as in ESL and some ESP, needs-analysis techniques can identify genuinely felt, and indeed often pressing, needs which the teacher can try to meet, the functionalist approach provides a coherent educational model (though, even here, the term 'needs' is sometimes over-worked and tends to ignore other important factors such as learner-demands or learner-aspirations, 'realistic' or otherwise). In much of EFL, on the other hand, and, by the same token, modern language teaching, the link between ascribed and perceived needs is more tenuous, and functionalist terminology is perhaps more usefully thought of as a means of setting course objectives than of analysing 'needs'. In this context, modern language teaching has moved one step ahead of EFL in exploring the possibilities of functional grading, and there is now a thriving movement in many local authority areas which is applying functionalist ideas to the definition of intermediate language learning goals.[57]

One of the common misconceptions associated with the 'notional/ functional approach', however, is that the specification of functional objectives ensures the adoption of a communicative methodology in order to reach them. This confusion over what is the proper province of the syllabus and what is the responsibility of method, may be due in some measure to the apparent failure of applied linguistics to keep more than one variable in play at the one time. In the sixties, for example, the syllabus was not an issue that caused more than marginal concern. There was a general consensus about what it should contain, and most discussion was limited to questions of ordering and presentation. There was, however, a lively controversy over methods of teaching which was reflected in a number of ambitious research projects. An influential study by Scherer and Wertheimer, published in 1964, for instance, found little difference between traditional and audiolingual approaches after two years of instruction, and a similar project in Pennsylvania later in the decade produced more or less the same results, as well as casting doubts on some of the more optimistic expectations of language laboratory enthusiasts.[58] A more detailed study that caused considerable discussion in its home-country was the Swedish GUME Project which compared the learning of grammar by implicit ('direct method') methods and by explicit ('traditional') ones.[59] The results tended to favour the latter, which upset a few people, but did not have much impact on the general direction of language teaching in the seventies.

Disappointment with the inconclusive outcomes of large-scale research projects and dissatisfaction with their orthodox control/experimental group design may have contributed to the decline in interest in methodological research in the seventies. Or, perhaps, it was simply a scarcity of funds. For whatever reason, the ballast shifted to the other side of the ship, so to speak, and most energy and inventiveness was devoted to the design of syllabuses and the production of classroom materials. 'Localized' research to establish the efficiency of new teaching programmes, for example, or the workability of new materials, was probably more common than it had been in the past. But it was not a time when anyone asked the 'big' questions like 'Is communicative language teaching worthwhile?' or 'Do overseas students really need special-purpose courses?' There was rather more model-making than data-collecting. The Council of Europe team, for instance, used the results of the vocabulary selection techniques developed in the past, but did not offer new ones.[60] The use of questionnaire techniques to establish what customers wanted from their language courses was a useful new departure, but again largely a matter of local initiative. Communicative principles produced new designs for tests, but, as yet, little is known about their validity, though they seem rather more interesting to do.[61]

The most significant research work in the seventies did not concern language teaching, but language learning, and led to the investigation of a theoretical base for the study of second language acquisition. The earliest serious studies in bilingualism had been done in the forties by W. F. Leopold.[62] Thereafter, little was said about the subject, and there were few if any descriptive studies out of which the first thoughts towards a theory might emerge. In the sixties however, the intellectual climate changed. Chomsky's work in linguistics attracted great attention among psychologists, notably men like George E. Millar and Eric Lenneberg, and discussions on language acquisition took on an urgency and enthusiasm that had been absent before. The destruction of the behaviourist view that learning a language resulted from rather simple responses to the environment, and its replacement by the notion of a meaning-seeking 'mind' which was biologically 'programmed' to create some kind of linguistic order out of the chaotic language data in the outside world, appealed to the imagination of many cognitive psychologists and set a new direction in child language acquisition research which has been explored in some detail since. It was only a matter of time before similar ideas would be influential in the second language field.

In 1967, partly under the stimulus of work being done by Julian Dakin with immigrant children in Glasgow, S. Pit Corder published a paper which contained the bold, and optimistic, statement: '*Given motivation*, it is inevitable that a human being will learn a second language if he is exposed to the data',[63] (his emphasis). The natural human ability to learn a language in infancy was available (given the will) for the acquisition of other languages later on, and, just as no one expected an infant to advance to 'perfection' without a long series of intermediate approximations, so no one should expect a second language learner to do anything different. Making 'mistakes' was a sign of activity, possibly even of learning, and the study of such errors was a legitimate, and indeed necessary, preliminary to a theory of second language acquisition. After this paper ('The significance of learners' errors'), Corder went on to claim a special status for the language of the learner.[64] It was not merely 'bad English', 'bad French', etc. but a communication system in its own right. In 1972, Selinker, who had previously studied with Corder in Edinburgh, christened this learner-language 'interlanguage'[65] and the term was adopted by many of the specialists who had been attracted into the field in the early seventies. Observational studies of second language acquisition began to appear in increasing numbers, and with them a more complex theoretical model. This was enriched further from the mid-seventies onwards by a closer interest in the strategies used by second language learners in their efforts to communicate with 'inadequate' linguistic resources.[66] Most of the work has centred around the development of syntax and phonology, but recently there has been some consideration of the role of discourse in the expansion of the second language learner's communicative repertoire.[67]

One of the interesting, and potentially fruitful, questions that interlanguage research has asked is whether there is a natural order of acquisition in unstructured, 'real life' second language situations and, if so, whether the variability that occurs when learners use the new language is, on closer inspection, more systematic than it appears at first sight. The evidence so far is encouraging in the sense that it points to some commonality in the learning histories of different learners with different mother tongues, and to greater systematicity than had been thought. However, second language learning appears to be susceptible to 'fossilization', as Selinker called it, when, for reasons that are not entirely clear, improvement ceases.[68]

The practical implications of second language acquisition studies have yet to be explored fully. It is likely, in the first instance anyway, that their principal value will be illuminative rather than operational, more helpful in providing teachers with insights into the learning processes of their students than in stimulating new materials or methods, though these might appear eventually. In particular, the interlanguage notion itself suggests the possibility of a more explicit and more reliable definition of progress. At present, progress is typically assessed in terms of how much of a given syllabus has been assimilated (achievement testing), or how much improvement has been made between two administrations of the same proficiency test. If there is a pattern of progress which is independent of any particular course syllabus (though not unrelated to the input provided by classroom instruction), it ought, in principle at least, to be possible to chart it in terms of recognizable 'milestones of attainment'.

Secondly, there is a need for the reassessment of the significance of error (Corder's original point). Clearly this does not mean that 'mistakes don't matter', appealing though the thought may be in some respects. If learning proceeds by a process of hypothesis-testing or 'trial-and-error', the response of the teacher in providing appropriate feedback is clearly crucial in promoting the development of the learner's internalized linguistic system.

The main feature of second language research to date has been the revival of the Leopold tradition of detailed case studies though some moves have been made towards the elaboration of more general models. One such that has attracted recent attention is Krashen's 'Monitor Model'[69] which starts from a familiar distinction between spontaneous language acquisition and conscious language learning which we have already encountered in, for instance, Palmer's work. A novel feature of Krashen's 'Monitor', however, is the restriction of 'learning' to exclude everything except conscious grammatical rules. ('Language study' might have been a less misleading term.) Of greater general interest is Krashen's revival of Palmer's notion of 'subconscious assimilation'[70] in a comprehension-based approach to foreign language teaching. As with Palmer, early instruction should include a 'silent period' during which production would be minimal and the emphasis would be put on the acquisition of an internalized 'grammar' through processing sufficient amounts of interesting 'comprehensible input', each example of which would be 'roughly' more demanding than the one before. No attempt should be made to control the input through a system of grammatical grading, but only through the requirement that it should be comprehensible. Learning the grammar would, it is argued, follow naturally. Like others influenced by post-Chomskyan notions of developing internalized competence, Krashen has nothing to say about lexical control which had been central to the thinking of both Palmer and Sweet, for whom the learning of vocabulary was 'the real intrinsic difficulty'.[71]

The work in second language acquisition raises again the issue alluded to earlier, namely the contrast between a 'weak' interpretation of the communicative approach to language teaching and a 'strong' one. According to the former view, learners must not only learn English, they must also learn 'how to use it'. There is an unstated assumption here that the learners already know English in some sense, and that it is the teacher's primary duty to ensure that this 'knowledge' is usefully employed for communicational purposes. In other words, the basic aim of a language teaching course is to promote (competent) *communicative performance*. The 'strong' view, on the other hand, maintains that knowledge of the second language is the outcome of communicative activity, not the prerequisite for it. Learners must use their communicative capacities in order to learn the new language or, to use the original term in its original sense, they must develop their *communicative competence*. The contrast is stated here in deliberately stark, confrontational terms. In reality, no doubt, both processes are going on at the same time. Nevertheless, the practical implications of the contrast between a performance view of communication and a competence view are serious and far-reaching.

The original motivation for adopting a communicative approach in the early seventies was remedial, an attempt to overcome the inadequacies of existing structural syllabuses, materials, and methods. As Widdowson, for example, put it in 1972: 'The problem is that students, and especially students in developing countries, who have received several years of formal English teaching, frequently remain deficient in the ability to actually use the language, and to understand its use, in normal communication, whether in spoken or written mode'.[72] Improving their practical command of communicative performance made particular sense to students learning English in Britain, who were enrolled in short-term courses: holiday courses for example, or pre-sessional programmes in preparation for their later studies at university or college. In this way they would make the best use of the advantages of a native-speaking community and native-speaking teachers. In addition, there was a high degree of motivation among the students themselves. They had 'already done' the grammar at home, and were disinclined to go over it all again. Instead, they wanted to improve their practical skills, especially in spoken English, and build up their confidence in using the language. This new market, and also the new emphasis on language use rather than form, encouraged course writers to produce materials with greater intrinsic interest, topics which engaged the students' attention, for example, pair-work activities, games, simulations, authentic listening and reading materials and so on, which brought learners into closer contact with real English. The influence of these new ideas swiftly spread elsewhere, to the teaching of EFL in secondary schools abroad, for instance, adult evening centres, and so on.

There is no reason why communicative performance cannot be promoted on the basis of a traditional language syllabus, provided that the linguistic material is suitably selected, presented and exercised. A syllabus with a semantic or functional bias, for example, allows the teacher to make the links between the 'new points' in a lesson and the attendant communicative exercises more explicit and systematic. Performance-related communicative teaching is in many ways more dependent on assumptions about method, however, than on theories of the syllabus.[73] In particular, it assumes that the monolingual principle of the 'direct method' is extended into social areas of language use which were neglected in the past. However, this in turn means that the performance abilities of the teachers must be of native or near-native standard, and the demands made on their 'sociolinguistic competence' can be very steep.

Issues such as these are particularly sensitive outside Europe. The Third World has frequently been the victim in the past of the over-enthusiastic promotion of 'packaged' methods originally devised for quite different circumstances, and there have been instances of the same kind of 'salesmanship' with communicative approaches. Increasingly, however, the initiative for change has emerged locally, and with it, a different pattern of co-operative enterprise. Recent examples have included the ESP projects at the University of Malaya and the Universidad de los Andes in Colombia which have already been referred to, and the Crescent Project, which originated in Qatar to produce materials for use in schools.[74]

Of particular interest, however, is a project in schools in South India whose progress will be watched closely elsewhere. It starts from a 'strong' interpretation of the communicative approach which means, among other things, that the children follow a communication syllabus, not a language one. Their course is organized round a series of communicative tasks which are graded in order of conceptual difficulty, beginning with very simple tasks like labelling and moving to more complex ones such as map-making.[75] The language used by the teacher in helping the children to accomplish the tasks provides the necessary input, and, in the initial stages, the primary emphasis is on comprehension. As the children's 'internal grammar' matures, their capacity to generate language of their own strengthens and, given time, the early deviance in surface forms is replaced by forms closer to the standard.

This project, directed by N. S. Prabhu and located at the Regional Institute of English in Bangalore, began in 1979 and is still continuing at three centres in South India. Initial results have been encouraging, but some of its characteristics will cause comment if not controversy, in particular, the low priority it attaches to social communication. It is in some ways a rather austere programme, in keeping with the constraints imposed by its location. This has given it strength. If Corder is right in saying that 'given motivation, it is inevitable that a human being will learn a second language if he is exposed to the data', the eventual outcome of the Bangalore project should show not only that it can be done, but that it can be done with the simplest means. But whatever happens, Bangalore has set the context for one of the most interesting arguments of the eighties, if not beyond.

The overall impact of the communicative approach has been to enrich and extend the traditions of language teaching initiated by the reformers at the end of the last century. The spoken language, for example, is promoted with more determination now than at any time since the Reform Movement. The principle of the connected text has not only withstood the challenge of structuralist 'sentence-patterns' but has been significantly extended into a principle of connected discourse which is already influential and will become more so in the future. Arguments over 'simple English' are still vigorously pursued, though the earlier consensus that 'simplicity' means merely graded grammar and controlled vocabulary has given way to a discussion on the relative contributions of linguistic and cognitive complexity. Finally, the monolingual principle, the unique contribution of the twentieth century to classroom language teaching, remains the bedrock notion from which the others ultimately derive. If there is another 'language teaching revolution' round the corner, it will have to assemble a convincing set of arguments to support some alternative (bilingual?) principle of equal power. There is no sign of such a revolution at the moment, but perhaps somebody said something like that the day before Viëtor published *Der Sprachunterricht muss umkehren!*

## Notes

1 Hornby (1950).
2 *In Honour of A. S. Hornby*, edited by Peter Strevens (1978). See 'The Hornby Educational Trust: the first ten years' by Peter Collier, David Neale, and Randolph Quirk.
3 Cf. Sampson (1980: 252).
4 See Angiolillo (1947).
5 Moulton (1961: 97).
6 Bloomfield (1942: 16).
7 Ibid.: 12.
8 Fries himself said, 'It (the Oral Approach) *is not primarily a new method as such*', (his emphasis). Fries (1955: 11).
9 Moulton (1961: 102). See, however, Darian (1972: 72–82) for a description of English teaching to immigrants before 1940.
10 Published under the auspices of the American Council of Learned Societies and edited by Martin Joos.
11 Moulton (1961: 101).
12 Mackin quoting from a prepared paper by Bruce Pattison in Center for Applied Linguistics (1959: 151).
13 Chomsky (1965: 8).
14 Ibid.: 4.
15 From Chomsky (1966) reprinted in Allen and Corder (eds. 1973: 234).

16  Cazden in Cazden *et al.* (eds. 1972: vii). The paper, 'On communicative competence', was later published in a number of sources including Pride and Holmes (eds. 1972: 269–93).
17  Hymes in Cazden *et al.* (eds. 1972: xii).
18  See Hartog (1917: 5–22).
19  Malinowski (1923).
20  Firth (1957: 182).
21  Reprinted in Palmer (ed. 1968: 126–36).
22  Ibid.: 206–209.
23  See Firth (1957: 195).
24  For example, Halliday (1973: 52–4).
25  Although 'sociolinguistics' was a new label, the tradition of socio-cultural language studies was a long one in American linguistics, owing most perhaps to the work of Edward Sapir (e.g. *Language*, 1921). During the Bloomfieldian period, the Sapir tradition was rather overshadowed, but it was never broken.
26  From 3.2 per cent of the gross national product in 1954 to 6.5 per cent in 1970. *The Changing Anatomy of Britain* by Anthony Sampson (1982: 114), published by Hodder and Stoughton.
27  For example, The Newsom Report on the secondary modern schools (*Half Our Future*) and the Robbins Report (*Higher Education*), both 1963.
28  The Nuffield Foreign Languages Teaching Materials Project, funded by the Nuffield Foundation (1963–67) and the Schools Council (1967–70). See the paper by A. Spicer (the Project Director) in H. H. Stern (ed.) *Languages and the Young School Child* (Oxford University Press, 1969: 148–61).
29  For example, the experience gained from the exploration of visual techniques in language teaching. Cf. Wright (1976).
30  *Vorwärts, Adelante*, and *Vperyod*.
31  Director: John Ridge; Organizer: June Derrick.
32  *The Social Background of Immigrant Pupils* (The Scope Handbook).
33  By David Mackay, Brian Thompson, and Pamela Schaub, published by Longman for the Schools Council.
34  By P. S. Doughty, J. J. Pearce, and G. M. Thornton, published by Edward Arnold.
35  Halliday and Hasan (1976: 11).
36  Quoted in Pride and Holmes (eds. 1972: 278).
37  Quoted in Widdowson (1979: 92).
38  See, for example, 'Directions in the teaching of discourse' (1973), reprinted in Widdowson (1979: 89–100).
39  Widdowson (1979: 98).
40  From 'The teaching of English as communication' (1972), reprinted in Brumfit and Johnson (eds. 1979: 117).

41 Final Report to the SSRC, August 1972, by J. McH. Sinclair, I. J. Forsyth, R. M. Coulthard, and M. Ashby, University of Birmingham. Later republished as *Towards an Analysis of Discourse* (Sinclair and Coulthard (1975)).

42 *English in Focus*, published by Oxford University Press from 1974 onwards. See also Allen and Widdowson 'Teaching the communicative use of English', in Brumfit and Johnson (eds. 1979: 122–42). *English in Physical Science* by J. P. B. Allen and H. G. Widdowson, Oxford University Press, 1974. *English in Education* by Elizabeth Laird, Oxford University Press, 1977.

43 *Concepts in Use* (1979), *Exploring Functions* (1979), *Discovering Discourse* (1979), and *Discourse in Action* (1980) published by Oxford University Press.

44 From 'The authenticity of language data', paper presented to the TESOL Convention, 1976. Reprinted in Widdowson (1979: 163).

45 See for example Candlin *et al.* (1978).

46 Funded by the Schools Council, 1968–72. See Schools Council Working Paper 29 (Evans/Methuen Educational, 1970).

47 The kit consists of four boxed components: *Listening with Understanding*, *Concept Building*, *Communication*, and a *Dialect Kit*. The *Communication* component includes what are probably the earliest examples of the 'information-gap' activities which became popular a number of years later.

48 The University of Malaya English for Special Purposes Project (UMESPP). The materials were originally published by the University of Malaya Press as *Reading for Academic Study* (1979). A central feature of this project is the prominence it gives to spoken interaction (in the form of group discussion, information exchange activities, collaborative project work, etc.) as an essential dimension of efficient reading development. See Nelson (1980).

49 Jespersen (1924: 55).

50 More accurately, the Council for Cultural Co-operation of the Council of Europe.

51 The phrase 'unit/credit system', which occurs frequently in Council of Europe materials, refers to a system for organizing educational programmes into more or less self-sufficient units related to specific learner-groups, and for awarding credits as each unit is taken. In principle, such credits would serve as transnational qualifications.

52 French: *Un niveau-seuil* by Daniel Coste, Janine Courtillon, Victor Ferenczi, Michel Martins-Baltar, Eliane Papo, and Eddy Roulet. Spanish: *Un nivel umbral* by P. J. Slagter. German: *Kontaktschwelle, Deutsch als Fremdsprache* by Markus Baldegger, Martin Müller, Günther Schneider, and Anton Näf. Italian: *Livello Soglia* by N. Galli de Paratesi. All published by The Council of Europe, Strasbourg.

53 From Trim's introduction to Trim *et al.* (1973: 17). Reprinted in Brumfit and Johnson (eds. 1979: 100).
54 Wilkins (1976: 18, footnote 13).
55 For example, The *Strategies* series by Brian Abbs and Ingrid Freebairn (Longman 1977 onwards) and the *Network* series by John Eastwood, Valerie Kay, Ronald Mackin, and Peter Strevens, Oxford University Press, 1980 onwards). Also, in a different format, the work of Wilkins' colleagues at the Centre for Applied Language Studies at Reading University: *Communicate 1/2* (1979–80) and *Approaches* (1980) by Keith Morrow and Keith Johnson, both published by Cambridge University Press.
56 Published by Heinemann Educational Books with the subtitle 'An example of theory and practice in functional language teaching for elementary learners'. The materials grew out of work at the Pathway Further Education Centre in Southall in London, where a special unit was set up in 1970, the forerunner of the National Centre for Industrial Language Training.
57 See, for example, Harding *et al.* (1980). The 'graded objectives' movement includes schemes in, for example, Oxfordshire, the East Midlands, the Lothian Region in Scotland, and many other places.
58 The Pennsylvania Foreign Language Project was a large-scale study which began in 1965 under the title 'Teaching Strategies Utilizing Three Language Laboratory Systems'. It reported formally in 1968. See Smith (1970).
59 The GUME (Göteborg, Undervisnings-Method i Engelska) Project produced a series of studies of implicit and explicit grammar learning by both children (for example, Lindblad (1969)) and adults (for example, Von Elek and Oskarsson (1973)).
60 Cf. Van Ek in Trim *et al.* (1973: 102–4).
61 A validation study of the English Language Testing Services (ELTS) Test developed by the British Council is in progress at the Institute for Applied Language Studies at Edinburgh University.
62 *Speech Development of a Bilingual Child: A Linguist's Record.* A series of studies published over ten years from 1939.
63 Corder (1967), republished in Corder (1981: 5).
64 'Describing the language learner's language' published in *CILT Reports and Papers*, No. 6, 1971. Republished in Corder (1981: 26–34).
65 Selinker (1972).
66 For example, Tarone *et al.* (1976), also Corder (1978), 'Strategies of communication', reprinted in Corder (1981: 103–6).
67 'Discourse analysis and second-language acquisition' by Evelyn Hatch in Hatch (1978: 401–35).
68 Selinker (1972).
69 Krashen (1981, 1982).

70 Palmer (1917/ 1968: 90–5).
71 Sweet (1899/ 1964: 64–5).
72 Widdowson (1972), 'The teaching of English as communication', reprinted in Brumfit and Johnson (eds. 1979: 117–21, p. 117).
73 Brumfit makes this point strongly in his contribution to Brumfit and Johnson (eds. 1979: 183-91), and also proposes lesson models which, to some extent, reflect the 'weak'/'strong' contrast being drawn here.
74 The Crescent Project was a large-scale scheme which involved collaboration between Oxford University Press and specialists from different countries in the Middle East. The materials represent a carefully judged fusion of new ideas and local priorities.
75 The most accessible account of the Bangalore Project to date is in Johnson (1982: 135–44) in a paper called 'The Procedural Syllabus', the term employed by the Project Director, N. S. Prabhu, to describe his syllabus of graded 'communicational' tasks.

# Epilogue

## On rational and natural approaches to language teaching

Learning a new language naturally by living, working, and interacting with other people who speak it as their mother tongue is a normal, everyday occurrence, more common perhaps than learning languages in classrooms. The success of informal learning, and particularly of the child acquiring its mother tongue, has always impressed language teachers, and attempts to reproduce the same effect by creating the same causes have been a regular feature of language teaching history. There was, for example, the glimpse that Morhof gave us of Nicholas Clenard's Latin lesson in the early sixteenth century (see Chapter 14), and the Montaigne story is a living legend. John Locke's live-in, native-speaking tutor was an obvious solution for families who could afford it, and his advice to 'talk the language into' children doubtless worked on many occasions. Locke's context was, however, an easy one for informal teaching. Much more challenging is the thought that appropriate conditions can be created in school classrooms of the normal modern pattern.

Sauveur's revival of natural methods around 1870, though others like Marcel and Blackie had been arguing the same point earlier without much success, depended on his personal enthusiasm, energy, and inspiration. His 'conversation', or, as it might be called today, 'discourse' model of teaching-through-talking lacked an analytical framework which could be put to use elsewhere. The systematization imposed by Berlitz, Palmer, and the other Direct Method teachers preserved Sauveur's monolingual principle, but idealized his intuitive conversations into classroom question-and-answer work based on an ordered series of language 'patterns'. Nature was, in effect, tamed by reason derived from the conscious study of language and language learning encouraged by the teachings of Sweet and the others in the rationalist Reform Movement.

Paradoxically, Palmer himself started a new quest for natural methods by identifying the spontaneity of natural spoken language with the formation of automatic speech habits through constant practice in infancy. The same general theme was taken up by Bloomfield later and it became the orthodoxy of the structuralist approach. However, by equating natural speech-habits with idealized sentence patterns, the approach destroyed the spontaneity it was seeking by divorcing language from its use in social communication. One reaction to this failure was the revival in the sixties of the situational techniques of the sixteenth and seventeenth centuries: models of social interaction presented in an idealized dialogue form. Such dialogues, however, create an imaginary world of predictable interchange, a rehearsed, theatrical substitute for the real world of improvisation. The contemporary communicative movement, in at least one of its many interpretations, has returned to the original Sauveurian concept of spontaneous spoken interaction, only in a more sophisticated form. The need for a rational basis for one's activities, if only to justify them to a critical outside world, is, however, as strong as ever, and it remains to be seen what form it will take this time. The evidence at present points to the elaboration and application of theories of discourse, but it is a little early to know for sure.

Nature in language teaching, it would seem, is intractable. Reason typically intervenes in the shape of linguistically organized syllabuses, sociologically responsible curricula, or psychologically well-argued methods. The blame, if indeed there is any, is put at the door of the education system with its restrictions, examinations, regulations, and other forms of intervention. There may be some justice in these complaints, but there is perhaps another reason why natural methods of language teaching have tended to meet with only intermittent success.

Natural language acquisition through orate interaction occurs in pre-literate infancy. The experience of becoming literate at school brings with it an awareness of language which is quite alien to the pre-school child, a consciousness of linguistic form and a measure of deliberate control over the use of language in different spoken and written contexts.[1] This does not mean that the literate older learner cannot acquire a second language under informal (orate) conditions; success, in some measure at least, is commonplace. Nevertheless, there are two significant consequences of literacy for 'natural' second language teaching derived too literally from attempts to recreate the conditions of informal learning. The first is social: educational institutions are by definition literacy-promoting and, in a sense, literacy-dependent. It is possible that some of the success of informal methods with young children at primary level, where there is still a considerable amount of non-linguistic activity going on, depends on learning conditions which are still sensitive to orate modes of interaction. Later on, this is not the case.

The second consequence is psychological. Under learning conditions which are modelled on 'natural' informal situations, the learner must be prepared to set his literacy aside. Individuals vary in their ability and willingness to do this (there are also powerful cultural pressures and inhibitions). The linguistic consciousness that accompanies literacy is a defence against error and other causes of discomfort. Teachers adopting monolingual methods, particularly with older learners, have long been aware of the problem, but perhaps less aware of how deep it can go. It is not merely 'overdependence on the written word' that can be cured by withholding the printed text (though this may well be useful in some instances). What is at issue is a more complex relationship between strategies of language learning derived from past experience, and strategies appropriate to the task in hand. Engaging in a fiction that the learner is 'illiterate' may impose considerable, and perhaps unnecessary, strain.

One of the implications of this line of argument is to consider approaches which are natural in the sense that they are primarily concerned with the communication of meanings, but which do not go out of their way to replicate earlier pre-literate contexts of use. The exchange of ideational meanings is more amenable to the conditions of the typical classroom than interpersonal socialization (particularly if it is role-played or simulated). The first step towards the communication of meanings is the ability to interpret them. As Marcel put it, 'The mind should be impressed with the idea before it takes cognizance of the sign that represents it'.[2] As familiarity with the signs, and their relationships in systems of signs, grows over time, the ability to use them in the expression of ideas will develop naturally. Provided the learner's attention is engaged by the task in hand, the meanings being communicated are not obscure, the signs used in their communication are clear, and the confidence of the learner not abused by the fear of error, nature will take its course. It is up to reason to provide the most propitious conditions.

## Notes

1 Cf. Donaldson (1978). Also, Goody and Watt (1963).
2 Marcel (1853: 217).

# A chronology of English language teaching

The following chronology is not narrowly restricted to English language teaching alone, but contains items that have, directly or indirectly, influenced the subject. Other historical events are also noted to give a context. Summary titles only are used.

1362  Court proceedings to be conducted in English.
1386  Chaucer begins work on the *Canterbury Tales*.
1396  First *manière de langage* (manual of French dialogues).
1399  Accession of Henry IV.
1413  Accession of Henry V.
1415  Battle of Agincourt;
      Second *manière de langage*.
1417  First extant Privy Council record in English.
1422  Brewers' decision to keep records in English.
1436  *The Book of Margery Kempe*, first extant biography in English.
*c.*1483  Caxton's *Tres bonne doctrine*.
*c.*1498  de Worde's *Lyttel Treatyse*.
1530  Palsgrave's *Lesclaircissement de la langue francoyse*.
1540  *Septem Linguarum*, one of the earliest polyglot dictionaries to include English;
      'Lily's *Grammar*' authorized by Royal Proclamation (Henry VIII).
1551  Hart's *Opening*.
1553  Meurier's *Treatise*, no extant copy of this edition;
      Accession of Mary I.
1554  Florio family flees to France;
      *A Very Profitable Book*, anonymous English–Spanish manual.
1558  Accession of Elizabeth I.
*c.*1566  Arrival of Holyband in England.
1569  Hart's *Orthography*.
1570  Hart's *Method*;
      Ascham's *Schoolmaster*.
1572  Massacre of St. Bartholomew.
1573  Holyband's *French Schoolmaster*.
1576  Holyband's *French Littleton*.

1578 Florio's *First Fruits*.
1580 Bellot's *English Schoolmaster*, first extant textbook specifically designed to teach English to foreigners;
Bullokar's *Book at Large*;
Montaigne's *Essais*.
1582 Mulcaster's *Elementarie*.
1585 Petrus Ramus translated into English.
1586 Bellot's *Familiar Dialogues*;
Bullokar's *Pamphlet for Grammar*, first grammar of English.
1591 Florio's *Second Fruits*.
1592 Birth of Comenius.
1593 Eliot's *Ortho-epia Gallica*;
Shakespeare's *Richard III*.
1598 Edict of Nantes.
1603 Florio's translation of Montaigne;
Accession of James I and VI.
1605 Bacon's *Advancement of Learning*;
Shakespeare's *Macbeth*.
1606 Jonson's *Volpone*.
1616 Death of Shakespeare;
First volume of Jonson's *Works*.
1618 Outbreak of the Thirty Years' War.
1621 Gill's *Logonomia Anglica* (2nd, revised edition. Orig.publ. 1619).
1622 Mason's *Grammaire Angloise*;
Webbe's *Appeal to Truth*.
1623 Probable first draft of Jonson's *Grammar*;
Webbe's *Petition to the High Court of Parliament*;
First Folio of Shakespeare.
1627 Webbe's *Children's Talk*.
1631 Comenius's *Janua Linguarum* published in London under title of *Porta Linguarum*, edited by John Anchoran.
c.1632 Comenius's *Great Didactic* completed.
1633 Comenius's *Janua Linguarum* and *Vestibulum*.
1640 Jonson's *English Grammar*.
1641 Comenius in London.
1642–8 Comenius in Elbing.
1646 Poole's *English Accidence*, earliest attempt to teach children English grammar before Latin grammar.
1648 End of Thirty Years' War.
1649 Trial and execution of Charles I.
1650 Comenius travels to Saros Patak. Starts on the *Orbis Pictus*.
1653 Wallis's *Grammatica Linguae Anglicanae*.
1657 Collected works of Comenius (*Opera Didactica Omnia*) published in Amsterdam. Comenius himself settles in the city.

1658   *Orbis Pictus* published in Nuremberg.
1659   *Orbis Pictus* translated into English, published in London.
1660   Restoration of Charles II.
1662   Incorporation of the Royal Society.
1668   Wilkins' *Essay*.
1670   Death of Comenius.
1672   Festeau's *Nouvelle Grammaire Angloise*.
1685   Revocation of the Edict of Nantes;
       Miège's *Nouvelle Méthode*;
       Cooper's *Grammatica*.
1687   Offelen's *Double-Grammar*, first grammar of English for German-speakers.
1688   Miège's *English Grammar*.
1693   Aickin's *Grammar*;
       Locke's *Some Thoughts Concerning Education*.
1706   König's *Englischer Wegweiser*, widely used text in eighteenth century, also translated into Swedish.
1711   'The Brightland *Grammar*'.
1712   Swift's *Proposal*;
       Maittaire's *Grammar*.
1718   Boyer and Miège's *Double-Grammar*.
1728   First grammar of English for Italian speakers (Altieri's *Grammatica*).
1731   First grammar of English for Portuguese speakers (de Castro's *Grammatica*).
1733   Anonymous *Accidence*.
1747   Johnson's *Plan of a Dictionary*.
1755   Johnson's *Dictionary of the English Language*.
1761   Priestley's *Rudiments*.
1762   Lowth's *Short Introduction to English Grammar*;
       Buchanan's *British Grammar*.
1766   First indigenous Russian grammar of English by Permskii.
1783   Meidinger's *Praktische französische Grammatik*, the first 'grammar-translation' course.
1791   Walker's *Critical Pronouncing Dictionary*.
1793   Fick's *Sprachlehre*, following Meidinger, first application of 'grammar-translation' methods to English.
1795   Murray's *Grammar*.
1797   Miller's *The Tutor* published in Serampore. Earliest (?) English language textbook outside Europe and N. America.
1801   Pestalozzi's *How Gertrud Teaches Her Children*.
1819   Cobbett's *Grammar of the English Language*.
1828   Webster's *American Dictionary of the English Language*.
1830   Jacotot's *Enseignement universel, langue étrangère*.

1834 First appearance of Ahn's *Method* (French for German speakers).

1835 First appearance of Ollendorff's *Method* (German for French speakers).

1845 Henry Sweet born.

1852 Roget's *Thesaurus*.

1853 Marcel's *Language as a Means of Mental Culture*;
Ploetz's *Elementarbuch* (French for German speakers).

1858 Start of Oxford and Cambridge Local Examinations.

1862 Cambridge Overseas Examinations begin.

1864 Prendergast's *Mastery of Languages*.

1865–6 Heness's experiment with 'natural methods' at Yale.

1874 Sauveur's *Teaching of Living Languages*.

1877 Sweet's *Handbook of Phonetics*.

1878 First Berlitz school opened in Providence, Rhode Island, U.S.A.

1880 Gouin published in Paris.

1882 Viëtor's *Der Sprachunterricht* published under Quousque Tandem pseudonym.

1884 Franke's *Praktische Spracherlernung*;
Sweet's paper to the Philological Society 'On the practical study of language'.

1885 Sweet's *Elementarbuch*.

1886 Second, acknowledged, edition of *Der Sprachunterricht*;
Passy founds Phonetic Teachers' Association in Paris;
Jespersen helps to found Quousque Tandem Society in Stockholm.

1887–8 Klinghardt's experiment in Reichenbach.

1888 Widgery's *Teaching of Languages in Schools*.

1897 International Phonetic Association established.

1899 Sweet's *Practical Study of Languages*;
Passy's *De la méthode directe dans l'enseignement des langues vivantes*. ~~Rev't of ELT professor in Britain~~

1902 Palmer opens language school in Verviers.

1904 Jespersen's *How to Teach a Foreign Language*.

1906 Daniel Jones starts lecture courses at London University. *University College (Univ of Edin)*

1913 Watson's founding paper on behaviourism.

1914 Outbreak of First World War; Palmer returns to England;
Bloomfield's *Introduction to the Study of Language*.

1915 Palmer joins Phonetics Department, University College, London.

1917 Palmer's *Scientific Study*;
Jones's *English Pronouncing Dictionary*;
Inauguration of School of Oriental Studies, University of London.

1921  Palmer's *Oral Method* and *Principles of Language-Study*.
1922  Palmer becomes Linguistic Adviser to the Japanese Ministry of Education.
1923  IRET founded in Tokyo.
1924  Palmer's *Grammar of Spoken English*.
1926  West's *Bilingualism*, report on the teaching of English in Bengal.
1927  Early New Method materials published in India.
1930  Ogden's *Basic English* published.
1931  Cambridge Proficiency Examination held overseas for first time (available in United Kingdom since 1913).
1932  First start made on teacher-training for EFL at Institute of Education, London.
1933  Bloomfield's *Language*.
1934  West's attack on Ogden;
      Carnegie Conference opens in New York;
      Foundation of British Committee, later British Council.
1935  Carnegie Conference reconvenes in London;
      Ogden's reply to West (*Counter-Offensive*);
      Inauguration of British Council by Prince of Wales.
1936  *Interim Report* (Carnegie) published; (Palmer, West, Thorndike)
      Palmer leaves Japan.
1938  Eckersley's *Essential English (1)*; (for refugees in England)
      Palmer's *New Method Grammar*.
1939  Cambridge Lower Examination started;
      Outbreak of Second World War.
1940  British Council incorporated by Royal Charter.
1941  English Language Institute founded at University of Michigan.
1942  Bloomfield's *Outline Guide*.
1943  The Army Specialized Training Program (ASTP).
1944  First Chair of General Linguistics in Britain (London) (J. R. Firth appointed);
      Basic English issue raised in House of Commons;
      Palmer's lecture tour of Brazil, Uruguay, and Argentina.
1945  Fries's *Teaching and Learning English as a Foreign Language*.
1946  First issue of *English Language Teaching*.
1948  Establishment of Chair with special responsibilities for English as a foreign language at London University (First Holder: Bruce Pattison);
      First issue of *Language Learning*;
      Hornby's *A Learner's Dictionary of Current English* published in London. *Advanced Learner's* from 1952.
1952  Fries's *Structure of English*.
1953  *General Service List of English Words* (West) published.

1954 Hornby's *Guide to Patterns and Usage in English* and *Progressive English (1)*.
1957 School of Applied Linguistics, University of Edinburgh.
1960 Stack's language laboratory guide;
Association of Recognized English Language Schools (ARELS) founded.
1961 CREDIF audio-visual course *Voix et Images de France*.
1963 Gattegno's *Silent Way*;
Nuffield Foreign Languages Teaching Materials Project (Director: A. Spicer);
Hayes Report on language laboratories in America.
1964 Halliday, McIntosh and Strevens' *Linguistic Sciences and Language Teaching*;
First Congress of the Association Internationale de Linguistique Appliquée (AILA) in Nancy, France;
Nuffield Programme in Linguistics and English Teaching (Director: M. A. K. Halliday).
1965 Chomsky's *Aspects of the Theory of Syntax*;
Mackey's *Language Teaching Analysis*.
1966 Centre for Information on Language Teaching (CILT) (Director: George Perren);
Teachers of English to Speakers of Other Languages (TESOL) established in America;
Chomsky's paper to the N.E. Conference;
Hymes' 'On communicative competence' read at Yeshiva University.
1967 First Annual Meeting of the British Association for Applied Linguistics (BAAL);
Association of Teachers of English as a Foreign Language (ATEFL, since 1971 IATEFL);
Royal Society of Arts (RSA) Certificate in Teaching English as a Foreign Language;
Alexander's *New Concept English*;
Corder's 'The significance of learners' errors'.
1968 Broughton's *Success with English*;
Huddleston *et al. Sentence and Clause in Scientific English*.
1969 *Scope, Stage 1*;
Conference on Languages for Special Purposes;
Ewer and Latorre's *A Course in Basic Scientific English*.
1971 Council of Europe Symposium at Rüschlikon in Switzerland.
1972 *Concept 7–9*;
Sinclair *et al., The English Used by Teachers and Pupils*;
Quirk *et al., Grammar of Contemporary English*;
Richterich's 'Model for the definition of the language needs of adults';

Widdowson's 'Teaching of English as communication';
Wilkins' 'Linguistic and situational content of the common core in a unit/credit system';
Selinker's 'Interlanguage'.

1973   Dakin's *Language Laboratory and Language Learning*;
Trim *et al.*, *Systems Development in Adult Language Learning*;
Van Ek's 'The "Threshold Level" in a unit/credit system';
Conference on 'The Communicative Teaching of English' sponsored by AILA/BAAL and organized by C. N. Candlin, University of Lancaster.

1974   Allen and Widdowson's *English in Focus*.

1975   Van Ek's *Threshold Level* for English;
Jupp and Hodlin's *Industrial English*.

1976   Wilkins' *Notional Syllabuses*;
Halliday and Hasan's *Cohesion in English*.

1978   Widdowson's *Teaching Language as Communication*;
Munby's *Communicative Syllabus Design*;
National Association for Teachers of English as a Second Language to Adults (NATESLA).

1979   RSA Certificate in the Teaching of English to Adult Immigrants and Preparatory Certificate for the Teaching of English as a Foreign Language to Adults (pilot);
Regional Institute of English, Bangalore, Project (Director: N. S. Prabhu);
Brumfit and Johnson's *The Communicative Approach to Language Teaching*.

1980   *Applied Linguistics* (journal).

# Biographical notes ·

Special attention has been given in these notes to individuals whose contribution to the subject may not have been sufficiently acknowledged in the main text. Widgery and Jespersen for instance, deserved a chapter to themselves but space did not permit, and I hope some amends have been made here. Secondly, famous names such as Johnson and Swift that can be found in any biographical dictionary are dealt with only briefly.

Specific sources are quoted for many of the entries, including, in particular, obituary notices in journals such as *Le Maître Phonétique*, *Englische Studien*, *English Language Teaching (Journal)*, etc.; Sebeok's two-volume *Portraits of Linguists* (1966) was also an important source. General reference works consulted include the *Dictionary of National Biography*, *Chambers Biographical Dictionary* (1974), and many similar publications, British, American, and European. Alston's editorial notes (Alston (ed. 1967–72)) have also been invaluable.

## AHN, Johann Franz   1796–1865

With H. G. Ollendorff (q.v.), Ahn was one of the leading, and most widely imitated, language textbook writers of the mid-nineteenth century. A schoolteacher in Aachen near the Dutch–German border, he began his writing career with a popular manual for Dutch (*Neue holländische Sprachlehre*) in 1829, and followed it with a series of readers and conversation books for other languages, including English. In 1834 he brought out the first edition of his *New, Practical, and Easy Method* (to teach French to German speakers) which became the model for courses in every major modern and classical language. His textbooks are short, easy to follow, and relatively free of grammatical jargon, though they follow the typical grammar–translation pattern of grammatical rules accompanied by practice sentences. In their day they were considered 'lightweight' and were often 'adapted' (i.e. expanded) for use in schools.

## ASCHAM, Roger   1515–1568

Ascham (pronounced 'æskəm) was a major figure in the intellectual life of Tudor England and the leading classical scholar of his time. He was tutor to the Princess Elizabeth (1548–50) and served as her secretary after she became Queen, a role he had previously filled for her Catholic sister, Mary I. Ascham's reputation rests chiefly on his posthumous work *The Schoolmaster*, published in 1570, in which he defined the principles of a classical humanist education, and outlined a curriculum 'specially purposed for the private bringing up of youth in Gentlemen and Noble mens houses'. He is well-known for promoting the use of 'double translation' (translating into the mother tongue and back into the foreign language). The fame of *The Schoolmaster* encouraged many of the foreign-language authors of the late sixteenth century to copy the title, for example, Holyband's *French Schoolmaster* (1573) and Bellot's *English Schoolmaster* (1580).

### BASEDOW, Johann Bernhard   1723–1790

Basedow (pronounced 'bazɜdɔ) was born in Hamburg. He was a gifted teacher with unorthodox views and had a rather uneven career. Under the influence of Rousseau's *Émile* (1762), he founded a school called the Philanthropinum at Dessau which followed a 'natural' curriculum that included crafts, outdoor activities, and a conversational approach to language teaching. He was also influenced by Comenius and included pictures in his materials following *Orbis Pictus*, but they were less closely integrated into the text. The school became well known, but did not outlive him and was closed in 1793. (See Quick (1895).)

### BELLOT, Jacques   (dates unknown).

Gentleman of Caen in Normandy. (He signed his books *I.B.Gen.Ca.*: Iacques Bellot Gentilhomme Cadomois.) Bellot arrived in England as a refugee in 1577 or 1578 and resided with Sir Philip Wharton. His works include the earliest extant textbooks expressly written for the teaching of English as a foreign language: *The English Schoolmaster* (1580) and *Familiar Dialogues* (1586). The former is dedicated to the Duke of Alençon, brother to Henry III of France and one of Elizabeth's unsuccessful suitors. A friend of Holyband's, Bellot wrote a dedicatory poem for *Campo di Fior* (1583). His other works were for the teaching of French: *French Grammar* (1578), *Le Jardin de Vertu* (1581, a book of readings dedicated to Elizabeth) and *A French Method* (1588). Nothing is known of him after the early 1590s. Presumably he returned to Normandy.[1]

### BERLITZ, Maximilian Delphinus   1852–1921

Born in southern Germany into a family of teachers, Berlitz emigrated to the United States in the early 1870s and opened a language school in Providence, Rhode Island in 1878. His first employee ( a Frenchman called Nicholas Joly) introduced him to a monolingual method of teaching languages, similar to that pioneered in the sixties and seventies by Heness and Sauveur (q.v.). Berlitz systematized the method and developed an extensive series of textbooks from 1882 onwards, teaching all the major European languages, some of the 'minor' ones, and a number of non-European languages as well. The Berlitz school system started in America, then spread to Germany and the rest of Europe. In the 1890s there were around fifty schools: sixteen in America, seventeen in Germany, five in Britain, and the rest in France, Hungary, Austria, and Holland. By the time he died, his organization had expanded to include schools in the Middle East, Australia, and Latin America.[2]

### BLACKIE, John Stuart   1809–1895

Educated in Scotland and Germany, Blackie was called to the bar in 1834. Some years later he became Professor of Humanity (Latin) at Aberdeen and, in 1852, Professor of Greek at Edinburgh, a post he held for thirty years. He published regularly on language teaching, consistently espousing what he called 'The Method of Nature'. A review he wrote in 1845 is remarkable for its detailed scheme for an oral approach starting with 'object lessons'. His later work, however, is disappointing. He merely repeats his earlier views and does not appear to have kept in touch with the subject.

### BLOOMFIELD, Leonard   1887–1949

Born in Chicago into a distinguished family of academics and artists, his uncle Maurice was a noted Sanskrit scholar and President of the Linguistic Society of America, Bloomfield's early work was in Germanic linguistics and he studied at Leipzig and Göttingen. At the age of 34, he became Professor of German and Linguistics at Ohio and in 1927 moved to the University of Chicago. His last appointment was as Sterling Professor of Linguistics at Yale from 1940 till his death in 1949.

An early work, *An Introduction to the Study of Language* (1914), greatly influenced Harold Palmer (q.v.), providing a link between the British and American schools of language teaching. Bloomfield's interest in applications of linguistic science is evident in the final chapter of his classic *Language* (1933) and the influential pamphlet *Outline Guide for the Practical Study of Foreign Languages* (1942), which became a set text for the Army Specialized Training Program (ASTP). He also produced a beginners' course in German (1923), two of the Spoken Language Series (Dutch and Russian) and materials for the teaching of reading in primary schools.

Bloomfield was by nature an unassuming, even slightly withdrawn man, but his influence on the whole field of linguistics – though temporarily 'out of fashion' – has been immense.[3]

**BOAS, Franz**   1858–1942

Born in Minden in Westphalia, Boas began his academic career as a physicist and a geographer. In 1883–4 he travelled to Baffin Island in northern Canada on a fieldwork expedition which changed the direction of his research and his thinking in general: '(it) definitely turned the interest of the scientist from geography to ethnology, and the leading place in his wide ethnological work to linguistics'.[4] He returned to Germany, but two years later (1886) emigrated to the United States. In 1896 he was appointed to a post at Columbia University where he remained until his death, combining his teaching with a long association with the American Museum of Natural History. Boas' intellectual background allowed him to approach the description of hitherto 'unknown' languages unencumbered by traditions of European philology. Careful and unprejudiced observation, meticulous standards of accuracy in making records, and respect for 'the facts' were among the hallmarks of the American School of descriptive linguistics which he founded and passed on either directly through students such as Edward Sapir (q.v.) or indirectly through his publications. His most influential work was probably his introduction to the first part of the *Handbook of American Indian Languages* (1911), but in a tradition in which example was as important as precept, his own descriptive work, particularly on a British Columbian language called Kwakiutl, was equally significant. He helped to found the *International Journal of American Linguistics* and the Linguistic Society of America, becoming its President in 1928.

**BULLOKAR, William**   *c.*1530–1609

A resident of Chichester in Sussex, Bullokar was one of the spelling reformers active in the late sixteenth century, a group that also included Sir Thomas Smith and John Hart (q.v.). His principal work, *Book at Large* (1580), proposed a 'black letter' orthography which was rather complicated, though Gill (q.v.) thought well of it. Bullokar can also claim the distinction of writing the first grammar of English (*Pamphlet for Grammar*, 1586), a short sketch based on Lily's Latin grammar.[5]

**COBBETT, William**   1763–1835

Born in Farnham, Surrey, the son of a small farmer. Cobbett left home at the age of nineteen intending to go to sea, but ended up in the army instead. While doing basic training, he learnt Lowth's *Grammar* by heart and his advanced literacy earned him promotion to sergeant-major while serving in New Brunswick in 1785. He left the army in a hurry in 1791 and went to France where he learnt the language. (He later wrote a grammar of French). From France he emigrated to the United States and taught English as a foreign language to French immigrants before launching his career as a political journalist with some fiercely right-wing attacks on Tom Paine and his sympathizers. After prosecutions for libel, he returned to England in 1800 and founded the *Weekly Political Register* in 1802. His politics swung 180 degrees and the paper took up radical causes with much gusto and some effect. Cobbett spent two years in jail for sedition and the threat of yet another court case sent him back to America in 1817.

While staying on Long Island, Cobbett wrote his *Grammar of the English Language* (1819) in the form of letters to his young son James Paul. The book was a great success and is reputed to have sold 10,000 copies in the first month of publication. It became one of the leading works of popular linguistics in the nineteenth century and is a 'bridge' between Lowth and the present century.

Cobbett came back to England in 1819 bringing with him the remains of Tom Paine, intending to raise enough money for a memorial to his hero, but the rather macabre project failed. After several unsuccessful attempts, he entered Parliament as MP for Oldham in 1832. Apart from the *Grammar* his best-known work is *Rural Rides* (1830), a classic account of rural life before the advent of the railway.[6]

## COLET, John   c.1467–1519

The Dean of St. Paul's from 1505, he refounded St. Paul's School in 1509 as a non-ecclesiastical establishment. William Lily (q.v.), with whom Colet was associated in the development of *A Short Introduction of Grammar* (popularly known as 'Lily's Grammar'), was the first Headmaster. Colet's contribution was a short Latin accidence (*Aeditio*) written around 1510.

## COMENIUS, Jan Amos   1592–1670

(Czech name, *Komensky*). Born in Nivnice, Moravia, Comenius was orphaned at the age of twelve. His early education was poor and his teachers brutal, an experience he never forgave nor forgot. He was rescued by the Unity of Brethren and sent to grammar school at Přerov, where, at the age of sixteen, he began to learn Latin. He continued his studies at Heidelberg and Herborn and, after his return, was ordained into the Brethren and sent as teacher and pastor to the town of Fulnek, not far from his home village. After the outbreak of hostilities in 1618, he became a refugee and finally escaped after seven years on the run. He became an exile in Leszno, a centre for the Brethren in Poland where he wrote his first two major didactic works, the *Janua Linguarum Reserata* (published in Leipzig in 1633, though a version appeared in London edited by John Anchoran in 1631 under the title *Porta Linguarum Reserata*), and the Czech version of his *Great Didactic* which was published, in a Latin translation, in 1657 as part of his collected works *Opera Didactica Omnia*.

In 1641 Comenius spent nine months in London at the invitation of Samuel Hartlib (q.v.) with a view to founding a pansophical college. The Civil War intervened, however, and he left to take up a post writing textbooks for the Swedish government. He worked in Elbing (then part of Sweden, now of Poland) until 1648 and wrote a lengthy theoretical work entitled *Linguarum Methodus Novissima* (Newest Method of Languages), Chapter 10 of which has become well-known as the *Analytical Didactic*. He proposed a 'new method' *Janua* and *Vestibulum* (his beginners' book), but the originals were too well-established for the revised versions, which in many ways contradicted his earlier precepts, to attract much attention.

Disappointed at the failure to secure independence for Moravia at the end of the Thirty Years' War in 1648, he accepted a commission to establish a new curriculum at a school in Saros Patak, a small Hungarian town north-east of Budapest. He stayed three years (1650–53) during which he began his celebrated *Orbis Sensualium Pictus*. It was not published until 1658 partly because it required a great many woodcuts which took time to design and produce. By the time it appeared, Comenius was in Amsterdam. He had returned to Leszno in 1653 to assist in yet another political move, but the town was ransacked and burnt in 1656 and Comenius lost many of his papers. He survived the journey to the Netherlands with difficulty, and lived for another thirteen years, occupying his time mainly on religious and philosophical works. He died at the age of seventy-eight in 1670. His last great work on pansophical philosophy disappeared after his death and did not turn up until the thirties in Germany. It was eventually published in Prague itself in 1966.[7]

## COOPER, Christopher   *c.*1646–1698

Born in Hertfordshire and educated at Cambridge University, Cooper became Headmaster of Bishop Stortford Grammar School about 1680, and Vicar of St. Michael's Church in the same town in 1686. His *Grammatica Linguae Anglicanae* appeared in 1685, but it was overshadowed by the more famous book of the same name by Wallis (q.v.). However, in Dobson's view 'Cooper's work was not inferior even to Wallis's in its general phonetic theory; it was in fact more exact. But Wallis had won the credit of the innovator'.[8] Two years later in 1687, Cooper published an English translation of the orthographical sections of the *Grammatica* as *The English Teacher* which was intended for 'Gentlemen, Ladies, Merchants, Tradesmen, Schools, and Strangers (that have so much knowledge of our English tongue as to understand the Rules)'. His life appears to have been uneventful and devoted to his teaching and pastoral duties in Bishop Stortford.

**FICK, Johann Georg Christian** 1763–1821

A German textbook author who applied J. V. Meidinger's (q.v.) sentence-method system to the teaching of English in *Praktische englische Sprachlehre* (1793), creating the earliest 'grammar-translation' course for English.

**FIRTH, John Rupert** 1890–1960

Born and educated in Yorkshire, Firth graduated from Leeds University with a first-class degree in history in 1911. He entered the Indian Education Service in 1913 where he remained until 1928, though his educational work was interrupted by war service in India itself, East Africa, and Afghanistan. From 1920–28 he was Professor of English at the University of the Punjab and subsequently returned to a Senior Lectureship at University College, London. He worked full-time in Daniel Jones's Phonetics Department until 1932 when he began at the School of Oriental (and African) Studies as a part-time lecturer in linguistics. In 1938 he became a Senior Lecturer in the School, specializing in linguistics and Indian phonetics. In 1940 he became a Reader and in 1944 was appointed to the newly-founded Chair of General Linguistics (the first in Britain). In 1956 he became Professor Emeritus. In 1946 Firth was awarded the O.B.E. for his part in developing a Japanese language training programme for R.A.F. personnel during the war. He was awarded an Honorary LL.D. (Doctor of Laws) by the University of Edinburgh where he taught briefly in 1959–60 at the School of Applied Linguistics. He died suddenly in December 1960 at the age of seventy.

Firth's principal contribution to descriptive linguistics was his theory of prosodic analysis, but his influence spread far beyond his own subject. His strong, forthright personality became a legend in his own lifetime and he left a distinctive school of linguistic thought with many adherents among the present generation of British linguists and applied linguists, notably M. A. K. Halliday. His principal publications were collected in 1957 as *Papers in Linguistics, 1934–1951*.

**FLORIO, John** *c*.1553–1625

Born in London, son of Michaelangelo Florio, Protestant refugee, pastor, and Italian tutor to Lady Jane Grey. The family fled to the continent in 1554 and lived in Strasbourg and Switzerland. His early education is unknown but he may have attended Tübingen University. He returned to England in the early 1570s and tutored in Italian at Oxford. His first textbook, *First Fruits*, appeared in 1578 and is dedicated to the Earl of Leicester. In 1583 he started work at the French Embassy in London. *Second Fruits*, his second, and last, language teaching manual appeared in 1591. By 1594 Florio was in the employ of the Earl of Southampton, which brought him into contact with literary leaders, particularly Ben Jonson whose intellectualism and love of books he shared. The first version of his Italian–English dictionary *A World of Words* came out in 1598; it was later enlarged and renamed *Queen Anna's New World of Words* (1611) in honour of his new employer Queen Anne, wife of James VI and I, whose children he tutored. His great literary work was a translation of Montaigne's *Essays* written at the behest of Lucy, Countess of Bedford, and published in 1603. Six years after losing his employment at Court he died of the plague in Fulham in 1625. King James' refusal to pay his fees meant he was in considerable financial difficulties. He was survived by his second wife and a daughter. Florio was one of the most talented and versatile figures in the history of language teaching: teacher, textbook writer, lexicographer, translator, bibliophile and, like Joseph Conrad in our own century, though on a smaller scale, a bilingual writer whose literary achievements helped to mould and extend the English language.[9]

### FRANKE, Felix   1860–1886

Born in Sorau, Silesia. An influential theorist of the Reform Movement, Franke wrote his pamphlet *Die praktische Spracherlernung, auf Grund der Psychologie und der Physiologie der Sprache dargestellt* in 1884, two years before his death from tuberculosis at the age of 26. He formed a friendship by correspondence with Jespersen (q.v.), who later edited a revised version of the pamphlet (1886) and prepared a Danish translation.

### FRIES, Charles Carpenter   1887–1967

After receiving two degrees from Bucknell University in Pennsylvania and spending a short time in Chicago, Fries moved to the University of Michigan where he took a doctorate in 1922. He was to remain associated with Michigan in one way or another for the remainder of his life. In 1941 he helped to found the famous English Language Institute and the following year he published his *Intensive Course in English for Latin-American Students* (1942) followed, not long afterwards, by *An Intensive Course in English for Chinese Students* (1946), written in collaboration with Yao Shen. The previous year Fries himself had published his most influential pedagogical work, *Teaching and Learning English as a Foreign Language* (1945), in which he had put forward a scheme of work which aimed to teach the basic patterns of English 'within approximately three months'. In the public mind, if not in Fries's own view, the most salient features of his approach were its stress on intensive, short-course study and on training in the spoken language. His own term 'The Oral Approach', as well as his links with the school of thought that had produced the well-known Army programme (the ASTP), underlined these impressions in the profession at large.

Fries himself, however, did not see his work in quite the same light. To him, what was important was the application of modern linguistic research in the production of teaching materials, and the contrastive studies that preceded the creation of these materials. His frustration at being misunderstood is evident in an article for *Language Learning* called 'American linguistics and the teaching of English' (1955). He was the first applied linguist in the modern sense and used the term 'applied linguistics' in the subtitle of *Language Learning – A Quarterly Journal of Applied Linguistics* (1948). The first editorial board consisted of Fries himself, W. F. Twaddell, and K. L. Pike.

Under Fries and his successors as Directors of the English Language Institute, Robert Lado and Albert H. Marckwardt, the work and prestige of the Institute continued to grow. Language laboratory techniques were pioneered from the late forties and, in particular, the teaching technique known by everyone in the profession as 'pattern practice'. More important than methods, however, were the descriptive linguistic analyses that preceded them. Fries produced two important studies, *American English Grammar* (1940) and *The Structure of English* (1952), two of the most influential analyses of the English language in the twentieth century.

Fries was an enthusiastic traveller and teacher. He lectured at the University of Puerto Rico in 1951, spent two years as Research Professor at the University of Mainz in 1954–5, and was closely involved with developments in English teaching in post-war Japan. He was accepted as a member of professional societies in many countries including Britain. In the United States he had been a founder member of the Linguistic Society of America and became its President in 1939.

Although the Structural Approach, as the Fries-Lado model is normally called, was rather unenterprising methodologically, the new rigour that Fries brought to the linguistic content of teaching materials carried the art of writing pedagogical grammars to an altogether different level of professional expertise from anything it had attained before.[10]

## GIL(L), Alexander  1565–1635

Born in Lincolnshire and educated at Corpus Christi, Oxford, Gill succeeded Mulcaster (q.v.) as High Master of St. Paul's School in 1608. (John Milton was a pupil between 1620 and 1625.) He devised what many consider the best system of reformed English spelling, published in the revised edition of his *Logonomia Anglica* (1621).[11]

## GOUIN, François   1831–1896

Born in Normandy in France, Gouin became a classics teacher in Caen while continuing his own studies at the university. He was advised by his professors to pursue his philosophical interests further by studying in Berlin, and set out for Germany some time in the early 1850s. He stopped off in Hamburg in order to learn German and began the saga of disaster that he describes at the beginning of his book *L'Art d'enseigner et d'étudier les langues* (1880). A holiday episode involving his three-year-old nephew led to the notion that experience, and therefore language, could be organized sequentially. The 'Series Method' that emerged from these observations required the analysis of events into sequences of component events, and their presentation to the learner in the form of (mainly) narrative texts. The technique became familiar in direct method teaching, for example *I am walking to the door, I am opening the door*, etc.

After completing his studies, Gouin stayed on in Berlin as a teacher of French as a foreign language, and seems to have moved in fairly high Hohenzollern circles at the Court. These contacts eventually led to a request by the Rumanian Government to act as an official adviser. He left Berlin in 1864, but his stay in Bucharest was terminated by a revolution and he moved briefly to England and finally Geneva. He established a school of languages there and composed his book which he published privately at his own expense. It was eventually brought out in Paris in 1880 and an English translation (*The Art of Teaching and Studying Languages* by Howard Swan and Victor Bétis) appeared in London in 1892. In the 1880s Gouin became Director of the Ecole Supérieure in Elboeuf in Normandy and, later, Professor of German at the Ecole Supérieure Arago in Paris. Gouin Schools grew up in various countries, including Britain, and a French course in the London school gave Daniel Jones (q.v.) his first introduction to language studies.

Gouin was in his fifties during the great days of the early Reform Movement, but there is no evidence that he came into contact with it. He died at the relatively early age of sixty-five. It has been suggested (Darian 1972) that he spent some time in America, but his translators do not mention this trip in the Preface to the 1892 London edition.

Gouin is difficult to evaluate. His book is very self-indulgent and perhaps ill-served by its English translators. Nevertheless, it contains flashes of insight which have kept its reputation alive in the present century. He is sometimes credited (for example, by Darian) with having founded the Direct Method, but, while his Series Method shared some of the same characteristics (it was, for instance, monolingual), there is no sign of the basic Direct Method concept of conversation.

Perhaps because the Reform Movement made relatively little impact in America, Gouin enjoyed a greater reputation as an innovator there than on this side of the Atlantic. According to Darian the method became 'the most popular approach to EFL teaching in the early part of the century', partly under the influence of a teacher called Henry H. Goldberger.

In a European context, Gouin appears rather more as the last in a line of nineteenth-century enthusiasts with an interesting, but narrowly-conceived, proposal for the reform of language teaching which had a superficial appeal, but little lasting significance.[12]

## HAMILTON, James   1769–1829

Born in London and educated in Dublin. While working as a business man in Hamburg in the late 1790s, he was taught German by a French emigré general whose method amounted to little more than a word-for-word translation of the text. The technique appealed to Hamilton who later adapted it for use in books by reviving the ancient device of interlinear translation. The only unusual feature of the system was Hamilton's insistence on literal translation rather than a literary re-working of the foreign language text. This may have given it a 'scientific' air. At all events, Hamilton was an excellent entrepreneur and he succeeded in making his system famous in America, which he visited in 1815–17, Canada, and back in London, where he managed to attract classes of fifty to one hundred customers. For some reason which is not entirely clear, the 'Hamilton System' caught the attention of nineteenth-century language teachers (one is reminded a little of the 'Gouin System') and it is frequently alluded to in the literature.

## HART, John   died 1574

Very little is known about his life, but it is likely that he was born in Northolt, near London, probably in or around 1500. His father died in October, 1500, making 1501 the latest possible date. He may also have attended Cambridge and met Sir Thomas Smith and Sir John Cheke, both interested in orthographical reform. In 1551 he wrote *The Opening . . . of our English Tongue* which was never printed. It is essentially a draft for his *Orthography* of 1569 in which he argued for the serious reform of English spelling and made his own proposals for an improved system. Between the two works, Hart travelled for a time in Europe and seems also to have done the state some service for which he was rewarded with the title of Chester Herald in 1566. His last work was his *Method* (1570), a primer for the teaching of reading using his reformed spelling system. [13]

## HARTLIB, Samuel   c.1600–1670

Born in Elbing (where Comenius (q.v.) spent seven years of his life) and educated at Cambridge where he became acquainted with Baconianism, Hartlib was the 'entrepreneur' of the Protestant nonconformist intellectual establishment surrounding the Parliamentarians at the time of the Civil War. He was responsible for bringing Comenius to England in 1641, for example, and he was also the addressee of Milton's essay *Of Education* (1644). With John Dury, a Scotsman with connections in Elbing, and Comenius, he was the third of the three philosophers whom Trevor-Roper (1967) described as 'the invisible college' surrounding Cromwell.[14]

### HOLYBAND, Claudius (dates unknown)

Original name Claude de Sainliens (or Desainliens). A native of Moulins in the Loire Valley in France, Holyband left home, probably in 1565 or early 1566, as a Huguenot refugee. He established his first school in England at Lewisham near London and it became sufficiently well-known to attract a royal visit by Elizabeth I. He entered the household of Lord Buckhurst some time in the early 1570s. Buckhurst was the grandfather of Robert Sackville, the boy whose education had been mapped out by Roger Ascham (q.v.) in *The Schoolmaster*. It was presumably this connection, as well as the fame of Ascham's work, that prompted Holyband to entitle his first textbook *The French Schoolmaster* (1573). By 1576, the date of Holyband's second textbook, *The French Littleton*, he was running a second language school, this time in St. Paul's Churchyard, the centre of the London book-trade and the home of a number of refugee schools. He had opened a third school by 1580, 'at the sign of the Golden Ball'. Though he advertised himself as a 'Professor of English', he never wrote a book specifically to teach the language. He did, however, include it in his polyglot 'reader' *Campo di Fior* in 1583, alongside Italian, Latin, and French. He also wrote an *Italian Schoolmaster* in 1580. Most of his later works, however, are linguistic studies of French which are intended to form an advanced course in the language for learners who had completed one of the earlier books. They include *A Treatise for Declining of Verbs* (1580), *De Pronuntiatione Linguae Gallicae* (1593, dedicated to the Queen) and *A Dictionary French and English* (also 1593). The last work provided the (unacknowledged) basis for Randle Cotgrave's *Dictionary of the French and English Tongues* (1611). Holyband probably left England for France after the Edict of Nantes in 1598. He was married twice, the second time to an Englishwoman called Anne Smith.[15]

### HORNBY, Albert Sidney 1898–1978

Born in Chester, A. S. Hornby (or ASH) completed his education with a degree in English Language and Literature from University College, London in 1922. He left to see the world, travelling on the Trans-Siberian Railway to the Far East. In 1923 he arrived in Tokyo and started teaching English literature. A growing interest in language brought him into contact with Palmer's (q.v.) Institute (IRET) of which he became a regular and enthusiastic member. In the early thirties,

Hornby became closely involved with Palmer's vocabulary research at IRET and proposed a 1,000-word list of essential items which he had begun to work on independently. The two men collaborated on the project which was eventually published in 1937 as *Thousand-Word English*.

Hornby became effectively Palmer's 'crown prince' at IRET and, after Palmer's departure in 1936, developed ideas and projects which they had initiated together. He became editor of the Institute's *Bulletin*, for example, which became the model for *English Language Teaching* when it was founded in 1946 with Hornby as its first editor, a task he relinquished in 1950 to devote himself to materials writing.

He also continued to work on the major project of his life, the dictionary, which went through a number of versions: *An Idiomatic and Syntactic English Dictionary* (Kaitakusha, Tokyo: 1942), *A Learner's Dictionary of Current English* (Oxford University Press, London: 1948), *The Advanced Learner's Dictionary of Current English* (Oxford University Press, London: 1952, 2nd edn 1963), all with E. V. Gatenby and Hugh Wakefield, and, finally, *The Oxford Advanced Learner's Dictionary of Current English* (Oxford University Press, Oxford: 1974) with the assistance of A. P. Cowie and J. Windsor Lewis.

Hornby left Japan on the outbreak of the war in the Far East and joined the British Council, who posted him to Iran where he worked (at the University of Teheran and other centres) until 1945. He became Linguistic Adviser to the Council on his return to London. His editorial work with *ELT* occupied much of his time for the next five years and his numerous articles in the journal, notably an early series on 'Linguistic Pedagogy' established the ground-rules for the British version of direct-method English language teaching: new linguistic items and patterns presented 'situationally' in class first, followed by oral work based on a text and exercises in speech and writing.

The basic patterns of English were described in Hornby's pedagogical grammar *Guide to Patterns and Usage in English* (1954), and presented in texts and practice materials in his three-volume course *Oxford Progressive English for Adult Learners* (1954 onwards), later expanded into four volumes with the assistance of Ronald Mackin as an *Alternative* version. His situational classroom material is contained in a four-volume series called *The Teaching of Structural Words and Sentence Patterns* (1959 onwards). In large designs as in small, Hornby's work had an intellectual coherence and a framework of steel.

Hornby's influence on the profession itself was profound. He worked quietly, travelling from place to place, meeting groups of teachers and talking, sometimes formally but more often informally. He was greatly loved, kind, modest, and gently humorous. His most characteristic decision was the establishment of the Hornby Educational Trust in

1961 which used income from royalties to provide financial assistance to individuals and projects of value to the future of the profession. His aim was 'to have the money used for education and go back to the countries from which it comes'.[16]

Hornby was a Fellow of University College, London, and was awarded an honorary Master's Degree by Oxford University in 1977.[17]

## JACOTOT, Jean Joseph   1770–1840

Born and educated in Dijon where he organized a revolutionary youth movement in 1788. He was, briefly, Professor of Latin at Dijon at the age of nineteen, a captain in the revolutionary army in 1792 and Deputy Director of the Polytechnique at Dijon in 1794. Forced to leave France after the Restoration (1818), he settled in Louvain where he developed an original system for teaching French as a foreign language. He devised a philosophy of universal education (*enseignement universel*) while in exile which was applied to various subjects including the mother tongue (1823), music, drawing, and painting (1824), foreign languages (1830), and mathematics (1841). He was the originator of the slogan 'All is in all' (or, 'learn one thing thoroughly and relate everything else to it'). He returned from exile in 1830.[18]

## JESPERSEN, Otto   1860–1943

Born in Randers, Denmark. His father, a district judge, died when Jespersen was only ten, and his mother, who had taught Latin to Hans Christian Andersen, two years later. While he finished school at Frederiksborg, he often lived with an uncle. At the age of seventeen, he started a law degree and he served as a shorthand reporter in Parliament for seven years. In 1887, he took a Master's degree in French with English and Latin, by which time he had made contact with the Reform Movement in France and Germany. In 1884 he had started a correspondence with the young Felix Franke (q.v.) and letters were exchanged every week for two years until Franke died. Later Jespersen was to say at his Farewell Lecture in 1925, 'I was spiritually more akin to him than anyone else'. Under Franke's influence he had written a short grammar of English (*Kortfattet engelsk grammatik* (1885)). In 1886, he helped to found the 'Quousque Tandem Society' in Sweden dedicated to the new methods. He also joined Passy's (q.v.) new Phonetic Teachers' Association in the same year.

After taking his degree in 1887, he travelled extensively. He visited London in 1887 and met Sweet (q.v.), and Ellis. He also went to Oxford to see James Murray (editor of the *Oxford English Dictionary*) and heard Sayce lecture. In 1888 he visited Germany, where he met Viëtor (q.v.) and Klinghardt (q.v.), and France, where he attended some of Passy's classes. He later returned to Berlin to study Old and Middle English.

On his return home to Copenhagen, he worked for a time teaching English and French in secondary schools and published a thesis on case in English in 1891. Two years later, at the age of thirty-three, he became Professor of English at Copenhagen University, a post he held for the next thirty-two years.

Jespersen had started his publishing career in the 1880s. In 1887, for instance, he had a lengthy article on the new methods called 'Der neue Sprachunterricht' published in *Englische Studien* (Vol.X, 412–37). His thesis came out in an expanded form in 1894 under the title *Progress in Language with Special Reference to English*. Then came his *Phonetik* (1897–9), and in 1901 his principal contribution to the Reform Movement, a book called *Sprogundervisning*, translated into English as *How to Teach a Foreign Language* (1904). Also in 1904 he began his monumental *Modern English Grammar* (1909–49) a work that was not completed until after his death, *Lehrbuch der Phonetik* and *Phonetische Grundfragen*. *The Growth and Structure of the English Language* followed in 1905.

A further spate of inspiration occurred in the twenties with the appearance of *Language: Its Nature, Development, and Origin* (1922), *The Philosophy of Grammar* (1924), and *Mankind, Nation, and Individual* (1925). After his retirement in 1925 he renewed his interest in international auxiliary languages and developed his own contributions to the field, Novial, which stood for New (NOV), International Auxiliari Lingue (IAL). Shaw was delighted, partly because Novial is closer to English than some of the other international languages, and partly because he liked Jespersen: 'Professor Jespersen has common sense, which is a great advantage in a professor', (Haislund p. 281) he declared. His later works include *Essentials of English Grammar* (1933), *Analytic Syntax* (1937), and *Efficiency in Linguistic Change* (1941). He died in 1943 at the age of eighty-three.

In linguistics Jespersen was the greatest of a distinguished group of contemporary north European anglicists and in language teaching, he wrote the book (*How to Teach a Foreign Language*) which gave the Reform Movement a human face. He was a dedicated idealist in the best Scandinavian tradition and Novial was intended as a serious contribution to international peace. On the occasion of his seventieth birthday, Edward Sapir wrote in a Danish newspaper: 'Your work has always seemed to me to be distinguished by its blend of exact knowledge, keenness of analysis, ease and lucidity of style, and by an imaginative warmth that is certainly not common in scientific writing'.[19]

**JOHNSON, Dr. Samuel**   1709–1784

Born in Lichfield, the son of a bookseller, Johnson moved to London in 1737. He published his *Plan of a Dictionary*, addressed to the Earl of Chesterfield, in 1747. The first edition of the great *Dictionary of the English Language* (2 folio volumes) appeared in 1755, when Johnson was forty-five. In later life he undertook the famous Scottish tour with James Boswell (1773).

**JONES, Daniel**   1881–1967

Born in London, D.J., as he was universally known, came from an interesting family background. His father (like Henry Sweet's) was a lawyer and one of the founders of the All England Tennis Club and the Wimbledon Championships. His uncle, on his mother's side, was Richard D'Oyly Carte, the Gilbert and Sullivan impresario. His first degree (at King's College, Cambridge) was in mathematics (1903) and he followed in his father's footsteps as a law-student, being called to the bar in 1907.

D.J.'s interest in language happened by accident. He attended a Gouin school in London in 1898 to learn French and discovered that he was good at it. In 1900 he studied German for a month at a language school run by William Tilly in Viëtor's (q.v.) home town of Marburg and discovered 'phonetic methods' for the first time. He maintained his contact with Tilly and through him met Paul Passy (q.v.) in Paris, with whom he studied the subject in detail in 1905–6. He later married Passy's niece Cyrille in 1911.

On his return to London in 1906, he persuaded University College to allow him to give lectures in the phonetics of French. They were a success with local foreign language teachers and he was encouraged to continue. From these small beginnings he built up a department, employing an increasing number of people, including for a time Harold Palmer (q.v.). During the first ten years of his work in London, he established and developed the concept of the 'cardinal vowels' (i.e. 'a set of fixed vowel-sounds having known acoustic qualities and known tongue and lip positions'[20]) which was his principal contribution to the theory of phonetic analysis.

Throughout his life D.J. was always a practical phonetician in the tradition of Sweet, Passy, and the other reformers. He was, for instance, a member of the BBC Advisory Committee on Spoken English from its foundation in 1926, a member and later President (1946) of the Simplified Spelling Society and Assistant Secretary (1907–27), Secretary (1927–49), and President (1949–67) of the International Phonetic Association. He held honorary degrees from the Universities of Zürich (1936) and Edinburgh (1958), and other academic honours.

As A. C. Gimson said in his obituary notice, in *Le Maître Phonétique*, the main source for the information in this note, 'wherever English is taught, his name is mentioned with respect and gratitude' (p. 6). His major works in English language teaching have maintained their popularity ever since their first appearance in the creative decade before and during the First World War which saw the founding of the profession. In particular, these include *The Pronunciation of English* (1909), *An Outline of English Phonetics* (1918), and the classic *English Pronouncing Dictionary* (1917). [21]

**JONSON, Ben** 1572–1637
Born in Westminster, Jonson was the author of the first vernacular English grammar printed in standard orthography. Originally written in 1623, but lost in a fire in 1625 and rewritten in the early 1630s, the *English Grammar* finally appeared in the second volume of his *Works*, published posthumously in 1640. The first volume (1616) contains the famous plays and other literary works.

**KLINGHARDT, Hermann** 1847–1926
Schoolteacher from Reichenbach, Silesia. One of the leading members of the Reform Movement, Klinghardt wrote many papers, articles, reviews, etc. for *Englische Studien* in the 1880s and 1890s, organized conferences, and tirelessly promoted the ideas of the reformers among the teaching profession. He carried out a detailed trial of the new methods in his *Realgymnasium* in 1887–88 with a class of fourteen-year-old beginners of English which was written up in *Ein Jahr Erfahrungen mit der neuen Methode* (1888) and extended in *Drei weitere Jahre Erfahrungen mit der imitativen Methode* (1892). This study was the first of its kind undertaken in schools.

**LILY, William** c.1468–1522
Lily was popularly credited with the sole authorship of the so-called Royal Grammar, or 'Lily's Grammar', whose proper title is *A Short Introduction of Grammar*. In fact, the *Grammar* derived from the work of a committee set up by Henry VIII in the late 1530s in an attempt to enforce uniformity of standards in Latin teaching in England. Its final shape also owes much to the work of John Colet (q.v.) and Erasmus as well as Lily himself. It was prescribed by Royal Proclamation in 1540 and continued in use for over two centuries. Before becoming the first Headmaster of St. Paul's School in 1510, Lily had travelled extensively in the eastern Mediterranean (including a pilgrimage to the Holy Land) and had learnt Greek. He became the first teacher of Greek in London.

**LOCKE, John** 1632–1704
Born in Somerset and educated at Westminster School and Oxford University, Locke lectured in Greek at Oxford (1660–64) and also

became physician to the Earl of Shaftesbury. Later he lived in exile in France (1675–79) and Holland (1683–88). He returned to England after the 'Glorious Revolution' in 1688. Main publications: *Essay Concerning Human Understanding* (1689); *Some Thoughts Concerning Education* (an 'open letter' of advice to Edward Clarke, Somerset, on the best way to bring up his young son (1693)).

## LOWTH, Robert   1710–1787

Born in Winchester and educated at Winchester College and New College, Oxford, Lowth was a Hebrew scholar and orientalist and was appointed Professor of Poetry at Oxford in 1741. He held various posts in the Church from 1744 onwards, eventually becoming Bishop of Oxford in 1766 and Bishop of London and Dean of the Chapel Royal in 1777. He declined the Archbishopric of Canterbury in 1783. His immensely influential *Short Introduction to English Grammar* was published anonymously in 1762. His other writings are mainly on biblical topics or related to the study of Hebrew poetry.

## MARCEL, Claude Victor André   1793–1876

French Consul at Cork in Ireland. As a young man, Marcel served in the Imperial Army and was badly wounded in Holland in 1814. Two years later, he was sent to the French Consulate at Cork for the first time, where he worked in a variety of posts for the remainder of his life. His practical language learning abilities were recognized early, and his superior wrote in a report in 1830: 'he speaks and writes (English) extremely well (and) has even published in the language'. Marcel opened a language school in Cork and succeeded in attracting many influential members of the local establishment to his classes. In 1840, he was promoted to 'consul honoraire', but his ambitions to reach 'consul titulaire' were frustrated, though he made plans to give up his 'unsuitable' teaching activities if required. His reward for long service came in 1850 (after a change of regime at home) in the form of the title Chevalier de la Légion d'Honneur. Three years later, he published his major work, *Language as a Means of Mental Culture and International Communication* (1853), written in English.

The two volumes of *Language as a Means of Mental Culture* are a neglected masterpiece in the history of language teaching and education. The work is inaccessible (few libraries possess it), and hence little known, except at second hand through the comments of late-nineteenth century writers who repeat a popular view that Marcel's 'Rational Method' consisted solely of teaching reading at the expense of the spoken language. This both distorts and grossly underestimates his contribution to the literature of the field.

Marcel based his methodology of language teaching on a detailed analysis of the language learning process in terms of 'four branches' ('skills' in modern jargon), and much of his-work is devoted to their definition and ordering. He distinguished between 'impression' and 'expression' (modern 'reception/production'), and between speech and writing, creating the four branches of hearing, speaking, reading, and writing. His criteria for ordering the branches were determined by (i) the maturational development of the learner and (ii) the educational value of the resulting classroom activities. Hence, for young children and some adults he recommended a Pestalozzian 'natural' approach beginning with the two speech skills, 'object lessons', etc., while for older students from secondary school upwards, he promoted reading to the first position as the most worthwhile of the four (cf. West (1926)). This decision was consistent with his view that 'impression' should always precede 'expression', but it had the unfortunate result of appearing to require the teaching of reading in complete isolation from the spoken language.

Marcel followed his great work with a series of studies published in France, notably *Méthode rationelle suivant pas à pas la marche de la nature pour apprendre à lire, à entendre, à parler et à écrire l'anglais* (Rational Method of Teaching Reading, Listening, Speaking, and Writing in English following the Path of Nature Step-by-Step, 1872), and materials for classroom use. A very early study, *Practical Method of Teaching the Living Languages* (London: Hurst Robinson, 1820), appears to be a sketch for his views on teaching children and adults with practical rather than educational aims. As Tickoo (1982b) says: 'the neglect of Marcel and his work is a sad reflection on the historians of our field'.[22]

### MEIDINGER, Johann Valentin   1756–1822
Originator of the sentence-based approach to language teaching known to us as 'the grammar–translation method'. Author of *Praktische französische Grammatik* (1783), and other courses for the teaching of French and German as a foreign language.[23]

### MIÈGE, Guy   1644–c.1718
Born and educated in Lausanne, Switzerland. Diplomat, lexicographer, language and geography teacher, and textbook writer, Miège came to England after the Restoration in 1661. He was engaged on diplomatic work with the English ambassador in Scandinavia and Russia for two years (1663–65). After his return, he wrote a series of French–English dictionaries, culminating in *The Great French Dictionary* (1688). His textbook for English as a foreign language, *Nouvelle Méthode pour apprendre l'Anglois* (1685), marked a major step forward in the subject. It was later translated as *The English Grammar* (1688). In tandem with a work for the teaching of French by Abel Boyer, the *Nouvelle Méthode* continued in use well into the eighteenth century as

*Nouvelle Double Grammaire Françoise–Angloise et Angloise–Françoise* (1718).[24]

**MULCASTER, Richard**   *c*.1530–1611
Born in Cumberland and educated at Eton, King's College, Cambridge, and Christchurch, Oxford, Mulcaster was an orientalist as well as a classical scholar. He was appointed Headmaster of the Merchant Taylors' School in 1561, a post he held for twenty-five years. He resigned in 1586 and turned to the church. He came back to education as High Master of St. Paul's School in 1596 and retired, aged seventy-eight, twelve years later. He wrote two educational works, a short study of general principles called *Positions . . . for the Training Up of Children* (1581) and the famous *First Part of the Elementarie* (1582). The *Elementarie* was intended as a complete curriculum for a vernacular system of education in England, but only the first part was ever produced. It concentrates on the teaching of basic literacy, and contains a reformed system of spelling which systematized, but did not radically alter, the existing one. As such, it was more practically influential than most of the thorough-going 'phonetic' systems of the time. As a man Mulcaster was a sincere but rather pedantic pedagogue, and may possibly have been Shakespeare's model for Holofernes in *Love's Labour's Lost*. The *Elementarie* can be heavy-going at times, but there is no doubting Mulcaster's passionate belief in English as the true basis for a national education system.[25]

**MURRAY, Lindley**   1745–1826
Born into a Quaker family of Scots origins in Swatara, Pennsylvania, Murray's life fell into two quite different phases. In his youth he built up a successful legal practice and amassed a considerable fortune. At the age of thirty-nine, however, he came to Britain and settled in Holgate, near York, a town with a long tradition of Quaker connections. He became very active in support of philanthropic causes in York, particularly on behalf of the mentally ill, and wrote extensively on religious topics. In 1795 he published his *English Grammar, adapted to the different classes of learners*, a work which proved so well-suited to the needs of schools at the time that it swiftly became the best-known and most widely-used grammar of its time, and earned Murray the nickname 'Father of English Grammar'. It was derived from Lowth (q.v.) and extended Lowth's footnote technique into a system in which different portions of the text were directed at different levels of learner, the levels being indicated by variations in type-size (hence the subtitle). Two years later, in 1797, he brought out an equally successful collection of *English Exercises* and, later still, *An English Reader* (1799), and *An English Spelling Book* (1804), which rivalled Webster's and went to over forty editions. Murray's health was

never good, and, during the last sixteen years of his life be became a recluse. He died at the age of eighty-one.

**OGDEN, Charles Kay**  1889–1957
Born in Lancashire, his father was a housemaster at Rossall School (a boys' public school). Educated at Magdalene College, Cambridge where he graduated with a first-class degree in classics, Ogden was one of the most remarkable intellectuals of his time. His published works include important studies on Jeremy Bentham (on whom he was an acknowledged authority) and, with I. A. Richards, a classic early semantics text, *The Meaning of Meaning* (1923). His greatest contribution to intellectual life was probably his editorial expertise: he founded the *Cambridge Magazine* (1912), edited the journal *Psyche* for many years (from 1920), and from 1921 was the editor of the prestigious and influential International Library of Psychology, Philosophy, and Scientific Method, which included works by Jung, Piaget, Malinowski, Wittgenstein, and many others. In the twenties Ogden devised Basic English as an international auxiliary language which would also act as a 'first step' towards standard English. Basic was presented publicly in *Basic English* (1930) and a long series of teaching texts followed during the thirties and early forties. Churchill became an enthusiast and the matter eventually reached the House of Commons (1944). Thereafter, interest waned, though it still retains its supporters.

Basic was the 'cause célèbre' in English language teaching in the thirties. Ogden rather over-reacted to an attack by Michael West (q.v.) in 1934 and circulated an elaborate and intemperate reply (*Counter-Offensive*) in 1935. Basic attracted an enthusiastic following for a time, but always suffered from the criticism that it was not 'real English'.[26]

**OLLENDORFF, Heinrich Gottfried**  1803–1865
Biographical information is difficult to find. Ollendorff published his *New Method of Learning to Read, Write, and Speak a Language in Six Months* for the first time in 1835 at the age of thirty-two. Thereafter, he continued to exploit its success for the rest of his life. His first courses taught German to French speakers (1835), German to English speakers (1838), French to English speakers (1843), and English to French speakers (1848). Other leading languages were added later. Like Franz Ahn's (q.v.) his work was widely copied and adapted.

**PALMER, Harold Edward**  1877–1949
Born in London and educated privately in Hythe in Kent, Palmer was sent to Boulogne in his late teens to improve his French. On his return he worked for a time as a reporter for the local newspaper, and pursued his interest in geology and fossil-collecting. In 1902 he went to teach English as a foreign language at the Berlitz School in Verviers in

Belgium, where, the following year, he set up a language school of his own. This independence allowed him to develop new ideas for teaching materials, in particular for the teaching of vocabulary. He joined the International Phonetic Association in 1907 and established a regular correspondence with Daniel Jones (q.v.). On his enforced return to England in 1914, he contacted Jones at University College, London, and was taken on the staff as a lecturer in spoken English in 1915. He also gave a series of lectures on language teaching methodology to local language teachers which formed the basis for his first major work, *The Scientific Study and Teaching of Languages* in 1917. With Sweet's *Practical Study*, it is one of the classics of an applied linguistic approach to language teaching. By the time he left for Japan in 1922, he had completed his foundation work with a methodological handbook, *The Oral Method of Teaching Languages* (1921) and his most influential work, *The Principles of Language-Study* (1921), in which he outlined a model for the psychology of language learning which would support the development of practical classroom activities.

He began his work in Japan as Linguistic Adviser to the Ministry of Education and, in 1923, was appointed Director of the Institute for Research in English Teaching (IRET). The Japanese reaction to his Oral Method was mixed, but the Institute itself succeeded in making an international reputation as the only establishment of its kind in the world. In his early years at IRET Palmer developed the classroom exercises for the Oral Method with his daughter Dorothée which were published as *English Through Actions* in 1925 (republished in 1959). Later he revived his work in vocabulary control and produced a series of word lists which led to the publication of *Thousand-Word English* (1937), written in collaboration with A. S. Hornby (q.v.). In 1934–35 he participated in the Carnegie Conferences in New York and London and made an important contribution to the *Interim Report on Vocabulary Selection* (1936) which was eventually to appear as *The General Service List of English Words*, edited by Michael West (1953).

Palmer returned from Japan in 1936 with an honorary doctorate from the Imperial University of Tokyo, and became a consultant and author for Longmans, Green, which was engaged on the development of West's *New Method* programme. Among his contributions to the scheme were his *New Method Grammar* (1938) and a series of three *New Method English Practice Books* (there were many more, see Mackin (ed. 1969: 161–6)). He also wrote a bilingual course which was published in six languages including a Spanish version, *Curso Internacional de Inglés* (1944). Towards the end of his life, he made a lecture tour of South America for the British Council, but he was a sick man and could not complete it. He died suddenly in 1949 at the age of seventy-two.

Palmer's work in applied English linguistics was as important in its way as his pedagogical interests. There were, in particular, three major studies in the field which have proved of lasting significance: *English Intonation, with Systematic Exercises* (1922), *A Grammar of Spoken English* (1924), and *A Grammar of English Words* (1938).

Altogether, no other single individual did more to create the English language teaching profession in the present century.[27]

**PASSY, Paul Édouard**   1859–1940
Born in Paris, the son of Frédéric Passy, economist and first winner of the Nobel Peace Prize, Paul Passy was educated at home in a large family, and learnt to speak four languages (French, English, German, and Italian) in his early youth. Later he studied Sanskrit and Gothic at the École des Hautes Études. He became an English teacher as an alternative to military service at the age of nineteen. He devised his own phonetic alphabet, and became one of the most committed members of the Reform Movement. He was converted to Christianity, and joined the Christian Socialist movement in 1897. Much of his later life was devoted to social and evangelical work, and he was described as 'saintly' by his former student Daniel Jones (q.v.) in an appreciation in *Le Maître Phonétique* in 1941. In 1886 Passy founded the Phonetic Teachers' Association, forerunner of the International Phonetic Association (1897), and also established a journal, *The Phonetic Teacher* (later *Le Maître Phonétique* (1889)). His best-known work relates to the teaching of French, notably *Le français parlé* (1885), *Les sons du français* (1887), and *Elementarbuch des gesprochenen Französisch* (1893). But he also wrote for learners of English (*Éléments d'anglais parlé* (1886)), and was very interested in applying phonetics to the teaching of reading in the primary school (*Premier livre de lecture* (1884)). He once wrote a study of primary methods in American schools for the French Ministry of Education called *L'Instruction primaire aux États-Unis* (1885). He was related to Daniel Jones by marriage, and worked closely with him and other members of the IPA during the early decades of this century.[28]

**PESTALOZZI, Johann Heinrich**   1746–1827
Born in Zürich, Pestalozzi was only six when his father died. He later studied philosophy and philology before starting out as a farmer. He was deeply affected by the rural poverty of eighteenth-century Switzerland, and his educational work (heavily influenced by Rousseau's *Emile* (1762)) was dedicated to its alleviation. His efforts at running a school were not very successful, but his impact on education through his writings has continued to the present day. His best-known work, *How Gertrud Teaches her Children*, was published in 1801. Pestalozzi will always be associated in the public mind with his notion

of 'object lessons' in which children explored the physical qualities of things in the world about them, a concept comparable to Comenius's (q.v.) ideas in the *Orbis Sensualium Pictus*, though it is unlikely that he knew of Comenius's work. There is a clear link with the Direct Method in language teaching through the Pestalozzian teacher Gottlieb Heness who adapted the 'object lessons' to the teaching of German to American children at Yale in 1865–6, and later founded a language school with Sauveur (q.v.).[29]

**PLOETZ, Karl Julius**   1819–1881
A native of Alsace, Ploetz was one of the most prolific textbook writers of the nineteenth century, his principal customers being the German *Gymnasien*. He wrote the 'archetypal' grammar-translation course *Elementarbuch der französischen Sprache* in 1853, and was also well-known for his vocabulary books. He wrote entirely for learners of French, though his son Gustav Carl Ploetz produced an *English Vocabulary* in 1878 as well as continuing the Ploetz tradition with a series of textbooks for French in collaboration with Otto Kares.

**PRENDERGAST, Thomas**   1806–1886
As an official in the Indian Civil Service in Madras, Prendergast had devised a system of language teaching based on memorizing sentences which contained examples of as many grammatical rules as possible and from which other sentences could be 'evolved'. On his return to Britain, he described his system in *The Mastery of Languages* (1864) and developed 'Mastery' courses for French (1868), German (1868), Spanish (1869), Hebrew (1871), and Latin (1872). The system attracted some attention but was attacked by the Reform Movement for its use of isolated sentences. Prendergast's work is rather more impressive than most of the other 'bright ideas' of the nineteenth century, not so much for the sentence-making techniques as for the theoretical observations underlying the method.

**RAMUS, Petrus** (*Pierre de la Ramée*)   1515–1572
Born into a poor family in northern France, Ramus became a servant in the house of a wealthy scholar and taught himself by studying at night. This unconventional basic training plus great intellectual talents made him a formidable and unconventional thinker. At the age of twenty-eight he published his *Dialectic*, an outspoken attack on Aristotelianism which caused an uproar and led to the supression of his work at the Sorbonne. Friends in high places, notably the Cardinal of Lorraine, looked after his interests and he was appointed Professor at the Collège Royal in 1551. In addition to his works in logic and philosophy, Ramus also wrote on mathematics, astronomy (he was a Copernican), and grammar. His rigorously systematic approach to intellectual challenges

and his concern for the facts of linguistic structure (as opposed to semantic speculation) have made him a popular figure among modern linguists. His descriptive system rests essentially on a hierarchical sequence of binary distinctions, for example, words can be divided into two classes, those which show number and those which do not. Those which show number can be divided into two further classes, nouns and verbs, etc. His *Latin Grammar*, originally published in Paris in 1559, appeared in an English translation in 1585, the same year as his *Rudiments of Latin Grammar*, a primer written in catechistic form. Ramus himself was murdered in the St. Bartholomew's Day Massacre in 1572, having returned to Paris the previous year after a period of self-imposed exile in Germany and Switzerland to escape from the repression.

### RATKE (or RATICH), Wolfgang  1571–1635
A German educationist who attempted, without it seems great success, to put Bacon's principles in the *Advancement of Learning* into practice. His writings influenced contemporaries like Joseph Webbe (q.v.) and Comenius (q.v.).

### ROGET, Peter Mark  1779–1869
Roget was born in Soho, the son of a Swiss Protestant pastor and an English mother (Susan Romilly). After his father's death, the family moved to Edinburgh where Roget took a degree in medicine in 1798. His working life was devoted to scientific and medical affairs in Manchester and, from 1808, in London. He was elected a Fellow of the Royal Society in 1815 and served as its secretary for twenty-two years (1827–49). On his retirement he pursued his interest in devising a taxonomy of ideas which eventually took the form of the famous *Thesaurus of English Words and Phrases* which he published in 1852 at the age of seventy-three. Twenty-eight editions of the work appeared during his lifetime, and it has become one of the classic reference books for the English language. (See Emblen (1970)).

### SAPIR, Edward  1884–1939
Sapir was born in Lauenburg in Pomerania, but his family emigrated to the United States when he was five years old. He completed his full-time education in 1904 when he graduated from Columbia University where he had come into contact with Franz Boas (q.v.). Following Boas' lead, Sapir spent the next six years working on descriptions of various American Indian languages spoken in West Coast states such as Washington, Oregon, and California. In 1910 he moved to Canada as Chief of the Division of Anthropology at the Canadian National Museum in Ottawa where he remained for the next fifteen years. During this time, which was not entirely happy, he developed a serious

interest in poetry and music. He also wrote and published his major work in linguistics (and only full-scale book), *Language, an Introduction to the Study of Speech* (1921). Some of his optimism returned when he resumed direct contact with students first at the University of Chicago and, from 1931, at Yale. In his later work he became increasingly interested in the broader relationships between language, culture, and personality, and in particular the exploration of a view that 'the "real world" is to a large extent unconsciously built up on the language habits of the group. No two languages are ever sufficiently similar to be considered as representing the same social reality. The worlds in which different societies live are distinct worlds, not merely the same world with different labels attached'.[30] Later this notion was pursued in detail by his student Benjamin Lee Whorf (1897–1941), and it became common practice to refer to it as the 'Sapir-Whorf hypothesis'. Unlike Bloomfield (q.v.) Sapir was never directly involved in language teaching activities. Nevertheless, the influence of his work has been profound, particularly concerning the educational role of language in society, reflected in part through the writings of modern sociolinguists like William Labov and Dell Hymes.[31]

## SAUSSURE, Ferdinand de   1857–1913

Born into a family with a distinguished record in the natural sciences, Saussure began his academic career by studying physics and chemistry in his native Geneva. He switched to linguistics, however, in 1876 and entered Leipzig University, the centre of the Junggrammatiker ('Neogrammarian') movement in historical linguistics which greatly influenced Viëtor (q.v.) and others in the Reform Movement. In 1880 he was awarded his doctorate *summa cum laude* for a thesis on a topic in Sanskrit studies. After teaching in Paris, he became Professor at Geneva and began his famous lecture series in 1907. The third series ended in 1911 and he died in 1913. His seminal *Cours de linguistique générale* was compiled from students' lecture notes by two colleagues Charles Bally and Albert Sechehaye (who had not themselves attended the lectures), and were published in 1916.

Saussure's unchallenged eminence as 'The Father of Modern Linguistics' has ensured that the influence of his work has been felt, directly or indirectly, in every branch of linguistic studies including language teaching. His emphasis on the (synchronic) study of language as a social fact revolutionized linguistics which had hitherto been preoccupied with (diachronic) processes of historical change. More specifically, his fundamental distinction between the language system (*langue*) and actual speech events (*parole*) has conditioned much of the thinking in theoretical linguistics this century. In the applied field, however, he remained a somewhat remote figure until Chomsky's analogous distinction between competence and performance focused renewed attention on the relationship between 'real' data and 'underlying systems'.

## SAUVEUR, Lambert   1826–1907

Sauveur arrived as an immigrant in America in the late 1860s and settled in New Haven, Connecticut, where he met Gottlieb Heness, who had recently carried out a successful experiment in the 'natural method' teaching of German to a group of children of staff members at Yale. Heness needed a native Frenchman to join him in setting up a language school to exploit the new approach. Sauveur had all the necessary enthusiasm and panache that the 'conversational' style of teaching required and their School of Modern Languages in Boston was a success. He also held summer schools to spread the gospel. It is possible that Nicholas Joly, another French immigrant who arrived about ten years later than Sauveur, was a student, or heard about the methods. At all events, Joly started teaching in the same way nearby in Providence, Rhode Island, as the first employee of the young Maximilian Berlitz (q.v.). Though Heness started the new system, it was Sauveur who made it well-known through his work and his writing, in particular his *Introduction to the Teaching of Living Languages without Grammar or Dictionary* published in 1874 alongside his 'textbook' *Causeries avec mes élèves* (Chats with my pupils), a curious collection of 'conversation skeletons' which were intended to act as the starting-point for the classroom conversations. Sauveur was clearly a born teacher, but had little analytical power and his lesson comments are not always easy to understand.

## SEIDENSTÜCKER, Johann Heinrich Philipp   1763–1817

One of the founders of the sentence-based 'grammar-translation' method in Germany. Part 1 of his book *Elementarbuch zur Erlernung der französischen Sprache* appeared in 1811 with Part 2 following in 1814 (a third was added posthumously in 1829). It was an influential textbook and the model for the immensely successful work of Karl Ploetz (q.v.) later in the century.

## SWEET, Henry   1845–1912

Born in London on September 15th, 1845. Sweet's father was a barrister and his mother a Scotswoman. After leaving school, he studied philology at Heidelberg University for a short time and, after a spell in a mercantile office in London, entered Balliol College, Oxford, at the age of twenty-four. He graduated with a fourth-class degree in 1873. Sweet's energies at Oxford were devoted more to his private enthusiasm for language than his prescribed studies, and he had already published two academic papers on philology before completing his university degree. During the 1870s he wrote three works which were to become standard textbooks in their various fields: *A History of English Sounds* (1874), *An Anglo-Saxon Reader* (1876), and *A Handbook of Phonetics* (1877), which also contains *A Popular Exposition of the Principles of Spelling Reform* demonstrating an interest in applied language studies which continued throughout his life. His next contribution to the applied field came in 1884 when, as a past President of the Philological Society, Sweet presented a paper on the occasion of the address in honour of James Murray, the then President. Sweet entitled his paper 'On the practical study of language', a topic that had interested him for the past fifteen years. He had, however, deliberately delayed the publication of his paper until his textbook *Das Elementarbuch des gesprochenen Englisch*, which exemplified his theoretical principles, was ready. It appeared the following year (1885) and was the book which Onions, in a famous phrase in his entry on Sweet in the *Dictionary of National Biography*, said 'taught phonetics to Europe'. After a further fifteen years of thought and development, the 1884 paper appeared as a book under a slightly different title, *The Practical Study of Languages* (1899), and established itself as the most substantial contribution to the study of language teaching methodology yet produced and a classic text in applied linguistics.

Sweet's failure to gain academic recognition in Britain, and in particular his rejection for the Chair of English Language and Literature at Merton College, Oxford in 1885, astonished his European contemporaries and embittered his relationships with his colleagues at home. A further failure in 1901 (the third altogether since he had earlier tried for a Professorship at London in 1876) was not really surprising, given the hostility he had provoked. He was, however, rewarded with a Readership in Phonetics , a post he held until his death from pernicious anaemia in 1912. Sweet's academic work continued throughout this period and his major works included *A New English Grammar* (1892/98), *The History of Language* (1900), and *The Sounds of English* (1908) as well as *The Practical Study*. As Onions says in his biographical note: 'Few scholars, native or foreign, have left their mark so plainly and permanently upon the study of the grammar and lexicography of Old English, of the relation of grammar to the laws of thought, and of the history of English in all its forms and periods'.[32] And, one might add, of the history of language teaching.

As a man, Sweet was, according to Shaw, 'not in the least an ill-natured man: very much the opposite I should say'. This casts him in a much pleasanter light than the post-Merton history of bickering seems to suggest. However, Shaw goes on to point out: 'he would not suffer fools gladly; and to him all scholars who were not rabid phoneticians were fools'.[33] Also, Sweet's poor eyesight led him to screw up his eyes which gave him a rather fierce appearance. He was certainly not the debonair Henry Higgins of *My Fair Lady*, but the dedicated, even ruthless, teacher of pronunciation of *Pygmalion* probably contains at least some of the 'touches of Henry Sweet' that Shaw said he used in his portrait of Higgins. He married in 1887, but the couple had no children.[34]

## SWIFT, Jonathan 1667–1745

Swift's connection with the history of language teaching was his *Proposal for Correcting, Improving, and Ascertaining the English Tongue* published in 1712 in the form of a letter to the Earl of Oxford and Mortimer. He suggested that a body be set up along the lines of the French Academy to regulate and improve the language. The death of Queen Anne in 1714 robbed the plan of its political support, and it was never seriously revived.

## VIËTOR, Wilhelm 1850–1918

Born in Kleeburg, Germany on December 25th 1850. Viëtor started his career as a teacher of English in *Realschulen*, and then spent two years (1872–74) teaching German in schools in England. His school experience convinced him that traditional methods of language teaching were not only ineffective but needlessly stressful, and that the children were being overworked to no good purpose. While on a touring holiday in North Wales during a period as 'dozent' at University College, Liverpool, he wrote the pamphlet *Der Sprachunterricht muss umkehren! Ein Beitrag zur Überbürdungsfrage* (Language Teaching Must Start Afresh! A Contribution to the Question of Stress and Overwork in Schools) which set the Reform Movement alight in Germany in 1882. In order to give himself the necessary freedom, he had used a pseudonym, Quousque Tandem, which became as famous as Viëtor himself. He revealed his true identity in the second edition in 1886. Two years earlier he had been appointed to the Chair of English Philology at the University of Marburg, a post he held until his death in 1918.

His academic work included *Elemente der Phonetik* (1884), enlarged and revised in 1893, which, with Sweet's *Handbook* was one of the founding classics of scientific phonetics. He was also an authority on the language of Shakespeare and published a number of studies in the field. He always retained his concern for language teaching methodology and held a series of summer schools in Marburg at the turn of the century. His lectures were published as *Die Methodik des neusprachlichen Unterrichts* (Modern Language Teaching Methodology) in 1902. In 1888 he succeeded the founder Paul Passy as President of the International Phonetic Association (as it was to become).

## WALKER, John   1732–1807

Born in Colney Hatch near London, Walker was a teacher of elocution and an actor as well as the author of a *Rhyming Dictionary of the English Language* which has survived to the present day. His chief claim to fame, however, was his *Critical Pronouncing Dictionary and Expositor of the English Language* (1791), which played the same authoritative role in pronunciation as Johnson's *Dictionary* did in lexicography and was not superseded until Daniel Jones (q.v.) produced his *English Pronouncing Dictionary* in 1917.

## WALLIS, John   1616–1703

Born in Ashford in Kent, Wallis was educated at Emmanuel College, Cambridge, graduating in 1637. Eight years later he took holy orders, and in 1649 he was appointed Savilian Professor of Geometry at Oxford University. His grammar, *Grammatica Linguae Anglicanae*, written for foreign students of English, continued to influence scholars well into the next century. Dr. Johnson, for instance, held it in high esteem. Thereafter it was largely forgotten until its reputation revived in the present century as one of the early grammars that did not look at English through Latin eyes. J. A. Kemp recently produced the first translation since the eighteenth century: *John Wallis's Grammar of the English Language* (1972).

Wallis was a founder member of the Royal Society but his later linguistic work (he was as much a phonetician as a grammarian) was overshadowed by a quarrel with William Holder (1616–1698) over who should rightfully claim the credit for a cure for surdo-mutism.[35]

## WEBBE, Joseph   *c.* 1560–1633

Little is known of his early life, but he was probably educated at Bologna University (being a Catholic he was barred from entry to an English university). It is possible he was a member of the famous Catholic family of Webb from Dorsetshire, but this cannot be proved. His work as a private tutor of Latin led him to devise a model system for teaching the language without the use of grammar, and he outlined his scheme in his *Appeal To Truth* in 1622. The following year he was granted a thirty-one-year patent on his method by Parliament after his *Petition to the High Court of Parliament* (1623). He published five texts using his system between 1626 and 1629, including a set of Latin dialogues called *Pueriles Confabulatiunculae* (Children's Talk) translated from Evaldus Gallus, published in 1627. He opened a school in Old Bailey (a street at that time) in 1626.[36]

## WEBSTER, Noah   1758–1843

Born in Hartford, Connecticut, and graduating from Yale in 1778, Webster first qualified in law and was admitted to the bar in 1781. In addition to his legal activities, he worked as a teacher and a journalist until 1798, when he retired to New Haven to devote himself to his literary work. Both his major works achieved phenomenal public success. The first was his *American Spelling Book* (1787, derived from Part 1 of *A Grammatical Institute of the English Language* (1783)), popularly known as 'The Blue-Backed Speller' on account of its blue paper covers. The second was his *American Dictionary of the English Language*, published in 1828. Between the two publications, Webster's views on spelling reform had changed. He promoted the cause of reform in an essay in 1789 for the first time, and was a tireless advocate thereafter. Spellings such as *labor, public* (in contrast to *publick*, also adopted in British English), and *theater* have survived in standard American English, but others, for example, *crum* and *frend*, did not find public favour. Webster's other works include *Dissertations on the English Language* (1789), which includes the *Essay on a Reformed Mode of Spelling*, and *A Compendious Dictionary of the Engish Language* (1806).[37]

## WEST, Michael Philip   1888–1973
On completing his education at Christ Church, Oxford, West went to India as an officer in the Indian Education Service. He eventually became Principal Inspector of Schools in Chittagong and Calcutta, Principal of the Teachers' Training College in Dacca and Honorary Reader in Education at Dacca University. He published two books on education: *Education and Psychology* (1914) and *Language in Education* (1929). In 1923, the Imperial Education Conference recognized 'the desirability of scientific investigation of the facts of bilingualism with reference to the intellectual, emotional, and moral development of the child, and the importance of the questions of practical educational method arising out of the investigation of such facts'. West's report, *Bilingualism – with special reference to Bengal* (1926), grew out of this statement of imperial policy. He took the Bengali learner's needs for English as his starting-point and concluded that a reading knowledge of the language was of overriding importance. In practical terms, this meant the development of improved materials and West's *New Method* scheme based on a strict control of vocabulary, was the outcome. Readers were published in Calcutta from 1927, but without West to promote them, it is doubtful whether they did any lasting good. West submitted his report in the form of a thesis to the University of Oxford and was awarded a degree of Doctor of Philosophy in 1927.

During the thirties West's talent for writing teaching materials made him the best-known and most prolific author in English as a foreign language of his time: *New Method Conversation Course* (6 parts) (1933), *New Method (Alternative) Readers 1–7* (1935–39), *New*

*Method Composition (Alternative Edition)* (4 parts) (1938) are some of his earlier titles. There were also books for teachers, for example, *Learning to Read a Foreign Language* (1926), and *Learning to Speak a Foreign Language* (1933). With C. E. Eckersley (q.v.) he made Longmans, Green one of the leading publishers in the field, a position that its successor still holds.

He also continued his research in vocabulary control, with two specific objectives in mind. One was the specification of a 'Minimum Adequate Vocabulary' for basic courses in English, and the other the discovery of a 'defining vocabulary', the concept behind his New Method *Dictionary* (1935) and one of his main contributions to the Carnegie Report. Provoked by the challenge of Ogden's (q.v.) *Basic English*, West took the initiative in calling the 1934 Carnegie Conference in New York, an event which brought him and Palmer (q.v.) into a close partnership. The General Service List that emerged from the reconvened Conference in 1935 in London (included in the *Interim Report on Vocabulary Selection*, 1936) became his project and, after frequency statistics had been supplied by Lorge, it was eventually published in 1953 as *The General Service List of English Words*.

In his later years, West undertook a number of tours abroad under British Council auspices and continued to write. He was a regular contributor to *English Language Teaching* and other journals, and his short teacher-training manual *Teaching English in Difficult Circumstances* (1960), which includes the Minimum Adequate Vocabulary as an appendix, was a useful contribution to a neglected field. He lived in Painswick in the Cotswolds and was well-known in the local community as a lively and colourful personality.[38]

## WIDGERY, William Henry   1856–1891

Born and educated in Exeter in Devon, where his father enjoyed a reputation as the poet-painter of Dartmoor, Widgery won an exhibition to St. John's College, Cambridge, in 1874, and, despite a year off through illness, graduated Seventh Senior Optime in the Mathematical Tripos in 1879. Like Daniel Jones (q.v.) Widgery moved into linguistic affairs after an initial training as a mathematician. He became a teacher at Dover College for a short time and then returned to Exeter and studied French, German, Spanish, and Italian. He also wrote an essay on the First Quarto of *Hamlet* for which he won the Harness Prize at Cambridge. In 1880 he returned to teaching in London, and continued his language learning activities, this time in Anglo-Saxon, Gothic, and Icelandic. He later added Sanskrit and Hebrew.

In addition to his formidable academic achievements, Widgery was also a very effective practical classroom teacher and active in educational affairs in London. He was, for example, Librarian and a member of the Council of the Teachers' Guild, the body to which he addressed the first draft of his *Teaching of Languages in Schools* in the form of a speech at their 1888 Conference. Later, he expanded his ideas in a series of articles in the *Journal of Education* and the final pamphlet appeared in December of the same year. Widgery was immensely well-read in the literature of language teaching in general and the Reform Movement in particular. He also made personal contact with the Movement by attending a conference in Berlin in 1886. The basic aim of his pamphlet was to apply the new ideas to the practical problems of the modern language classroom, a task he was particularly well-equipped to do. As he said himself, 'unfortunately, our phoneticians are as little schoolmasters as our schoolmasters phoneticians', and his comments on the new methods are full of detailed advice on the teaching of pronunciation, the use of phonetic wall-charts, how to handle transcription, the development of reading, the expansion of vocabulary, and so on. In spite of this intense concern for improvement in modern language teaching, Widgery remained a Comenian at heart in his belief that the study of language begins with the mother tongue: 'Around English and around English alone, can our teaching be properly concentrated'.

His pamphlet is unique in two important respects. The first is his extensive survey of the history of language teaching since classical times, a study that Klinghardt described in *Englische Studien* as 'as intelligent as it is learned'. And the second, which greatly impressed his contemporaries, is the bibliography, which is twenty pages long and organized chronologically. Nothing like it had appeared before, and it clearly represents an immense amount of preparatory research and a deep commitment to the subject. Its value in preparing this book has already been acknowledged.

Widgery died in 1891 from a kidney complaint that was not treated as expertly as it should have been. He was only thirty-five years of age and, had he lived, his influence on the development of language teaching in Britain would have been profound.[39]

## WILKINS, John   1614–1672

Born near Daventry and educated at Magdalen Hall, Oxford. Wilkins sided with Parliament during the Civil War and married a sister of Oliver Cromwell. He was made Master of Trinity College by Cromwell's son, Richard, in 1659. After the Restoration he lost the Mastership but made his peace with the new regime and became Dean of Ripon and later Bishop of Chester. He was a founder member of the Royal Society for which he wrote the *Essay towards a Real Character and a Philosophical Language*. After being delayed by the Great Fire in 1666, it was eventually presented to the Society in 1668.

## Notes

1 Sources: Lambley (1920); Bjurman (1977).
2 Sources: Berlitz Organization (1978); Pakscher (1895).
3 Source: 'Leonard Bloomfield' by Bernard Bloch (Sebeok ed. 1966: 508–18).
4 Source: 'Franz Boas' approach to language' by Roman Jakobson in Sebeok (ed. 1966: 128).
5 Sources: Dobson (1957: 93–117); Danielsson and Alston (eds. 1966); Turner (ed. 1980).
6 Sources: Taylor (1976); Woodcock (1967).
7 Sources: Keatinge (1910); Sadler (1969); Trevor-Roper (1967).
8 Source: Dobson (1957: 280).
9 Source: Yates (1934).
10 Sources: Moulton (1961); Anthony (1968).
11 Source: Dobson (1957: 131–55).
12 Sources: Swan (Preface to Gouin 1892); Darian (1972).
13 Sources: Danielsson (1955); Dobson (1957: 62–88).
14 Source: Trevor-Roper (1967).
15 Sources: Lambley (1920); St. Clare Byrne (1953).
16 Strevens (ed. 1978: 3).
17 Sources: Hornby (1966); Strevens (ed. 1978); *The Times* 15.9.78.
18 Source: Payne (1830).
19 Source: Haislund (1943).
20 *Outline of English Phonetics*, 6th edition, Cambridge: Heffer, 1948:28.
21 Source: Gimson (1968).
22 Sources: Ministère des Affaires Étrangères de la Republique Française (archives et documentation), private communication; Tickoo (1982 b).
23 Source: Junker (1904).
24 Source: Lambley (1920).
25 Source: Scragg (1974).
26 Source: Florence and Anderson (eds. 1977).
27 Sources: Hornby and Jones (1950); Redman (1967); Anderson (1969).
28 Source: 'Paul Passy' by Daniel Jones in Sebeok (ed. 1966: 139–47).
29 Source: Silber (1960).
30 Sapir (1929), quoted in Sampson (1980: 82–3).
31 Sources: Sampson (1980, Chapter 4); 'Edward Sapir' by C. F. Voegelin, in Sebeok (ed. 1966: 489–92).
32 *Dictionary of National Biography, 1912–1921*: 520.
33 Shaw: Preface to *Pygmalion*. Penguin edition 1967 p. 7.
34 Sources: Wrenn (1946); Henderson (ed. 1971); Onions's entry in the *Dictionary of National Biography, 1912–1921*.

35  Source: Kemp (1972).
36  Source: Salmon (1961/79: 15–31).
37  Source: Venezky (1980).
38  *Times* Obituary, 24.3.73.
39  Sources: Hill (1894); Tozer (1903).

# Appendix

# Language teaching must start afresh!

A translation of Wilhelm Viëtor's
*Der Sprachunterricht muss umkehren!*

A.P.R. Howatt and David Abercrombie
with the assistance of Beat Buchmann

# Translators' Note

*Der Sprachunterricht muss umkehren! Ein Beitrag zur Überbürdungs-frage*, to give Wilhelm Viëtor's influential pamphlet its full title, is often cited as the key document that prompted the reform of language teaching in Germany and elsewhere in the late nineteenth century. It has not, however, been published in English before, so far as we are aware, and we hope that by filling this gap we can help to clarify the origins of the Reform Movement and strengthen the links between the early work of Viëtor in Germany and the later developments in Britain led by Henry Sweet, some of which had already been forged by the time the pamphlet was republished in Heilbronn in 1886. Viëtor quotes the Preface to Sweet's *Handbook of Phonetics* (1877) in his text (p. 359), for example, and we have deliberately taken the English translation of the title used by Sweet when he referred to the pamphlet in his address 'On the practical study of language' to the Philological Society in May 1884, two years after the original publication in 1882.[1]

Although the impact of the pamphlet has long been acknowledged and the general drift of its argument is familiar, what it actually said is much less widely known and consequently open to misinterpretation. It has been suggested, for instance, that Viëtor was an early champion of the Direct Method whereas it is evident from the text that he was proposing a rather different solution to the methodological problems that grammar-translation language teaching had created in the class-room. In particular, he was passionately concerned with language teaching in schools (the Direct Method was mostly used with adults) as the subtitle *Ein Beitrag zur Überbürdungsfrage* shows. *Überbürdung* is a difficult term to translate clearly for a modern English-speaking readership. It refers to a long-standing educational controversy in

Germany concerning the amount of work youngsters were expected to do both at school and at home in the evenings. Liberal opinion at the time held that much of the burden placed on schoolchildren derived from the inefficiency of schools and their teaching methods. In the interests of the children's health and general well-being, the workload not only should but could be reduced without any loss in academic standards or achievement. 'Overwork' gives part of the meaning of the term, but does not perhaps cover the notion of injury to health, so we have added the word 'stress'. Viëtor alludes to this controversy many times in the text and expected his views to provoke a storm of opposition from conservative factions.

The Preface to the second edition shows that the trouble Viëtor foresaw indeed occurred. This may, in part at least, have contributed to his decision to 'come clean' and use his real name on the title-page as well as his by now famous pseudonym. Quousque Tandem is part of a quotation from the opening sentence of Cicero's first speech to the Senate on the Catiline conspiracy in 63 BC in which he successfully provoked Catilina to leave Rome: '*Quousque tandem abutere, Catilina, patientia nostra* (How much longer are you going to abuse our patience, Catilina?)' The choice of pseudonym with its implications of Ciceronian invective set the tone for the pamphlet itself and expressed Viëtor's own exasperation at the appalling state of affairs in language classrooms (classical and modern) which he discusses with such passion and energy in the pamphlet. It is difficult to capture this pamphleteering style in a modern translation. At times it reads like a political manifesto, and at other times like an academic article with properly acknowledged sources and so on. One apparently small but important problem is the extensive use which Viëtor makes of the exclamation mark. (Conventions governing its use are quite different in German and English.) We have retained most of Viëtor's exclamation marks on principle, but omitted a few where it would have made the English text look exaggerated or insincere. We have also altered the paragraphing occasionally. Viëtor used a punctuation mark (an extended dash sign) which indicated a piece of text half-way between a paragraph and a new sentence. References have been modernized and collected in a separate bibliography at the end.

All translations have to choose between a faithful rendering of the original and an effectively readable text in the new language. This is made more difficult when, as in this case, the original is nearly a century old and the technical terminology of the subject has changed and expanded in the meantime. We hope, however, that the modern reader will not only discover what Viëtor had to say, but also find some echo of the emotion he invested in his work which makes it a unique document in the history of linguistics and language teaching.

Finally, we should like to acknowledge the painstaking and sensitive assistance provided by Beat Buchmann in the preparation of this translation. His sharp and experienced eye has rescued the text from many errors, and any which remain are, of course, entirely our responsibility.

A.P.R.H., D.A.

### Note

1. Sweet (1884: 581), with Sweet's *'teaching of languages'* modified to *'language teaching.'*

*Figure 28 Title-page of Wilhelm Viëtor's* Der Sprachunterricht muss umkehren!

DER

# SPRACHUNTERRICHT

## MUSS UMKEHREN!

———

EIN BEITRAG

ZUR

ÜBERBÜRDUNGSFRAGE

VON

## QUOUSQUE TANDEM

(WILHELM VIETOR).

ZWEITE UM EIN VORWORT VERMEHRTE AUFLAGE.

HEILBRONN

VERLAG VON GEBR. HENNINGER

1886.

*Language teaching must start afresh!*
A contribution to the question of stress and overwork in schools.

To the author of *Die Überbürdung der Schuljugend*
Friedrich Wilhelm Fricke
As a mark of like conviction and sincere respect
Q.T.

## Preface to the second edition

Four years have gone by since I first wrote down the following pages during a holiday visit to Llangollen in the beautiful valley of the Dee. Six years' service as a probationary teacher, member of staff, and head at various German secondary schools[1] had recently been completed by my appointment to the staff of the newly-founded University College in Liverpool. This gave me the opportunity for reflection. What impelled me to put pen to paper was the conviction that language teaching in our country had taken the wrong road and the desire that I personally could make some contribution towards promoting a change of direction. While I was in the process of writing the manuscript, it occurred to me that my words would have a much greater impact if their authorship were not credited to me personally. With Quousque Tandem on the title-page, the tone of the pamphlet could be sharper and more outspoken, even perhaps a little outrageous. I apologize if this has upset people at times. I cannot accept the charge of being 'anti-teacher' (even the most obdurate of them), though I would always champion the cause of young people. However, my main aim is, and always has been, to concern myself solely with the problem in hand. These circumstances help to explain and justify the somewhat flattering references in the text to my own work.

I would be the first to admit that this new edition of my pamphlet, or new impression since that is essentially what it is, gives me great satisfaction. I am pleased to think that it has actually played a role in prompting a Reform Movement which has grown in strength since then. It would be pointless and unnecessary to continue using a pseudonym which friends far and wide have either guessed or revealed.
*Wiesbaden, Easter 1886, W. Viëtor.*

'Children at school are overworked! This issue seems to turn up virtually every day, but for all its good intentions, the public is worrying about things it doesn't really understand. Leave the schools to get on with things alone! Both the education authorities and the teaching staff have taken the danger of overwork extremely seriously for years. Whatever the causes may be – the growth of teaching materials, overlarge classes, unsupervised homework, the inordinate pursuit of pleasure – they are not the fault either of the system or of the individual school.'

I'm sorry, sir, but we are not talking about an averted threat, but a melancholy fact. Overwork exists, and though not alone, the school system has to bear some share of responsibility for it. Let us avoid, however, making over-generalized charges and counter-charges, and look closely, if we may, at one specific aspect of the school system, namely language teaching. This seems worth doing considering that it takes up almost two-thirds of the Gymnasium timetable, around seven thousand hours altogether, excluding homework. It could be argued that this is already an excessively high demand to make, but you would no doubt raise the question of priorities, and, if I were to point out that actual achievement in foreign languages, even after six to nine years' instruction, was still pretty mediocre, you would presumably counter this by demanding scornfully if I had ever heard of the 'formal principle'.[2] That is why I prefer to stick to the facts.

## Linguistic aspects

Although our discussion will be almost exclusively concerned with foreign language teaching, it might be worth taking a brief look first at the way in which the grammar of the mother tongue is taught at elementary level in primary or preparatory schools.

Ask any class of schoolchildren what a word consists of. You will either get no answer at all – in the long run that might be the best answer – or you will get the answer 'letters'. Suppose you were to give an example, *schwarz* for instance.[3] The child will stick to his original view and tell you that *schwarz* consists of *s,c,h,w,a,r,z*. He has no idea that this is a matter of orthographical convention that has nothing to do with the language as such. Possibly the teacher has explained the distinction between written letters and spoken sounds. In that case, ask the child about the sounds, and back will come the answer: *s/c/h/w/a/r/z/*. He will not know that the three letters *s,c,h* stand for a single sound, or that the letter *z* stands for two sounds. Nor will the teacher either, though both will know that sometimes the pronunciation is 'like this' and sometimes 'like that'.

This appalling confusion between writing and speech has been firmly implanted in the child's mind by his spelling book. Woe betide him if he fails to remember that *a,e,i,o,u*, and *y* are vowels and the other letters, or 'sounds', are consonants. Try asking the child – or the teacher for that matter – what the basis for the distinction is: 'Well, you can't pronounce consonants on their own' (how do you manage to say *Sh!*, then, when you want someone to be quiet?), or, 'every syllable must have a vowel' (what about *Psst!*?)[4] In short, you hear all kinds of phonetic nonsense which is matched only by the rubbish talked about 'syllables' at school. Practice follows theory. Teachers insist on distinctions (such as that between *ei* (ăi) and *ai* (āi), for instance), which disappeared from the pronunciation more than five hundred years ago. If they ever have the misfortune to consult a French or an English grammar, they will be misled by what they read into teaching the 'soft' *b,d,g* at the end of German words and syllables in place of the 'hard' stops and fricatives used right up to the present time. Or they may take a musical fancy to the 'sharp' Hanoverian pronunciation of *s–p* or *s–t*, and require their pupils to produce these plattdeutsch provincialisms in place of the *shp* and *sht* which have been normal in High German since before Luther's day.

Schoolmasterly wrong-headedness about local dialects has succeeded in persuading people to accept the long *dās* (alongside the formally identical *daß*), *ēs*, *ān*, *vōn*, *hīn*, *ūn*, etc. into 'educated German'! It would surely be better (and this is really the whole point) if everybody used 'literate standards of educated colloquial speech – that priceless treasure which is our common heritage – and really spoke his mind'. This demand originates from no less a figure than Schleicher (1879), while he considers it to be of the greatest importance that sounds which were identically pronounced even in the Middle High German period should sometimes be written as *ß* and at other times as *ss(s)*, because Middle High German script did not use *ß* and *ss(s)* but *z* and *ss(s)*, and because the former derived from a *t* in Primitive Germanic ('Urdeutsch') while the latter was originally an *s*! Would philology not be better employed identifying a generally acceptable 'spoken German', that is a spoken version of the written language which would follow the phonetic rules of modern High German, and require the schools to use it as the basis for their teaching?

However, for the time being, this would be considered as yet another 'diversion' from the teaching of German grammar in schools, which does not normally deal with the study of 'pronunciation' at all, but leaves it all to the practical teaching of reading. The teaching of German grammar typically begins with the 'parts of speech', i.e. their names, with no serious explanation and no logical framework. After all, they're in the book! After this list of contents, each part of speech is dealt with individually. The fact is, the distinction between strong and weak nouns is absurd in modern German, and there is a fully-fledged and vigorously expanding declension with *s* – but our German grammar books 'based on historical principles' pay absolutely no attention. They prefer to complain about the disappearance of old endings and the importation of foreign loanwords – both of which can only be welcomed by any sensitive friend of our language. After 'the pronoun' and 'the verb', with any luck we come eventually to the interjection, and then the syntax appears. Subject and predicate, object and attribute: what a source of confusion! What a struggle! Of course it is, when the labels are presented first and forms are more important than explanations. Finally, thank God, we have finished with grammar. Now we can start all over again in the secondary school! All the same muddles reappear, and for every one that is straightened out, a new one takes its place. As far as the primary school is concerned, anyway, teaching grammar and particularly German grammar is a pointless torture. It is not understood, so it cannot contribute to the children's mental development. And the idea that they learn living German that way cannot possibly be taken seriously. Fortunately, that is well taken care of elsewhere!

When it comes to foreign language teaching, the generally accepted view is that the same mistaken approach based on the written language, the same kind of school grammars, will be able to work miracles and teach a new language. They never have, and they never will. And even if you actually succeeded in stuffing the pupils' heads with the best grammars and the most comprehensive dictionaries, they still would not know the language! As the well-known philologist Sayce (1879) says: 'Language consists of sounds, not of letters, and until this fact is thoroughly impressed upon the mind, it is useless to expect that languages will ever be studied aright. Language, moreover, is formed and moulded by the unconscious action of the community as a whole, and like the life of the community is in a constant state of change and development. Consequently, we cannot compress the grammar of a language into a series of rigid rules, which, once laid down by the grammarians, are as unalterable as the laws of the Medes and Persians. On the contrary, grammar is what the community makes it; what was in vogue yesterday is forgotten today, what is right today will be wrong tomorrow. But above all, language, except for the purposes of the lexicographer, consists not of words but of sentences. We shall never be able to speak a foreign tongue by simply committing to memory long lists of isolated words. Even if we further know all the rules of the grammarians, we shall find ourselves unable in actual practice to get very far in stringing our words together or in understanding what is said to us in return'.[5]

I can already see the 'formal principle' lurking in the background and so hasten to return to the facts. Here is an example from an English grammar: 'Chapter 1: Phonology. Paragraph 1: The English Alphabet'. The English alphabet? Surely they are the same twenty-six letters as in the Latin-based German alphabet (a curious contradiction here) that the children learnt when they started to read in the primary school. 'Ah yes, but the pronunciation is different.' You mean the names of the letters? Certainly, but isn't the symbol A always the symbol A, the symbol B always the symbol B, and so on? And the characteristic English digraphs for single sounds such as *sh* and *th* are of course as neglected in an 'English' Alphabet as their German counterparts (*sch* for example) are in a 'German' one. Not until later in the book is the 'pronunciation' of each letter set out and discussed at very great length in an attempt to reduce the chaos of the English orthographical system to a set of exact correspondences between letters (or letter sequences) on the one hand and sounds (or sound sequences) on the other. The children actually have nothing new to learn except the English names of the letters. Since the letter names are merely English words consisting of English sounds, the pupil should be taught the English sound system if he is to pronounce them properly. And what does the grammar book do about it? It attaches German transliterations in brackets after each letter: A (*eh*), B (*bih*), C (*ßih* or even *sih*), and so on.[6] The problem is, however, as we know from our experience in the primary school, that reading German means 'translating' the written text into Westfalian, Swabian, Silesian, or whatever dialect the child speaks, with the result that the children refer to the 'English letters' by meaningless Swabian, Westfalian, and Silesian 'names'. Nor can we expect the teacher to do much about it. Fewer than five per cent of them know or demand more than the textbook provides. What they will do, though, is insist that the children parrot the twenty-six letter names, in whatever dialect suits them, all the way up the secondary school.

Next the book moves on to the teaching of pronunciation. Now, surely, the children will learn the nature of English sounds and their relationships both to each other and to the sounds of their own dialect. Will they be told that the 'long vowels', which they have so far associated only with their own *oh*, *ah*, etc., are diphthongs in English (*ai*, *ou*), or that English makes a clear distinction between voiced or sounded consonants and voiceless or unsounded ones, a feature which is totally absent from the German of the south or central part of the country? Not a bit of it. It will merely be mentioned in passing that *ch* sounds like *tsch*, *sh* like *sch*, and *th* 'is pronounced like *s* or *t* with the tip of the tongue pressing against the upper teeth' – and nonsense of every kind – while earnest attempts are made through rules and word lists to make the children see when this or that letter is pronounced like this or that German sound, *k* or *s*, *i* or *ei*, etc. What is more, these dreadful methods are made .even worse through errors and mistakes of detail. If, for instance, the 'guides to pronunciation' given in the grammar book were to keep the German *s* and *ß* distinct, at least the north German children would learn something accurate for a change. However, the average author is as unlikely to be a north German as an Englishman; and his sources are no better. Sources! It is really incredible that all the scientific findings in the study of speech during the past few decades seem to have been completely disregarded in most school grammars and dictionaries. We make do with a pronunciation manual such as Walker's, originally published in 1791 (!) in order to study a language like English which has developed with all the energy of its native steam-engines. But for hair-raising mistakes 'such as 'the *o* in *go* slides from *a* to *o*; *ai* sounds like *eh* in *gain* and *äi* in *lay*' (I am quoting from the second edition of a so-called 'textbook') there is no other authority than the author's own ignorance. Only the worst is good enough for our schoolchildren!

After hours, if not weeks, of bitter toil, the 'pronunciation' is finished. But what has the pupil achieved? Only scraps of dubious knowledge for *Punch* to mock ('Vaiter!' – 'Yessir!' – 'After zis, I vish to become a Velsh rappit!'), and, moreover, the completely false impression that the characteristic features of English 'pronunciation' can be discerned in its orthography, and the laughable assumption that he has now learnt to pronounce and to read English.

As in English, so in French. From the beginning of the Alphabet to the end of the 'Pronunciation' section – the same methods and the same results. The only difference is, we have French in place of English. The errors wear different colours, that is all. Voiced mediae; weak, strong, and aspirated voiceless tenues; voiced, and weak and strong voiceless spirants, all correctly or incorrectly pronounced as the child's native dialect dictates ('Chai bas gonfianze' as Planus once said). That is the French consonant system. '*Ang, äng, ong, öng* with no trace of a *g*' is the familiar recipe for distinguishing the clearly monophthongal nasal vowels (as though any German other than a Westfalian would ever pronounce the *g* in *ng*!). Open and closed *e*, *o*, and *ö*, light and dark *a* are all confused with each other, (though Ploetz, for example, gets this right); *oi* (*ua*) is used for *oa*, *ng* (palatal *n*) for *nj*, etc., a German word stress is placed on the last complete syllable, and so on. In short, the French language, which is foolishly thought to be easier to learn how to pronounce because the spelling is slightly more phonetic, is reduced to 'nonsensical gibberish' as Kraüter, writing in *Sprache und Schrift* (1880), says, quoting the complaint of the worthy Schartenmeyer:

'Sprecht ihr aber doch Französisch,
Soll's nicht lauten wie Chinesisch,
Träng, Detalch und Reglemang
Ist ein sonderbarer Klang.'[7]

In a word, the pronunciation of English and French taught in our schools is gruesome. (This is also the conclusion of Trautmann (1877), Viëtor (1879, 1880), and Kühn (1882).) It seems we need no further evidence to show that learners fail to grasp that contemporary speech is no more than an isolated moment in the ongoing process of phonetic change, and never attain any real understanding of the spoken language as it really is.

The classical languages are fortunately in a better position than English and French to withstand assaults on their pronunciation as their orthographies are rather closer to their sound systems. However, the principle that German sound-spelling rules can be projected on to foreign language writing systems has done its share of damage here as well. The rules for assigning vowel quantity in Latin have been stated scientifically, and things like *scribēre*, *utiquē*, and so on, are no longer taught. Yet you still have *bōnus* and *mŏs*, *cāvet* and *mĕnsā*, and so on and so forth, following the German principle that vowels are 'long in open, stressed syllables, short in closed ones' without the slightest attention to the facts of Latin. (Bouterwek and Tegge (1878) appear not to have grasped this.) Initial *sp* and *st* are germanized as *schp* and *scht*, and *s–ch* typically becomes *sch*. We know that the Latin *c* was pronounced *k* (pure tenuis) right up to the Middle Ages, but I would not advise anyone to mention 'Kikero' in place of 'Tsitsero' in front of an audience of classical scholars! κικερων in Greek is of course acceptable, after all, κ = k in the orthography! That is what we have done to Latin, and it is absurd indeed, as Bouterwek and Tegge say, that 'so much is made of the elegant structure of Latin verse, the rhythmical charm of the language, etc.' But 'empty phrase-making and verbiage' are all part of the business these days!

In Greek, where both ω and ο, η and ε are given and accents are included, vowel quantity is expressed rather better. But who distinguishes between αι and ει, or between οι and ευ? Who remembers to pronounce φ and χ as aspirates (p + h, k + h)? Our German *t* (aspirated tenuis) in initial position by chance almost coincides with a true ϑ, but we pronounce initial τ exactly like that, and initial π and κ not as a pure tenuis, and in the whole of central and south Germany, the weak tenuis serves for β, γ, δ as well as for Latin, French, and English *b, g, d*. If the third-form schoolboy were to create the same confusion in writing and mix up β, π, and φ, δ, τ and ϑ, ευ, and οι, etc. with similar obstinacy on paper, I wager no one would give him a second chance to redeem himself: the entire staff of the school would sink into deep despair and earnestly advise the poor parents to remove their son from the school forthwith, – 'Look here, Smith, it's quite a different kettle of fish!' Writing is infinitely more important than speech! Instead of trying to reform the barbaric pronunciation of Greek, or, in the case of writing, to get rid of the Greek alphabet from the schools (as Kräuter, op. cit. has suggested) and replace it with a Latin-based phonetic script (why the outcry? Gothic, Sanskrit, Arabic, Hindustani, etc. have all been latinized without the scientific world collapsing), instead of this, the pupils are forced to use detached forms rather than the more comfortable cursive Greek script. It is more 'historical', and the boys have to struggle over it for longer! How long are we going to wait before they introduce wax tablets and styluses into the Latin classroom or get pupils to carve their homework in capital letters on slabs of stone?

This is the fraudulent English, French, Latin, and Greek 'phonetics' on which the school grammars build their description of accidence.

Let us begin with English, the simplest and most transparent of languages in this respect. The 'definite and indefinite articles' head the parts of speech list, and the declension of the noun appears in the eyes of school grammars to depend on the mysterious juxtaposition of the definite article and the prepositions *of* and *to* before nouns, so the chances are that the account of accidence will start off with the following: 'Declension of the Definite Article' (the second edition of the grammar already quoted 'declines' the indefinite article: *a, an*!):

| Singular. | | Plural. | |
|---|---|---|---|
| Nominative: | *the* | Nominative: | *the* |
| Genitive: | *of the* | Genitive: | *of the* |
| Dative: | *to the* | Dative: | *to the* |
| Accusative: | *the* | Accusative: | *the* |

It is presumably a blind belief in tradition which deludes people into thinking that anything at all is being declined here. One might just as well argue that *Berlin* can be declined in German as:

| Nominative: | *Berlin* |
|---|---|
| Genitive: | *ab* (or, *von*) *Berlin* |
| Dative: | *zu* (or, *nach*) *Berlin* |
| Accusative: | *Berlin* |
| Locative: | *in Berlin* |
| Instrumental: | *mit* (or, *durch*) *Berlin* |

etc. etc., *ad infinitum*! Now we know how to decline nouns. All we have to do is stick our properly declined article in front of the noun, singular and plural, and the job is done. Splendid! The only trouble is, nothing has actually been declined at all! 'Phrases like *of the child* or *to my friend* in modern English are merely relationships between a preposition and a case and are not in themselves cases: the former is not the genitive of *the child* (that would be *the child's*) and the latter is not the dative of *my friend* since this has merged with the accusative to form the objective, or, if you like, has been absorbed by the accusative, which in turn takes the same form as the nominative, *my friend*' (Viëtor 1879). Apart from the so-called 'Saxon genitive', which is dying out, formal contrasts in the declension of the English noun are restricted to the remarkably regular formation of plurals. In our school grammars, however, with their emphasis on the written language, rules and exceptions are absurdly confused. 'The pupil learns, for example, that the regular plural is formed by adding *s* and *es* after the four(!) sibilants *s*, *sh*, *x*, and *ch*. He naturally supposes that *horse* and *judge*, for instance, are regular and do not count as 'exceptions' under the sibilant rule, whereas in fact they do end in sibilants and form their plurals by adding *ez* or *iz* (where *z* stands for a voiced or sounded *s*). That the *e* in *horses* and *judges* is 'pronounced' is another 'exception' he has to learn along with the others.' He is not told that the same triple set of rules applies not only to the regular formation of plurals but also to the genitive singular, irregularly formed plurals and the Third Person Singular of the Simple Present Tense, namely:

> *ez* after sibilants *z*, *s*, *ž*, and *š*, for example, *foxes*.
> *z* after voiced sounds other than *z* and *ž*, for example, *dogs*.
> *s* after voiceless sounds other than *s* and *š*, for example, *cats*.
> (*ž* represents the voiced, and *š* the voiceless, broad fricative, cf. German *sch*).

The Past Tense and the Past Participle are formed in an analogous manner:

> *ed* and after *d* and *t*, for example, *ended*.
> *d* after voiced sounds other than *d*, for example, *loved*.
> *t* after voiceless sounds other than *t*, for example, *asked*.

These, along with the *-ing* forms, the comparative (*er*, *est*) and adverbials (*ly*) complete the inflectional apparatus of English' (Viëtor, op. cit.) The sub-classification of verbs into strong and weak, which has no basis in the contemporary language and may conceivably be equally inappropriate to other earlier 'periods of grammar', might also be mentioned in passing along with other errors in pedagogical grammars of English already pointed out by Viëtor.

Things are little better so far as French is concerned, as these brief comments will indicate. The clever 'declension' of *the* in English is repeated with *le*, *la*, and *les* in French. 'But surely *du*, and *au*, *des* and *aux* are genuine genitives and datives?' No more than *vom* for *von dem* and *im* for *in dem* are genuine genitives and locatives. None of this is any use: French nouns no longer show case formally and as a rule the plural is not marked at all, except in a liaison by the addition of a voiced *s* (*roi*, *rois*). Furthermore, the feminine of the adjective only appears to be formed by adding a final *e*. 'If French orthography reflected the spoken language accurately,' comments Kräuter (1880), 'it would make sense to say that the feminine form of the adjective in present-day French is distinguished from the masculine partly by a change in the final consonant, partly by the addition of final *d*, *g*, *s*, etc. (with or without a modification of the vowel sound) but mainly by nothing at all. We can be grateful to historical grammar for explanations of this kind, so long as it is not obscure or confusing. Conjugation in French is also different from the picture presented in the grammars: the singular, for example, has in most cases lost its person markers, or at any rate combined the first and second persons in a single form.' (Try producing the following forms which I cannot reproduce here in Kräuter's phonetic transcription, if you want corroborating evidence: *je, tu, il* – *donne, donnes, donne; punis, punis, punit; vends, vends, vend; donne, donnes, donne; punisse, punisses, punisse; vende, vendes, vends*; etc., etc.). It is sad to see the traditional 'four conjugations' listed so 'companionably' side-by-side. Only the *-er* form, and, if Chabaneau is right, the *-ir* form (*punir*) are still alive; the others are flotsam of the past carried along on the stream of language. It is pointless to try and explain the present in terms of the past! There is an Augean stable of rules, groupings, sound-change laws (or, rather, 'letter-change laws', see Kühn 1882) classes and exceptions to cleanse! The final and most serious misapprehension about the nature of conjugation in present-day language is to combine simple and compound tenses following the inappropriate model of Latin and Greek grammar. There is no justification for this in morphology and only very little in syntax: form and meaning are indivisible, like body and soul; together they create speech, for which writing is merely an outer garment.

I have returned to the classical languages and it is time we saw how their morphology is treated in the school grammars. Once again, better orthography has provided some protection against a complete misrepresentation of the facts. Yet here the principal shortcoming of the schools is an irresponsible lack of the restraint which ought to be the hallmark of a good teacher. Even Curtius' Greek grammar, which in many ways is an enormous improvement on the past, is far too old-fashioned in this respect. What twelve-year-old needs to know that the River Elaver is neuter, that *ligo* (*pickaxe*) is masculine, or that the plural of *ren* (*kidney*) is normally *renes* or whether the dative and ablative plural of *veru* (*cooking spit*) ends in *-ubus* or *-ibus*, and so on? Are facts of this kind really worth teaching? Will these words occur in the pupils' readers? In which case could not the teacher help? (Ah, but they might turn up in the next 'unseen', so there is no question of helping the boys.) The need for little jingles handed down from year to year shows how impossible it is to cover all this material at school. There is no better witness to the dire poverty of school grammars of Latin than this:

'Die Wörter auf *as, aus*, x, (or *ix?*), *is*
Sind *feminini generis*,
Ingleichen alle, wie bekannt (!),
Auf s, wovor ein Konsonant.'

Or, an even more edifying variation:

'Die (!) *as* und *is* , die *aus* und *x*,
E – *s*, dazu sonst weiter nichts, (!!),
Und *s* davor ein Konsonant,
Die werden weibliche genannt(!).'[8]

Why not have a rule that says: 'words of the "third" declension with the nominative in *s* are feminine'? (The fact that words which refer to males are masculine either derives from a superordinate rule or is self-evident.) – But there is nothing of the kind in the grammar book and the jingle is so much nicer, isn't it? Worthy gentlemen of philology – don't you realize how absurd you all are?

In syntax, too, traditional rules have done their fair share of damage. Most of them are mere recipes with no grasp of underlying principle. Verbs in English and French which are followed by the prepositions *to* or *à* 'take the dative', leaving a perfectly comprehensible sentence like *I am told* as an inexplicable puzzle no matter how much twisting and turning one may do; *if* and *quoique*, *ut* and *ἐάν* still 'govern' the subjunctive, etc., etc. Year after year the pupils are fed mistakes which the teachers, with their customary attitude to grammar, know to be wrong. Bouterwek and Tegge (op. cit.) complain that 'it is impossible to stop people teaching *–μεθον* as a first person dual in the passive and middle voices', and they continue, 'how many teachers insist on distinguishing between *σύν* and *μετά* (our much-cited Englishman is extremely helpful on this point in the second edition of his book where he meets a long-felt need by stating that *on* answers the question *where?* and *upon* the question *whither?*), and they cannot make up their minds to give up their sharp-witted investigations into these Greek prepositions which have been conclusively settled by Mommsen'. The authors I have mentioned find it 'remarkable that with so many mistakes being made in the schools, the teachers themselves do not shoulder some if not all of the blame'. At least part of the reason is that their lordships are not only unaware of a great many of their mistakes, but continue to force these things down the children's throats as important 'truths', at great cost to themselves and their pupils.

## Pedagogical aspects

Force – an ugly word, but an apt one. 'Suppose a cabinet-maker wanted to teach his craft to his apprentice, how would he apply the Donatus system?' is the question asked by Brassai in a pamphlet called *The Reform of Language Teaching* published in 1881. 'I'll tell you. First of all he would lay out samples of the different types of wood that a cabinet-maker uses, group them and classify them according to their weight, colour, hardness, etc. Having done that, he would bring out his tools and equipment. The principal types would comprise: (1) those made entirely from wood (for example, the workbench, clamps, racks, etc.), (2) those made partly from wood and partly from steel, some of which have a cutting edge (for example, saws, knives, and planes) while others are pointed (drills and chisels, for example) and then further sub-categories. The apprentice would be made familiar with all these things in theory, and instruction would continue until he could enumerate all the various groups and components correctly without of course ever having made a cut with a knife or a hole with a drill. In short, without ever having used the tools he had been told so much about.'

Well, language teaching methods at present are not much better than the Donatus approach. Their principal aim is to teach the contents of the school grammar book and a necessary fund of vocabulary. To discover how one sets about this task, one only has to look at the textbooks themselves. A list of grammatical rules is apportioned to each 'lesson' or 'chapter'. Practice sentences follow, first in the foreign language, then in German. The relevant vocabulary is given at the foot of the text, with or without reference numbers, or, more usually, lodged in an appendix. This means it has to be learnt by heart.

Most teachers treat this rote-learning as a preparation for going through the lesson material itself. We are reminded of the philologist Sayce's warning: 'Language does not consist of isolated words'. I should like to add that it particularly does not consist of the appallingly pronounced isolated words which pupils have to swot up at home after hearing the teacher read them aloud in class once or twice. But let us leave the question of language on one side for a moment. What do the pupils get out of all this? I shall leave the answer to a practical educationalist who has made a conscientious and thorough trial of the noxious methods that prevail in the teaching of Latin. In the first place, isolated words create no lasting interest in young learners. This means that a quite unnecessary effort is required to learn and retain them which in turn robs the child of time for the enjoyment he might have found in other aspects of his language lessons. He is never asked to think or exercise his judgement: all the ideas and thoughts which emerge from his work are immediately and forcibly squashed. Günther (1881) makes this argument in his book on the teaching of Latin and comes to the conclusion that: 'teaching isolated words and word-forms is a grievous offence against psychology and pedagogy'. – Yes, and when half the class 'don't know their words', the unfortunate probationary teacher, being forbidden to beat these 'slackers', throws psychology and pedagogy out of the window and makes them copy them out one, two, three hundred times!' If a further illustration is needed, take the demands made by the school authorities that words which have been learnt should constantly be repeated, since they have noticed that, as pupils move up the school, their vocabulary becomes poorer. I am afraid that repetition is merely prescribing an extra dose of the original bad medicine!

After memorizing the words, with or without being 'taken through' the lesson, the pupils learn the grammatical rules by heart. Not only is this approach the wrong way of treating language, that much is clear, but it is also pedagogically harmful in itself. Instead of having to discover things for himself by his own independent thought and effort, the pupil is, as Günther (op.cit.) put it, presented with everything on a platter. 'He will never be able to exclaim "I've got it!" because he will never have learnt how to look'. He will take no interest in the new rule or even acknowledge its existence. 'He will read or listen patiently to whatever is set before him, and mechanically parrot what the teacher or the book tells him, without exercising his mind in any way except to memorize slavishly what he did not understand in the first place. Still less, of course, can he see why a rule holds or grasp its underlying reality. All he has to do is mindlessly read his rules, mindlessly memorize them, and mindlessly use them as models for his translation exercises'.

As Günther says, once the pupil has translated the first two or three sentences, that is, once he has worked out which rule is being used, all he needs to do, obviously, is mechanically translate the remaining fifty or more sentences dealing with exactly the same point following the same model as before. 'Only when he starts a new section which deals with a different rule or a different point is the pupil's mind exercised at all by this kind of teaching. A new chord is struck, the pupil concentrates briefly on the effort of translating the first few sentences, and then the whole silly story starts all over again'. Ninety-nine per cent of our textbooks are like this. There are, however, variations. One recent English textbook seems to have gone to great lengths to avoid the 'single rule' pitfall (according to a review in *Litteraturblatt für germanische und romanische Philologie*). After twenty-four pages of preparatory pronunciation exercises in the first lesson we find: the alphabet, eight detailed references to the preparatory exercises, fifteen 'main rules', of which three (Rules 9, 5, and 14) are 'provisional', and eight more rules with eighteen footnotes and exceptions, and many further references to the preparatory exercises, – altogether six-and-a-half pages of 'pronunciation', a further two-and-a-half pages of 'grammar' and then the exercises! And on it goes! This book is recommended by reviewers in the warmest possible terms, though not by Günther himself it should be said.

Now we come to the content of the sentences! 'It almost looks', Günther remarks, 'as if someone took a wicked delight in collecting together all the most heterogeneous scribbles he could find, mixing them in with the most trite and vapid bits and pieces of information, and flinging the whole lot together without rhyme or reason (and often, one might add, making a great many grammatical mistakes). But these sentences have not actually been written and published as funny stories and carnival jokes, they are meant to be studied and worked through seriously week-in and week-out for years, wasting the time and mental energy of everyone in the class. Who could seriously deny that, if schoolbooks of this kind contribute anything at all, it is nothing but mental confusion, frivolity and distraction, superficiality and boredom? Fortunately, however, the pupil fails to recognize the serious damage being done to his mind by books and lessons of this sort; but it must be deeply deplored that methods of this kind continue to be maintained against all sound pedagogical and psychological judgement'.

If this is true of oral work in class, it is still more true of written homework exercises. I could name one large well-run Gymnasium where the fifth-form recently opened a fund – guess what for? The Niederwald Memorial? No, for the purchase of a class duplicator! It is difficult to resist a smile, or even a hint of *Schadenfreude*, at the thought that even if the teacher were as ingenious as his pupils, he would still have to mark the duplicated exercises one-by-one. However, there is a serious side to all this. Homework exercises, that breeding-ground for errors, that scourge for teacher and student alike, are a double, a triple offence against youth!

Nothing that language teaching has to offer later on, reading in particular, can undo or make up for the damage that has already been done. Nor does it have any intention of doing so. It is very unclear what purpose work with the reading text is supposed to fulfil in foreign language teaching, except, in my view, to exemplify the grammatical rules yet again. It seems there is no desire to encourage students to take an interest in the content. Stick to the method! Does it matter that the more thoughtful student might come to the conclusion one heavy summer's afternoon that the whole of Caesar, Livy, and Cicero is contained in the paragraphs of Ellendt-Seyffert? The isolated study of style, phraseology, and synonymy – these are cultivated as the disciplines of language teaching. More rags and bones! I have before me a bookshop catalogue crammed with titles such as *Handbook of Latin Style for the Upper Gymnasium Student, The Principal Rules of Latin Syntax to Learn by Heart, with a selection of phrases to accompany the grammar of Ellendt-Seyffert, The Essential Phraseology of Nepos and Caesar as the basis for the independent collection of the phraseology of Livy and later Cicero, and as a guide for beginners in free composition in Latin, especially of an historical nature, intended principally for the fifth form – ordered by subject matter.* Stupidity of this kind has not yet found its way into modern language teaching. However, modern language phraseologies and synonym collections are now beginning to shoot up like mushrooms on decaying bogland. One pseudo-Englishman has translated *Wohnzimmer* as *living-room* and *das tägliche Brot (le pain quotidien)* as *standing dish*! Never mind! 'It has already been introduced in twenty, thirty, forty schools'. What can be done about it? We already know what dreadful phrase-making goes on under the name of 'Latin Prose Composition'. Even our best examination candidates can no more write a letter in English or French than they can ask the way in London or Paris without stammering or stuttering. And their smattering of literature would be better acquired through translation.

Enough is enough. There is no other conclusion: when our harassed school-children eventually leave school, the languages of ancient Rome and Greece as well as the living languages of England and France are as 'foreign', in the literal meaning of the word, as they were at the start. For six or even nine years they have eaten husks, and never tasted a single grain. Goethe warned against an education that 'points to the goal instead of enjoying the path towards it'. How much worse, then, an education that does not even have a goal to point to!

*   *   *

Things are beginning to look a little brighter for language teaching, thank God! It is only a question of time before modern languages come to dominate the classics in our secondary schools. I will not repeat all the arguments made by our friends in the *Realschule* on behalf of English and French. There is, however, one point I should like to make to the champions of the classics which was emphasized by Stengel (1881) and is repeated in the following comment by Sayce (op.cit.): 'To learn a dead language in anything like a proper way is a very hard matter. We must first be able to think in other languages than our own and know what language really is; in other words, we must have a sound acquaintance with living tongues. Until we realize that Greek and Latin are in no essential respect different from English, or French, or German, that they do not consist in a certain number of forms and rules learnt by rote out of a school-grammar, or even in the polished phrases of a few literary men, but in sounds once uttered and inspired with meaning by men who spoke and thought as we do, the long years spent over Latin and Greek are as good as wasted. It were far better to fill our minds and store our memories with something that will be practically useful to us in after life and at the same time afford that mental training of which we hear so much. To begin our education with the dead tongues and afterwards fill up the odd intervals of time with a modern language or two is to reverse the order of science and nature. The necessary result is to produce a total misapprehension of the real character of speech, a permanent inability to gain a conversational knowledge of foreign idioms, and a false and generally meagre acquaintance with the classical languages themselves. It is not wonderful that the small modicum of Latin and Greek acquired during years of painful work at school should so frequently disappear altogether as soon as school is left, and, considering the erroneous views this small modicum of learning implies, it is perhaps hardly to be regretted that it should'.[9] Stengel (op.cit.) also gives pride of place to

French before Latin: 'As soon as it has really clarified its aims and stopped apeing completely inappropriate methods derived from the teaching of Latin and Greek, which has led to a deep and widespread misunderstanding of the nature of language and its relationship to human thought, modern foreign language teaching will open the minds of young people in a very different and more educationally valuable way than the philosophical grammar of the Middle Ages, long condemned by contemporary philology, could possibly hope to do'. Ostendorf recommends teaching French as the first foreign language, Viëtor recommends English. Fricke (1881) proposes that *only* modern languages should be taught.

Of more immediate and practical importance are the proposals for the reform of language teaching itself. As Sweet said in the Preface to his *Handbook of Phonetics* (1877): 'If our present wretched system of studying modern languages is ever to be reformed, it must be on the basis of preliminary training in general phonetics, which would at the same time lay the foundation of a thorough practical study of the pronunciation and elocution of our own language – subjects which are totally ignored in our present scheme of education'.[10] In Germany Trautmann published his 1877 *Anglia* article, which has already been mentioned, with its practical concern for language teaching in schools, followed by Viëtor's *English Grammar 1* (1879) based on phonetic principles and his articles in *Englische Studien* and *Zeitschrift für neufranzösische Sprache und Litteratur*, the latter containing pedagogical advice on the teaching of French pronunciation. Viëtor has also recommended that the teaching of morphology should be based on the spoken rather than the written language, that is to say on a reformed phonology, and has carried this out in his *Grammar* though restricting himself only to the most important features. Most recently Kühn (op.cit.) has, as a result of practical experience and expressly under Viëtor's influence, recommended the 'new methods' in the strongest terms. Clearing away the rubble of the past, he has started building a fresh approach to French syntax following the motto 'Principles in place of rules'.

Even more voices, and not a few of them classicists, have taken up the cry: 'Death to rules and isolated sentences! The basis of all language teaching must be the connected text!' Apart from Mager and Schrader, I would cite, together with Günther: Eckstein's *Teaching of Latin* (in Schmid's *Encyclopaedia*), Perthes' *Reform of Latin Teaching* as well as practical textbooks such as Giesecke's *Latin Primer*, Meurer's *Latin Reader*, Barth's *Latin Reader and Practice Book for First and Second Forms*, as well as Bolle's *Texts from Apuleius for Elementary Grammar School Classes*, from the Celle Programme. Appropriate materials for Latin and Greek are scanty, I am afraid, as they are for French, too. Plötz' *Reading and Exercise Book* is at least a step in the right direction;

Kühn also mentions Lehmann's *Coursebook and Reader* based on the Perceptual Method, which is in my view rather dubious, Willm's *Premières lectures françaises* and Wiemann's *French Chrestomathy*. There are a number of attractive poems in Marelle's *Le petit monde*, which repairs some of the damage caused by his *French Essays*. For English, Viëtor has since 1879 been promising us, besides the second volume of his *Grammar*, a *Reading and Practice Book* which will, one hopes, exclude everything that is not attractive to children and youngsters. English literature offers a treasure-trove of rhymes and stories, puzzles and songs! Spring, summer, autumn, and winter, and what they bring in the way of work, fun, and play; home, farm, garden, meadow and wood, land and water, earth and sky – they all come alive in reality and in poetry for the delight of the young people of England. They should be known to our own German youth as well. 'Raindrops on the Window', 'Hush-a-bye-baby', the story of 'The Spider and the Fly': they will recognize these and hundreds more as their own. They make more sense than a chapter of Nepos, and will be learnt much better than a page of gender rules! I do not accept that their first Reader needs to be a continuous text as Günther, for example, suggests. On the contrary, that would mean going from one extreme to another. Nor do I go along with Kühn when he proposes that the reading texts should be constructed round systematically graded grammar points. After going through the pronunciation and possibly some of the main morphological points, I would suggest the following lesson plan.

The pupils should not be required to do any preparatory homework. In the class the teacher should read a short text aloud slowly, clearly, and as often as required. The pupils should listen with their books closed. The teacher should gloss any new words which cannot be made clear from the context, but he should leave the class to compete with suggestions for a complete translation under his guidance. Only then should the pupils open their books. The text should be read aloud again, either by the teacher or by one of the better pupils. The others – and there will be great eagerness to take part– should also have a chance of reading and translating later. Once he has made sure that everyone has understood the individual words, the teacher should ask questions about the content of the text, still with the pupils' books open. (In certain circumstances, the questions may have to be put in German first, then in the foreign language.) Answers should be given in the foreign language in complete sentences. Afterwards, the pupils should close their books again, and try to retell the story in the foreign language. The teacher should choose the more confident pupils first, but later on also encourage the more timid ones. Next the class should do some writing. This should consist of the answers to the same questions which were done earlier in the lesson. They should be written on the blackboard first and then copied into the pupils' exercise books. The text should be revised in the next lesson. There should be a glossary with a phonetic transcription at the back of the book (at a later stage, a dictionary), so that the children can revise the new words at home. They should not have to prepare texts at home or learn word lists by heart. However, once most of the children are confident they can 'do it', they might be set a short poem or an appropriate piece of prose to learn by heart at home, and they can perform it in front of Mother or one of their sisters. There should be no written homework at all. Written practice exercises such as Günther and others still include at the end of each reading text should, in my view (and Viëtor's), be mercilessly rejected. I also agree completely with those who, unlike Kühn, condemn the practice of translating connected German texts into the foreign language. If we can bring our pupils to think and express themselves in the foreign language in addition to their mother tongue, we shall have accomplished what we set out to do. Translation into the foreign language is an art which is inappropriate for the school classroom. Gradually, the teacher will have to develop a freer approach to the handling of texts in class, but he should never lose sight of the two basic aims: comprehension and text reproduction. Needless to say, the latter will become increasingly free and spontaneous as the pupils' powers of thought and expression expand. Where then is the grammar? It grows naturally out of the reading texts themselves. At short, regular intervals the teacher should revise the texts with a specific grammar point in mind, and present the results of this study systematically alongside earlier work so that the grammar builds up over the course of time. Also, it goes without saying that the foreign language should always be spoken in class. The more reluctant the classical language teaching profession is to follow this precept, the more doubtful their claim to a place in the schools at all.

Let me now fire one parting shot. Whenever there is a proposal to reduce class hours for one reason or another, there is, we are told, an outcry from the teachers involved. 'I need all the hours I can get!' 'I've already lost this or that hour anyway!' 'I can't manage as it is!' 'It quite simply won't work!' It has got to work, not only in individual cases, but in general. Even if homework were reduced to a minimum, as I should like to see, we should still have a very long way to go. The current school timetable already eats into other activities. Sport, relaxation, physical education: running and jumping, gymnastics and fencing, walking and games – they are still begging in vain for their rightful place, in spite of Hasse, Koch, and Hartwich. Admittedly, the individual teacher cannot cope with this alone, but there is nevertheless a great deal that he can do. Let language teachers make a start! Let them show how half-an-acre, well-tilled and tended, can prove more fertile than a whole one over which handfuls of seeds have been scattered indiscriminately. Then even the authorities will see the point. And afterwards, as a reward, take the children out into the woods and on to the sports field. You will find a sure welcome and will not come away empty-handed. Perhaps you may then discover that it has been worthwhile to sacrifice a couple of ancient and harmful prejudices in return for the gratitude of the children for even the smallest acts of affection and kindness that they so richly deserve.

## Notes

1 *Realanstalten.*

2 'The formal principle' (*das formale Prinzip*) is a difficult phrase to translate adequately as Viëtor appears to be alluding to two different issues at the same time. The first is a contemporary view of 'formal education' (*formale Bildung*) which believed in mental training as an analogous extension of physical training. It is clear that Viëtor followed enlightened opinion of his time in rejecting this notion with its theory of 'faculties' (*Vermögenstheorie*). (See '*Formale Bildung*' by E. Ackermann in Rein (1904: 866–76).) However, from a note he attached to the third edition of his pamphlet in 1905, it seems Viëtor was also referring to a controversy in linguistics about the status of grammatical categories. The 'formalists' believed that grammar reflected logic (hence, language teaching 'trained the mind' in logical thinking, etc.), while the reformers held that grammatical categories were linguistic and not derived from other disciplines. I am grateful to G. Richardson of Hull University for drawing my attention to this note, and for other very helpful comments.

3 *Schwarz* = black. *sch* = /ʃ/ and *z* = /ts/.

4 In the original 'Sh! When you are shooing chickens', and 'Bst! wer kommt da still und stumm? (Who's that coming softly and silently?)', an allusion to a children's rhyme.

5 Sayce (1879: 93).

6 '*ßih* or even *sih*'. The letter *ß* represents a voiceless *s*-sound, whereas the *s* in *sih* would be voiced, making '*zee*' the 'name' of the letter C.

7 Literally, 'If you want to speak French, it should not sound like Chinese. *Träng* (*train?*), *Detalch* (*détail?*) and *Reglemang* (*règlement?*) sound very strange'.

8 Literally, 'Words ending in *as*, *aus*, *x*, *is*, and *s* after a consonant are feminine'.

9 Sayce (1879: 93).

10 Sweet (1877: v–vi).

# Bibliography

**Bouterwek, R. and Tegg, A.** 1878. *Die altsprachliche Orthoepie und die Praxis.* Berlin: Weidmann.

**Brassai, S.** 1881. *Die Reform des Sprachunterrichts in Europa. Ein Beitrag zur Sprachwissenschaft.* Kolozsvár. (Note: this pamphlet introduced Gouin to German language teachers.)

**Fricke, F. W.** 1881. *Die Überbürdung der Schuljugend.* Berlin: Hofmann.

**Günther, J. H. A.** 1881. 'Der Lateinunterricht am Seminar' in *Jahrbuch des Vereins für Wissenschaftliche Pädagogik.*

**Kraüter, J. F.** 1880. 'Sprache und Schrift' in *Zeitschrift für Orthographie.*

**Kühn, K.** 1882. 'Zur Methodik des französischen Unterrichts' in *Programm des Realgymnasiums,* Wiesbaden.

**Sayce, A. H.** 1879. 'How to learn a language'. *Nature* May 29, 1879: 93–94.

**Schleicher, A.** 1879. *Die deutsche Sprache* (4th edn. by J. Schmidt, orig. publ. 1860), Stuttgart: Cotta.

**Stengel, E. M.** 1881. 'Die Ziele und Wege des Unterrichts in den neueren Sprachen' in *Pädagog. Archiv.*

**Sweet, H.** 1877. *Handbook of Phonetics.* Oxford: Clarendon Press.

**Trautmann, M.** 1877. 'Schulbücher und Lautliches'. *Anglia* Vol. 1: 582–598.

**Viëtor W.** 1879. *Englische Grammatik I.* Leipzig: Teubner.

**Viëtor W.** 1879. 'Die wissenschaftliche Grammatik und der englische Unterricht'. *Englische Studien* III 1880: 106–124.

**Viëtor W.** 1880. 'Schriftlehre oder Sprachlehre?' in *Zeitschrift für neufranzösische Sprache und Litteratur.*

**Walker, J.** 1791. *A Critical Pronouncing Dictionary.* London: Robinson.

# Bibliography

**Abbreviations:**

CILT   = Centre for Information on Language Teaching and Research.
ELT(J)  = English Language Teaching (Journal).
HMSO  = His/Her Majesty's Stationery Office.
IRAL   = International Review of Applied Linguistics.
IRET   = Institute for Research in English Teaching (Tokyo).
TPS    = Transactions of the Philological Society.

**Scolar Press:** Books included in the Scolar Press facsimile series *English Linguistics, 1500–1800*, edited by R. C. Alston, are identified by their series numbers and dates of publication by Scolar Press, Menston, England.

**Abbs, B. and I. Freebairn.** 1977 onwards. The *Strategies* series: *Starting S.* 1977; *Building S.* 1979; *Developing S.* 1980; *Studying S.* 1982. London: Longman.

**Abercrombie, D.** 1948a. 'Forgotten phoneticians'. *TPS* 1948; 1–34. Reprinted in Abercrombie 1965: 45–75.

**Abercrombie, D.** 1948b. 'The social basis of language'. *ELT* III/1: 1–11. Reprinted as 'Linguistics and the teacher' in Abercrombie 1956: 1–15.

**Abercrombie, D.** 1949a. 'Teaching pronunciation'. *ELT* III/5: 113–22. Reprinted in Abercrombie 1956: 28–40.

**Abercrombie, D.** 1949b. 'Some first principles'. Part 1: *ELT* III/6: 141–6; Part 2: *ELT* III/7: 169–71. Reprinted in Abercrombie 1956: 16–27.

**Abercrombie, D.** 1949c. 'What is a 'letter'?' *Lingua* II: 54–63. Reprinted in Abercrombie 1965: 76–85.

**Abercrombie, D.** 1956. *Problems and Principles. Studies in the teaching of English as a second language.* London: Longmans, Green.

**Abercrombie, D.** 1965. *Studies in Phonetics and Linguistics.* London: Oxford University Press.

**Abercrombie, D.** 1981. 'Extending the Roman alphabet: some orthographic experiments of the past four centuries', in Asher and Henderson (eds.) 1981: 207–24.

**Ahn, F.** 1829. *Neue holländische Sprachlehre. Zum Selbstunterricht für Deutsche.* Krefeld: Schütter.

**Ahn, F.** 1834. *Handbuch der englischen Umgangssprache.* Cologne: Dumont-Schauberg.

**Ahn, F.** 1834. *Praktischer Lehrgang zur schnellen und leichten Erlernung der französischen Sprache.* Cologne: Dumont-Schauberg. (The first of the series known in English as *New, Practical, and Easy Method.*)

**Ahn, F.** 1849. *A New, Practical and Easy Method of Learning the German Language (1).* Frankfurt: Brockhaus and Avenarius.

**Aickin, J.** 1693. *The English Grammar: or, The English Tongue Reduced to Grammatical Rules.* London: printed for the Author (Scolar Press 21, 1967).

**Aitchison, J.** 1981. *Language Change: Progress or Decay?* London: Fontana.

**Alexander, L. G.** 1967. *New Concept English.* Four volumes. London: Longman.

**Allen, J.P.B. and S.P. Corder** (eds.). *The Edinburgh Course in Applied Linguistics*: Vol. 1, 1973, *Readings for Applied Linguistics*; Vol. 2, 1975, *Papers in Applied Linguistics*; Vol. 3, 1974, *Techniques in Applied Linguistics*; Vol. 4, 1977, edited by J. P. B. Allen and A. Davies, *Testing and Experimental Methods*. London and Oxford: Oxford University Press.

**Allen, J.P.B. and H.G. Widdowson** (eds.). 1974 onwards. *English in Focus*, including *English in Physical Science* 1974 by J.P.B. Allen and H.G. Widdowson and *English in Education* 1977 by E. Laird. Oxford: Oxford University Press.

**Allen, W.S.** 1947. *Living English Structure*. London: Longmans, Green.

**Allen, W.S.** 1954. *Living English Speech*. London: Longmans, Green.

**Alston, R.C.** (ed.) 1967–72. *English Linguistics 1500–1800*. A Collection of Facsimile Reprints. Menston: Scolar Press.

**Alston, R.C.** 1967. 'Polyglot Dictionaries and Grammars; Treatises on English written for Speakers of French, German, Dutch, Danish, Swedish, Portuguese, Spanish, Italian, Hungarian, Persian, Bengali and Russian'. Vol. II of *Bibliography of the English Language from the Invention of Printing to the Year 1800*. Bradford: Ernest Cummins.

**Alston, R.C.** 1974. *A Bibliography of the English Language from the Invention of Printing to the Year 1800*. Corrected reprint of Vols I–X. Ilkley: Janus Press.

**Altieri, F.** 1728. *Gramatica Inglese per gl'Italiani*. London: William Innys.

**Anderson, D.** 1969. 'Harold E. Palmer: a biographical essay', in Palmer and Redman 1932/69: 133–61.

**Angiolillo, P.F.** 1947. *Armed Forces' Foreign Language Teaching: critical evaluation and implications*. New York: S. F. Vanni.

**Anon.** 1554. *A Very Profitable boke to lerne the maner of redyng, writyng, & speakyng english & Spanish*. London (Scolar Press 292, 1971).

**Anon.** 1646. *The English Schole-master, or certeine rules and helpes, whereby the natives of the Netherlands, may bee, in a short time, taught to read, understand and speake, the English tongue*. Amsterdam.

**Anon.** 1733. *The English Accidence, being the Grounds of our Mother Tongue: or, a Plain and Easy Introduction to an English Grammar*. London: J. Roberts (Scolar Press 10, 1967).

**Anthony, E. M.** 1968. 'Charles Carpenter Fries, 1887–1967'. ELT XXIII/1: 3–4.

**Arnauld, A. and C. Lancelot.** 1664/1753. *A General and Rational Grammar, containing the Fundamental Principles of the Art of Speaking*. London: for J. Nourse, 1753 (Translation of the 'Port Royal Grammar', 2nd edition, 1664.) (Scolar Press 73, 1968).

**Arnold, T.** 1736. *Grammatica Anglicana concentrata, oder kurz-gefasste englische Grammatica*. Leipzig.

**Ascham, R.** 1570. *The Scholemaster, or plaine and perfite way of teachying children, to understand, write, and speake, the Latin tong*. London: Iohn Daye.

**Asher, R. E. and E. J. A. Henderson** (eds.). 1981. *Towards a History of Phonetics*. Edinburgh: Edinburgh University Press.

**Axtell, J. L.** (ed.) 1968. *The Educational Writings of John Locke*. Cambridge: Cambridge University Press.

**Bacon, F.** 1605. *The Advancement of Learning*. (See Kitchin (ed. 1973)).

**Bantock, G. H.** 1980. *Artifice and Nature, 1350–1765*. Studies in the History of Educational Theory, Vol. 1. London: Allen and Unwin.

**Barker, E.** 1766. *Nuova e facile Grammatica della lingua Inglese per gl'Italiani*. Siena: Bindi.

**Barker, E.H.** (ed.) 1832. Amended reprint of Webster 1828 under title *A Dictionary of the English Language*. Two volumes. London: Black, Young, and Young.

**Barlement, N. de** 1511. *Vocabulaire de nouveau ordonné et derechief recorigé pour aprendre legierement à bien lire, escripre, et parler françoys et flameng*. Anvers.

Barrutia, R. 1965. 'A neglected classic'. *IRAL* III.1: 63–74.

Bartels, A. 1850. *The Modern Linguist.* London: D. Nutt.

Bates, M. and T. Dudley-Evans (eds.). 1976 onwards. *Nucleus.* London: Longman.

Baugh, A. C. and T. Cable. 1978. *A History of the English Language.* Third edition. London: Routledge and Kegan Paul.

Bell, A. M. 1867. *Visible Speech: the Science of Universal Alphabetics.* London: Simpkin, Marshall & Co.

(Bellot. J.) 1580. *The Englishe Scholemaister. Conteyning many profitable preceptes for the naturall borne french men, and other straungers that haue their French tongue, to attayne the true pronouncing of the Englishe tongue.* Made, and sette forth, by I.B.Gen.Ca. London: Thomas Purfoote (Scolar Press 51, 1967).

(Bellot, J.) 1586. *Familiar Dialogves, for the Instruction of them, that be desirous to learne to speake English, and perfectlye to pronounce the same:* Set forth by James Bellot Gentleman of Caen. London: Thomas Vautrollier (Scolar Press 141, 1969).

Bennett, H.S. 1970. *English Books and Readers 1603–1640.* Cambridge: Cambridge University Press.

Berlitz, M.D. 1882. *Méthode pour l'enseignement de la langue française dans les écoles Berlitz,* première partie. Boston: Schoenhof. With E. Dubois.

Berlitz, M.D. 1888/92. *The Berlitz Method for Teaching Modern Languages.* English part. Books 1–2, 1888–90. Rev. American edn, First Book, New York/Boston: Berlitz/Schoenhof, 1892.

Berlitz, M.D. 1907. *The Berlitz Method for Teaching Modern Languages.* Illustrated edn for children. English Part. New York: Berlitz. Extracts reprinted in Hesse (ed.), 1975: 313–21.

Berlitz Organization. 1978. 'Berlitz history in brief. 100 years of a language teaching revolution'. New York: Berlitz Organization (mimeo).

Bernardo, C. da S.T. de M. 1762. *Grammatica Ingleza ordenada em Portuguez,* Lisbon: F. L. Ameno.

Bertram, C. 1749. *Rudimenta grammaticae Anglicanae,* Copenhagen: A. H. Godiche.

Billows, F. L. 1961. *The Techniques of Language Teaching.* London: Longmans, Green.

Bjurman, M. 1977. *The Phonology of Jacques Bellot's Le Maistre d'Escole Anglois (1580).* Stockholm Studies in English, XL. Stockholm: Almqvist and Wiksell.

Blackie, J. S. 1845. 'On the teaching of languages'. *The Foreign Quarterly Review* XXXV: 170–87.

Blake, N. F. 1965. 'The "Vocabulary in French and English" printed by William Caxton'. *English Language Notes* 3: 7–15.

Bloch, B. and G. L. Trager. 1942. *Outline of Linguistic Analysis.* Baltimore: Linguistic Society of America.

Bloomfield, L. 1914. *An Introduction to the Study of Language.* New York: Holt.

Bloomfield, L. 1933. *Language.* New York: Holt.

Bloomfield, L. 1942. *Outline Guide for the Practical Study of Foreign Languages.* Baltimore: Linguistic Society of America.

Bolling, F. 1678. *Friderici Bollingi fuldkommen Engelske Grammatica.* Copenhagen.

Bongers, H. 1947. *The History and Principles of Vocabulary Control.* Woerden: WOCOPI.

Boyer, A. and G. Miège. 1718. *Nouvelle Double Grammaire Françoise-Angloise et Angloise-Françoise.* Amsterdam/Rotterdam: R. G. Wetstein/J. Hofhout.

Bradley, H. (ed.) 1900. *Dialogues in French and English by William Caxton.* Early English Text Society, Extra Series, No. LXXIX. London: Kegan Paul, Trench and Trübner.

Brereton, C. 1930. *Modern Language Teaching in Day and Evening Schools, with special reference to London.* London: London University Press.

Breul, K. 1906. *The Teaching of Modern Foreign Languages and the Training of Teachers.* Third edition, orig. publ. 1898. Cambridge: University Press.

Brightland, J. 1711. *A Grammar of the English Tongue, with Notes, Giving the Grounds and Reason of Grammar in General.* London: for John Brightland. Also attributed to Charles Gildon as co-author (Scolar Press 25, 1967).

British Council, The. 1968 onwards. *English Language Units.* General Editor: C. E. Nuttall. London: Longman for the British Council.

British Council, The. 1969. *The Turners.* London: Longman for the British Council.

Brotanek, R. (ed.) 1905. *George Mason's 'Grammaire Angloise'.* Halle: Niemeyer.

Broughton, G. 1968–70. *Success with English.* Three volumes. Harmondsworth: Penguin.

Brumfit, C. J. 1980. *Problems and Principles in English Teaching.* Oxford: Pergamon Press.

Brumfit, C. J. and K. Johnson (eds.). 1979. *The Communicative Approach to Language Teaching.* Oxford: Oxford University Press.

Buchanan, J. 1762. *The British Grammar: or, an Essay in Four Parts, towards Speaking and Writing the English Language Grammatically.* London: for A. Millar (Scolar Press 97, 1968).

Bullokar, J. 1616. *An English Expositor.* London: Iohn Legatt.

Bullokar, W. 1580. *Booke at Large, for the Amendment of Orthographie for English speech.* London: Henry Denham.

Bullokar, W. 1586. *Pamphlet for Grammar.* London: Henry Denham.

Burstall, C., M. Jamieson, S. Cohen, and M. Hargreaves. 1974. *Primary French in the Balance.* Slough: National Foundation for Educational Research.

Candlin, C. N., J. M. Kirkwood, and H. M. Moore. 1978. 'Study skills in English: theoretical issues and practical problems', in Mackay and Mountford (eds.) 1978: 190–219.

Canzler, F. G. 1787. *Neue englische Sprachlehre.* Göttingen: Brose.

'Carnegie Report, The'. 1936. See Palmer *et al.* 1936.

Castro, J. de 1731. *Grammatica Lusitano-Anglica,* London: F. Fayram and W. Meadows.

Catford, J.C. 1950a. 'Intelligibility'. *ELT,* V/1: 7–15.

Catford, J.C. 1950b. 'The background and origins of Basic English'. *ELT* V/2: 36–47.

Cawdrey, R. 1604. *A Table Alphabeticall, conteyning and teaching the true Writing and Understanding of hard vsuall English Wordes.* London: Adam Islip.

Caxton, W. *c.*1483. *Tres bonne doctrine pour aprendre briefment fransoys et engloys.* (See Bradley (ed.), 1900.)

Cazden, C. B., V. P. John, and D. Hymes (eds.). 1972. *Functions of Language in the Classroom.* New York: Teachers' College Press, Columbia.

Center for Applied Linguistics. 1959. *Proceedings of the Conference on English Teaching Abroad.* Washington, D.C.: Center for Applied Linguistics.

Charlton, K. 1965. *Education in Renaissance England.* London: Routledge and Kegan Paul, and Toronto: University of Toronto Press.

Chomsky, N. 1957. *Syntactic Structures.* The Hague: Mouton.

Chomsky, N. 1959. 'A review of B. F. Skinner's "Verbal Behaviour"'. *Language* 35/1: 26–58.

Chomsky, N. 1965. *Aspects of the Theory of Syntax.* Boston, Mass.: MIT Press.

Chomsky, N. 1966. 'Linguistic theory'. *North-East Conference on the Teaching of Foreign Languages,* Working Committee Reports, edited by Robert C. Mead, Jr: 43–9. Reproduced in Allen and Corder (eds.), Vol. 1, 1973: 234–40.

Christophersen, P. 1956. *An English Phonetics Course.* London: Longmans, Green.

Clair, C. 1965. *A History of Printing in Britain*. London: Cassell.

Cobbett, W. 1819. *A Grammar of the English Language, in a Series of Letters*. London: Thomas Dolby.

Cockeram, H. 1623. *The English Dictionarie*. London: for Nathaniel Butter (Scolar Press 124, 1968).

Coles, E. 1674. *The Compleat English Schoolmaster*. London: Peter Parker (Scolar Press 26, 1967).

Coles, M. and Lord, B. 1974 onwards. *Access to English*. Four vols. Oxford: Oxford University Press.

Collier, P., D. Neale, and R. Quirk. 1978. 'The Hornby Educational Trust, the first ten years', in Strevens (ed.) 1978, *In Honour of A. S. Hornby*: 3–7. Oxford: Oxford University Press.

Collinson, W. E. 1945. 'Basic English as an international language'. *TPS* 1945: 121–36.

Collyer, J. 1735. *The General Principles of Grammar; especially adapted to the English Tongue*. Nottingham: Tho. Collyer (Scolar Press 59, 1968).

Comenius, J.A. 1631. *Porta Linguarum Trilinguis Reserata et Aperta (The Gate of Tongves vnlocked and opened, or else a Seminarie or seed-plot of all Tongues and Sciences)*. London: George Millar. An early trilingual (Latin, English, French) version of Comenius's *Janua Linguarum*, brought out by John Anchoran (Scolar Press 250, 1970).

Comenius, J.A: 1633. *Janua Linguarum Reserata Aurea*. Leipzig. The edition consulted for the present book was published in London in 1662.

Comenius, J.A. 1633. *Januae Linguarum Reseratae Aureae Vestibulum*. Leszno. The edition consulted for the present book, containing a Preface dated 4th January, 1633, was published in Amsterdam in 1642.

Comenius, J.A. 1648–9. *Linguarum Methodus Novissima*. Completed in 1648 and printed in Leszno, probably in 1649. Reprinted as *Novissima Linguarum Methodus* in Comenius's *Opera Didactica Omnia* in Amsterdam in 1657. See Jelinek, 1953.

Comenius, J.A. 1657. *Didactica Magna* (The Great Didactic). Published in *Opera Didactica Omnia*, Amsterdam, 1657. Originally written in Czech, 1628–32. See Keatinge, 1896/1910.

Comenius, J.A. 1658. *Orbis Sensualium Pictus*. Nuremberg. See Hoole, 1659.

Connelly, T. 1784. *Gramática que contiene reglas faciles para pronunciar y aprender metódicamente la lengua Inglesa*. Madrid: en la Imprenta Real.

Cooper, C. 1685. *Grammatica Linguae Anglicanae*. London: Benj. Tooke (Scolar Press 86, 1968).

Cooper, C. 1687. *The English Teacher, or, the Discovery of the Art of Teaching and Learning the English Tongue*. London: John Richardson (Scolar Press 175, 1969).

Corder, S. P. 1967. 'The significance of learners' errors'. *IRAL* V/4: 161–70.

Corder, S. P. 1981. *Error Analysis and Interlanguage*. Oxford: Oxford University Press.

Cotgrave, R. 1611. *A Dictionarie of the French and English Tongues*. London (Scolar Press 82, 1968).

CREDIF. 1961. *Voix et Images de France: cours audio-visuel de français premier degré*. London: Harrap. Orig. publ. St. Cloud, 1958.

CREDIF. 1963. *Bonjour Line*. Paris and London: Harrap-Didier.

Cressy, D. 1977. 'Literacy in seventeenth-century England: more evidence'. *Journal of Interdisciplinary History*, VIII/1: 141–50.

Dakin, J. 1973. *The Language Laboratory and Language Learning*. London: Longman.

Dakin, J., B. Tiffin, and H. G. Widdowson. 1968. *Language in Education*. London: Oxford University Press.

Danielsson, B. 1955. *John Hart's Works on English Orthography and Pronunciation (1551.1569.1570).* Two volumes. Stockholm: Almqvist and Wiksell.

Darian, S.G. 1972. *English as a Foreign Language: History, Development and Methods of Teaching.* Norman: University of Oklahoma Press.

Desainliens, C., (see Holyband, C.).

Dilworth, T. 1751. *A New Guide to the English Tongue.* Thirteenth edition, orig. publ., 1740. London: Henry Kent (Scolar Press 4, 1967).

Dinneen, F. P. 1967. *An Introduction to General Linguistics.* New York: Holt, Rinehart, Winston.

Dobson, E. J. 1957. *English Pronunciation 1500–1700, Vol. 1: A Survey of the Sources.* Oxford: Clarendon Press.

Donaldson, M. 1978. *Children's Minds.* Glasgow: Fontana/Collins.

Duncan, D. 1731. *A New English Grammar.* London: Nicholas Prevost (Scolar Press 17, 1967).

Ebers, J. 1792. *Englische Sprachlehre für die Deutschen, nach Sheridan's und Walker's Grundsätzen.* Berlin: F. Oehmigte.

Eckersley, C. E. 1933. *A Concise English Grammar for Foreign Students.* London: Longmans, Green.

Eckersley, C. E. 1938–42. *Essential English for Foreign Students.* Four volumes. London: Longmans, Green.

Eckersley, C. E. 1955. *Essential English for Foreign Students.* Teacher's Book 1. Revised edition. London: Longmans, Green.

Eliot, J. 1593. *Ortho-epia Gallica, ELIOTS FRVITS for the French.* London: John Wolfe (Scolar Press 114, 1968).

Elton, G. R. 1967. *The Practice of History.* London: Collins/Fontana in association with Sydney University Press.

Emblen, D. L. 1970. *Peter Mark Roget, the Work and the Man.* London: Longman.

Ewer, J. R. and G. Latorre. 1969. *A Course in Basic Scientific English.* London: Longman.

Faucett, L. 1933. *The Oxford English Course.* Four volumes. London: Oxford University Press.

Faucett, L. and I. Maki. 1932. *A Study of English Word-Values, statistically determined from the latest extensive word-counts.* Toyko: Matsumura Sanshodo.

Fell, J. 1784. *An Essay towards an English Grammar.* London: for C. Dilly (Scolar Press 16, 1967).

Fenning, D. 1771. *A New Grammar of the English Language.* London: for S. Crowder (Scolar Press 19, 1967).

Festeau, P. 1667. *A New and Easie French Grammar.* London: for Thomas Thornycroft (Scolar Press 282, 1971).

Festeau, P. 1672. *Nouvelle Grammaire Angloise, enrichié de Dialogues Curieux touchant l'Estat, & la Cour d'Angleterre.* London: Thomas Thornycroft.

Fick, J.C. 1793. *Praktische englische Sprachlehre für Deutsche beyderley Geschlechts. Nach der in Meidingers französischen Grammatik befolgten Methode.* Erlangen.

Firth, J.R. 1934. 'The word "phoneme"'. *Le Maître Phonétique*, 46, 1934. Reprinted in Firth, 1957a: 1–2.

Firth, J.R. 1946. 'The English School of Phonetics'. *TPS*, 1946. Reprinted in Firth, 1957a: 92–120.

Firth, J.R. 1950. 'Personality and language in society'. *The Sociological Review*, xlii, 2, 1950. Reprinted in Firth, 1957a: 177–89.

Firth, J.R. 1957a. *Papers in Linguistics, 1934–1951.* London: Oxford University Press.

Firth, J.R. 1957b. 'Applications of general linguistics'. *TPS* 1957: 1–14.

Firth, J.R. 1959. 'The treatment of language in general linguistics', in Palmer (ed.) 1968: 206–9.

Florence, P.S. and J.R.L. Anderson (eds.). 1977. C.K. Ogden: A Collective Memoir. London: Elek Pemberton.

Florio, J. 1578. His firste Fruites: which yeelde familar speech, merie Prouerbes, wittie Sentences, and golden sayings. Also a perfect Induction to the Italian, and English tongues. London: Thomas Dawson (Facsimile edition by Da Capo Press, Amsterdam and New York, 1969).

Florio, J. 1591. Second Frvtes, to be gathered of twelue trees, of diuers but delightsome tastes to the tongues of Italians and Englishmen. London: for Thomas Woodcock (Facsimile edition by Da Capo Press, Amsterdam and New York, 1969).

Florio, J. 1598. A Worlde of Wordes, or Most copious, and exact Dictionarie in Italian and English. London.

Florio, J. 1603. The Essayes or Morall, Politike and Millitarie Discourses of Lo: Michaell de Montaigne . . . done into English. London: Val. Sims.

Florio, J. 1611. Queen Anna's new World of Words, or Dictionarie of the Italian and English tongues. London (Scolar Press 105, 1968).

Franke, F. 1884. Die praktische Spracherlernung auf Grund der Psychologie und der Physiologie der Sprache dargestellt. Heilbronn: Henninger. Third edition (1896) with foreword by Otto Jespersen, Leipzig: O.R. Reisland.

Fries, C.C. 1940. American English Grammar. New York: Appleton-Century Co.

Fries, C.C. 1942 onwards. An Intensive Course in English for Latin-American Students. Ann Arbor: University of Michigan Press.

Fries, C.C. 1945. Teaching and Learning English as a Foreign Language. Ann Arbor: University of Michigan Press.

Fries, C.C. 1948. 'As we see it'. Language Learning, I/1: 12–16.

Fries, C.C. 1952. The Structure of English, an introduction to the construction of English sentences. New York: Harcourt, Brace.

Fries, C.C. 1955. 'American linguistics and the teaching of English'. Language Learning, VI/1: 1–22.

Fries, C.C. 1959. 'Preparation of teaching materials, practical grammars and dictionaries, especially for foreign languages'. Language Learning IX/1: 43–50.

Fries, C.C. and Y. Shen. 1946. An Intensive Course in English for Chinese Students. Four volumes. Ann Arbor: University of Michigan Press.

Frisby, A.W. 1957. Teaching English. Notes and comments on teaching English overseas. London: Longmans, Green.

Frith, U. (ed.) 1980. Cognitive Processes in Spelling. London: Academic Press.

Gaillard, J.D. 1875. The French Language by the Association of Ideas. London: George Philip & Son.

Garmonsway, G.N. (ed.) 1947. Aelfric's Colloquy. Second edition. London: Methuen.

Gatenby, E.V. 1952. A Direct Method English Course. London: Longmans, Green.

Gattegno, C. 1963. Teaching Foreign Languages in Schools. The Silent Way. Reading: Educational Explorers Ltd.

Gauntlett, J.O. 1957. Teaching English as a Foreign Language. London: Macmillan.

Gil(l), A. 1621. Logonomia Anglica. First edition, 1619. London: John Beale (Scolar Press 68, 1968).

Gimson, A.C. 1962. An Introduction to the Pronunciation of English. London: E. Arnold.

Gimson, A.C. 1968. 'Daniel Jones'. Obituary notice in Le Maître Phonétique, Jan–July, 1–6.

Goody, J. and I. Watt. 1963. 'The consequences of literacy'. *Comparative Studies in Society and History*, 5, 3, 1963, 304–45. Reprinted in Goody (ed.) *Literacy in Traditional Societies*, 1968. Cambridge: Cambridge University Press. First paperback edition, 1975: 27–68.

Gougenheim, G., R. Michéa, P. Rivenc, and A. Sauvageot. 1956. *L'élaboration du français elémentaire*. Paris: Didier. (See also Ministère de l'éducation nationale, 1954.)

Gough, J. 1754. *A Practical Grammar of the English Tongue*. Revised by John Gough. Dublin: Isaac Jackson (Scolar Press 13, 1967).

Gouin, F. 1880/92. *The Art of Teaching and Studying Languages*. Translation by H. Swan and V. Bétis. Orig. publ. in Paris, 1880. London: George Philip.

Greaves, P. 1594. *Grammatica Anglicana*. Cambridge: Iohannis Leggat.

Green, F.C. 1964. 'Anglomaniacs and francophiles', in F. C. Green (ed.), *Eighteenth-Century France, Six Essays*. 1964: 29–69. New York/London: Ungar/Constable. Orig. publ. 1929.

Gurrey, P. 1947. 'The University of London Institute of Education'. *ELT* I/3: 72–5.

Gurrey, P. 1955. *Teaching English as a Foreign Language*. London: Longmans, Green.

Grönlund, J. U. 1885. *Lärobok i Engelska Språket, efter Prof H. G. Ollendorffs nya method, utarbetad af J. U. Grönlund*. Eighth edition. Stockholm: Hjalmar Kinberg.

Haislund, N. 1943. 'Otto Jespersen'. *Englische Studien* LXXV: 273–83.

Hakuta, K. 1974. 'Prefabricated patterns and the emergence of structure in second language acquisition'. *Language Learning* 24/2: 287–97.

Halliday, M.A.K. 1961. 'Categories of the theory of grammar'. *Word* 17: 241–92.

Halliday, M.A.K. 1973. *Explorations in the Functions of Language*. London: Edward Arnold.

Halliday, M.A.K., A. McIntosh, and P. Strevens. 1964. *The Linguistic Sciences and Language Teaching*. London: Longman.

Halliday, M.A.K. and R. Hasan. 1976. *Cohesion in English*. London: Longman.

Hans, N. 1951. *New Trends in Education in the Eighteenth Century*. London: Routledge and Kegan Paul.

Harding, A., B. Page, and S. Rowell. 1980. *Graded Objectives in Modern Languages*. London: CILT.

Hart, J. 1551. *The Opening of the unreasonable writing of our inglish toung*. Unprinted manuscript.

Hart, J. 1569. *An Orthographie, conteyning the due order and reason, howe to write or paint thimage of mannes voice, most like to the life or nature* (London).

Hart, J. 1570. *A Methode or comfortable beginning for all unlearned, whereby they may bee taught to read English, in a very short time, with pleasure*. London: Henrie Denham.

Hartog, P. J. 1917. 'The origins of the School of Oriental Studies'. *Bulletin of the School of Oriental Studies* 1/1: 5–22.

Hasan, R. 1968. *Grammatical cohesion in spoken and written English, part one*. Programme in Linguistics and English Teaching, Paper 8. London: Longman for the Schools Council.

Hatch, E. M. (ed.) 1978. *Second Language Acquisition, A Book of Readings*. Rowley: Newbury House.

Hayden, D. E., E. P. Alworth, and G. Tate (eds.). 1968. *Classics in Linguistics*. London: Peter Owen.

Hayes, A.S. 1963. *Language Laboratory Facilities*. Washington, D.C.: U.S. Government Printing Office. Also, London: Oxford University Press, 1968.

Hazlitt, W. 1821. 'The character of Cobbett'. *Table Talk* Essay VI: 115–34. London: John Warren.

Henderson, E. J. A. (ed.) 1971. *The Indispensable Foundation, A selection from the writings of Henry Sweet.* London: Oxford University Press.

Heness, G. 1875. *Der Leitfaden für den Unterricht in der deutschen Sprache ohne Sprachlehre und Wörterbuch.* Second edition. Boston: Schönhof and Möller.

Hesse, M. G. (ed.) 1975. *Approaches to Teaching Foreign Languages.* Amsterdam: North-Holland Publishing Co.

Hexham, H. 1647. *An English Grammar, appended to a copious English and Nether-Duytch Dictionary.* Rotterdam.

Hicks, D. 1956 onwards. *Foundations of English.* London: Longmans, Green.

Hill, W.K. 1894. *William Henry Widgery, Schoolmaster.* London: D. Nutt.

Hillenius, F. 1664. *Den Engelschen ende Ne'erduitschen Onderrichte ... The English and Low-Dutch Instructor.* Rotterdam: Bastiaen Wagens.

HMSO. 1918. *Modern Studies: being the Report of the Committee on the Position of Modern Languages in the Education System of Great Britain.* London: HMSO.

Hodges, R. 1644. *The English Primrose.* London: Richard Cotes (Scolar Press 183, 1969).

Holmes, D. T. 1903. *The Teaching of Modern Languages in Schools and Colleges.* Paisley: A. Gardner.

Holyband, C. 1573. *The French Schoolemaistr, wherein is most plainlie shewed the true and most perfect way of pronouncinge of the French tongue, without any helpe of Maister, or Teacher: set foorthe for the furtherance of all those whiche doo studie privately in their owne study or houses.* London: William How (Scolar Press 315, 1972).

Holyband, C. 1576. *The French Littelton. A most easie, perfect and absolute way to learne the French tongue.* London: T. Vautrollier (Scolar Press 220, 1970). (See St. Clare Byrne 1953.)

Holyband, C. 1580. *De Pronuntiatione Linguae Gallicae.* London: T. Vautrollier.

Holyband, C. 1593. *A Dictionarie French and English.* London: for Thomas Woodcock (Scolar Press 231, 1970).

Hoole, C. 1659. *Johann Amos Comenius's Visible World. Or, a Picture and Nomenclature of all the Chief Things that are in the World; and of Mens Employments therein.* London: for J. Kirton. (Translation of *Orbis Sensualium Pictus.*) (Scolar Press 222, 1970.)

Hoole, C. 1660. *A New Discovery of the old Art of Teaching Schoole.* London: Andrew Crook (Scolar Press 133, 1969).

Horn, E. 1926. 'A basic writing vocabulary'. *Monographs in Education*, No. 4. University of Iowa Press.

Hornby, A.S. 1946/7. 'Linguistic pedagogy'. A series of six articles in *ELT* Vols I and II.

Hornby, A.S. 1950. 'The situational approach in language teaching'. A series of three articles in *ELT* IV: Issues 4–6.

Hornby, A.S. 1952. 'Situations – artificial or natural?' *ELT* VI/4: 118–24.

Hornby, A.S. 1953. 'Vocabulary control – history and principles'. *ELT* VIII/1: 15–21.

Hornby, A.S. 1954. *Guide to Patterns and Usage in English.* London: Oxford University Press.

Hornby, A.S. 1954–6. *Oxford Progressive English for Adult Learners.* Three volumes. London: Oxford University Press.

Hornby, A.S. 1959–66. *The Teaching of Structural Words and Sentence Patterns.* Four volumes. London: Oxford University Press.

Hornby, A.S. 1966. 'Looking back'. *ELT* XXI/1: 3–6.

Hornby, A.S. 1974. *The Oxford Advanced Learner's Dictionary of Current English.* With the assistance of A. P. Cowie and J. Windsor Lewis. Oxford: Oxford University Press.

Hornby, A.S., E. V. Gatenby, and H. Wakefield. 1948. *A Learner's Dictionary of Current English*; 1952, *The Advanced Learner's Dictionary of Current English*. London: Oxford University Press. (See also Hornby, 1974.)

Hornby, A.S. and D. Jones. 1950. 'H. E. Palmer'. Obituary notice in *ELT* IV/4: 87–90.

Hornby, A.S. and R. Mackin. 1964 onwards. *Oxford Progressive English for Adult Learners, Alternative Edition*. Four volumes. London: Oxford University Press.

Howell, J. 1662. *A New English Grammar, prescribing as certain Rules as the Language will bear, for Forreners to learn English*. London: for T. Williams, etc.

Huddleston, R. D., R. A. Hudson, E. O. Winter, and A. Henrici. 1968. *Sentence and Clause in Scientific English*. Communication Research Centre, University College, London.

Hymes, D. 1966/72. 'On communicative competence'. Paper originally read at the Research Planning Conference on Language Development among Disadvantaged Children, Yeshiva University, June 1966. Reprinted, in part, in Pride and Holmes (eds.) 1972: 269–93.

Hyndman, M. 1978. *Schools and Schooling in England and Wales: A Documentary History*. London: Harper and Row.

Jacotot, J. J. 1830. *Enseignement universel, langue etrangère*. Paris.

James, W. 1890. *The Principles of Psychology*. Two volumes. New York: Holt.

Jelinek, V. 1953. *The Analytical Didactic of Comenius*. Chicago: University of Chicago Press.

Jespersen, O. 1887. 'Der neue Sprachunterricht'. *Englische Studien* X: 412–37.

Jespersen, O. 1904. *How to Teach a Foreign Language*. London: Allen and Unwin.

Jespersen, O. 1907. 'John Hart's pronunciation of English'. *Anglistische Forschungen*, xxii.

Jespersen, O. 1909–49. *A Modern English Grammar on Historical Principles*. Seven volumes. Copenhagen: Munksgaard; London: Allen and Unwin.

Jespersen, O. 1924. *The Philosophy of Grammar*. London: Allen and Unwin.

Jespersen, O. 1928. *An International Language*. London: Allen and Unwin.

Jespersen, O. 1933. *Essentials of English Grammar*. London: Allen and Unwin.

Jespersen, O. undated. *The Selected Writings of Otto Jespersen*. London: Allen and Unwin.

Johnson, K. 1982. *Communicative Syllabus Design and Methodology*. Oxford: Pergamon Press.

Johnson, K. and K. Morrow. 1979. *Approaches*. Cambridge: Cambridge University Press.

Johnson, S. 1747. *The Plan of a Dictionary of the English Language*. Addressed to the Right Honourable Philip Dormer, Earl of Chesterfield. London: for J. and P. Knapton *et al.* (Scolar Press 223, 1970).

Johnson, S. 1755. *A Dictionary of the English Language, in which the Words are deduced from their Originals and Illustrated in their Different Significations by Examples from the Best Writers. To which are prefixed a History of the Language and an English Grammar*. London: W. Strahan.

Jones, D. 1909. *The Pronunciation of English*. Cambridge: Cambridge University Press.

Jones, D. 1917. *An English Pronouncing Dictionary, on strictly phonetic principles*. London: Dent.

Jones, D. 1918. *Outline of English Phonetics*. Leipzig and Berlin. Second edition, Cambridge: Heffer, and Leipzig: Teubner.

Jones, D. 1941/66. 'Paul Passy'. *Le Maître Phonétique*, third series, 75, 1941, 30–9. Reprinted in Sebeok (ed.) 1966 II: 139–47.

Jones, H. 1724. *An Accidence to the English Tongue*. London: for John Clarke (Scolar Press 2, 1967).

**Jones, Sir W.** 1786/88. The Third Anniversary Discourse to the Bengal Asiatic Society. Delivered in 1786, published in *Asiatic Researches, or Transactions of the Bengal Asiatic Society*, Vol. 1, Calcutta, 1788. Reprinted in Hayden *et al.* (eds.) 1967: 58–70.

**Jonson, B.** 1640. *The English Grammar*. From *The Workes*, pp. 31–84. London (Scolar Press 349, 1972).

**Junker, H. P.** 1904. 'Englischer Unterricht, geschichtlicher Abriss'. In Rein (ed.) 1904 Vol. II: 406–21.

**Jupp. T. C. and S. Hodlin.** 1975. *Industrial English, an example of theory and practice in functional language teaching for elementary learners*. Assisted by Jacek Opienski and Elizabeth Laird. London: Heinemann Educational Books.

**Kaeding, K.** 1898. *Häufigkeitswörterbuch der deutschen Sprache*. Steglitz.

**Keatinge, M. W.** 1910. *The Great Didactic of John Amos Comenius*. Second edition, first published in 1896. London: Adam and Charles Black.

**Kelly, J.** 1981. 'The 1847 alphabet: an episode of phonotypy', in Asher and Henderson (eds.) 1981: 248–64.

**Kelly, L. G.** 1969. *25 Centuries of Language Teaching*. Rowley: Newbury House.

**Kelly, L. G.** 1971. 'English as a second language: an historical sketch'. *ELT* XXV/2: 120–32.

**Kemp, J. A.** (ed.) 1972. *John Wallis's Grammar of the English Language*. Facsimile reprint with an Introduction, based on the sixth edition, 1765. London: Longman.

**King, P.** 1971. *The Development of the English Economy to 1750*. London: Macdonald and Evans.

**Kinsella, V.** (ed.) 1978. *Language Teaching and Linguistics: Surveys*. Compiled for CILT/ETIC. Cambridge: Cambridge University Press.

**Kirkby, J.** 1746. *A New English Grammar, or, Guide to the English Tongue, with Notes*. London: for R. Manby & H. S. Cox (Scolar Press 297, 1971).

**Kitchin, G. W.** (ed.) 1973. *Francis Bacon: The Advancement of Learning*. London: Dent.

**Klemm, L. R.** 1903. *European Schools*. New York: D. Appleton.

**Klinghardt, H.** 1887. 'Techmer's und Sweet's Vorschläge zur Reform des Unterrichts im Englischen'. *Englische Studien* X: 48–80.

**Klinghardt, H.** 1888. *Ein Jahr Erfahrungen mit der neuen Methode*. Marburg: N. G. Elwert'sche Verlag.

**Klinghardt, H.** 1892. *Drei weitere Jahre Erfahrungen mit der imitativen Methode*. Marburg: N. G. Elwert'sche Verlag.

**Klinghardt, H.** 1893. 'Der neue Sprachunterricht im Ausland'. *Englische Studien* XVIII: 62–92.

**König, J.** 1706. *Ein volkommener Englischer Wegweiser für Hoch-Teutsche*. London: for Wilhelm Frieman & B. Barker.

**Köhler, J. B.** 1799. *Die Grundsätze der englischen Sprache*. Lübeck and Leipzig: F. Bohn.

**Kraak, I.** 1748. *An Essay on a Methodical English Grammar for the Swedes*. Gothenburg: J. G. Lange.

**Krashen, S.D.** 1981. *Second Language Acquisition and Second Language Learning*. Oxford: Pergamon Press.

**Krashen, S.D.** 1982. *Principles and Practice in Second Language Acquisition*. Oxford: Pergamon Press.

**Kroeh, C.F.** 1887. 'Methods of teaching modern languages'. *Transactions and Proceedings of the Modern Language Association of America* III: 169–85.

**Kryazhev, V. S.** 1791. *Rukovodstvo k aglinskomu yazyku*. Moscow: Okorokov.

**Kryazhev, V. S.** 1795. *Aglinskaya grammatika*. Moscow: Riediger and Claudius.

**Kullin, L. J.** 1744. *Et Kort och Tydeliget Begrep af en Engelsk Grammatica*. Stockholm: Lars Salvius.

Labov, W. 1969. *The Study of Non-Standard English*. National Council of Teachers of English (USA).

Lado, R. 1957. *Linguistics Across Cultures: applied linguistics for language teachers*. Ann Arbor: University of Michigan Press.

Lado, R. and C.C. Fries. 1954–58. *An Intensive Course in English*. Four volumes. Ann Arbor: University of Michigan Press.

Lambley, K. 1920. *The Teaching and Cultivation of the French Language in England during Tudor and Stuart Times*. Manchester: Manchester University Press; London: Longmans, Green.

Law, A. 1965. *Education in Edinburgh in the Eighteenth Century*. London: University of London Press.

Lawson, J. and H. Silver. 1973. *A Social History of Education in England*. London: Methuen.

Leathes, S. (Chairman). 1918. *Modern Studies*. See HMSO (1918).

Leopold, W. F. 1939–49. *Speech Development of a Bilingual Child: A Linguist's Record*. Four volumes. Vol. 1 (1939), Vol. 2 (1947), Vols. 3/4 (1949). Evanston, Ill.: Northwestern University Press.

Lily, W. and J. Colet. 1549. *A Shorte Introdvction of Grammar, generally to be vsed in the Kynges Maiesties dominions . . . to atteyne the knowlege of the Latine tongue*. London. Brought together from a variety of sources and known traditionally as 'Lily's Grammar' or the 'Royal Grammar' (Scolar Press 262, 1971).

Lindblad, T. 1969. *Implicit and Explicit – An Experiment in Applied Psycholinguistics*. GUME – Projektet 1. Gothenburg: Göteborgs Universitet, Engelska Institutionen.

Locke, J. 1693. *Some Thoughts Concerning Education*. London: Awnsham and John Churchill. Reprinted in Axtell (ed.) 1968: 111–325.

Lockhart, L.W. 1933. *Basic for Economics*. London: Kegan Paul, Trench, Trubner.

Lockhart, L.W. 1950. *The Basic Teacher*. London: The Basic English Publishing Co.

Lorge, I. 1949. *A Semantic Count of the 570 Commonest English Words*. New York: Columbia University Press.

Lowth, R. 1762. *A Short Introduction to English Grammar, with critical notes*. London: J. Hughs (Scolar Press 18, 1967).

Mackay, D., B. Thompson, and P. Schaub. 1970. *Breakthrough to Literacy*. Longman for the Schools Council.

Mackay, R. and A. J. Mountford (eds.). 1978. *English for Specific Purposes, A Case Study Approach*. London: Longman.

Mackey, W. F. 1965. *Language Teaching Analysis*. London: Longman.

Mackin, R. and A. Weinberger. 1949. *El Inglés para Médicos y Estudiantes de Medicina*. London: Longmans, Green.

Maittaire, M. 1712. *The English Grammar, or an Essay on the Art of Grammar, applied to and exemplified in the English Tongue*, London: W.B.

Malinowski, B. 1923. 'The problem of meaning in primitive languages'. Supplement to C. K. Ogden and I. A. Richards, *The Meaning of Meaning*. London: Routledge and Kegan Paul, 1923, 296–336.

Marcel, C. 1853. *Language as a Means of Mental Culture and International Communication; or, Manual of the Teacher and the Learner of Languages*. London: Chapman and Hall.

Marcel, C. 1869. *The Study of Languages Brought Back to its True Principles*. New York: D. A. Appleton.

Mason, G. 1622. *Grammaire Angloise*. London: Nat. Butter (Scolar Press 261, 1971).

Mauger, C. 1653. *The True Advancement of the French Tongue*. London: Tho. Roycroft.

**Maver, W.** (ed.) 1809. *Johnson's English Dictionary*. Two vols. Glasgow: R. Chapman.

**McCarthy, P.A.D.** 1944. *English Pronunciation. A practical handbook for the foreign learner*. Cambridge: Heffer.

**Meidinger, J. V.** 1783. *Praktische französische Grammatik*. Frankfurt.

**Miège, G.** 1685. *Nouvelle Méthode pour apprendre l'Anglois, avec une Nomenclature, Françoise et Angloise; un Recueil d'Expressions familières; et des Dialogues, familiers et choisis*. London: for Thomas Bassett (Scolar Press 216, 1970).

**Miège, G.** 1688. *The English Grammar, or the Grounds and Genius of the English Tongue*. London: J. Redmayne (Scolar Press 152, 1969).

**Miller, J.** 1797. *The Tutor, or a New English and Bengalee Work, well adapted to teach the natives English* (Serampore) (Scolar Press 276, 1971).

**Milton, J.** 1644. 'Of Education'. Reprinted in *John Milton, Selected Prose* edited by C. A. Patrides 1974: 181–95. Harmondsworth: Penguin.

**Milton, J.** 1669. *Accedence commenc't Grammar*. London.

**Ministère de L'Éducation Nationale.** 1954. *Le français fondamental (1er degré)*. Paris: Institut pédagogique national.

**'M.L.L.'** 1973 'Michael West'. *ELTJ* XXVIII/1: 3–5.

**Mohrmann, C., A. Sommerfelt, and J. Whatmough** (eds.). 1961. *Trends in European and American Linguistics, 1930–1960*. Utrecht: Spectrum.

**Montaigne, M. de** 1580. *Essais*. Translated with an Introduction by J. M. Cohen (1958) in the Penguin Classics Series. Harmondsworth: Penguin.

**Moore, J. and H. G. Widdowson** (eds.). 1979–80. *Reading and Thinking in English*. Four volumes. Oxford: Oxford University Press.

**Moritz, K. P.** 1784. *Englische Sprachlehre fur die Deutschen*. Berlin: A. Weber.

**Morrow, K. and K. Johnson.** 1979/80. *Communicate*. Two vols. Cambridge: Cambridge University Press.

**Moulton, W. G.** 1961. 'Linguistics and language teaching in the United States, 1940–1960'. In Mohrmann *et al.* (eds.) 1961: 82–109.

**Mulcaster, R.** 1581. *Positions wherein those primitive circumstances be examined, which are necessarie for the training up of children*. London: T. Vautrollier.

**Mulcaster, R.** 1582. *The First Part of the Elementarie, which entreateth chefelie of the right writing of our English tung*. London: T. Vautrollier (Scolar Press 219, 1970).

**Munby, J.** 1978. *Communicative Syllabus Design*. Cambridge: Cambridge University Press.

**Murray, K. M. E.** 1977. *Caught in the Web of Words: James A. H. Murray and the Oxford English Dictionary*. New Haven and London: Yale University Press.

**Murray, L.** 1795. *English Grammar, adapted to the different classes of learners*. York: Wilson, Spence and Mawman (Scolar Press 106, 1968).

**Murray, L.** 1797. *English Exercises*. York: Wilson, Spence and Mawman.

**Myers, A.R.** (ed.) 1969. *English Historical Documents 1327–1485*. Vol. 4 of English Historical Documents, edited by D. C. Douglas. London: Eyre and Spottiswoode.

**Nelson, T.** (publishers). 1980 onwards. *Skills for Learning*. Five volumes. London.

**Nesfield, J. C.** 1898. *Manual of English Grammar and Composition*. London: Macmillan.

**Nesfield, J. C.** 1898. *English Grammar, Past and Present*. London: Macmillan.

**Nesfield, J. C.** 1954. *English Grammar Series*. New edition. London: Macmillan.

**Nida, E.A.** 1946. *Morphology*. Ann Arbor: University of Michigan Press.

**Offelen, H.** 1687. *A Double Grammar for Germans to Learn English and for Englishmen to Learn the German Tongue*. London.

**Ogden, C.K.** 1930. *Basic English, a general introduction with rules and grammar*. London: Kegan Paul, Trench and Trubner.

**Ogden, C.K.** 1931. *Basic English Applied (Science)*. London: Kegan Paul, Trench and Trubner.

Ogden, C.K. 1932. *Bentham's Theory of Fictions*. London: Kegan Paul.

Ogden, C.K. 1935. *Counter-Offensive*. London: The Orthological Institute.

Ogden, C.K. and I.A. Richards. 1923. *The Meaning of Meaning*. London: Routledge and Kegan Paul.

Oldmixon, J. 1712. *Reflections on Dr Swift's Letter to the Earl of Oxford, about the English Tongue*. London (Scolar Press 254, 1970).

Ollendorff, H.G. 1835. *Nouvelle Méthode pour apprendre à lire, à écrire, et à parler une langue en six mois, appliquée a l'allemand*. Paris: the Author.

Ollendorff, H.G. 1838. *A New Method of Learning to Read, Write and Speak a Language in Six Months, adapted to the German*. London: Whittaker. See also Grönlund (1885).

Ollendorff, H.G. 1848. First adaptation of the *New Method* to teach English. Intended for French speakers. Paris.

Owen, H. and J. Bell (eds.). 1967. *Wilfred Owen: Collected Letters*. London: Oxford University Press.

Pakscher, A. 1895. 'Die Berlitz-methode'. *Englische Studien* XXI: 310–20.

Palermo, E. 1779. *The Amusing Practice of the Italian Language*. London: for T. Cadell.

Palmer, F. R. (ed.) 1968. *Selected Papers of J. R. Firth, 1952–59*. London: Longman.

Palmer, H.E. 1917/1968. *The Scientific Study and Teaching of Languages*. London: Harrap. Republished by Oxford University Press, 1968, edited by D. Harper.

Palmer, H.E. 1921. *The Oral Method of Teaching Languages*. Cambridge: Heffer.

Palmer, H.E. 1921/1964. *The Principles of Language-Study*. London: Harrap. Republished by Oxford University Press, 1964, edited by R. Mackin.

Palmer, H.E. 1922. *Everyday Sentences in Spoken English*. Cambridge: Heffer. (Third edition, 1927, with F. G. Blandford.)

Palmer, H.E. 1924. *A Grammar of Spoken English, on a strictly phonetic basis*. Cambridge: Heffer.

Palmer, H.E. 1930. *IRET First Interim Report on Vocabulary Selection*. Tokyo: IRET.

Palmer, H.E. 1931. *Second Interim Report on Vocabulary Selection*. Tokyo: IRET.

Palmer, H.E. 1932a. *The Grading and Simplifying of Literary Material*. Tokyo: IRET.

Palmer, H.E. 1938. *The New Method Grammar*. London: Longmans, Green.

Palmer, H.E. 1944/65. *Curso Internacional de Inglés*. First published by Evans Bros., London in 1944, later republished by Oxford University Press, 1965, edited by R. Mackin.

(Palmer, H.E.) Obituary by A. S. Hornby and D. Jones in *ELT* IV/4 Jan. 1950: 87–92.

Palmer, H.E. and A. S. Hornby. 1933. *The IRET Standard 1,000 Word Vocabulary*. Tokyo: IRET.

Palmer, H.E. and A. S. Hornby. 1937. *Thousand-Word English*. London: Harrap.

Palmer, H.E. and D. Palmer. 1925/59. *English Through Actions*. Toyko: IRET, 1925. Republished by Longmans, Green, 1959.

Palmer, H.E. and H. V. Redman. 1932b/1969. *This Language-Learning Business*. London: Harrap. Republished by Oxford University Press, 1969, edited by R. Mackin.

Palmer, H.E., M. P. West, and L. Faucett. 1936. *Interim Report on Vocabulary Selection for the Teaching of English as a Foreign Language*. Report of the Carnegie Conference, New York 1934, and London 1935. London: P. S. King and Son. (See also West (ed.), 1953.)

Palsgrave, J. 1530. *Lesclaircissement de la langue francoyse*. London (Scolar Press 190, 1969).

Passy, P. 1884. *Premier livre de lecture*. Paris: Firmin-Didot.

**Passy, P.** 1885. *L'Instruction primaire aux États-Unis*. Paris: C. Delagrave.

**Passy, P.** 1886. *Éléments d'anglais parlé*. Paris: Librairie Shakespear.

**Passy, P.** 1887. *Les sons du français*. Paris: Firmin Didot, for the Association fonétique des professeurs de langues vivantes.

**Passy, P.** 1899. *De la méthode directe dans l'enseignement des langues vivantes.* Paris: Colin. Published as a special supplement to *Le Maître Phonétique*, May 1899.

**Passy, P.** 1929. *La phonétique et ses applications*. Cambridge: International Phonetic Association.

**Passy, P. and F. Beyer.** 1893. *Elementarbuch des gesprochenen Französisch*. Cöthen: O. Schultz.

**Passy, P. and H. Michaelis.** 1897. *Dictionnaire phonétique de la langue française.* Hanover/Berlin: C. Meyer.

**Pattison, B.** 1952. 'English as a foreign language in the University of London'. *ELT* VI/3: 75–9.

**Paul, H.** 1880. *Prinzipien der Sprachgeschichte*. Halle: Niemeyer.

**Payne, J.** 1830. *A Compendious Exposition of the Principles and Practice of Professor Jacotot's Celebrated System of Education, originally established at the University of Louvain in the Kingdom of the Netherlands*. London: R. Stephens.

**Permskii, M.** 1766. *Prakticheskaya angliskaya grammatika*. St. Petersburg: at the Naval Academy for Young Noblemen.

**Perren, G.** (ed.) 1969. *Languages for Special Purposes*. CILT Reports and Papers No. 1. London. CILT.

**Peyton, V. J.** 1761. *Elements of the English Language, explained in a new, easy, and concise manner, by way of dialogue*. London: Payne and Cropley, and J. Walter.

**Pike, K. L.** 1947. *Phonemics*. Ann Arbor: University of Michigan.

**Pistorius, F. L. A.** 1794. *Deutliche englische Sprachlehre, oder Grammatik*. Erfurt: G. A. Keyser.

**Pitman, I.** 1837. *Stenographic Shorthand*. London: S. Bagster.

**Ploetz, K. J.** 1853. *Elementarbuch der französischen Sprache, nach Seidenstückers Methode bearbeitet*. Berlin: Herbig.

**Poole, J.** 1646. *The English Accidence: or, a short, plaine and easie way, for the more speedy attaining to the Latine tongue, by the help of the English*. London: R.C. (Scolar Press 5, 1967).

**Poutsma, H.** 1914–29. *A Grammar of Late Modern English*. Five volumes. Groningen: Noordhof.

**Prendergast, T.** 1864. *The Mastery of Languages, or, the Art of Speaking Foreign Tongues Idiomatically*. London: R. Bentley. (Mastery Series for French, 1868; German, 1868; Spanish, 1869; Hebrew, 1871; and Latin, 1872.)

**Pride, J.B. and J. Holmes** (eds.). 1972. *Sociolinguistics: Selected Readings*. Harmondsworth: Penguin.

**Priestley, J.** 1761. *The Rudiments of English Grammar, adapted to the Use of Schools, with Observations on Style*. London: R. Griffiths (Scolar Press 210, 1970).

**Priestley, J.** 1798–99. *Grammaire Angloise*. Paris. (Translation of the *Rudiments* for French-speaking learners of English.)

**Quick, R. H.** 1895. *Essays on Educational Reformers*. New edition, orig. publ. 1868. London: Longmans, Green.

**Quinault, R. J.** 1947. 'English by Radio' *ELT* I/5: 119–25.

**Quinault, R. J.** 1967. 'C. E. Eckersley, M.A.' *ELT* XXII/1: 2–3.

**Quirk, R., S. Greenbaum, G. Leech, and J. Svartvik.** 1972. *A Grammar of Contemporary English*. London: Longman.

**Ramus (de la Ramée), P.** 1585a. *The Latine Grammar of P. Ramus: translated into English*. London (Scolar Press 305, 1971).

Ramus (de la Ramée), P. 1585b. *The Rudiments of P. Ramus his Latine Grammar, Englished and newly corrected.* London: Robert Walde-graue (Scolar Press 306, 1971).

Redman, V. 1967. 'Harold E. Palmer–pioneer teacher of modern languages'. *ELT* XXII/1: 10–16.

Rein, W. (ed.) 1909. *Encyklopädisches Handbuch der Pädagogik.* Langensalza: H. Beyer. ('Überbürdungsfrage', Vol. 9: 311–25; 'Englisch', Vol. 2: 406–33).

Richards, I. A. 1943. *Basic English and its Uses.* London: Kegan Paul.

Richards, I. A. and C. M. Gibson. 1945. *English Through Pictures.* New York: Pocket Books, Inc. (Originally entitled *A Pocket Book of Basic English*).

Richterich, R. 1972. *A Model for the Definition of Language Needs of Adults Learning a Modern Language.* Strasbourg: Council of Europe.

Rippmann, W. 1910. *Elements of Phonetics, English, French and German.* Translated and adapted . . . from Prof. Viëtor's *Kleine Phonetik.* Fifth edition. London: Dent.

Roach, J. 1971. *Public Examinations in England 1850–1900.* Cambridge: Cambridge University Press.

Robins, R. H. 1967. *A Short History of Linguistics.* London: Longman.

Robinson, P. 1980. *ESP (English for Specific Purposes).* Oxford: Pergamon Press.

Roget, P. M. 1852. *A Thesaurus of English Words and Phrases.* London: Longman, Brown, Green, and Longman.

Rossiter, P. M. 1937. *Basic for Geology.* London: Kegan Paul, Trench and Trubner.

Russell, J. E. 1907. *German Higher Schools, the history, organization and methods of secondary education in Germany.* Second edition, orig. publ. 1899. New York: Longmans, Green.

Sadler, J. (ed.) 1969. *Comenius.* Educational Thinkers Series. London: Collier-Macmillan.

Salmon, V. 1961. 'Joseph Webbe: some seventeenth-century views on language teaching and the nature of meaning'. *Bibliothèque d'Humanisme et Renaissance* 23: 324–40. Reprinted in Salmon, 1979: 15–31.

Salmon, V. 1964. 'Problems of language-teaching: a discussion among Hartlib's friends', *Modern Language Review* 59: 13–24. Reprinted in Salmon, 1979: 3–14.

Salmon, V. 1966. 'Language-planning in seventeenth-century England: its context and aims', in Bazell *et al.* (eds.) 1966, *In Memory of J.R. Firth*, London, Longman. Reprinted in Salmon, 1979: 129–56.

Salmon, V. 1974. 'John Wilkins' "Essay" (1668): critics and continuators'. *Historiographia Linguistica* 1/2: 147–63. Reprinted in Salmon, 1979: 191–206.

Salmon, V. 1975. ' "Philosophical" grammar in John Wilkins' "Essay" '. *Canadian Journal of Linguistics* 20/2: 131–60. Reprinted in Salmon, 1979: 97–126.

Salmon, V. 1979. *The Study of Language in 17th Century England.* Amsterdam: John Benjamins B.V.

Sammer, R. 1783. *Kurzgefasste englische Sprachlehre.* Vienna.

Sampson, G. 1980. *Schools of Linguistics: competition and evolution.* London: Hutchinson.

Sapir, E. 1921. *Language: an introduction to the study of speech.* New York: Harcourt, Brace.

Sapir, E. 1929. 'The status of linguistics as a science.' *Language* 5: 207–14.

Sapir, E. 1931. 'The function of an international auxiliary language'. *Psyche* 11/4: 4–15.

Saussure, F. de 1916/1974. *Cours de linguistique générale.* Edited by C. Bally and A. Sechehaye. Glasgow: Fontana/Collins, 1974. Orig. publ. Geneva, 1916.

Sauveur, L. 1874. *Introduction to the Teaching of Living Languages without Grammar or Dictionary.* Boston: Schoenhof and Moeller.

Sauveur, L. 1874. *Causeries avec mes élèves.* Boston: Schoenhof and Moeller.

Scherer, G. A. C. and Wertheimer, M. 1964. *A Psycholinguistic Experiment in Foreign Language Teaching*. New York: McGraw Hill.

Scheurweghs, G. 1960. 'English grammars in Dutch and Dutch grammars in English in the Netherlands before 1800'. *English Studies* 41: 129–67.

Schofield, R. S. 1968. 'The measurement of literacy in pre-industrial England', in Goody (ed.) 1968: 310–25.

Schools Council, The. 1969–72. *Scope*. Stage 1 1969; Stage 2 1972; Stage 3 1972. London: Longman for the Schools Council.

Scott, T. (ed.) 1907. *The Prose Works of Jonathan Swift, D.D.* Vol. XI, Literary Essays. London: George Bell & Sons.

Scragg, D.G. 1974. *A History of English Spelling*. Mont Follick Series (3). Manchester: Manchester University Press, and New York: Barnes and Noble.

Sebeok, T. A. (ed.) 1966. *Portraits of Linguists: a biographical source book for the history of western linguistics, 1746–1963*. Two volumes. Bloomington and London: Indiana University Press.

Seidenstücker, J.H.P. 1811. *Elementarbuch zur Erlernung der französischen Sprache*. Book 1 1811, Book 2 1814, Book 3 1829. Hamm: Schulz.

Selinker, L. 1972. 'Interlanguage'. *IRAL* X/3: 209–31.

Sewel, W. 1705. *Korte Wegwyzer der Engelsche Taale . . . A Compendious Guide to the English Language*. Amsterdam: S. Swart.

Silber, K. 1960. *Pestalozzi: the Man and his Work*. London: Routledge and Kegan Paul.

Sinclair, J. McH. and R. M. Coulthard. 1975. *Towards an Analysis of Discourse, the English used by teachers and pupils*. Oxford: Oxford University Press.

Sinclair, J. McH., I. J. Forsyth, R. M. Coulthard, and M. Ashby. 1972. *The English Used by Teachers and Pupils*. Final Report to SSRC for period September 1970 to August 1972. Birmingham: University of Birmingham, Department of English Language and Literature.

Siret, L. P. 1773. *Élémens de la langue Angloise, ou Méthode pratique pour apprendre facilement cette langue*. Paris: Ruault.

Sledd, J. H. and G. J. Kolb. 1955. *Dr. Johnson's Dictionary: essays in the biography of a book*. Chicago: University of Chicago Press.

Smiles, S. 1859. *Self-Help*. London: John Murray.

Smith, F. 1978. *Reading*. Cambridge: Cambridge University Press.

Smith, G. 1752. *Den vollkommene Engelsche Spraakkonst . . . the compleat English Grammar*. Utrecht: A. de Knyff.

Smith, P. D. Jr. 1970. *A Comparison of the Cognitive and Audiolingual Approaches to Foreign Language Instruction—The Pennsylvania Project*. Philadelphia: The Center for Curriculum Development, Inc.

Smith, Sir T. 1568. *De recta et emendata linguae anglicae scriptione, Dialogus*. London.

Spencer, D. H. 1982. 'Retrospect: 1967–1982'. *IATEFL Newsletter* 75 October 1982: 13–16.

Spicer, A. 1969. 'The Nuffield Foreign Languages Teaching Materials Project', in Stern (ed.) 1969: 148–61.

Spira, T. (ed.) 1912. *I.B.Gen.Ca.: 'Le Maistre D'Escole Anglois', (1580)*. Halle: Niemeyer.

St. Clare Byrne, M. (ed.) 1953. *'The French Littelton' by Claudius Holyband, with an Introduction*. Cambridge: Cambridge University Press.

Stack, E.M. 1960. *The Language Laboratory and Modern Language Teaching*. New York: Oxford University Press. (Also, London: Oxford University Press, 1971.)

Stepney, W. 1591. *The Spanish Schoole-master*. London: R. Field (Scolar Press 274, 1971).

Stern, H. H. (ed.) 1969. *Languages and the Young School Child*. London: Oxford University Press.

Stern, H. H. 1983. *Fundamental Concepts of Language Teaching*. Oxford: Oxford University Press.

Stevick, E.W. 1980. *Teaching Languages: A Way and Ways*. Rowley: Newbury House.

Strevens, P. 1977/8. 'Special-purpose language learning: a perspective', in Kinsella (ed.) 1978: 185–203. Dated July 1977.

Strevens, P. (ed.) 1978. *In Honour of A. S. Hornby*. Oxford: Oxford University Press.

Strevens, P. 1978. 'The English language made plain for the teacher of English: the descriptivist and the linguistic traditions', in Strevens (ed.) 1978: 103–16.

Strevens, P. 1980. *Teaching English as an International Language, from practice to principle*. Oxford: Pergamon Press.

Strevens, P. 1981. 'Dr. W. R. Lee, Editor of ELT Journal 1961–1981, An Appreciation'. *ELTJ* 36/1: 3–4.

Swales, J. 1971. *Writing Scientific English*. London: Nelson.

Sweet, H. 1877. *A Handbook of Phonetics, including a Popular Exposition of the Principles of Spelling Reform*. Oxford: Clarendon Press.

Sweet, H. 1884. 'On the practical study of language', *TPS* 1882–84: 577–99.

Sweet, H. 1885. *Elementarbuch des gesprochenen Englisch*. Oxford: Clarendon Press.

Sweet, H. 1890. *A Primer of Phonetics*. Oxford: Clarendon Press.

Sweet, H. 1892, 1898. *A New English Grammar*. Two volumes. Oxford: Clarendon Press.

Sweet, H. 1899/1964. *The Practical Study of Languages. A Guide for Teachers and Learners*. London: Dent. Republished by Oxford University Press in 1964, edited by R. Mackin.

Swift, J. 1712. *A Proposal for Correcting, Improving and Ascertaining the English Tongue*. London: for Benj. Tooke. In Scott (ed.), 1907: 3–21

Swoboda, W. 1890. 'Die methode Toussaint-Langenscheidt'. *Englische Studien* XIV: 210–40.

Tarone, E., A. D. Cohen, and G. Dumas. 1976. 'A closer look at some interlanguage terminology: a framework for communication strategies'. *Working Papers in Bilingualism* 9, 76–91. Toronto: Ontario Institute for Studies in Education.

Taylor, A. J. P. 1976. 'William Cobbett', in Taylor (ed.) 1976, *Essays in English History*. Harmondsworth: Penguin. Essay first published in 1953.

Thorndike, E. L. 1921. *The Teacher's Word Book*. New York: Teachers' College, Columbia University.

Thorndike, E. L. 1932. *A Teacher's Word Book of 20,000 Words*. New York: Teachers' College, Columbia University.

Thorndike, E. L. and I. Lorge. 1944. *A Teacher's Word Book of 30,000 Words*. New York: Teachers' College, Columbia University.

Tiarks, Rev. J. G. 1834. *A Practical Grammar of the German Language*. London: J. Taylor.

Tiarks, Rev. J. G. 1837. *An Introductory Grammar of the German Language*. London: D. Nutt (Eleventh edition, 1864).

Tickoo, M. L. 1982a. 'Where practice prevailed: an appreciation of the work of Harold E. Palmer'. *ELTJ* 36/2: 112–18.

Tickoo, M. L. 1982b. 'James Hamilton and C. V. A. Marcel: a review of language teaching in the 1820s'. *World Language English* 1, 3: 174–8.

Titone, R. 1968. *Teaching Foreign Languages, an historical sketch*. Washington, D.C.: Georgetown University Press.

Toussaint-Langenscheidt, see Swoboda, 1890.

Tozer, F. 1903. Biographical introduction to second edition of Widgery's 1888 pamphlet. London: D. Nutt.

Trager, G. L. and H. L. Smith, Jr. 1951. *An Outline of English Structure*. Reprinted, Washington, D.C.: American Council of Learned Societies, 1957.

Trevelyan, G. M. 1956. *Illustrated History of England*. London: Longmans, Green.

Trevor-Roper, H.R. 1967. 'Three foreigners: the philosophers of the Puritan revolution', in *Religion, the Reformation and Social Change*. London: Macmillan 237–93.

Trim, J. L. M., R. Richterich, J. A. van Ek, and D. A. Wilkins. 1973/1980. *Systems Development in Adult Language Learning*. Strasbourg: The Council of Europe, 1973. Republished by Pergamon Press, Oxford, 1980.

Turner, J. R. (ed.) 1970. *The Works of William Bullokar, Vol. III: 'Booke at Large, 1580'*. Leeds: University of Leeds, School of English.

Turner, J. R. (ed.) 1980. *The Works of William Bullokar, Vol. II: 'Pamphlet for Grammar 1586'*. Leeds: University of Leeds, School of English.

University of Birmingham. 1972. *Concept 7–9*. Leeds: E. J. Arnold, for the Schools Council.

Ussher, G.N. 1785. *The Elements of English Grammar*. Gloucester: R. Raikes (Scolar Press 27, 1967).

Van Ek, J. A. 1973 *The 'Threshold Level' in a unit/credit system*. Strasbourg: Council of Europe.

Van Ek, J. A. 1975. *The Threshold Level in a European Unit/Credit System for Modern Language Learning by Adults*. Strasbourg: The Council of Europe. Republished as *Threshold Level English*, with L. G. Alexander, Oxford: Pergamon Press, 1980.

Van Heldoran, J. G. 1675. *Een nieuwe en gemakkelijke Engelsche Spraak-konst . . . a new and easy English grammar*. Amsterdam.

Venezky, R. L. 1980. 'From Webster to Rice to Roosevelt. The formative years for spelling instruction and spelling reform in the USA', in Frith (ed.) 1980: 9–30.

Viëtor, W. 1882. *Der Sprachunterricht muss umkehren! Ein Beitrag zur Uberbürdungsfrage*. Heilbronn: Henninger. Under pseudonym *Quousque Tandem*.

Viëtor, W. 1884. *Elemente der Phonetik und Orthoepie des Deutschen, Englischen und Französischen*. Heilbronn: Henninger.

Viëtor, W. 1887. 'Die älteste deutsch-englische und englisch-deutsche Grammatik (1686–7)'. *Englische Studien* X: 361–6.

Viëtor, W. 1902. *Die Methodik des neusprachlichen Unterrichts*. Leipzig: Teubner.

Viëtor, W. and F. Dörr. 1887. *Englisches Lesebuch*. Leipzig: Teubner.

Von Elek, T. and M. Oskarsson. 1973. *A Replication Study in Teaching Foreign Language Grammar to Adults*. The GUME/Adults Project. Gothenburg: Gothenburg School of Education, Department of Educational Research.

Von Humboldt, W. 1836. *Über die Verschiedenheit des menschlichen Sprachbaues*. Berlin.

Vorlat, E. 1975. *The Development of English Grammatical Theory, 1586–1737*. Leuven: University Press.

Walker, J. 1791. *A Critical Pronouncing Dictionary and Expositor of the English Language*. London: Robinson. New edn. 1856 (Tegg) (Scolar Press 117, 1968).

Wallis, J. 1653. *Grammatica Lingvae Anglicanae*. Oxford: Leon Lichfield (Scolar Press 142, 1969).

Watson, F. 1908. *The English Grammar Schools to 1660: their Curriculum and Practice*. Cambridge: Cambridge University Press.

Watson, F. 1909. *The Beginnings of the Teaching of Modern Subjects in England*. London: Pitman.

Watson, J. B. 1913. 'Psychology as the behaviorist views it'. *Psychological Review* XX/2: 158–77.

Webbe, J. 1622. *An Appeale to Truth, in the Controuersie betweene Art, and Use; about the best, and most expedient Course in Languages. To be read Fasting.* London: H. L. for George Latham (Scolar Press 42, 1967).

Webbe, J. 1627. *Pveriles Confabvlativncvlae, or Childrens talke: clavsed and drawne into Lessons, for such as desire to breed an habit in themselves . . . of that kind of Dialogicall, or common-speaking Latine.* London: F. K. (Scolar Press 74, 1968).

Webster, N. 1783. *A Grammatical Institute of the English Language, Part 1.* Hartford: Hudson and Goodwin (Scolar Press 89, 1968).

Webster, N. 1787. *The American Spelling Book.* New title for Webster (1783).

Webster, N. 1789. 'An Essay on the Necessity, Advantages and Practicability of Reforming the Mode of Spelling, and of Rendering the Orthography of Words Correspondent to the Pronunciation'. Appendix to *Dissertations on the English Language: with notes, historical and critical.* Boston: Isaiah Thomas & Co. (Scolar Press 54, 1967).

Webster, N. 1806. *A Compendious Dictionary of the English Language.* New Haven: Sidney Babcock.

Webster, N. 1828. *An American Dictionary of the English Language.* New York: S. Converse.

Wedgwood, C.V. 1957. *The Thirty Years' War.* Harmondsworth: Penguin.

Weisse, T. H. 1888. *A Complete Practical Grammar of the German Language.* Fourth edition (orig. publ. 1885). London and Edinburgh: Williams and Norgate.

West, M. 1914. *Education and Psychology.* London: Longmans, Green.

West, M. 1926. *Bilingualism (with special reference to Bengal).* Calcutta: Bureau of Education, India.

West, M. 1927. 'The position of English in a national system of education for Bengal'. Thesis for D.Phil., University of Oxford.

West, M. 1927 onwards. *New Method Readers.* Calcutta: Longmans, Green.

West, M. 1933a. *New Method Conversation Course.* Six parts. London: Longmans, Green.

West, M. 1933b. *On Learning to Speak a Foreign Language.* London: Longmans, Green.

West, M. 1935 onwards. *New Method Readers (Alternative Edition).* London: Longmans, Green.

West, M. 1938. *New Method Composition (Alternative Edition).* London: Longmans, Green.

West, M. (ed.) 1953. *A General Service List of English Words, with semantic frequencies and a supplementary word-list for the writing of popular science and technology.* London: Longmans, Green.

West, M. 1954. 'Vocabulary selection and the minimum adequate vocabulary'. *ELT* VIII/4: 121–6.

West, M. 1960. *Teaching English in Difficult Circumstances.* London: Longmans, Green.

West, M. and J. G. Endicott. 1935. *The New Method English Dictionary.* London: Longmans, Green.

West, M., E. Swenson *et al.* 1934. *A Critical Examination of Basic English.* Bulletin, No. 2, The Department of Educational Research, Ontario College of Education, University of Toronto. Toronto: University of Toronto Press.

Wharton, J. 1654. *The English-Grammar.* London (Scolar Press 241, 1970).

White, A. J. S. 1965. *The British Council, the First 25 Years, 1934–59. A Personal Account.* London: The British Council.

Widdowson, H. G. 1968. 'The teaching of English through science', in Dakin *et al.* (1968), *Language in Education.* London: Oxford University Press.

**Widdowson, H. G.** 1972. 'The teaching of English as communication'. *ELT* 27/1: 15–19. Reprinted in Brumfit and Johnson (eds.) 1979: 117–21.

**Widdowson, H. G.** 1978. *Teaching Language as Communication*. Oxford: Oxford University Press.

**Widdowson, H. G.** 1979. *Explorations in Applied Linguistics*. Oxford: Oxford University Press.

**Widgery, W. H.** 1888. *The Teaching of Languages in Schools*. London: D. Nutt.

**Wilkins, D. A.** 1972. *The linguistic and situational content of the common core in a unit/credit system*. Strasbourg: Council of Europe.

**Wilkins, D. A.** 1976. *Notional Syllabuses. A taxonomy and its relevance to foreign language curriculum development*. Oxford: Oxford University Press.

**Wilkins, J.** 1668. *An Essay towards a Real Character and a Philosophical Language*. London: for Sa: Gellibrand, and for John Martyn (Scolar Press 119, 1968).

**Wodroephe, J.** 1625. *The Marrow of the French Tongve*. Second edition. London. First published at Dort, 1623.

**Woodcock, G.** (ed.) 1967. *Rural Rides* by William Cobbett, with an introduction. Harmondsworth: Penguin.

**Wrenn, C. L.** 1946. 'Henry Sweet'. Presidential Address delivered to the Philological Society, Friday 10th May, 1946. *TPS* 1946: 177–201.

**Wright, A.** 1976. *Visual Materials for the Language Teacher*. London: Longman.

**Wyld, H.C.** (ed.) 1913. *The Collected Papers of Henry Sweet*. Oxford: Clarendon Press.

**Wynken de Worde.** *c.* 1498. *A Lytell treatyse for to lerne Englisshe and Frensshe*. London.

**Yamamoto, N. Y.** 1978. 'The oral method: Harold E. Palmer and the reformation of the teaching of the English language in Japan'. *ELTJ* XXXII/2: 151–8.

**Yates, F. A.** 1934. *John Florio. The Life of an Italian in Shakespeare's England*. Cambridge: Cambridge University Press.

**Zandvoort, R. W.** 1945/1957. *A Handbook of English Grammar*. Groningen: Wolters (1945, English–Dutch); London: Longmans, Green (1957, English only).

**Zhdanov, P. I.** 1772. *Angliska Grammatika*. St. Petersburg: at the Naval Academy for Young Noblemen.

**Zhdanov, P. I.** 1776. Translation of Thomas Dilworth's *New Guide to the English Tongue* (1740). St. Petersburg: at the Naval Academy for Young Noblemen.

## Addenda

**Danielsson, B.** and **R. C. Alston** (eds.). 1966. *The Works of William Bullokar, Vol. 1*. Leeds: University of Leeds, School of Education.

**Kiddle, L.B.** 1949. 'The laboratory of the Department of Romance Languages at Michigan'. *Language Learning* II/4: 121–7.

**Kingdon, R.** 1958. *The Groundwork of English Stress* and *The Groundwork of English Intonation*. London: Longmans, Green.

# Index

Main entries are shown by bold print. Works marked with an asterisk (*) are also entered separately.